IFIP
SERIES ON COMPUTER GRAPHICS

Editors: J.L. Encarnação G.G. Grinstein

Tosiyasu L. Kunii (Ed.)

Modeling in Computer Graphics

Proceedings of the IFIP WG 5.10
Working Conference
Tokyo, Japan, April 8-12, 1991

With 286 Figures, Including 57 in Color

Springer-Verlag

Tokyo Berlin Heidelberg
New York London Paris
Hong Kong Barcelona

Prof. Dr. Tosiyasu L. Kunii
Department of Information Science
Faculty of Science
University of Tokyo
Tokyo 113, Japan

Sereis Editors:

Prof. Dr. José L. Encarnação
Graphische Datenverarbeitung
Wilhelminenstraße 7
D-6100 Darmstadt
Germany

Prof. Dr. Georges G. Grinstein
Graphics Research Laboratory
University of Lowell
Lowell, MA 01854
USA

ISBN-13: 978-4-431-68149-6   e-ISBN-13: 978-4-431-68147-2
DOI: 10.1007/978-4-431-68147-2

Preface

Computer graphics has been making steady and rapid progress, and has now reached a stage in which it is possible to integrate the results of a very large amount of research and varieties of techniques into a smaller number of models by generalizing and abstracting the knowledge using computer graphics. Such a process is called "modeling," and can only be done properly through testing the models thus obtained against various applications. It is also necessary to look into related disciplines such as mathematics and physics to learn from other ways of modeling.

This volume is the result of an effort of IFIP WG 5.10 on Computer Graphics, chaired by Professor J.L. Encarnacao, under the auspices of TC 5, chaired by Mr. M. Tomljanovich, to advance knowledge of modeling in computer graphics by organizing an open working conference in Tokyo, Japan on April 8 through 12 in 1991, in cooperation with the Information Processing Society of Japan and the Institute of Electronics, Information, and Communication Engineers, Japan. In response to the call for papers, 32 high-quality original research papers were submitted from 12 different countries, 1 from Canada, 7 from China, 1 from England, 2 from France, 2 from Germany, 4 from Italy, 9 from Japan, 1 from Mexico, 1 from the Netherlands, 2 from Singapore, 1 from Switzerland, and 1 from the United States. After extensive peer review, 21 papers were selected for presentation at the conference and also for printing in this book. To highlight the areas of particular importance, 3 additional papers were invited.

This volume is divided into three parts. Part 1, on Disciplines of Modeling, contains the first five chapters: Mathematical Modeling (Chapter 1), Physical Modeling (Chapter 2), Geometric Modeling (Chapter 3), Solid Modeling (Chapter 4), and Animation Modeling (Chapter 5). Here, the disciplines such as mathematical, physical, geometrical, and solid modeling are rather well established and, in some sense, have gained knowledge from closely related individual disciplines. The discipline of animation is related to diverse disciplines which are all centered around life, such as biology, medicine, and theatrical art, and is in a rapidly growing phase. Part 2, on Roles of Modeling, includes three chapters: Rendering Models (Chapter 6), Display Algorithms (Chapter 7), and Visualization Models (Chapter 8). Novel features of the mature and essential roles of modeling in computer graphics are elucidated in these chapters. Part 3, on Modeling of Applications, consists of two chapters: Modeling of Art Painting (Chapter 9) and Modeling of Computer-aided Design (Chapter 10). You may wonder why it is "modeling of" and not "modeling for"? Perhaps, in the papers, the reason will become clear. There is an emerging progress in modeling which is noticeable in art and design. Instead of simply using the models, the process of modeling is applied to specify and represent the course of action for painting and for designing. This new advance is beginning to be made, although it is not yet as explicit as we would wish. In a sense, it is closely connected with the direction of advances in computer animation. Modeling is finally on a passage to the 4D (four-dimensional, namely x-, y- and z- plus time t-) world. So is the hardware for graphics; there are now 4D visualizers. We can also model "modeling" and can get into meta models and meta modeling. This book is fortunate in that it stands at the Continental Divide, separating the 3D and 4D worlds. It is essential to encourage your active participation in this movement in order to advance knowledge in 4D modeling, while also extending the application of 3D modeling, and I sincerely hope this volume will serve as an invitation.

Tosiyasu L. Kunii

Conference Organization

Organized by:

IFIP TC 5/WG 2.6

Department of Information Science, the University of Tokyo

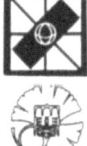

In Coorporation with:

Information Processing Society of Japan

The Institute of Electronics, Information
and Communication Engineers

Supported by: (alphabetical order)

Asahi Kasei Information Systems Co. Ltd.

Fujitsu Limited

Hitachi Microcomputer System Ltd.

Kubota Computer Inc.

Nihon Silicon Graphics K.K.

Nihon Sun Microsystems K.K.

Nissan Motor Co. Ltd.

Oki Electric Industry Co. Ltd.

Ricoh Co. Ltd. Software Division

Conference Committees

General Chairmen: J.L. Encarnação (Germany), Z. Tang (China)

Program Committee:

Program Chairman
T.L. Kunii (Japan)
Members
H. Chiyokura (Japan)
J.L. Encarnação (Germany)
B. Falcidieno (Italy)
A.E. Kaufmann (USA)
N. Magnenat-Thalmann
(Switzerland)
E. Nakamae (Japan)
Y. Shirai (Japan)

W. Straßer (Germany)
Z. Tang (China)
D. Thalmann (Switzerland)
G.T. Toussaint (Canada)
A. van Dam (USA)
T.C. Woo (USA)
G. Wyvill (New Zealand)

List of External Reviewers

Pierre van Berkel
Thomas. W. Calvert
Martin J. Dürst
Hirohisa Enomoto
Issei Fujishiro
Hironobu Gotoda
Richard Greene
Qinglian Guo
Gérard Hégron
Christine C. Hofmann
G.R. Hofmann
Hiroshi Imai
Emery Jou
Nami Kin
Kornél Klement
Jin Tae Lee
Kyu-Jae Lee

Myeong Won Lee
Junji Maeda
Kaoru Maeda
Ryo Mukai
G. Nagy
Satoshi Nishimura
Tsukasa Noma
C. Porzia
Jarek Rossignac
Hitoshi Saji
Yoshihisa Shinagawa
M. Spagnuolo
Lining Sun
Kangda Wang
Kazunori Yamaguchi
Kensyu Yoshida

Local Arrangement Committee

Local Arrangement Chairman: Y. Shinagawa (Japan)
Members: N. Kin (Japan), Q. Guo (Japan)

Table of Contents

Part 2: Roles of Modeling

Part 3: Modeling of Applications

Chapter 9: Modeling of Art Painting

Chapter 10: Modeling of Computer-Aided Design

PART 1

Disciplines of Modeling

Chapter 1

Mathematical Modeling

The Differential Model: A Model for Animating Transformation of Objects Using Differential Inforamtion

Yoshihisa Shinagawa and Tosiyasu L. Kunii

ABSTRACT

A new model named the differential model is presented for representing the transformation of objects using differential information. Differential information refers to the curvature and torsion of a curve, the first and the second fundamental forms of a surface and the first fundamental form of a solid object. Given the initial and the final states in the transformation of an object, we compute the initial and the final values of these differential variables. Then, we interpolate the initial and the final values to obtain the in-between values. Finally, the in-between shapes with the desired values of the differential variables are reconstructed. It is possible to represent wide changes in the global shape with simple interpolation of differential variables. It is also easy to represent isometric (preserving the line length or the first fundamental form) transformation. Simulating the transformation of the coiled filamentous structure of the acrosome of an abalone sperm illustrates the efficiency of this method.

Key Words and Phrases: transformation animation, differential, metric tensor, fundamental form, tangent line, curvature, torsion

1. INTRODUCTION

Modeling transformation of objects has been done using global variables such as the coordinate values of each part of an object; i.e., given the initial coordinate value $f_0(u)$ and the final coordinate value $f_1(u)$ of each point of the object, the transformation is modeled by the interpolation $f_t(u)$ of $f_0(u)$ and $f_1(u)$. This method does not work when there are wide changes in the global shape. For example, when we apply this method to the animation of bending a stick, it appears that the stick shrinks first and then elongates (see Fig. 1). Physically based modeling [Weil 1986; Issacs and Cohen 1987; Barzel and Barr 1988; Terzopoulos and Fleischer 1988; Miller 1988] uses differential information. They are used, however, for motion control only; i.e., the differential variables are computed from the given global variables and are used just for deciding the change in the values of the global variables [Terzopoulos, Platt, Barr and Fleischer 1987; Platt and Barr 1988]. Terzopoulos, Platt, Barr and Fleisher (1987), for example, used the Lagrange's form of the equation of motion

$$\frac{\partial}{\partial t}(\mu \frac{\partial \mathbf{r}}{\partial t}) + \xi \frac{\partial \mathbf{r}}{\partial t} + \frac{\delta E(\mathbf{r})}{\delta \mathbf{r}} = \mathbf{f}(\mathbf{r},t)$$

where $\mathbf{r}$ is the position of the particle, μ is the mass density, ξ is the damping density and $\mathbf{f}$ represents the net externally applied forces. The differential information is used only for the energy of the deformation (the third term of the left hand side). For a curve, for example, they used the strain energy

$$E(\mathbf{r}) = \int \alpha(s - s^0) + \beta(\kappa - \kappa^0) + \gamma(\tau - \tau^0) da$$

where s, κ, τ are the arc length, the curvature, the torsion respectively and α, β, ξ are the amount of resistance of the curve to stretching, bending, twisting, respectively. It is required to solve

t = 0

t = 0.5

t = 1

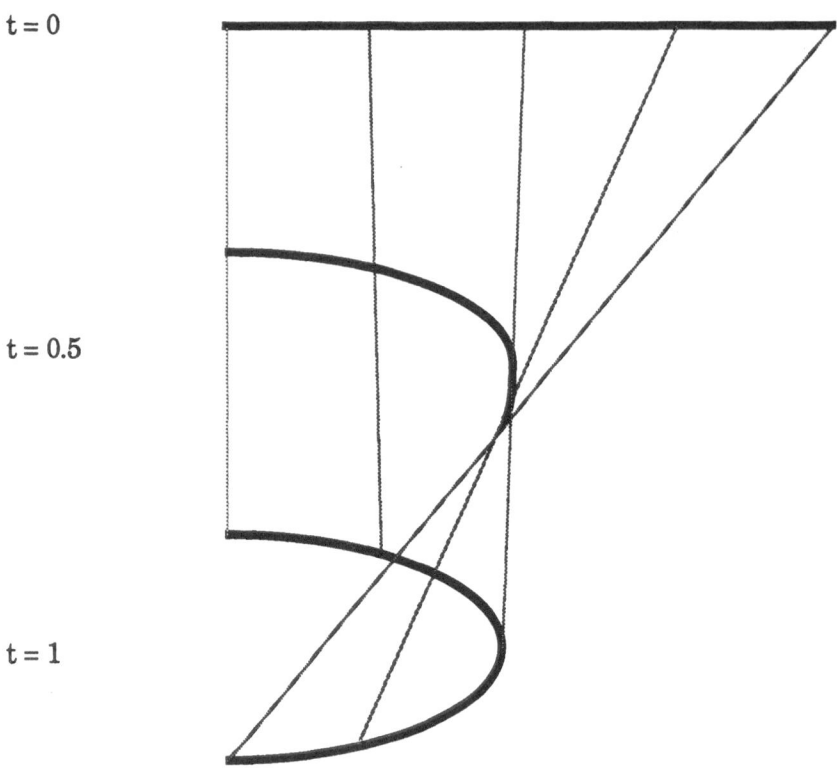

Fig.1. The transformation that cannot be represented
by a simple interpolation of global variables

complicated systems of equations of motion. Barr (1984) used Jacobian, which is the first derivative, to control the deformation. However, they did not take the second derivative and the isometric transformation into consideration.

In our approach, the roles of the global and the differential information are interchanged. Differential information here denotes variables such as the curvature and torsion of a curve, the first and the second fundamental forms of a surface and the metric tensor of a solid object. In the rest of this paper these variables are referred to as "differential variables." The differential variables represent local information. The global variables can be computed from the given differential variables. The fundamental theorems [e.g., do Carmo 1976] guarantees that the global shape of an object is decided uniquely by the differential variables. This is discussed in detail later. Given the initial and the final states of the transformation of an object, we first compute the initial and the final values of these differential variables. Then, we interpolate the initial and the final values to obtain the in-between values. Finally, the in-between shape is reconstructed that has the given values of the differential variables, which is used as a frame in the transformation animation. The main advantage of this method is that it is possible to represent wide changes in the global shape with simple interpolation of differential variables. It is also easy to represent isometric transformation which preserves the line length or the area of the object by simply keeping the arc length or the first fundamental form constant. An example of animating the transformation of the coiled filamentous structure in the acrosome of the abalone sperm is presented.

2. CHOOSING THE DIFFERENTIAL VARIABLES

First of all, we have to choose a set of differential variables which will decide the shape of the object uniquely. The choice depends on the dimension of the object.

CASE 1. 1-D (space curve)
The fundamental theorem of curves [do Carmo 1976] states that two curves have the same shape (differing only by a rigid body motion) if their curvature and torsion are identical. Therefore, we choose the curvature and torsion. Their definitions are as follows. First of all, the curve α is

$$\alpha : \mathbf{R} \rightarrow \mathbf{R}^3$$

and it is assumed to be parametrized by the arc length s.
The curvature is defined as

$$k(s) = |\alpha''(s)|$$

and when $k(s) \neq 0$, we define normal vector $n(s)$, a unit vector in the direction of $\alpha''(s)$ by

$$n(s) = \alpha''(s) / k(s).$$

In what follows, we shall restrict ourselves to curves without points where $k'(s) = 0$ holds. We shall denote by $t(s) = \alpha'(s)$ the unit tangent vector of α at s. The unit vector $b(s) = t(s) \times n(s)$ is called the binormal vector at s. Here, $\times$ denotes the outer product. Then the torsion $\tau(s)$ of α at s is defined by

$$b'(s) = \tau(s) n(s).$$

The set of the orthogonal unit vectors $\{t(s), n(s), b(s)\}$ is referred to as the Frenet trihedron and we use this as the local coordinate system at the point on the curve.

CASE 2. 2-D (surface)
The fundamental theorem of surfaces by Bonnet [e.g., do Carmo 1976] states that two surfaces have the same shape if their first and second fundamental forms are identical. Therefore, we choose the first and the second fundamental forms. Their definitions are as follows. First of all, the object assumed to be covered by a single coordinate neighborhood [e.g., do Carmo 1976]; the surface is parametrized by a map

$$x(u, v): \mathbf{R}^2 \rightarrow \mathbf{R}^3.$$

The first fundamental form at the point $p = x(u_0, v_0)$ is expressed by

$$E(u_0, v_0) = \mathbf{x}_u(u_0, v_0) \bullet \mathbf{x}_u(u_0, v_0)$$

$$F(u_0, v_0) = \mathbf{x}_u(u_0, v_0) \bullet \mathbf{x}_v(u_0, v_0)$$

$$G(u_0, v_0) = \mathbf{x}_v(u_0, v_0) \bullet \mathbf{x}_v(u_0, v_0)$$

where $\mathbf{x}_u = \partial \mathbf{x} / \partial u$, $\mathbf{x}_v = \partial \mathbf{x} / \partial v$ and $\bullet$ denotes the inner product. Let N be a unit normal vector at point p defined by

$$N(p) = \frac{\mathbf{x}_u \times \mathbf{x}_v}{|\mathbf{x}_u \times \mathbf{x}_v|}.$$ The expression of the second fundamental form is given by

$$e(u_0, v_0) = N \bullet \mathbf{x}_{uu}(u_0, v_0)$$

$$f(u_0, v_0) = N \bullet \mathbf{x}_{uv}(u_0, v_0)$$

$$g(u_0, v_0) = N \bullet \mathbf{x}_{vv}(u_0, v_0).$$

CASE 3. 3-D (solid)

The two solids have the same shape if their first fundamental forms are identical [e.g., Terzopoulos, Platt, Barr and Fleischer 1987]. Therefore, we choose the first fundamental form. Let the solid be parametrized by a map

$$\mathbf{x}(u, v, w): \mathbf{R}^3 \rightarrow \mathbf{R}^3.$$

The first fundamental form is given by

$$G_{ij} = \mathbf{x}_{t_i} \bullet \mathbf{x}_{t_j}$$

where $t_1 = u$, $t_2 = v$ and $t_3 = w$.

3. INTERPOLATION OF DIFFERENTIAL VARIABLES

Let u be the coordinate value of a point of the object and let $A_0(u)$, $A_1(u)$ be differential variables at the point indicated by u of the initial state (at time t = 0) and the final state (at time t = 1) respectively. Then the differential variable at time t is can be given by

$$f(x, t) A_0 + (1-f(x, t))A_1$$

where $f(u, 0) = 1$ for all u. $f : \mathbf{R} \rightarrow \mathbf{R}$ is a blending function which simulates the transformation. When the transformation is a linear interpolation from the initial state to the final state,

$$f(t) = \begin{cases} 1-t & (0 \le t \le 1) \\ 0 & (1 \le t) \end{cases} .$$

We can use

$$f(x) = \cos(\omega t)$$

to express oscillation and

$$f(x) = e^{-\gamma t}$$

for damped motion.

4. RECONSTRUCTION PROCEDURE

This section discusses the reconstruction of the entire shape of the object from the given differential variables. The reconstruction procedure differs according to the dimension of the object.

4-1. Space Curve

In order to reconstruct the shape of the object, we must discretize the differential variables. First, we divide the object into small elements at the interval of Δs. The elements are as shown in Fig. 2. Then, we use the values of differential variables A(0), A(Δs), A($2\Delta s$),... instead of the continuous function A. A(0), A(Δs), A($2\Delta s$),... are used as sample values of the differential variables of each element. Δs has to be sufficiently small. For simplicity, however, we assume that $\Delta s = 1$ in what follows.

For the discretization of the curvature and the torsion, it is convenient to use the angle between the vectors instead of these scalar value. Because of the discretization error, $t(s+\Delta s) - t(s)$ is not in the direction of $n(s)$, although for the limit $\Delta s \rightarrow 0$ the two directions coincide and we have $t'(s) = k(s)n(s)$. Therefore, we used the angle between $t(s+\Delta s)$ and $t(s)$; more formally,

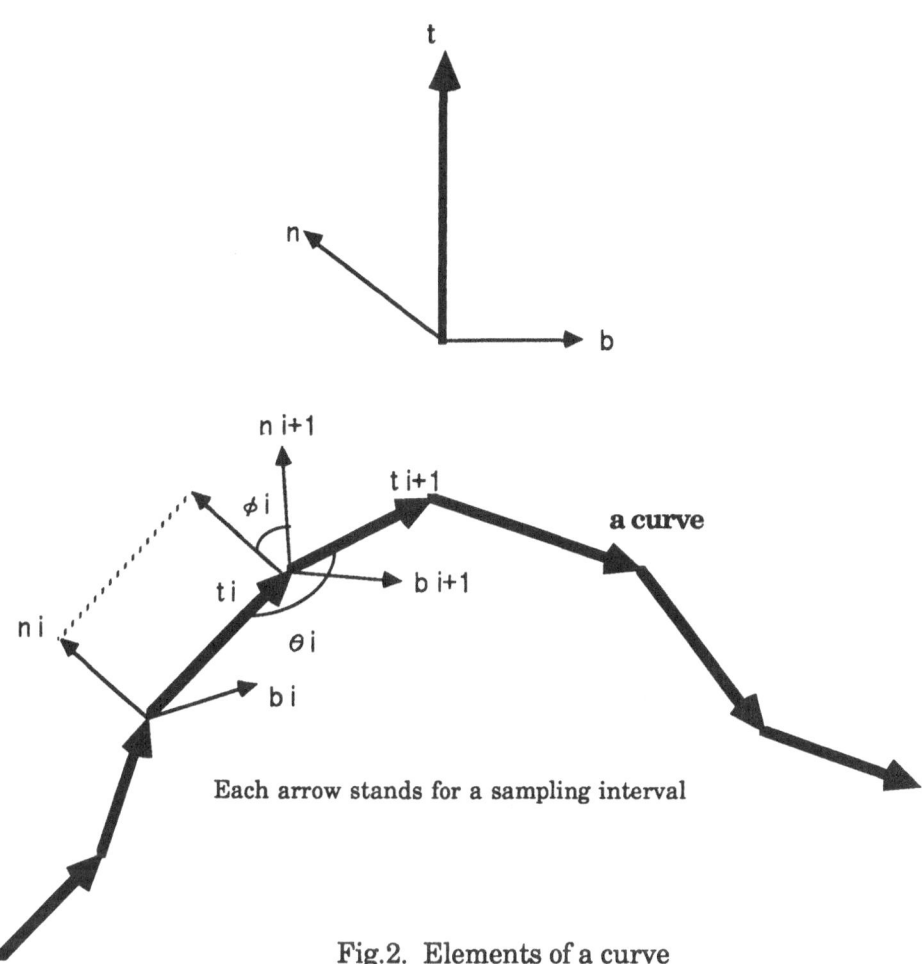

Each arrow stands for a sampling interval

Fig.2. Elements of a curve

$$\theta = \cos^{-1}(t(s+\Delta s), t(s))$$

was used. We call this value "curvature angle". When $t(s+\Delta s) = t(s)$ holds, $n(s)$, $b(s)$ cannot be defined. In that case, the value of ds is modified to avoid this. In the same way, we used

$$\phi = \cos^{-1}(b(s+\Delta s), b(s)).$$

We call this value "torsion angle". When $\kappa = 0$, we set $\tau = 0$ for ease of implementation.

Then, the reconstruction procedure is described as follows. We denote by θ_i the curvature angle and by ϕ_i the torsion angle, by $\{t_i, n_i, b_i\}$ the Frenet trihedron of the element i (i = 1,...,). Let us assume that element 1 through i are connected. Then the element i+1 is added as follows.
STEP 1. Set the element i+1 so that the angle between t_{i+1} and t_i is θ_{i+1}.
STEP 2. Rotate the element around t_i so that the angle between n_{i+1} and n_i is τ_{i+1}.

4-2. Surface

This section discusses the reconstruction of the surface from the given first and second fundamental forms. For simplicity, we take the discretization intervals Δu and Δv of the parameters u and v as 1. The element is as shown in Fig. 3. In what follows, the element corresponding to the point (u_i, v_j) is referred to as $L_{i,j}$, the origin of the element is referred to as $O_{i,j}$, the terminal points of the two arrows from the origin are referred to as $U_{i,j}$ and $V_{i,j}$ in the direction of $\mathbf{x}_u$ and $\mathbf{x}_v$ respectively, and $E_{i,j}$, $F_{i,j}$, $G_{i,j}$, $e_{i,j}$, $f_{i,j}$ and $g_{i,j}$ are the fundamental forms at the point (u_i, v_j) (see Fig. 3). The angle ϕ is given as

$$\cos \phi = F / \sqrt{EG} .$$

Also, the lengths of the arrows are decided so that $\overline{O_{i,j}U_{i,j}} = \sqrt{E}$ and $\overline{O_{i,j}V_{i,j}} = \sqrt{G}$ hold. The surface is reconstructed by forming a grid using these elements (see Fig. 3). The fundamental theorem by Bonnet demands E, F, G, e, f and g satisfy the Gauss equation, the Mainardi-Codazzi equations and the condition $EG - F^2 > 0$. When these conditions are satisfied, the reconstruction is straight-forward as follows.
STEP 1. Align $L_{i,0}$ ($i = 0,1,2,...$). To be more precise, $L_{i,0}$ is located next to $L_{i-1,0}$ so that $O_{i,0}$ coincides with $U_{i-1,0}$, the distance from $U_{i,0}$ to the plane that contains $L_{i-1,0}$ is $E_{i,0}$, the distance from $V_{i,0}$ to that plane is $F_{i,0}$ and the distance from $V_{i,0}$ to $V_{i-1,0}$ is $E_{i-1,1}$.
STEP 2. Let j = 1.
STEP 3. Align $L_{i,j}$ ($i = 0,1,2,...$). To be more precise, $L_{i,j}$ is located next to $L_{i,j-1}$ so that $O_{i,j}$ coincides with $V_{i,j-1}$, $U_{i,j}$ coincides with $V_{i+1,j-1}$ and the distance from $U_{i,j}$ to the plane that contains $L_{i,j-1}$ is $G_{i,j}$.
STEP 4. Let j ← j+1 and goto STEP 3.

When the discretization errors cannot be ignored, STEP 3 of the above procedure does not work well. Also, although the first and the second fundamental forms of the initial and the final states of the object satisfy the Gauss equation, the Mainardi-Codazzi equations and the condition $EG - F^2 > 0$, the interpolated values of the fundamental forms are not guaranteed to satisfy the Gauss equation and Mainardi-Codazzi equations (the condition $EG - F^2 > 0$ is satisfied). This is easily seen from the form of one of the Mainardi-Codazzi equations

$$e_v - f_u = e\,(\Gamma^1{}_{12}) + f\,(\Gamma^2{}_{12} - \Gamma^1{}_{11}) - g\,(\Gamma^2{}_{11}),$$

where the Christoffel symbols $\Gamma^i{}_{jk}$ are given by

$$\Gamma^1{}_{11}E + \Gamma^2{}_{11}F = E_u / 2,$$

$$\Gamma^1{}_{11}F + \Gamma^2{}_{11}G = F_u - E_v / 2,$$

$$\Gamma^1{}_{12}E + \Gamma^2{}_{12}F = E_v / 2 \text{ and}$$

$$\Gamma^1{}_{12}F + \Gamma^2{}_{12}G = G_u / 2.$$

Therefore, STEP 3 has to be modified to cancel the errors as follows.
STEP 3'. $L_{i,j}$ is located next to $L_{i,j-1}$ so that $O_{i,j}$ coincides with $V_{i,j-1}$, the direction of $\overline{O_{i,j}U_{i,j}}$ coincides with $\overline{O_{i,j}V_{i+1,j-1}}$ and the distance from $U_{i,j}$ to the plane that contains $L_{i,j-1}$ is $G_{i,j}$.

4-2. Solid

This section discusses the reconstruction of the solid from the given first fundamental form. As usual, we take the discretization intervals Δu, Δv and Δw of the parameters u, v, w as 1 for simplicity. The element is as shown in Fig. 4. In what follows, the element corresponding to the point (u_i, v_j, w_k) is referred to as $L_{i,j,k}$, the origin of the element is referred to as $O_{i,j,k}$, the terminal points of the three arrows from the origin are referred to as $U_{i,j,k}$, $V_{i,j,k}$ and $W_{i,j,k}$ in the direction of $\mathbf{x}_u$, $\mathbf{x}_v$ and $\mathbf{x}_w$, respectively (see Fig. 4). The positions of the terminal points of the arrows are determined so that

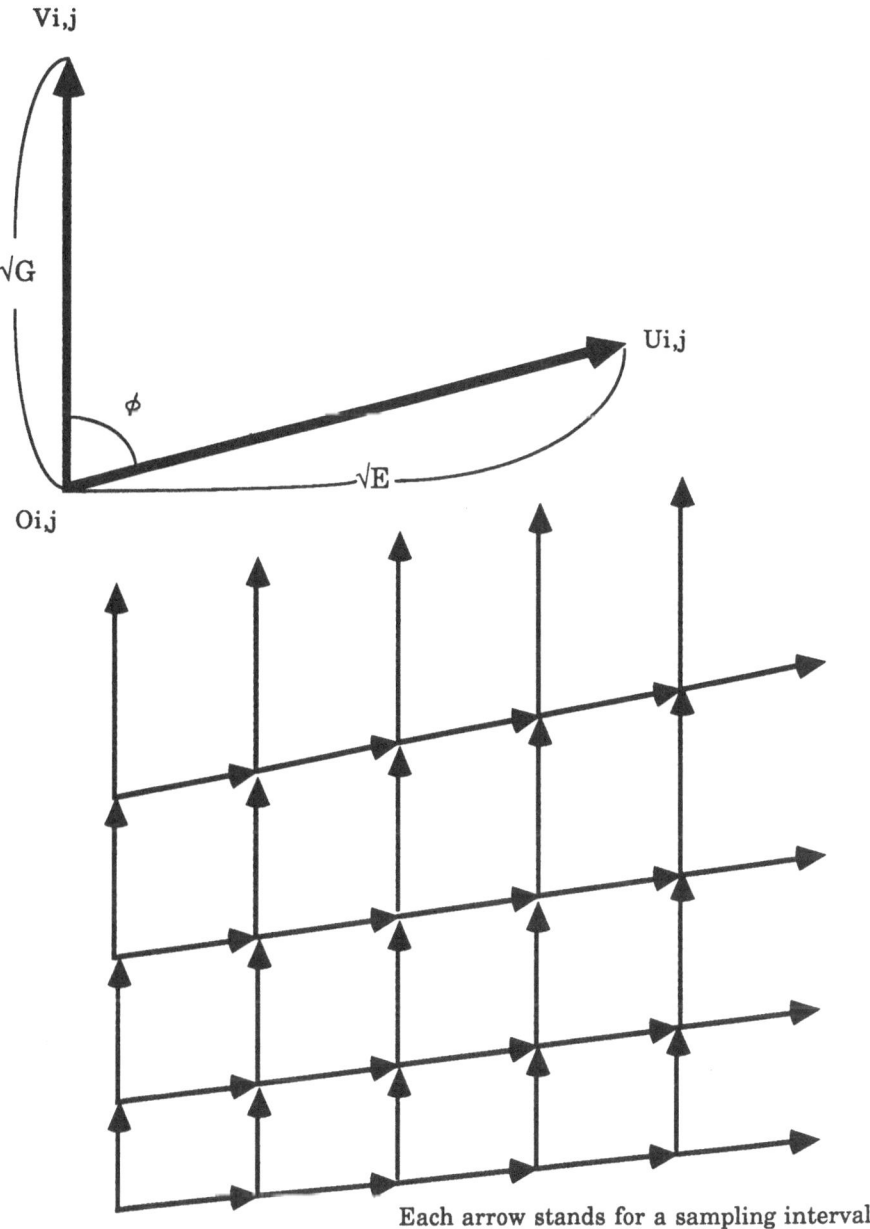

Each arrow stands for a sampling interval

Fig. 3. Elements of a surface

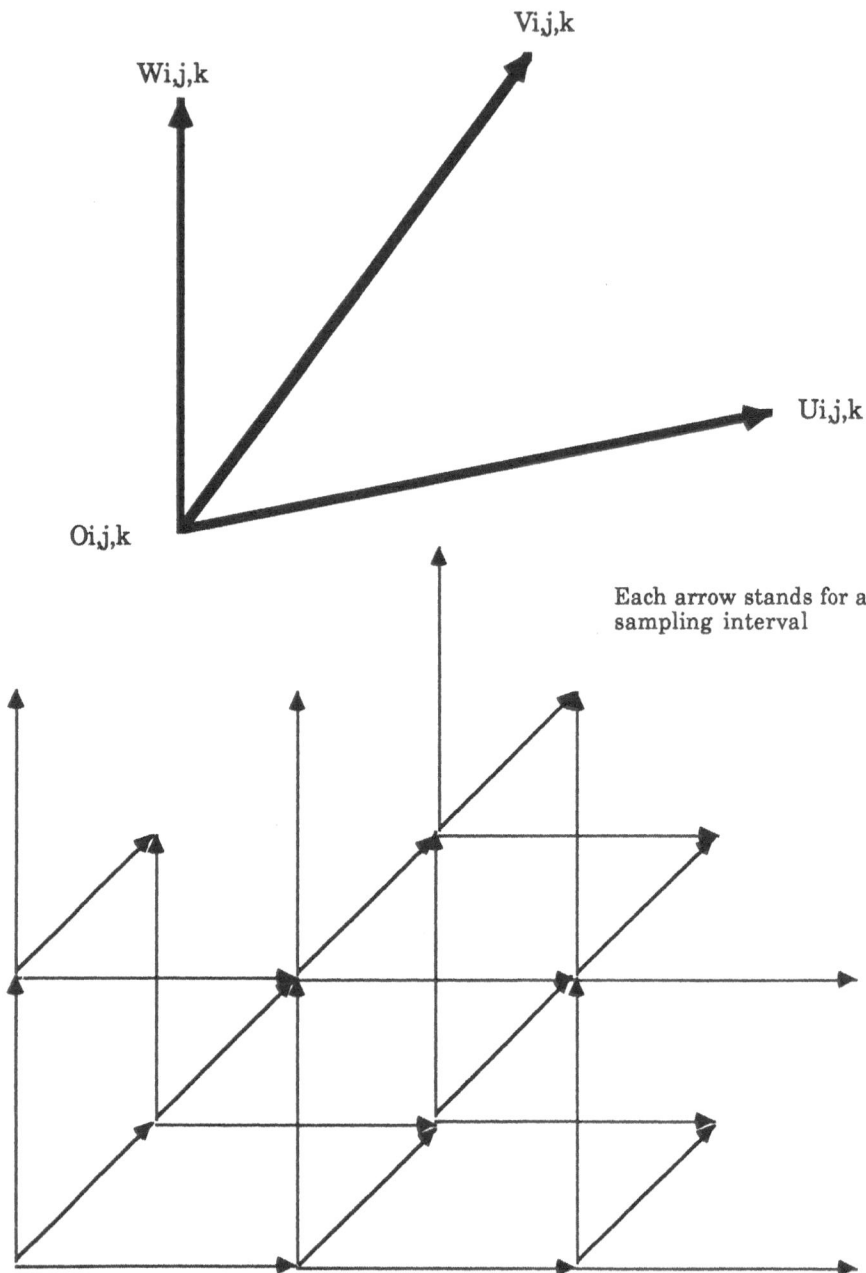

Fig. 4. Elements of a solid

$$\overline{O_{i,j,k}U_{i,j,k}} = \sqrt{G_{11}},$$

$$\overline{O_{i,j,k}V_{i,j,k}} = \sqrt{G_{22}},$$

$$\overline{O_{i,j,k}W_{i,j,k}} = \sqrt{G_{33}},$$

$$O_{i,j,k}U_{i,j,k} \times O_{i,j,k}V_{i,j,k} = G_{12},$$

$$O_{i,j,k}U_{i,j,k} \times O_{i,j,k}W_{i,j,k} = G_{13} \text{ and}$$

$$O_{i,j,k}V_{i,j,k} \times O_{i,j,k}W_{i,j,k} = G_{23}$$

hold. The solid is reconstructed by constructing a grid by these elements. (see Fig. 4).

STEP 1. Let $l = 0$.
STEP 2. Locate $L_{i,j,k}$ $(i + j + k = l)$. When deciding the location of $L_{i,j,k}$, the positions of $L_{i-1,j,k}$, $L_{l-1,j+1,k}$ and $L_{l-1,j,k+1}$ are determined at the same time, i.e.,

$$O_{i,j,k} == U_{i-1,j,k} \qquad (1)$$

$$V_{i,j,k} == U_{i-1,j+1,k} \qquad (2)$$

$$W_{i,j,k} == U_{i-1,j,k+1} \qquad (3)$$

$$O_{i-1,j+1,k} == V_{i-1,j,k} \qquad (4)$$

$$W_{i-1,j+1,k} == V_{i-1,j,k+1} \qquad (5)$$

$$O_{i-1,j,k+1} == W_{i-1,j,k} \qquad (6)$$

Here, '==' means that the positions of the right hand side and the left hand side must coincide with each other.
STEP 3. Let $l \leftarrow l+1$ and go to STEP 2.

By the same reason as the previous section, the STEP 2 of the above procedure might fail to work well. Therefore, STEP 2 has to be modified to cancel the errors. It can be modified as follows. The condition (1), (4) and (6) can be always satisfied. We try to satisfy the condition (2), (3) and (5) in this order. If it is impossible to satisfy one or more of the conditions, the element is located so as to minimize the sum of the squares of the errors with respect to each conditions. Here, the absolute value of the difference between the position on the right hand side and that on the left hand side of the above conditions is referred to as the size of the error.

5. DISPLAY EXAMPLE

As an example, the transformation of the coiled filamentous structure in the acrosome of abalone sperm heads is presented. The filamentous structure, which is referred to as the "truncated cone" in the apex of the acrosome was isolated from abalone sperm heads. Observation of the isolated truncated cone fraction by negative staining revealed that the truncated cone was composed of a helically coiled filamentous structure [Shiroya, Maekawa and Sakai 1989]. This structure elongates anteriorly from the opening of the acrosome and transforms into a cylindrical structure to closely encircle the acrosomal process during the acrosome reaction. The transformation of the truncated cone is shown in Fig. 5. It is not easy to model such a transformation by using global variables because the transformation cannot be expressed by simple interpolation of $f_0(u)$ and $f_1(u)$ where $f_0(u)$ and $f_1(u)$ are the global coordinate values of each point of the object. Fig. 5 shows the effectiveness of the use of differential vareables to model this type of transformation.

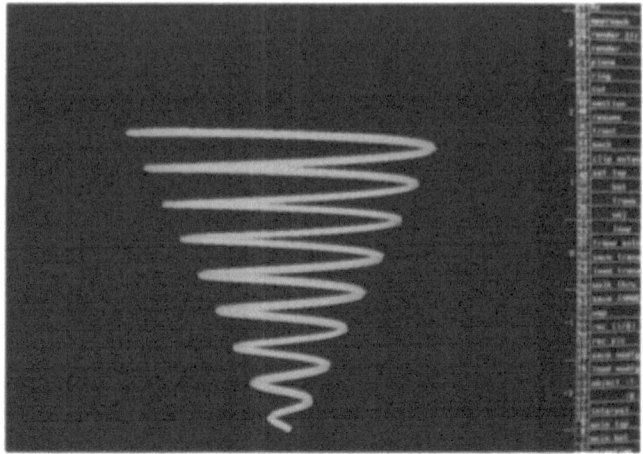

(a) The original shape of the truncated cone

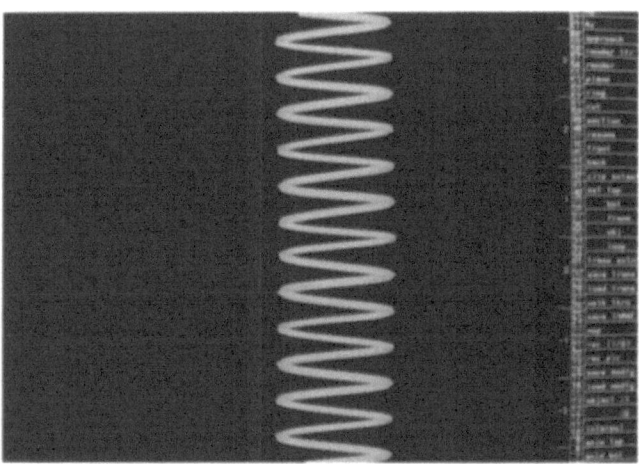

(b) The shape of the truncated cone after elongation

Fig. 5. The transformation of the truncated cone

6. CONCLUSIONS AND FUTURE WORK

A new method to model the transformation using only differential variables was presented. This method enables us to simulate wide changes in shape by a simple interpolation of the differential variables. The implementation and the study of the effective method to cancel the errors in the case of the 2-D and 3-D objects is left as future research. To provide a method for the objects which cannot be covered by a single coordinate neighborhood is another extension that we have in mind.

ACKNOWLEDGMENTS

The work is the result of our initial effort to present a model to simulate the transformation of the coiled filamentous structure of the acrosome of an abalone sperm. We wish to thank Prof. Y.T. Sakai of Wayo Women's University for explaining the problem to us.
We wish to express our gratitude to Graphica Co., Ltd. and Cadtech Inc. for offering the drum scanner, G-225C, Yokogawa Hewlet Packard Co., Ltd. for HP900 model 550 and Silicon Graphics Co., Ltd. for personal IRIS.
Special thanks are extended to Ms. Deepa Krishnan of the Kunii Laboratory of Computer Science, the University of Tokyo for help in copy editing the manuscript.

REFERENCES

Barr A (July 1984) Global and Local Deformations of Solid Primitives. *ACM Computer Graphics, Vol.18, No. 3* , pp.21-30

Barzel R, Barr A (August 1988) A Modeling System Base On Dynamic Constraints. *ACM Computer Graphics, Vol.22, No. 4* , pp.179-188

do Carmo MP (1976) *Differential Geometry of Curves and Surfaces.* Prentice-Hall, New Jersey London Sydney Toronto New Delhi Tokyo Singapore, p.273

Issacs PM, Cohen MF (July 1987) Controlling Dynamic Simulation with Kinematic Constraints, Behavior Functions and Inverse Dynamics. *ACM Computer Graphics, Vol.21, No. 4* , pp. 169-178

Miller GSP (August 1988) The Motion Dynamics of Snakes and Worms. *ACM Computer Graphics, Vol.22, No. 4* , pp. 215-224

Platt J, Barr A (August 1988) Constraint Methods for Flexible Models. *ACM Computer Graphics, Vol.22, No. 4* , pp.279-288

Shiroya Y, Maekawa S, Sakai YT (1989) Characterization of a Coiled Filamentous Structure, "Truncated Cone", in the Acrosome of Abalone Sperm. *Cell Structure and Function 14*, pp. 415-428

Terzopoulos D, Platt J, Barr A, Fleischer K (July 1987) Elastically Deformable Models. *ACM Computer Graphics, Vol.21, No. 4* , pp. 205-214

Terzopoulos D, Fleischer K (August 1988) Modeling Inelastic Deformation: Viscoelasticity, Plasticity, Fracture. *ACM Computer Graphics, Vol.22, No. 4* , pp. 269-278

Weil J (August 1986) The Synthesis of Cloth Objects *ACM Computer Graphics, Vol.20, No. 4* , pp. 49-54

Department of Information Science, Faculty of Science, The University of Tokyo, Tokyo, 113 Japan

Equivalence Classes in Object Space Modelling

Michel Lucas

ABSTRACT

Wo procent in this paper a new approach to geometric modelling, which we call declarative modelling. The aim is to describe objects pertaining to a given shape universe through sets of properties and constraints. The computer has to generate the potential answers to this description, and to present them to the user. Declarative modelling implies the development of tools allowings us to describe, generate, explore, visualize and understand classes of objects. The potential application areas are concerned with the construction of benchmarks for graphics, generation of scenes through the description of properties and constraints, the illustration of mental concepts. Examples concerning diverse universes of shapes are given (cellular automata, voxel matrices, polyhedra, segments configurations).

Keywords: geometric modelling, declarative modelling, universes of shapes, Artificial Intelligence.

1 . INTRODUCTION

There exist today efficient algorithms and machines allowing us to produce realistic pictures, attaining a high degree of sophication. The use of parallel techniques has led to real-time processing of complex scenes. In general, *complex* means: built from a great number of primitives (up to a million), such as planar polygons. The question is now: how do we get this bunch of polygons ?

Actual modelling systems offer powerful tools to describe 3-D scenes. Various modelling schemes may be used (Requicha 1980), and have been thoroughly studied. However, the need for more deeper understanding is still on. Major part of the research work today emphasizes computation techniques such as how to properly calculate the result of boolean operations ? We think that, although this is an important point, other ways have to be explored.

2 . DECLARATIVE MODELLING

Let us imagine...

a small town, coming from the old ages

thick walls are running all around, build from enormous stones,

impressive towers dominate hollow moats

narrow streets meander through tiny houses

...

Let us suppose now that we wish to translate this mental image into a geometric model, so that pictures could be produced by a computer. If we use actual modelling systems, such as CAD systems, we will have to transform this nice picture into a lot of geometric primitives, worrying about coordinates, edges, elementary shapes, boolean operators, so that we could enter the description of one such town into the computer language. We call this way of thinking <u>imperative modelling</u>. This process is pictured in Fig. 1:

      user   **idea**   ---> **object** ---> **model**

      computer   **model**   ---> **picture**

Fig. 1 imperative modelling

<u>Declarative modelling</u> is aiming at lightening the burden of the user, by allowing him to forget the geometric primitives. He will describe the desired object(s), using perhaps natural language. The computer will have to generate all (or part of) the objects corresponding to this description. In particular, it is now the responsibility of the computer to decompose the described scene into primitives, that is to say to build the corresponding geometric model. The schema is such as in Fig. 2:

      user   **idea**   --->   / **description**

      computer   **description** ---> **objects** ---> **model** ---> **picture**

fig. 2: declarative modelling

Let us quote some potential applications. We can characterize declarative modelling system as being systems which are expert in providing:

- benchmarks for graphics algorithms. In order to understand the complexity of graphics algorithms (such as ray-tracing algorithms), automatic generation of scenes having predicted properties could help us to really compare the efficiency of different programs.

- complex scenes. Here, *complex* not only means 'composed of numerous primitives', but also corresponds to the fact that it is sometimes difficult for the user to give the values determining complex shapes. The computer will help in finding these values.

- new shapes (art, architecture, design, ...): exploring a universe of shapes should lead us to discover shapes which have never been seen, because people have not thought of them.

The project ExploFormes, which is currently under investigation in Nantes (France), is aiming at providing algorithms for exploring universes of shapes. A universe of shapes is the set of all objects which can be built within a particular world, defined through some basic properties or elementary primitives. We are studying a variety of those universes, in order to be able to enlight as well basic problems of such an approach as common or particular solutions to these problems.

Two basic mechanisms are under study:
- automatic generation of all objects pertaining to a particular universe of shapes. This ensures us that all objects of the universe can be reached, if needed.

- selective exploration of this universe, using geometric, topological, mechanical properties in order to describe the desired objects. One example is the use of cutting techniques, which allow us not to travel into regions of the universe containing no objects of interest.

The general goal of the project is to study how is it possible to describe, generate and study objects pertaining to various universes of shapes. The corresponding programs are called Explorators. Some of them will be depicted later in this paper.

When designing an Explorator, the following tools are needed:
 . description
 . generation
 . understanding (visualization, learning)

3 . DESCRIPTION

In a first step, we may say that declarative modelling is modelling without coordinates or values. This means that we wish to use formal definitions of a classes of objects. These descriptions are given by means of lists of necessary and sufficient properties, defining completely these classes. Different problems occur when dealing with properties or constraints:

- there exist classes of properties: topological, geometric, mechanical ones, which allow us to give the more appropriate description of the desired objects. An Explorator will have to be able to understand words pertaining to a basic vocabulary, characterizing the universe to explore.

- there exist global or local properties. The first ones are associated with the elementary primitives allowing us to build objects. The second ones permit us to establish links with all or part of the primitives creating an object. Global or local properties will play an important role when trying to establish structuring or cutting rules (using for instance heredity).

- there is a need to be able to combine various properties or constraints. We must provide mechanisms to check the coherence of a set of constraints, or the derivation of new properties when combining given ones.

We shall give some examples of results we have obtained today. The first is linked with the PolyFormes project (Martin 88, Martin 89). The explored universe is that of regular or semi-regular polyhedra. This universe is well known from the mathematicians. A rich vocabulary exists, allowing us to describe with a few words complex shapes. Pict. 3 gives a typical example.

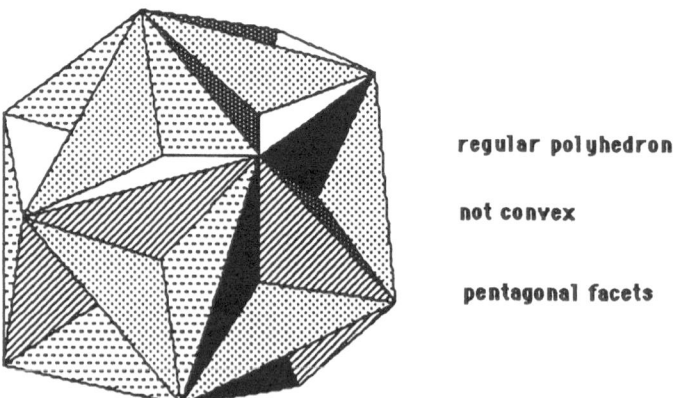

regular polyhedron

not convex

pentagonal facets

Pict. 3 - a polyhedron and its formal description

This polyhedron is entirely defined with the few words which are given in the picture. Martin D. and Martin P. have developed an Explorator based on an expert system and an inference engine allowing a user to give a list of properties concerning the shape of the polygons (regular, star, convex, ...), the sequence of polygons around a vertex, generic properties (dual of ...). This program can produce all the polygons corresponding to such a list, if there exists one.

In the case of the universe of polyhedra, the basic vocabulary was existing. The problem was to compute the corresponding values (coordinates, polygons). In general, we do not have such a vocabulary to our disposal. For instance, the AutoFormes project (Lucas 89, Martin 90) deals with pictures generated by linear cellular automata. It is very easy to write a program producing lots of pictures. However, if one would like to control the produced picture (for instance to produce textures), one needs to describe it: which components, how to do the lay-out, and so on. Martin JY has derived an Explorator allowing us, for instance, to draw patterns, such as the one appearing in Pict. 4.

Pict. 4 - an example of pattern

The Explorator computes if there exists a corresponding cellular automaton, and produces a list of evolution rules. Each of them is able to produce a set of pictures, every one containing copies of the initial pattern. An example of such a picture may be found in Pict. 5.

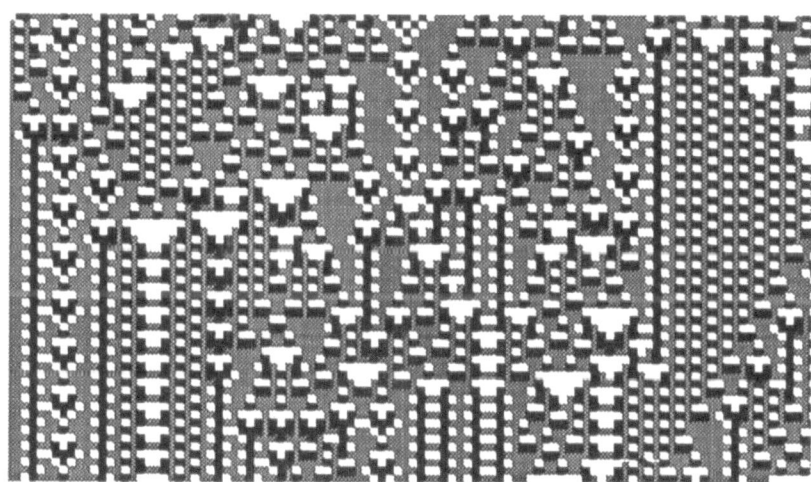

Pict. 5 - A picture containing the pattern of Pict. 4

One can see that we have here a kind of local control: the Explorator is able to produce pictures containing copies of the pattern. It would be nice to control the general arrangement of the patterns. Martin J.Y. has provided some mechanisms, such as the ability to produce appropriate evolution rules through the study of a picture produced by an unknown cellular automaton. However, we do not know today how to describe such pictures, using words: we miss a basic vocabulary.

In fact, this is a very general problem: for most of the applications, there does not exist a standard vocabulary. People do not know how to describe objects. This also explains why we have focused upon generation mechanisms: we think that the description system can be seen as a layer put upon the generation layer.

4 . GENERATION

The goal of the generation module is to create one (or many) object(s) pertaining to the studied universe. To create one object, we need:

- to choose a geometric modelling schema (primitives, coordinates), which will give the materials allowing us to build geometric models,

- to be able to transform the formal model into the geometric model, allowing us to associate a shape to each object responding to the laid down constraints.

Different ways may be used to create objects:

- random generation: objects are selected at the random from the universe,

- specific algorithms: programs are written, which deliver exactly the desired objects,

- generating trees, which allow us to structure the universe of shapes, so that we can achieve selective explorations.

4.1 Random Generation

This is a very popular way to explore universes. The reason is that it is very simple, in general, to write programs producing a great number of objects are created by randomly choosing coordinates and generic values. For instance, it is easy to create random objects using octrees, by choosing at the random if a node is empty, full, or to be divided. If you have a good random numbers generator, you can obtain very different objects.

There are some keys for random generation. The first one is parametrization. Objects have to be reduced to a few number of parameters. The generation process is essentially devoted to obtaining at the random values pertaining to a specific domain.

A second key is what can be called *randomness* control (!):

- random generation without control. This means that we do not know how the generator works. The result is that we do not know anything about the objects.

- random generation with control. This means that we know how the random generator works. In general, distribution laws are used, so that objects properties are known.

This technique is so simple, that in a first step people may wish to use it. However, there remain many difficulties:

- is it sure that every property can be expressed through random values ? how to combine properties ?

- we are not sure to find all configurations. This means that it could happen that a very interesting object (may be the only one existing) be missed.

This is not acceptable. This explains why we do not use random generation for exploring universes.

4.2 Specific Algorithms

The second way consists in writing algorithms taking into account the nature of the objects and the relationships with the properties. It leads in general to efficient algorithms, well adapted to the desired objects.

As an example, let us study the universe of shapes which are contained in a spatial enumeration matrix. The SpatioFormes project (Lucas 89) is aiming at providing tools to explore this enormous universe. For instance, much work has been devoted to objects which are defined using three projected shadows. Light Is supposed to come from three directions, parallel to the main axis. An example of such an object, which we call in french a *triplombre*, is given in Pict. 6.

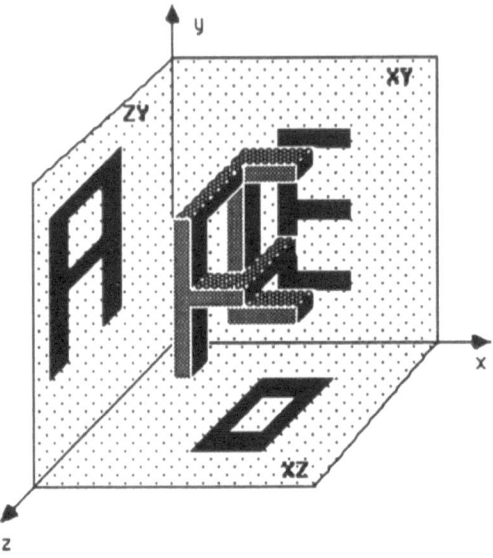

Pict. 6 - a *triplombre* and its defining shadows

If we suppose now that we have the description of the shadows (for instance as a set of three 2D pixel arrays), it is easy to write an algorithm able to produce some corresponding *triplombres*. This algorithm can be very efficient. However:

- it is clear that not all the objects of the universe of voxels can be reached using this algorithm. We cannot describe all the objects by using only three shadows (or views). Some would need more.

- it is clear that, in general, not only one object corresponds to a given set of shadows. One may understand here the notion of class of objects: all objects which share the property of having exactly the same three shadows can be considered as equivalent.

In the case of the triplombre, very interesting properties may be used:

- it has been demonstrated that there exists a unique object built with a maximum number of voxels. We call this object the *maximum triplombre*. The algorithm to produce the *maximum triplombre* is very simple and very efficient. An example of a *maximum triplombre* is given in Pict. 7a.

- it has been demonstrated that, in general, there are several *triplombres* built by using a minimum number of voxels. We call them *minimum triplombres*. The computation of *minimum triplombres* is very complex, and time consuming. An example of soe *minimum triplombres* is given in Pict. 7b.

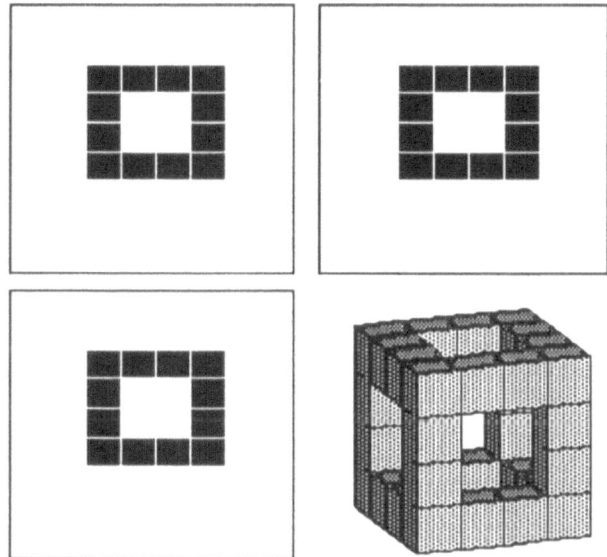

7a - An example of a *maximum triplombre*

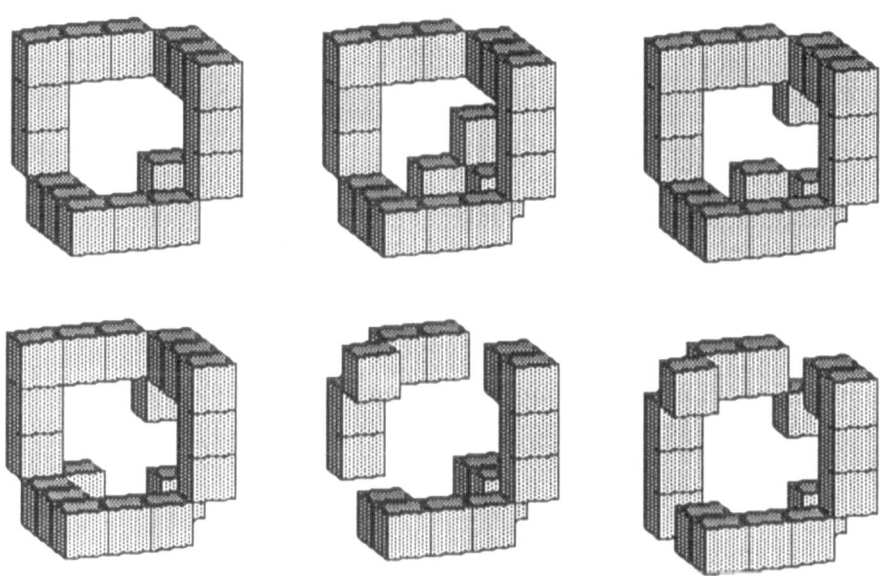

7b - six *minimum triplombres* corresponding to 7a

Pict. 7 - examples of *maximum* and *minimum triplombres*

A final example of *triplombre* is given in Pict. 8. This is to show that this graphical description may be very powerful even for so called complex objects !

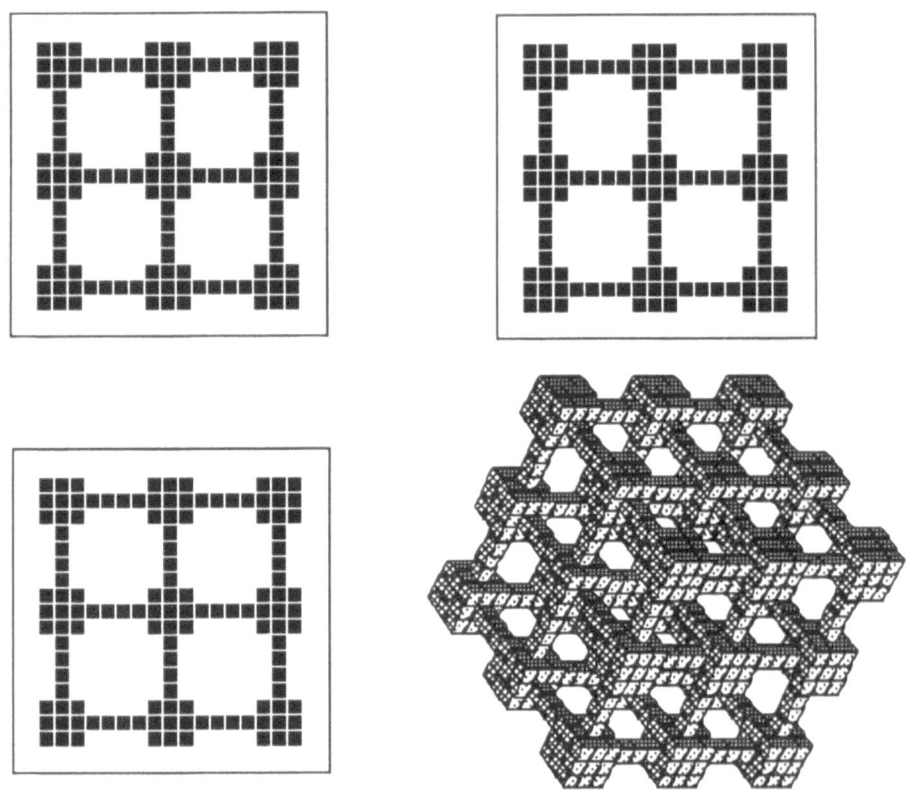

Pict. 8 - an example of complex *triplombre*

Although specific algorithms can be powerful tools, they suffer from several defects:

- they do not allow us to reach all the objects of a given universe. If we need to get all of them, we shall have to develop a collection of (independant) programs.

- it is sometimes very difficult to combine properties with the one corresponding to the specific algorithm. This is especially true if we have to merge several programs.

- they do not allow us to structure the universe, so that similar objects could be found easily. For instance, it would be nice to be able to group all the *minimum triplombres* in one region. In general, specific algorithms cannot offer this possibility.

This explains why, although we are using specific algorithms, we have tried to find more general mechanisms.

4.3 Generating Trees

One way to structure a set of objects is to organize it by using tree structures. We have applied this technique, considering two cases:

- finite universes (such as universes of voxels). It is easy to see that there exist trees allowing us to enumerate all configurations. In general, we use forests (set of trees). Configurations are generated through the traversal of the different trees. Various ways of generation exist, depending on how one adds or deletes objects at each node. If we aim at exploring only a part of the universe, we use exploring trees, that is to say trees associated with some filtering mechanism aiming at cutting useless branches.

- infinite universe (such as the universe of polyhedra). In this case, there does not exist an exhaustive tree. We use inference engines, allowing us to describe the world through rules and facts. We speak of deducing trees.

As an example of a generating tree, we shall consider some results of the FiloFormes project (Lucas 89). In this project, we are interested in generating configurations of segments on a grid (see Pict. 9).

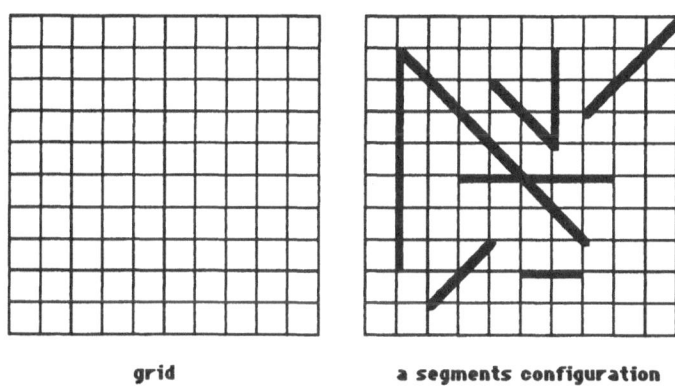

grid   a segments configuration

Pict. 9 - generating segments on a grid.

One potential application is the automatic generation of benchmarks (segments configurations) to compare algorithms computing the visibility of such sets (Kremer-Patard 88).

One way to organize the automatic generation of all potential configurations of segments is to use a tree, such that each node represents one configuration. For instance, let us study the very classical tree of Pict. 10. This tree gives all configurations of 1, 2, 3, ..., n elements (in the picture, n=4).

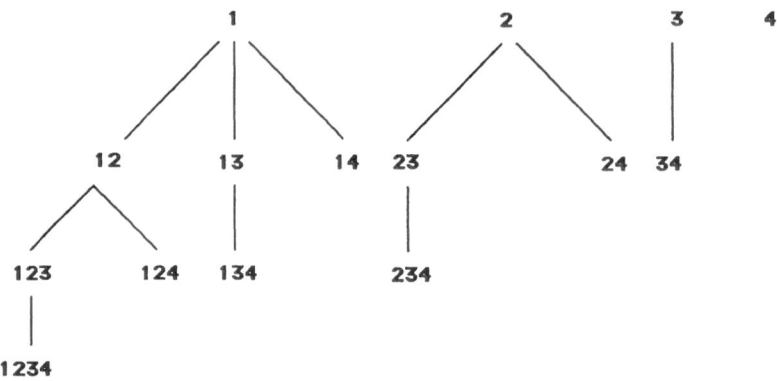

Pict. 10 - a configuration tree (n=4)

A formal definition of this tree is:

- a node is defined by a couple (P, k)
    . P $p_1 p_2 p_3 \dots p_k$ 1 p_i n
    . length   k   1   k   n

- continuation conditions

    . $\exists$ son (P,k)   <--> $p_k < n$
    . $\exists$ brother (P,k) <--> $p_k < n$

- building rules

    . elder-son (P,k) $p_{k+1} = p_k + 1$ $k = k+1$
    . brother (P,k) $p_k = p_k + 1$ k no change
    . root   ({1}, 1).

The advantages in using this tree are:

- we obtain all permutations without repetition, including 1 to n elements.

- only one element is added when descending of one level. This will allow us to use cutting techniques 'from above'. We can check at each node if some property is attained. If this property is to be inherited by the sons of the node, we can stop the exploration of the corresponding branch.

- it is easy to determine the maximum level to be reached from a node, or the number of next brothers. This will allow us to use cutting techniques 'from below': we shall not explore branches which cannot lead to objects having the desired property.

- prefixed traversal produces all combinations under lexicographical ordering (left justification, with 0 filling on the right)

To generate segments configurations, we use the following rules:

- every segment of the grid is associated with a number, starting from 1 to nbseg_max, maximum number of potential segments.

- a configuration is given by a set of numbers, each number representing a segment. We give interest only to configurations without repetitions.

We need now a numbering schema for enumerating all the potential segments. The number of such segments is as it follows:

$$\text{matrix} \quad mxn \quad <\text{------}> \quad (mxn)(mxn-1)/2 \text{ segments.}$$

Let us call nbseg_max this number of potential segments. It is clear that there exist nbseg_max ! ways to number the segments. One can wonder if the way to number the segments is of some importance. We shall demonstrate that it can be very useful !

For instance, let us look at three separate classes of segments, with a particular numbering schema:
- horizontal ones   (numbered from 1 to n1)
- vertical ones   (numbered from n1 to n2)
- other directions   (numbered from n2 to nb-max)

Pict. 11 shows how the tree is partitionned into regions.

segments   **generating tree**

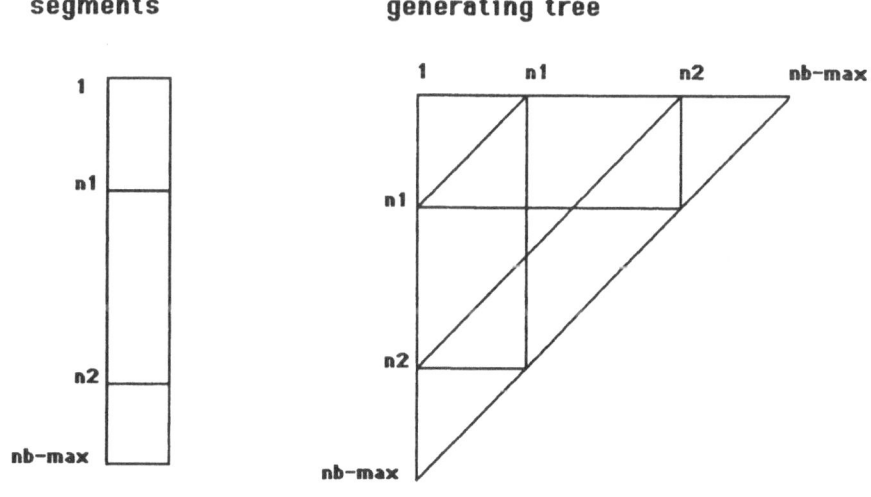

Pict. 11 - partitionning a generating tree

This numbering, combined with the fixed order produced by the traversal of the tree, will have as a consequence that it will be easy to find segments sharing a given property (for instance, vertical ones only) in the generating tree. We will have an efficient algorithm to produce configurations with or without some local properties: the desired configurations can be reached directly, without spending time in analysing uninteresting branches.

It is clear that not all properties obey this schema. One part of our work consists in trying to determine classes of properties (or constraints), so that we could identify general methods allowing us to implement efficient Explorators.

Through this example, we may see the importance of understanding how properties may be disseminated into generating trees. Algorithms for reorganizing trees through numbering schemes are under investigation. Some interesting results have been already obtained.

5 . UNDERSTANDING

When using imperative modelling, the user knows exactly how the designed object will look like: he is explaining all details to the computer. Using declarative modelling leads to a new problem: the user knows the properties he has used to describe the objects, but, in general, he does not know the shapes of the corresponding objects. Declarative modelling appeals to providing tools enabling a user to understand the computer generated objects. We shall discuss two kinds of those tools:

- visualizing tools, so that the user may look to the proposed objects to understand how they are built,

- learning tools, helping the user to explore the universe more efficiently.

5.1 Visualization

Basic techniques linked to the visualization problem are:

- propose different presentation modes, such as wire-frame, realistic presentation, squeleton, ... In general, the user need to look at different modes simultaneously, even on the same object. This will permit to automatically highlight some properties.

- show multiple views of the object.

- allow the visual exploration of a potentially great number of pictures. This point is the most difficult to handle. We do not know today how to solve this problem correctly.

- automatically choose a viewpoint. This is one of the most important features of an Explorator. It can be achieved by using the descriptive properties or by using properties deduced from the descriptive ones. The aim is to automatically emphasize the properties of the observed scene. Pict. 12 is an example of the usefulness of the automatic selection of a viewpoint.

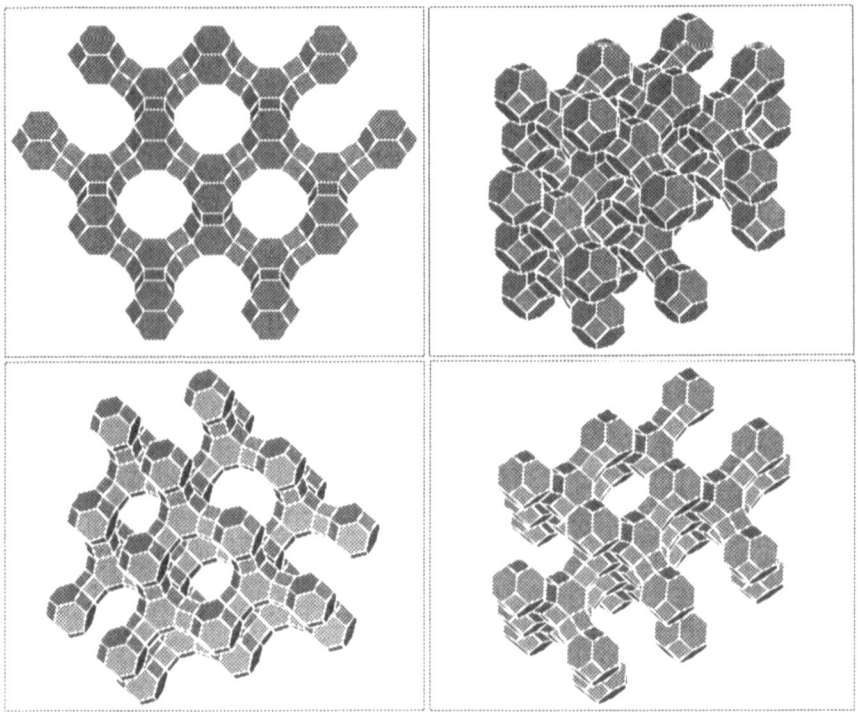

Pict. 12 - some views of the same object

In order to provide such a facility, we have developped in the PastoFormes project the notion of good viewpoint (Colin 88, Colin 90). It is a restriction of the notion of : there could exist an infinity of 'best viewpoints', or we could need to explore an infinity of viewpoints before finding one which could be the best one.

To compute a good viewpoint, we restrict the number of candidates by considering limited regions:

- observation directions: we choose only to try a few potential observation directions, depending on the type of observed objects. For instance, for objects described with octrees, 6 major directions may be choosen. Some adjustment is obtained by combining 2 or three of them.

- observation areas, depending on the studied property. Pict. 13 shows the observation areas which may be selected to highlight properties such as symmetry with respect with some axis, or flatness.

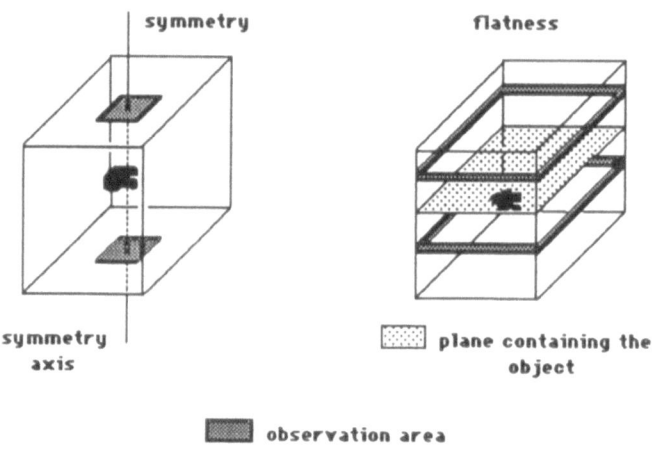

Pict. 13 - choosing an observation area

5.2 Learning

Another point of importance for an Explorator is the ability to learn. This learning skills will able the Explorator:

- to keep track of what has been explored in order not to produce again well known objects, or, in the contrary, to quickly produce again selected known objects. This will allow the user willing to discover new shapes to avoid regions of the universe containing well known or uninteresting shapes.

- to keep memory of interesting viewpoints. It could happen that selecting a good viewpoint take time. The Explorator could automatically associate to some object (or set of objects) a list of interesting viewpoints, provided that the user asks him to do.

- to enrich his knowledge, by learning new description rules, or new properties and their associated cutting or generating rules.

It is clear that this is a very important point. However, we have not yet begun to work deeply about this problem, although the need for these learning mechanisms appears very quickly when you develop an Explorator.

CONCLUSION

We have presented a new way to design modelling systems: the declarative modelling. Developping such systems (which we call Explorators) leads to the necessity to provide description, generation and understanding tools.

The major point of this approach is that the user has only to give a desciption through a list of properties and/or constraints. The understanding of this formal description and the translation into a classical geometric model are left to the computer. The user no longer deals with coordinates and values. He will get from the computer a set of objects, all sharing the desired properties.

We have presented generation techniques classified under using specific algorithms and generating trees. We have shown some techniques allowing us to structure a given universe, so that efficient techniques could help us to explore limited areas of this universe.

We have also outlined the importance of the understanding tools. Powerful visualization techniques have to be provided, especially concerning the automatic choice of a good viewpoint. Learning skills have also to be provided, in order to speed up the exploration process, or to enrich the knowledge of the Explorator.

We have illustrated our talk with some results, which prove that declarative modelling is a good approach. We hope that other researchers will join us, so that rapid progress will be made on this way. New application domains will become attainable. Computer graphics will become more and more useful.

Acknowledgements

I must express all my gratitude to Professor T.L. Kunii, who kindly invited me to come and participate to this workshop. I must also thank my colleagues (Colin, Martin, Martin, Martin and Plemenos !) and the numerous students who are exploring the universe of declarative modelling with much enthusiasm. They helped me to keep confidence in maintaining the chosen direction.

REFERENCES

Colin C. (1988) A System for Exploring the Universe of Polyhedral Shapes. In: Proceedings of Eurographics'88, North-Holland, Amsterdam, 209-220

Colin C. (1990) Modélisation déclarative de scènes à base de polyèdres élémentaires: le projet PastoFormes (Declarative modelling of scenes built with elementary polyhedra: the PastoFormes project). PhD Thesis, ENSM Nantes

Kremer-Patard G. (1988) Evaluation d'algorithmes de calcul de la visibilité d'un ensemble de segments du plan (Complexity of algorithms for computing visibility of sets of segments in a plane). Revue Internationale de CFAO et d'Infographie, vol. 3, n° 3,

Lucas M., Martin J.Y. (1988) Vers la maîtrise de la synthèse d'images à l'aide d'automates cellulaires (Towards mastering image synthesis produced by cellular automata). In: Proceedings of MICAD 89, Hermès, Paris, 615-636

Lucas M., Martin D., Martin P., Plemenos D. (1989) Le projet ExploFormes: quelques pas vers la modélisation déclarative (Project ExploFormes: some steps towards declarative modelling). Journées BIGRE, Strasbourg.

Martin J.Y. (1990) Synthèse d'images à l'aide d'automates cellulaires: le projet AutoFormes (Image generation using cellular automata: the AutoFormes project). PhD Thesis, ENSM Nantes

Martin D., Martin P. (1988) An Expert System for Polyhedra Modelling. In: Proceedings of Eurographics'88, North-Holland, Amsterdam, 221-232

Martin D., Martin P. (1989), Catalogue de polyèdres (A book of polyhedra). Research Report LIST-89-03

Requicha AAG (1980) Representations for Rigid Solids: Theory, Methods and Systems. Computing Surveys 12(4), 438-464

Ecole Nationale Supérieure de Mécanique, Laboratoire d'Informatique pour les Sciences de l'Ingénieur, 44072 Nantes Cedex, France

Chapter 2

Physical Modeling

Animation of Physical Systems from Geometric, Kinematic and Dynamic Models

BRUNO ARNALDI, GEORGES DUMONT, and GÉRARD HEGRON

Abstract

This paper presents the design of an extensible animation system in which rigid and deformable multibody systems are animated from their geometric models and the specification of kinematic and dynamic constraints. Theoretical, numerical and practical aspects of the system implementation are presented. One of its main features is the automatic derivation of the symbolic form of the motion equations from a physical model created interactively. This process is detailed by means of a simple example. Besides achieving motion control by the application of direct dynamics, the system provides animation of deformable objects, automatic motion control from a specified motion without having to determine the forces required to produce this desired effect, and object collision detection and response. Experimental results are presented to illustrate each type of animation control. Finally, the applicability of our animation system to scientific simulation is discussed.

Key-words : Modeling, Kinematics, Dynamics, Animation, Deformation, Interaction, Constraints, Symbolic calculation, Simulation.

1 Introduction

Object animation requires motion coordination. Traditional animation systems, where the animator explicitly controls motions and deformations, become inadequate when the scene contains many objects whose motions are due to actions, reactions, joint constraints and physical properties. For this reason, the use of simulation methods in animation has been considerably investigated recently.

Simulation models especially developed for solving specific natural phenomena have already been proposed by Fournier and Reeves [9, 10, 19] and by Miller [15]. A background on mechanics regarding the animation of rigid solid objects can be found in [1, 14, 25]. Recently, deformable models have been extensively featured in the literature and interesting results are already available. Terzopoulos [21, 22, 23] uses dynamical deformable models and a finite difference method to model the deformation under prescribed forces. Furthermore, he has proposed physically-based models of objects capable of inelastic deformation. Some authors have developed different constraint approaches for the animation of rigid or flexible bodies [5, 18, 26, 27].

The methods presented in this paper provide a means to incorporate some of these animation techniques within a single coherent system. Our animation system offers the following novel features :

- The automatic derivation, in symbolic form, of the motion equations from physical objects models created interactively ;

- The animation of rigid and deformable objects under an unified framework ;

- The automatic motion control of physical objects to produce a desired motion, taking into account dynamic properties without using inverse dynamics.

Our animation system also handles object collision detection and response at each time step.

In this paper, we first describe the principles of our system, with emphasis on the user interface and the mechanical formalism. Then, the implementation of the system is developed. The automatic derivation of symbolic motion equations is detailed using a simple example. Then, deformation, motion and collision controls are explained and illustrated with experimental simulations. Finally, the ability of our system to perform scientific simulation is discussed.

2 System Principles

2.1 Overview

The objective of this work is the animation of multibody systems using traditional motion control techniques as well as dynamics. As the animator may be neither a computer scientist nor a mechanical engineer, but an artist, the animation system must provide automatic motion computation from description of the mechanism.

The animator constructs the multibody system and specifies constraints so as to produce the desired motion. This modeling is achieved interactively in three steps : object shape design, object interrelationship description, and specification of kinematic and dynamic constraints evolving over the time.

The geometry, material composition and joint coordinate systems of the objects are designed by using a solid modeling system. The animator is provided with a standard joint library which has been described in [2].

To animate the mechanism, the animator specifies kinematic and dynamic constraints such as :

- gravity (direction and magnitude);

- springs, dampers, thrusts, forces and torques applied on joint degrees of freedom (DOF), the parameters of which (given in Table 1) may evolve over the time and therefore may be described by a trajectory in time;

- point forces applied to objects;

- nonholonomic constraints, such as rolling without sliding (for instance, for a wheel);

- for a specialist, hand-written constraint equations, if needed.

Table 1: DOF coefficients

Descr.	param.	note
spring	k	rigidity coefficient
	l_0	rest length of the spring
damper	v	damping coefficient
motor	F	force or torque

2.2 Mechanical formalism

In previous work published in *The Visual Computer* [2], we presented extensively the mechanical formalism employed. Let us remind that it was based on the **principle of virtual work**, associated with LAGRANGE's multipliers [4, 12]. We choose it because it can deal with "general multibody systems" [20, 28]. We propose here an alternative for writing the equation system. It uses the penalty method for taking the joints into account and is an improvement of the method based on the LAGRANGE's multipliers when we do not need to compute the constraint forces : it saves extra computation due to the multipliers which are extra variables. With this penalty method we obtain the system :

$$\mathcal{Q}_i - \frac{d}{dt}\left(\frac{\partial \mathcal{C}}{\partial \dot{q}^i}\right) + \frac{\partial \mathcal{C}}{\partial q^i} + k \sum_h f_h \frac{\partial f_h}{\partial q^i} + k \sum_l g_l \frac{\partial g_l}{\partial \dot{q}^i} = 0, \quad i = 1, 2, ..., n \tag{1}$$

where $q = (q^i)_{i=1,n}$ is the set of the lagrangian parameters of the multibody system, $\mathcal{C}$ is the kinetic energy, $\mathcal{Q}_i$ is the generalized given effect relative to q^i. The constraints are denoted by f_h (holonomic) and g_l (non-holonomic), and k is a chosen penalty constant.

Let us now explain the major improvement of this method with respect to the one inducing the multipliers. The system is of order only n and thus it is solved more quickly. Note that it leads to the same results and becomes equivalent to the previous system when k tends to infinity. Another important point is that no singularity occurs when the constraint equations are dependent ; even if one of these equations is duplicated, it is equivalent to multiplying k by 2. this allow to avoid the implementation of algorithms which can deal with redundancies. Furthermore, the penalty method tolerates some mechanical inconsistencies : the constraint violations, for instance, are detected on the graphical output. This is a more convenient detection method for an artist.

3 System Implementation

3.1 Overview

The animation system, written in the C programming language, allows the user to automatically derive and compute the motion equations from any rigid multibody system description. The flow of control of the system is illustrated in Figure 1. The system input is the user description of the mechanism in terms of objects, joints, constraints and initial state (positions, velocities, etc.). The following automatic process can be broken down into three main phases : extraction of mechanical properties of the objects, symbolic derivation of motion equations, and solution of these equations for each time step.

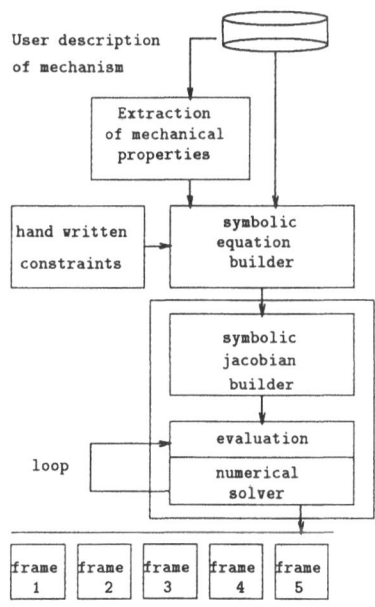

Fig. 1: Synoptic of the application

Mechanical properties

The mechanical properties of each object (center of gravity (COG), inertia matrix, principal coordinate system of inertia) are extracted from the object's geometric model. Inertia and mass are integrals over the volume. A discrete integration is performed by using a parallel ray tracing algorithm from a regular grid mapped on a face of the object bounding box. The ray tracing technique has been chosen because of its applicability to a large variety of solid models. Along each ray, inner parallelepipeds are computed according to the grid resolution and the intersection points between the ray and the object boundary. The physical properties of the parallelepipeds are calculated, then the object properties are derived using associativity of COGs and additivity of inertia matrices with respect to the global COG.

Formation of symbolic motion equations

The motion equations are then automatically generated in a **symbolic** form from the mechanism data structure (tree) according to the following steps :

- for each object, the COG and the angular velocities are computed symbolically by a tree traversal, according to the joints between objects and the relative positioning of local frames. Symbolic names are given to the system parameters during this phase ;

- from the previous results, the kinetic energy $\mathcal{C}$ of the whole mechanism is computed as the sum of each object kinetic energy ;

- for each object and each joint, the given work $\mathcal{W}_d$ (gravity, spring, damper, thrust, force and torque works) is evaluated . Its associated given actions $\mathcal{Q}_i$ are derived by performing a symbolic derivation of $\mathcal{W}_d$ with respect to generalized coordinates. For some effects (elastic joints for instance) there exists one potential $\mathcal{F}$ such as $\delta\mathcal{W}_d = \delta\mathcal{F}$ and for the viscous joints one dissipative function $\mathcal{D}$ such as $\delta\mathcal{W}_d = \frac{\partial\mathcal{D}}{\partial\dot{q}^i} \cdot \delta q^i$. So $\mathcal{Q}_i$ is written as :

$$\mathcal{Q}_i = \frac{\partial\mathcal{F}}{\partial q^i} + \frac{\partial\mathcal{D}}{\partial\dot{q}^i}$$

- holonomic and nonholonomic constraints are derived from the geometric and kinematic constraint specifications ;

- the last step consists in expressing the motion equations according to Equation 1.

At this step, a finite difference method is applied to discretize the equation with respect to time. A non-linear non-differential system of the form $f(q) = 0$ is obtained. Then the Jacobian matrix J, used for numerical resolution, is symbolically computed by using :

$$a_{ij} = \frac{\partial f_i}{\partial q_j}$$

where a_{ij} is the element of J (f_i is the i-th equation and q_j is the j-th coordinate). The symbolic computation is performed once only.

Resolution of the motion equations

For each time step, a numerical resolution of the nonlinear system is performed by using a *Newton Raphson* algorithm, as follows :

- evaluation of the symbolic jacobian matrix J ;

- solving of the numerical system : $J\Delta q = f$ where Δq is the unknown change of the coordinate vector q and f is the value (evaluated from its symbolic expression) of the vector built by the equations ($f(q)$). This computation is achieved using an LU decomposition of the Jacobian matrix.

3.2 Symbolic expressions

In this section, the advantages of a symbolic computation of the motion equations versus a pure numerical solution are discussed. Then the implementation of the symbolic calculus is described.

Why a symbolic construction ?

First, the operations performed under a symbolic form are exact. This is important for derivatives, because a reliable numerical derivation is difficult to perform. For instance, $\frac{d\sin(x)}{dx}$ will be represented exactly by $cos(x)$ and not by $\frac{sin(x+h)-sin(x)}{h}$.

Second, the equation simplifications, based on the particular form of the modeled system, are easily performed, and the structural knowledge of the mechanism is not lost during the calculation.

The use of a library of symbolic functions offers two main advantages :

- the programming of new features is made easier by the natural way of writing the corresponding routines. Moreover, it is shorter, and that reduces the programming errors. The example program to construct the motion equations, which refers to the inertia and given effect terms (see Equation 1), is given in Figure 2 to illustrate this assertion ;

```
nbequa = 0;
for(i=0;i<nbparam;i++) {
  /* -ddt(d/d(q')) ec + d/d(q) ec */
  interm2 = eq_plus(
              eq_mun(
              deq_dt(
              deq_dqp(ec,ident[i]))),
              deq_dq(ec,ident[i]));
  /* motion equation[i] =    interm2
                          + d/dq W
                          + d/dq' W */
  equa[i] = eq_plus(interm2,
              eq_plus(
              deq_dq(work,ident[i]),
              deq_dqp(work,ident[i])));
  nbequa++;
}
```

Fig. 2: Program of motion equation generator (extract)

- the system offers to the user two different ways of introducing information : graphical and manual. The manual writing of equations under a natural form is appreciated by the specialist who wants to introduce new equations which are not allowed by the graphical interface. An example of a hand-written constraint (where # represents : = 0) is presented in Figure 3. These equations are those of the prescribed car trajectory presented in Figure 11.

The data structure

The data structure is based on a binary tree, the leaves of which store three kinds of entities :

- a constant ;

- a variable which can be modified by external processes (mass, gravity, rigidity and damping coefficients, motor or thrust parameter linked to a trajectory). The variables allow th user to specify a model evolving through time ;

- a DOF of the mechanical system (unknowns, parameters).

```
        valid*((a+l*cos(theta)-h*sin(theta)-xcircle)*cos(theta+beta1)
        +(b+l*sin(theta)+h*cos(theta)-ycircle)*sin(theta+beta1)) #

        valid*((a+l*cos(theta)+h*sin(theta)-xcircle)*cos(theta+beta2)
        +(b+l*sin(theta)-h*cos(theta)-ycircle)*sin(theta+beta2)) #
```

Where **valid** allows to activate (or deactivate) the constraint, and **a**, **b**, **theta**, **beta1** and **beta2** are DOFs of the car. **l** and **h** are respectively the length and the width of the car. **xcircle** and **ycircle** are parameters of the trajectory.

Fig. 3: Hand written constraint equations on file

The other nodes are operators such as :

- arithmetical operators : $+, -, *, /$;

- functions : $\sin(x)$, $\cos(x)$, $\exp(x)$, $\tan(x)$, $\arctan(x)$, etc... (where x is an expression) ;

- derivatives : $\frac{d}{dt}$ or $\frac{\partial}{\partial q_i}$ where t is the time and q_i is a generalized coordinate of the mechanical system.

Such an implementation obviously requires a large memory space as the complexity of the mechanical models grows, but the equations produced are those of a structured physical system, which are known to share common terms. For this reason, the replacement of the binary tree structure by a Direct Acyclic Graph (D.A.G) is proposed : common equations are shared in the structure by means of pointers. To benefit from this implementation, two kinds of databases are defined : the mechanism database created by propagation along the links of the system (which is a D.A.G by construction) and the equation database. The operations performed during the equation building process are grouped into sets : for instance, time derivatives or derivations with respect to a given coordinate are performed once for the whole system of equation. This leads to the D.A.G structure. To this end, a pointer to the last calculated derivative is stored within each shared node of the mechanism D.A.G and each new shared node of the equation D.A.G.

3.3   A detailed example

Mechanism Description

In order to illustrate the features of the animation system, an example showing the animation of a simple mechanism, dubbed gyroscope, by direct dynamics is developed. The gyroscope presented in Figure 4 is composed of five objects : a cylindrical base, and two bars linked by pin joints. On each bar, a parallelipipedic object is linked by a sliding joint.

During the phase of geometric modeling, the animator is provided with a joint library. The description of the joint coordinate systems occurs during the modeling phase. Once the geometric model (including joints) is achieved, the five DOFs of the mechanism are available (see Table 2).

Only the relevant DOFs are created during the modeling step. For instance, the introduction of one pin joint (between object 0 and object 1) creates the DOF α_1 and the associated symbolic transformation matrix from object 0 to object 1 :

$$M_{l0->l1} = \begin{pmatrix} \cos(\alpha_1) & -\sin(\alpha_1) & 0.0 & 0.0 \\ \sin(\alpha_1) & \cos(\alpha_1) & 0.0 & 0.0 \\ 0.0 & 0.0 & 1.0 & 0.0 \end{pmatrix}$$

The objects are parametrized in their inertial reference frame. The joint reference frames R_l are introduced to define the joint location with respect to the local (inertial) reference frames R_g of the associated objects (see Figure 5). For instance, the pin joint, parametrized by α_1, is (partially) defined by its transformation matrix in the local (inertial) reference frame of object 0 :

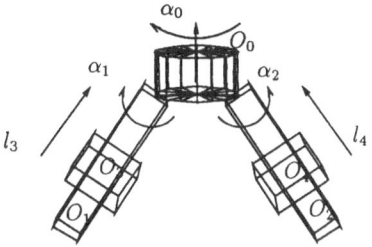

Fig. 4: Gyroscope

Table 2: List of the gyroscope parameters

name	description
α_0	rot DOF for the object 0
α_1	rot DOF between O_1 and O_0
α_2	rot DOF between O_2 and O_0
l_3	trans DOF between O_3 and O_1
l_4	trans DOF between O_4 and O_2

$$M_{l0->g0} = \begin{pmatrix} -1.0 & 0.0 & 0.0 & 1.0 \\ 0.0 & -1.0 & 0.0 & 0.0 \\ 0.0 & 0.0 & 1.0 & 0.0 \end{pmatrix}$$

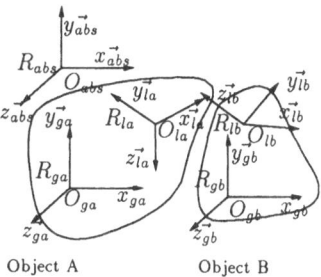

Object A   Object B

Fig. 5: Description of joint reference frame

Effects such as motor, springs, and dampers may be applied on the DOF, which may be furthermore constrained by thrusts. A summary of these given effects is to be found in Table 3 refering to the equations :

$$\mathcal{W}_{d-spring} = \frac{1}{2} * k * (q - r)^2$$
$$\mathcal{W}_{d-motor} = motor * q$$

The default initial state is defined by the rest position of the system (each DOF is equal to zero) and the external standard given effects. For instance gravity is represented by the vector : $\vec{g} = (0.0, 9.81, 0.0)$.

The chosen input for this system is a torque on DOF α_0 which obviously allows to generate motion. The inputs (which may vary over time) are conveniently defined by trajectories, as presented in Figure 6.

Table 3: DOF description

	effect	coef.	
α_0	motor	traject.	
α_1	thrust	p= 0.0	$\alpha_1 < p$
α_2	thrust	p= 0.0	$\alpha_2 < p$
l_3	spring	r= 0.0	k= 100.0
l_4	spring	r= 0.0	k= 100.0

Output of the mechanism modeler

The mechanical properties, presented in Table 4, are automatically computed by the system. The computation of these properties represents the first step of the animation process.

Table 4: Mechanical properties

O	mass	inertial coef.		
0	3.152412	1.048302	1.583837	1.060937
1	4.000000	0.666667	5.666636	5.666636
2	4.000000	0.666666	5.666636	5.666636
3	4.000000	2.666668	1.666639	1.666639
4	4.000000	2.666666	1.666630	1.666630

The next step consists in generating the symbolic expressions of the coordinates of the mass center in accordance with the DOFs. These vectors are needed to construct the velocities used later to generate the kinetic energy.

Output of the symbolic calculus

The structural knowledge about the mechanical system (degrees of freedom) allows the symbolic equation generator to calculate the mass center of each object (with respect to the DOF) and the rotational velocities. The translational velocities are the derivatives the coordinates of the mass center with respect to time. A subset of these automatically generated equations (set up by the program) is presented in the following :

- coordinates of the mass center for object 0 :
  $G_0/x = 0$, $G_0/y = 0.5$, $G_0/z = 0$;

- rotational velocity vector for object 0 :
  $\Omega_0/x = 0$, $\Omega_0/y = \dot{\alpha}_0$, $\Omega_0/z = 0$;

- coordinates of the mass center for object 4 :
  $$G_4/x = \cos(\alpha_0)(-2\sin(\alpha_2) - 1) - \cos(\alpha_0)\sin(\alpha_2)l_4$$
  $$G_4/y = 0.5 + \cos(\alpha_2)(l_4 + 2)$$
  $$G_4/z = \sin(\alpha_0)\sin(\alpha_2)l_4 - \sin(\alpha_0)(-2\sin(\alpha_2) - 1);$$

- rotational velocity vector for object 4 :
  $$\Omega_4/x = \sin(\alpha_2)\dot{\alpha}_0$$
  $$\Omega_4/y = 0.5(\cos(\alpha_2)\dot{\alpha}_0 + \dot{\alpha}_2) + 1.414214(\cos(\alpha_2)\dot{\alpha}_0 - \dot{\alpha}_2)$$
  $$\Omega_4/z = 0.5(\cos(\alpha_2)\dot{\alpha}_0 + \dot{\alpha}_2) - 1.414214(\cos(\alpha_2)\dot{\alpha}_0 - \dot{\alpha}_2).$$

Here is one motion equation built by the system (refering to DOF lz_3) :
$$-4\cos(\alpha_1)^2 lz3\dot{\alpha}_0^2 + 39.24\cos(\alpha_1) - 100l_3 - 4\ddot{l}_3 + 8\dot{\alpha}_1^2 + 8\dot{\alpha}_0^2 + 4l_3\dot{\alpha}_1^2 - 8\cos(\alpha_1)^2\dot{\alpha}_0^2 - 4\sin(\alpha_1)\dot{\alpha}_0^2 + 4l_3\dot{\alpha}_0^2$$

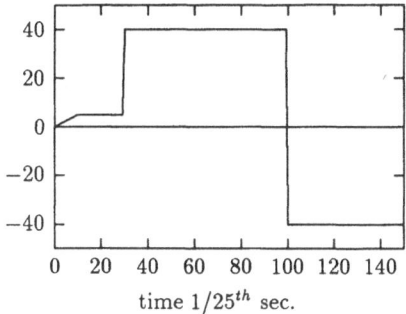

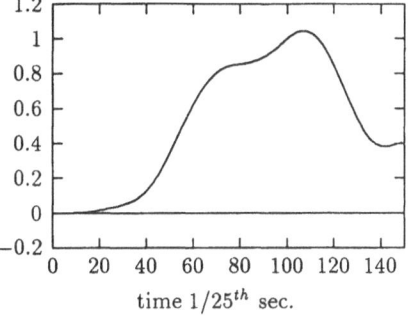

Fig. 6: Torque applied on DOF α_0 over the time

Fig. 7: Torque applied on DOF α_0 over the time

Table 5: interest of D.A.G structure

	memory	time for building motion equations	time for 200 frames	number of frames per second
Without D.A.G	131Ko	2.1s	63.4s	3
With D.A.G	46Ko	0.5s	7.2s	> 30

These results have been obtained on a Silicon Graphics Iris 4D/20 Personnal Computer.

Numerical results

The system calculates each parameter value at each time step. For instance, the evolution curve associated with parameter α_1 is presented in Figure 7.

Table 5 illustrates the efficiency of the D.A.G structure with respect to the resolution step. The D.A.G structure not only decreases memory occupancy but also increases computation time.

Some frames of the animation sequence are presented in Figure 18.

4 Deformation, Motion and Collision Control

The previous sections describes the ability of the animation system to control the motion of any multibody system using direct dynamics. Owing to the mechanical formalism chosen and to the symbolic writing of equations, the system can also handle deformable objects, automatic motion control and object collisions.

4.1 Deformable solids

Two different approaches have been developed for the animation of deformable solids by using mechanical laws.

The first was based on the finite element method [24, 29]. Our purpose here will not be to describe this method which is well known in the scientific community. Work in this field, using finite difference method, has already been presented by Terzopoulos who furthermore proposed modeling of such systems with the use of inelastic deformations. Our implementation was made under a numerical (classical) form [8].

The second approach is based on a mesh too, but it uses point masses linked by springs and dampers. This method is implemented under a symbolic form within the previous described system. The symbolic equations are derived from the object mesh and the initial state (location of the punctual masses, rest length of the springs) determined by mesh geometry. The solution of these equations is the same as was described previously. The only difference between rigid and deformable models lies in the construction of the symbolic equations from the geometric model.

The revolving and the fall to the ground of an elastically deformable cube illustrates this last approach (see Figure 8). At the beginning, the cube is held at a lower corner with a ball and socket joint. This joint is defined by :

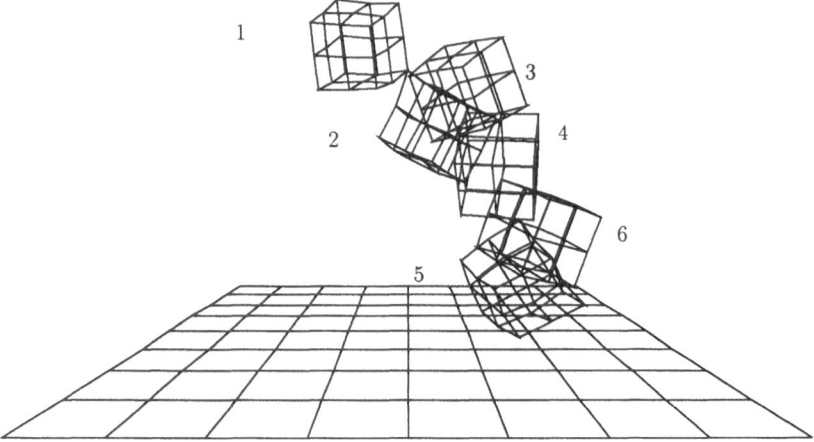

Fig. 8: Revolving and fall of a deformable cube

$$valid * (x - x_0) = 0$$
$$valid * (y - y_0) = 0$$
$$valid * (z - z_0) = 0$$

where (x, y, z) are the lower corner global coordinates, (x_0, y_0, z_0) are the initial lower corner global coordinates (coordinates of the joint), *valid* is a variable whose initial value is one.

The cube rotates, losing its shape around the point (x_0, y_0, z_0) under the action of gravity. Then the cube is dropped by setting the value of *valid* to zero ; i.e., the joint does not exist any more. The cube falls to the ground, bounces, and is bent out of shape. The interaction between the cube and the ground is achieved by adding a lower thrust (force control of collision, which is approximatively valid in this case) on each cube corner altitude coordinate. The use of symbolic equation writing and of variables whose trajectory is easily specified allows the system to perform this whole sequence automatically.

This technique can also be applied to deformable surfaces modeled by a mesh.

The animation of deformable solids or surfaces represented by a mesh of point masses linked by springs and dampers remains similar to the animation of rigid multibody system. The difference lies only in the way of specifying constraints and of deriving symbolic motion equations from these specifications and from object geometry. Moreover, with such deformable object modeling, interactions between rigid and deformable solids are performed in a simple way, because the DOFs are handled independently of the fact that they refer to deformable or rigid bodies. This is illustrated in Figure 9, where a rigid sphere bounces on an elastic surface. The non-interpenetration constraints relate the coordinates of the mass center of the sphere (three DOFs) to the surface.

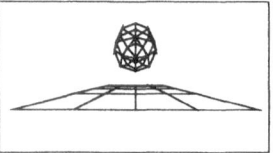 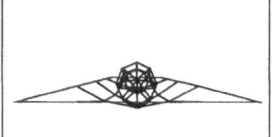 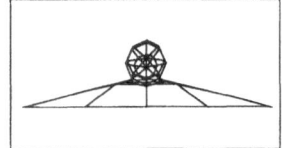

Fig. 9: Rigid sphere on a elastic surface

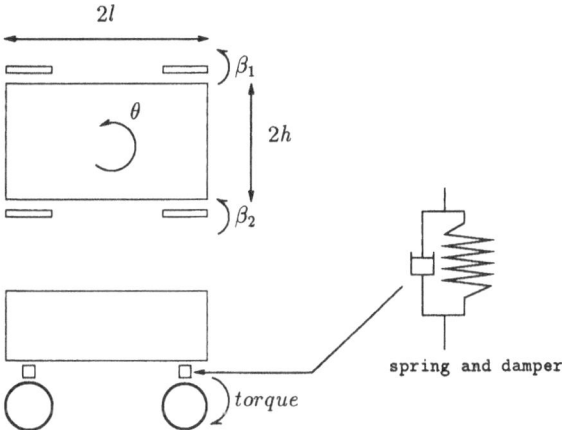

Fig. 10: Model of a car

4.2 Automatic Motion Control

The problem of motion control [5] consists essentially in controlling a dynamical system by means of prescribed **trajectories**. Such a task may always be written as $e = e(\ddot{q}, \dot{q}, q, t)$, which is a constraint that can be integrated into the motion equations as explained previously. The main difference with robotics, is to avoid the calculation of forces which generate a given effect, as inverse dynamics does. Nevertheless, the effects are taken into account with respect to the dynamic behavior of the system. The main problem is the task modeling which consists in writing the desired effect equations in terms of DOFs only.

In [3], we presented the motion control of an arm whose hand extremity $\vec{X} = (x, y, z)$ follows a 3D spacetime trajectory $\vec{X}_t = (x_t, y_t, z_t)$. The arm is a four link chain (clavicle, upper arm, lower arm, hand) with ball and socket joints (12 DOFs), and thrusts to ensure that motion lies within human capabilities. The task is modeled by three holonomic constraints : $x - x_t = 0$, $y - y_t = 0$ and $z - z_t = 0$ for all t, where x, y and z represent the symbolic expressions of hand extremity location automatically extracted from the root of the arm chain. In this case, task modeling remains obvious.

In order to show automatic control implications onto the user task specification and the task modeling, we present the motion control of a car. The car model presented in Figure 10 is a right parallelepiped suspended on wheels by four coupled spring-absorber. It is animated by exerting a torque mimicing the engine on front wheels. The guiding is assumed to be produced by a torque too, and regulated by a spring-absorber system. The wheels are rolling without sliding on the ground. Such a link can be modelled as : let (O, x, y) be a referential and let us consider a wheel of radius r rolling without sliding on the Ox axis. The contact condition is written as $y_c = r$ (where c is the center of the wheel) and the associated nonholonomic constraint as $r \cdot \dot{\theta} + \dot{x} = 0$. One condition constraining the orientation of the steering wheels is necessary : they roll on concentric circles, that is compatible with the conditions of rolling without sliding.

The nonholonomic constraints are, because of their generality and complexity, of great interest with respect to motion control.

The two-dimensional prescribed trajectory proposed here models the desired motion of car COG. We want to guide the motion without computing the efforts which realize this motion, but by direct writing of the task as a set of constraints, which will be introduced into the motion equations (see Equation 1). These constraint equations are written with respect to the DOFs governing the motion. They express the projection of the trajectory equation onto the space of DOFs.

In the following example, they are written with respect to β_1 and β_2, which are the steering angles expressed in the car reference frame.

When the trajectory is a circle, these constraints are written as follows :

$valid*((a+l*\cos(\theta)-h*\sin(\theta)-xcircle)*\cos(\theta+\beta_1)+(b+l*\sin(\theta)+h*\cos(\theta)-ycircle)*\sin(\theta+\beta_1)) = 0$

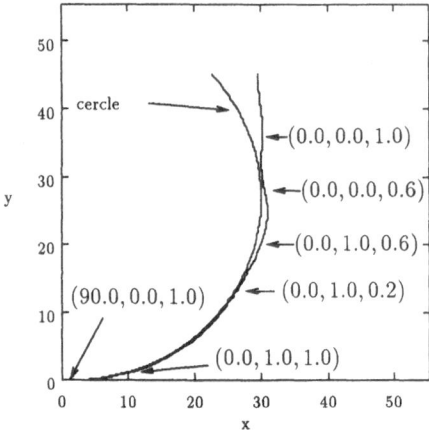

Fig. 11: Trajectory of car COG

$valid*((a+l*\cos(\theta)+h*\sin(\theta)-xcircle)*\cos(\theta+\beta_2)+(b+l*\sin(\theta)-h*\cos(\theta)-ycircle)*\sin(\theta+\beta_2)) = 0$
Where a and b are the global coordinates of wheel COG, θ defines the global orientation of the car and, $xcircle$ and $ycircle$ are the coordinates of the circle center.

These equations express that the global velocity of the car COG is tangent at (a, b) to the circle defined by its center $(xcircle, ycircle)$ and its radius R with $R = \sqrt{(xcircle - a)^2 + (ycircle - b)^2}$.

The results of motion computation are presentented in Figure 11. The regular curve is the trajectory performed by the car COG under task constraint which remains identical to the prescribed trajectory, i.e the circle. The irregular curve is a variation from the previous one obtained by changing and removing through time either the driving torque, or the rolling without sliding constraint, or the task constraint (circle tracking). These changes are referenced in the Figure 11 under the form "(torque, valid, weight of rolling without sliding constraint)" for each of them.

4.3   Object Interaction

Collision treatment is important in animation systems. Objects have to interact with each other, avoiding interpenetration. This problem has already been developed for rigid and deformable objects [11, 13, 16]. Note that a collision physically occurs at a given location and at a given time, and that the percussions (actions of collision) are the unknowns.

For solving the contact/collision problem, we have implemented a method based on the principle of virtual work. For a system submitted to collision from the outer, the variation of momentum is equal to the integration of the external efforts over the duration of collision, which is called percussion action :

$$\Delta(\frac{\partial \mathcal{C}}{\partial \dot{q}_i}) = \mathcal{P}_i$$

Let us recall that the momentum is the derivative of the kinetic energy with respect to the velocities.

A geometrical algorithm detects the collision effects and returns some necessary informations such as the collision plane, the normal vector, as well as the normal velocities of the collision points. When interpenetration is too severe (because of the time step) a backward-subdivision of the time step is performed so as to detect the spacetime position of the collision points. Then, collision laws are applied : conservation of momentum, reflexion of relative normal velocities by the use of an empirical law [12] : $(V_1 - V_2)^+ = -e(V_1 - V_2)^-$ where V_1 (resp. V_2) is normal velocity of the collision point on the first (resp. second) solid and + (resp. −) denotes the instant after (resp. before) the collision. The constant e is the coefficient of restitution characterizing the collision. This coefficient depends on the objects involved. If $e = 1$ the collision is elastic (see Figure 12) else the collision is inelastic (see Figure 13 for $e = 0$).

For each frame (time step t_n), we use the recursive procedure defined below. This procedure determines as a function of events (as collision) the way of subdividing the time step in order to treat the events, then induces the event treatment and returns the initial state compatible for the normal calculation of the next frame (time step t_{n+1}), as if nothing had occured :

```
procedure time_step_management()
begin
 if(not(collision))
  then if(collision_detection)
        then if (treatable)
              then collision_treatement()
              else collision = true
                   subdivide_time()
                   backward_calculation()
                   time_step_management()
        else next_time_step_calculation()
  else if(collision_detection)
        then if (treatable)
              then collision_treatement()
              else subdivide_time()
                   backward_calculation()
                   time_step_management()
        else subdivide_time()
             forward_calculation()
end
```

The procedure "collision_detection" returns the geometric information necessary to treat the collision. That is : the relative velocities of the objects and the normal vector at contact points. The boolean "treatable" represents a geometric criterion of interpenetration of objects at contact points. The procedure "collision_treatment" performs the treatment based on the principle of virtual work by changing the initial state of the DOFs for the next time step.

Fig. 12: Example of multiple collisions : restitution equal to 1

Fig. 13: Example of multiple collisions : restitution equal to 0

5   From animation to scientific simulation

In previous sections, the use of dynamics for animation was presented. As a general mechanical formalism is used, the utility of our animation system for scientific simulation has been evaluated

50

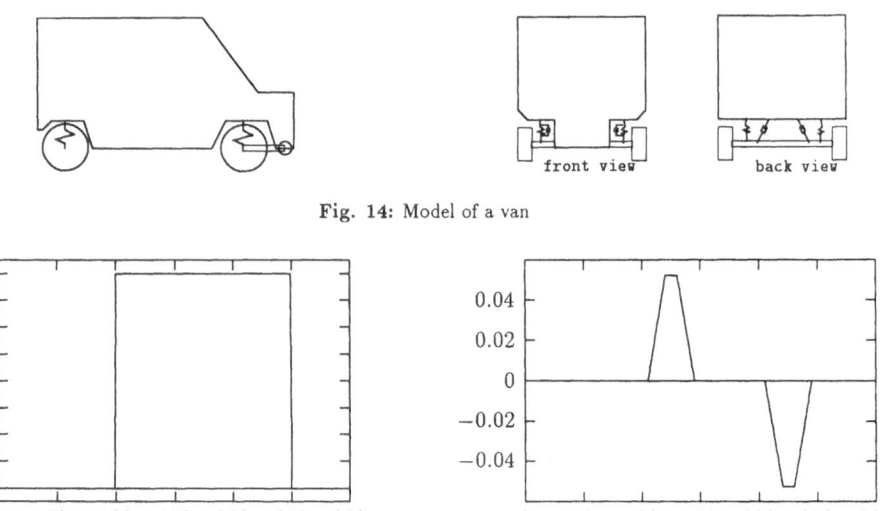

Fig. 14: Model of a van

Fig. 15: Propulsion force

Fig. 16: Turning angle

and compared to the ADAMS system [6, 17] using the simulation of a "van in overtaking". The van shown in Figure 14 has ten DOFs, which are the six DOFs of frame COG, the rotational DOF for each front wheel around a transversal axis at the extremity of the arm, and two DOFs for the rear axle for pumping (translation along a vertical axis) and for rolling (rotation around a longitudinal axis). Besides the gravity effect, the given effects are suspension forces (see springs and dampers in Figure 14), drift forces applied to each wheel at the contact point according to the drift angle (and to the turning angle for front wheels), vertical forces applied to each wheel center according to the tire stiffness, and the propulsion force given in Figure 15. The turning angle is presented in Figure 16.

The comparison of DOF accelerations is the most discriminating criterion. Therefore, the numerical results for transversal acceleration $\ddot{x}$ and longitudinal acceleration $\ddot{y}$ of the van COG are presented in Figure 17. They are equivalent for both systems. At the end of the van in overtaking simulation, the locations (x, y) of the frame COG are nearly identical (the relative difference is about 10^{-4}).

Real-time dynamics simulation plays a major role in the study and in the experimentation of physical systems ; for instance, in driving simulations [7]. To improve the efficiency of solving the motion equations, the D.A.G. traversal used to evaluate the Jacobian matrix from its symbolic representation can be automatically replaced by its equivalent numerical code. Using this, for the "gyroscope" computation leads to 600 frames per second (see Table 5). Even if numerical computation provides a considerable improvement in speed with respect to the symbolic version, the implementation of a parallel code remains necessary for complex mechanisms because the computation time grows exponentially with the number of system DOFs. This work is under progress.

6 Future work and conclusion

We have described an animation system in which the behavior of physical objects is computed from their geometric, kinematic and dynamic models. Generality is obtained by using a mechanical formalism based on the principle of virtual work associated with Lagrange multipliers or the penalty method :

- animation of general multibody systems with holonomic and nonholonomic constraints, and with open and closed chains ;
- automatic motion control from task modeling with a set of constraints ;

51

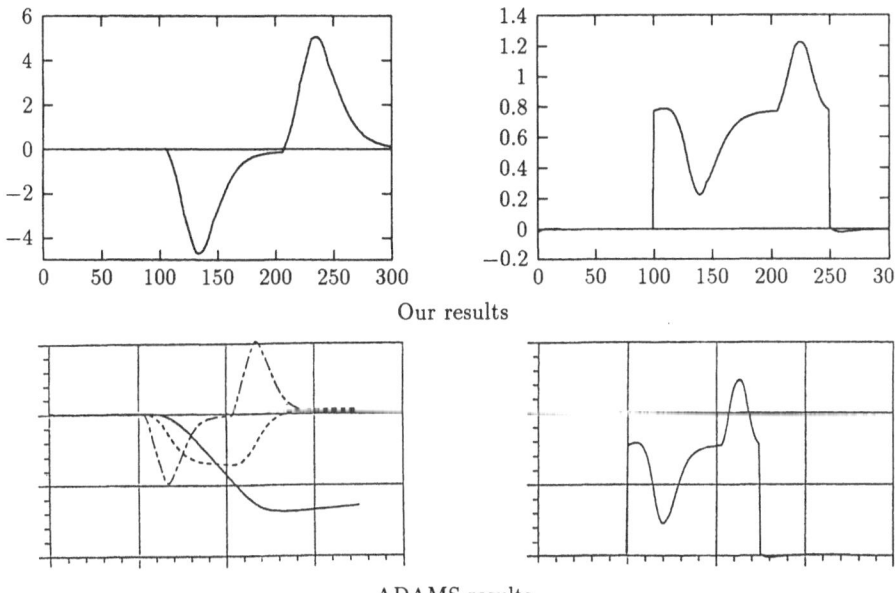

Our results

ADAMS results

Fig. 17: Comparisons between the system and ADAMS

- scientific simulation of physical objects.

The automatic derivation of the motion equations in a symbolic form from object models induces the following system facilities :

- implementation of a flexible and friendly user interface providing an artist with a graphically based interface to describe mechanism geometry and behavior constraints (trajectories), with possible intervention, for a specialist, by means of hand written symbolic equations ;

- exact mathematical operations (as derivation) and numerical stability ;

- event specification : addition or removal of constraints through time by using "variables" ;

- system extensibility : incorporation of collision detection and response in the motion resolution loop, and introduction of new kinds of joints and constraints.

The symbolic computation applied to deformable objects modeled as meshes of point masses linked by springs and dampers, allows the control of non rigid solids and surfaces. Furthermore, it allows control over the interactions between rigid and deformable objects, since they are handled in the same way.

The motion control is performed either explicitly by applying direct dynamics (Figure 4) and by task modeling (Figure 11), or implicitly by gravity effect and object interaction (Figure 8 and 9). The task modeling differences from one mechanism to another have been illustrated by the example of an arm along a 3D trajectory and the example of the car following a 2D trajectory (Figure 11). The animator should be provided with an automatic process which generates the constraint equations from task description (desired motion) and from the object model.

Acknowledgements

The van model and ADAMS simulation have been performed by R.V.I. (Renault Véhicules Industriels) and I.N.R.E.T.S. (Institut National de Recherches et d'Etudes sur les Transports et leur Sécurité). Special thanks go to Pierre Tellier for the ray-traced gyroscope animation sequence and to Jean-Luc Corre for illustrations.

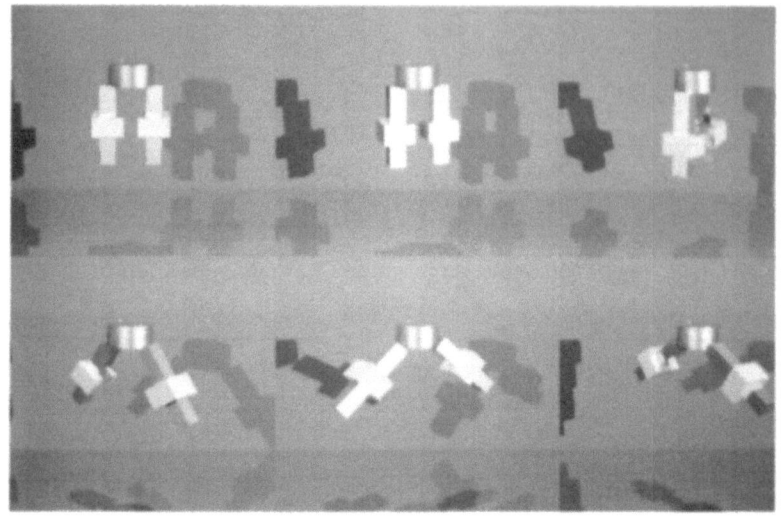

Fig. 18: Part of gyroscope sequence

References

[1] ARMSTRONG, W., AND GREEN, M. The dynamics of articulated rigid bodies for the purposes of animation. *The Visual Computer 1*, 4 (Dec. 1985), 231–240.

[2] ARNALDI, B., DUMONT, G., AND HÉGRON, G. Dynamics and unification of animation control. *The Visual Computer*, 5 (1989), 22–31.

[3] ARNALDI, B., DUMONT, G., HÉGRON, G., MAGNENAT-THALMANN, N., AND THALMANN, D. Animation control with dynamics. In *Computer Animation'89, State-of-the-art in Computer Animation* (1989), Springer-Verlag, Ed., Computer Graphics International, pp. 113–123.

[4] BAMBERGER, Y. *Mécanique de l'ingénieur 1 : systèmes de corps rigides.* Vol. 1, Hermann, 293 rue Lecourbe 75015 Paris, 1981.

[5] BARZEL, R., AND BARR, A. H. A modeling system based on dynamic constraints. In *SIGGRAPH'88* (Aug. 1988), Computer Graphics, pp. 179–188.

[6] CHACE, M. A. Methods and experience in computer aided design of large-displacement mechanical systems. In *Computer Aided Analysis and Optimisation of Mechanical System Dynamics*, E. Haug, Ed., Springer-Verlag, 1984, pp. 233–259.

[7] DEYO, R., BRIGGS, J. A., AND DOENGES, P. Getting graphics in gear : graphics and dynamics in driving simulation. In *SIGGRAPH'88* (Aug. 1988), Computer Graphics, pp. 317–326.

[8] DUMONT, G., ARNALDI, B., AND HÉGRON, G. Mechanics of solids for computer animation. In *PIXIM'89* (Sep. 1989), pp. 293–307.

[9] FOURNIER, A., BLOOMENTHAL, J., OPPENHEIMER, P., REEVES, W., AND SMITH, A. The modeling of natural phenomena. *ACM SIGGRAPH'87 Courses Notes 17* (1987).

[10] FOURNIER, A., AND REEVES, W. A simple model of ocean waves. In *SIGGRAPH'86* (Aug. 1986), Computer Graphics, p. 75.

[11] GASCUEL, M. P. Osea : un nouveau modèle de matière pour traiter les collisions entre objets déformables. In *PIXIM'89* (Sep. 1989), pp. 309–323.

[12] GERMAIN, P. *Mécanique*. Vol. 1, Ecole Polytechnique, 91128 Palaiseau Cedex, 1986.

[13] HAHN, J. K. Realistic animation of rigid bodies. In *SIGGRAPH'88* (Aug. 1988), Computer Graphics, pp. 299–308.

[14] HÉGRON, G., ARNALDI, B., AND DUMONT, G. Toward general animation control. In *C.G.I'88* (May 1988), Springer-Verlag, Ed., Computer Graphics International, Geneva, pp. 54–63.

[15] MILLER, G. S. P. The motion dynamics of snakes and worms. In *SIGGRAPH'88* (Aug. 1988), Computer Graphics, pp. 169–178.

[16] MOORE, M., AND WILHELMS, J. Collision detection and response for computer animation. In *SIGGRAPH'88* (Aug. 1988), Computer Graphics, pp. 289–298.

[17] ORLANDEA, N. *Development and Application of Node-Analogous Sparsity-Oriented Methods for Simulation of Mechanical Dynamic System*. PhD thesis, University of Michigan, 1973.

[18] PLATT, J. C., AND BARR, A. H. Constraints methods for flexible models. In *SIGGRAPH'88* (Aug. 1988), Computer Graphics, pp. 279–288.

[19] REEVES, W. Particle systems : a technique for modelling a class of fuzzy objects. In *SIGGRAPH'83* (July 1983), Computer Graphics, pp. 359–376.

[20] SCHIELEN, W. Computer generation of equations of motion. In *Computer Aided Analysis and Optimisation of Mechanical System Dynamics*, E. Haug, Ed., Springer-Verlag, 1984, pp. 183–215.

[21] TERZOPOULOS, D., AND FLEISCHER, K. Modeling inelastic deformation : viscoelasticity, plasticity, fracture. In *SIGGRAPH'88* (Aug. 1988), Computer Graphics, pp. 269–278.

[22] TERZOPOULOS, D., PLATT, J., BARR, A., AND FLEISCHER, K. Elastically deformable models. In *SIGGRAPH'87* (July 1987), Computer Graphics, pp. 205–214.

[23] TERZOPOULOS, D., AND WITKIN, A. Physically based models with rigid and deformable components. In *Graphics Interface'88* (June 1988).

[24] TOUZOT, G., AND DHATT, G. *Une Présentation de la Méthode des Eléments Finis*. Maloine S.A Editeur, 27 rue de l'Ecole de Medecine, 75006 Paris, 1984.

[25] WILHELMS, J., AND BARSKY, B. Using dynamic analysis to animate articulated bodies such as humans and robots. In *Graphics interface'85* (May 1985), pp. 97–104.

[26] WITKIN, A., FLEISCHER, K., AND BARR, A. Energy constraints on parameterized models. In *SIGGRAPH'87* (July 1987), Computer Graphics, pp. 225–232.

[27] WITKIN, A., AND KASS, M. Spacetime constraints. In *SIGGRAPH'88* (Aug. 1988), pp. 159–168.

[28] WITTENBURG, J. *Dynamics of Systems of Rigid Bodies*. Teubner, Stuttgart, 1977.

[29] ZIENKIEWICZ, O. C. *The Finite Element Method in Engineering Science, third edition*. Mc Graw-Hill, London, 1977.

ISISA/INRIA, Campus Universitaire de Beaulieu, 35042 Rennes Cedex, France

An Unified View of Multitude Behavior, Flexibility, Plasticity and Fractures Balls, Bubbles and Agglomerates

A. Luciani, S. Jimenez, O. Raoult, C. Cadoz, and J.L. Florens

Abstract

The work presented here, is a part of a "modeler-simulator", capable of representing and simulating a large variety of physical objects: The Cordis-Anima system.

Based on particle physics, atomic interactions and the decomposition by network of lumped physical components, the Cordis-Anima system enables modelisation and real time simulation of a large variety of objects and scenes, rigid or deformable with collisions, fractures, sticking ...

However, the atomic representation of the objects becomes more unwieldy if there is more discontinuous behavior or if the desired resolution in the shapes or deformations are greater. We have added to the previous principles, the three following points :

◊ "physical ball-meshing" which consists in an adaptive structural physical decomposition of matter.

◊ "agglomerate-compacting" which consists in regrouping severals balls by one interaction law.

◊ "physical-shaping" : the contour is seen as a physical interaction frontier between several agglomerates.

This provides access to a more macroscopic modelisation of large free form objects, or of objects whose structure is under dynamic modification.

Key words :

Computer animation - Physical models - physical interactions - Real time simulation - Physical shaping.

I. INTRODUCTION TO PHYSICAL MODELING

During its initial phase of evolution, image synthesis has gone from pixel manipulation to 3D modelisation. Whatever the importance of this leap forward, in terms of principles as well as the machines that materialise them, the breakthrough nonetheless was not sufficient to tackle the problem of animation adequately. Mathematical or geometric models, for the most part mainly directed towards indeformable objects - be they CAD models like CSG (Constructive Solid Geometry) and BR (Boundary Representation) or modelisation of natural objects using different interpolation functions (varieties of splines, Coons or Béziers surfaces) - are extremely unwieldy if used to describe high variability movements, the extreme case being highly deformable objects such as fluids or pastes.

Over the last two years, image synthesis has jumped another major hurdle, which is the introduction, in the object model, of behavioural properties. Some of these, such as the Reynolds multitude behaviour models [Reyn 87] or the Reeves "particle systems" [Ree 83] are formalisms that enable explicit cinematic restitution of the phenomena that may, or may not (e.g. anticipation phenomena) result from physical systems.

Others have tried to restitute the dynamics of physical systems by simulation, or what we refer to as "physical models". It is therefore clear that physical modeling can be considered as one sector of behavorial modeling. Indeed, from a conceptual standpoint it displays the same major advantages :

---

genericity : a physical model represents the class of movements - all the possible movements are potentially contained in the model.

coherence : the movements obtained are "more natural" than those offered by combinations of geometric transformations - temporal and dynamic aspects are still coherent because of the simulation process.

simplicity : these models take charge of the intrinsic behaviour of the objects, interactions between objects, internal forces and so on, with only one formalism.

modularity : two models of two different objects can be mixed in a unique scene, i.e. each part of a complex scene can be developped an tested separatly.

However there are distinct differences and these are to be found in the field of representation and in the algorithms. Non-physical models are based on systems of rules - we might even add on systems of arbitrary non limited behavorial rules. In physical modeling there is a canonical (in a mathematical sense) base of rules composed of physical rules. Variables are strictly state variables. These can be extensive variables (such as position, speed or deformation) and intensive variables (such as forces or constraints).Physical interactions cannot include anticipations such as actions to avoid obstacles or anticipatory behaviour proper to living beings.

From a simulation standpoint, we solve a set of great number of diferential equations and the algorithmic models are time implicit.

Physical modeling and simulation appeared in 1979 with the first developement of the Cordis-Anima system [Cad 79,81 - Luc 81]. Cordis-Anima is a system based on physical modeling for producing sound and/or animated images. Some time later, physical calculus was used at Ohio State University as a complement to other animation methods [Sch 84].

A great deal of research results have begun to accumulate in this field [Luc 84,85 - Cad 84 - Flo 86 - Ter 87,88 - Bar 88 - Mil 88 - Hah 88 - Arn 88 - DAH 89 - Flo 89 - Jim 89] since 1984. The net result is that the idea and the interest of physical models in synthesising a moving image is today acknowledged and has unanimously proved its initial worth.

In terms of physics, there are several computer representations available, and this obviously depends on the aim of the application. For example,

models and their implementation can be very different if we use computers to predict the behaviour of a physical system in as precise terms as possible (i.e. and application in numerical calculation) or if we want to use the computer as a modelor-simulator for physical systems and animation.

The Cordis-Anima system and the work presented in this paper have opted for the second goal. It follows that the modularity and the constructability of the models, in addition to real time in simulation, are major constraints in the computer representation of the physics.

The first part of this paper is devoted to the formal aspect in a computer physical modeler-simulator. The second part deals with the major optimisation needs occasioned by the constraints of real-time and of complex object simulation.

II THE CORDIS-ANIMA FORMALISM

It is pertinent to consider that a physical model of a physical object is itself a physical object, that is, it moves and is deformed when subjected to physical actions.

To achieve our objective of a modeler-simulator, we can therefore consider that such an object may be symbolised by a dipole, or more generally by an n-poles system, which associates the two sets of dual variables, extensives and intensives : $O(P,F) = F$

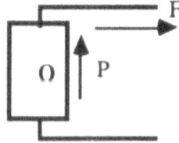

figure 1 : a physical object

It follows that all objects or sets of objects can be built by interconnected n-pole blocks which are in series, parallel, or in parallel/series.

This formalism conveys the structural discretisation needed in a modeler-simulator.

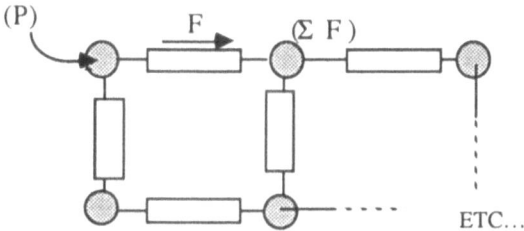

figure 2 : structural discretisation of physical object

This approach forces us to explicitly choose what each block contains, which is, in fact, the question of the minimal matter element and the underlying basis to interactions.

Physics, and the various chapters of mechanics offer many ways to define the minimal material element and to select and associate these two variables. The choice depends on the phenomena that interest us. This implies an option on a basic discretisation and modelisation principle for the real universe. However, the modularity constraint (cf. I) means that the expression of these laws should be the same on all levels of object description. These laws must be applicable to any network of the above type, even if this network represents only a part of an object, a complex set of objects or the entire scene.

A usual choice (but not our own) is the "infinitesimal solid". The two dual variables are constraints and deformations. The integration of the behavorial laws of infinitesimal solids provide a macroscopic solid behavior.

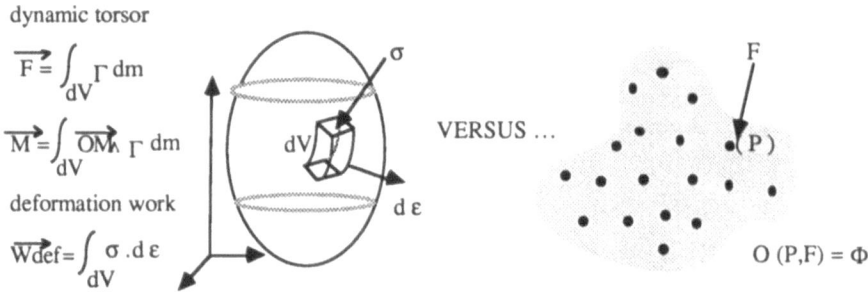

dynamic torsor

$$\vec{F} = \int_{dV} \Gamma \, dm$$

$$\vec{M} = \int_{dV} \vec{OM} \wedge \Gamma \, dm$$

deformation work

$$\vec{Wdef} = \int_{dV} \sigma \, .d\varepsilon$$

VERSUS ...

$$O(P,F) = \Phi$$

figure 3 : infinitesimal solid versus punctual representation of matter

The Cordis-Anima system, presented below, has opted for a "particle physics". The minimal element of matter is a punctual mass. Dual variables are positions and centered forces. Interactions links several of these elements of matter to make up an object or a scene.

Physical particles have mass and receive forces. They can physically interact and be submitted to gravity or all other kinds of forces.

In other "particle models", [Ree 83] for example, the particle systems have been chosen to simulate complex systems with a very high number of simple elements which are not necessarily supposed to be physical elements.

Cordis - Anima [Cad 81, Luc 84, Cad 84, Flo 89] has adopted the 3 following axioms as modelisation principles of physical space.

1 - Modelisation of matter in punctual masses : the minimal matter element is the punctual mass. It is represented by a discrete component, named the "matter component", whose physical parameter is the mass value. The calculation describing the behaviour of the component is provided by the fundamental dynamics equation Force = Mass*Acceleration, expressed in terms of "finite differences". This calculation is oriented to provide the mass position from the forces that are applied to it. This component therefore presents itself as an oriented dipole [force -> position].

2 - Modelisation of the continuous behavior of the material : the material, that is normally defined by parameters of elasticity, viscosity, or others is represented by discrete components without mass, named the "material component", whose characteristics are elasticities or viscosities, considered under their continuous aspects, with neither thresholds nor hysteresis. The calculations are provided by the basic equations describing continuous behaviour F = -K*D (the force is proportional to the distance) and F= -Z*V (the force is proportional to the relative speed) . These calculations are oriented to provide forces from the positions. These components present themselves as oriented quadripoles [two positions ->two forces].

3 - Modelisation of the structure of matter and of objects : the "material components" that enable modelisation of the material are equipped with a double logical function. The first is to "link up" the components representing the punctual masses. The second is to carry out this liaison

according to a transition status logic that enables the parameters of the material to be modified in function of conditions affecting the parameters or variables. This enables homogeneous access to non-linear behaviour, continuous or discontinuous behaviour without any addition of basic primitives. Collisions, non-linear parameter modifications, such as elastic behaviour over large displacements, all non continuous behaviour, with or without hysteresis (like plasticity) can thus be processed by this unique formalism.

There are thus no specific collision or fracture algorithms for rigid and deformable objects. This choice of modelisation enables us to modelise the microscopic structure of matter of an object in the same way as the non-linear macrostructure of a scene. It clearly evidences the proximity between phenomena situated on different levels - an elastic collision, a rupture (exceeding the elasticity threshold), or plasticity for example.

The fact that the components can be represented in terms of quadripoles and dipoles enables us to define simple connexions between components. The representation of physical objects by a network of interconnected boxes is particularly adapted to model construction modularity. The extremely restricted number of base algorithms lend themselves well to vectorisation.

The network which describes an object or a set of objects in physical interaction can be simulated component by component, and this is a great advantage as regards the model experimentation, depending on the modular design.

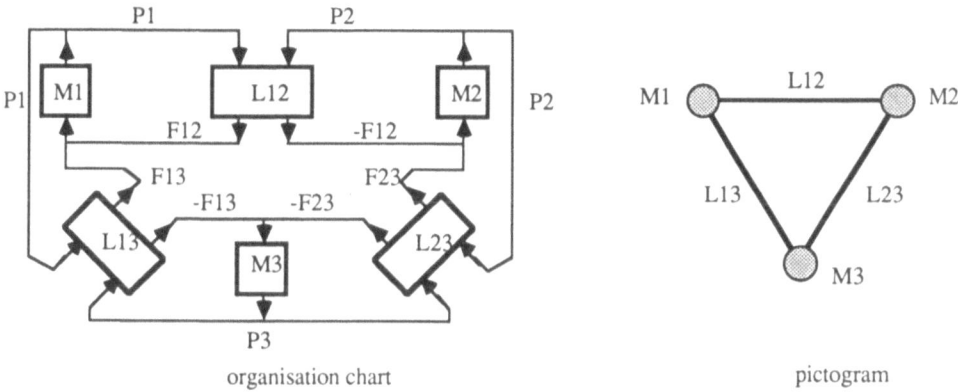

organisation chart   pictogram

figure 4 : an example of a Cordis-Anima model

Major consequences arise from these principles :

- The interaction between the human operator and the simulated objects is similar to the interactions between physical objects.
- The simulated physical objects are physically manipulable.
- By using gestual transducers, a user can apply forces, or positions to the object. This object responds by movement and deformation.
- Such an object is perceptible in a proprio-tactilo-kinesthetic manner. By using force feeback transducers, the user can actually feel forces and displacements.

There is hence no control problem. The gestual bandwith is large enough to convey expressive manipulations. This formalism is more general and therefore enables modelisation and simulation of all types of objects, be they rigid or deformable. This equally applies to objects linked by any type of interaction, linear or otherwise.

In contrast, this kind of atomic description and simulation of a scene becomes more unwieldy if there are:
- more complex discontinuous behaviour events (for example, dry friction between a track vehicle and a non-homogeneous ground).
- a great number of masses and interactions as for example in the agglutination of finely granulated bodies (powders, fluids, ...).

Because of the above, two more specific optimisations have been developed [Jim 89] as a special supplement to the Cordis-Anima modeler-simulator. They are totally compatible with the Cordis-Anima formalism but they provide access to a more macroscopic modeling of free form physical objects or of objects and scenes whose structure is under frequent modification.

These are suitable when there are :
- a great number of the same elements (homogeneous materials for example).
- or in the case of non-linear interactions, when the non-linearities depend only on a condition over one variable (collisions for example).

Depending on the importance of these case, these optimisations can be seen as another modeling principle, which we have named "agglomerate with univariable non-linear interactions".
Nonetheless, as a part of the Cordis-Anima modeler-simulator, they fulfil the general conditions of modularity; they do not restrict the domain of representation and they can use the force feedback interaction devices for physical real time interactions with the operator.

III.   AGGLOMERATES WITH UNIVARIABLE NON-LINEAR INTERACTIONS.

The context is one of buildable, manipulable, and interactional physical objects. The basic principles remain the same as those described and discussed above - the choice of particle dynamics in opposition to solid dynamics ; the use of interaction between particles to define complex objects or set of objects ; the modelisation by network of lumped physical components.

III.1   Balls, bubbles and agglomerates

The fundamental change brought in, compared to the previously described Cordis-Anima formalism, resides in a new way of breaking down a piece of matter. The principled is rooted in the construction of agglomerates, that are pieces of matter which present themselves as a milieu. The minimal matter element here is the "physical ball".
We replace the Cordis-Anima physical points, nominatively coupled to another physical point, by composite entities named "balls". A ball is never alone. What we designate as "balls" are a group of

punctual masses that come into interaction amongst themselves via a distributed interaction function. The prime parameter of this function is the interaction zone.

Each ball is a punctual mass plus a spherical non-entrance zone (impenetrability). In the case of a non-exit zone, we refer to "bubbles" (figures 5). This zone appears only when interaction occurs. A set of scattered balls is merely a group of punctual masses .

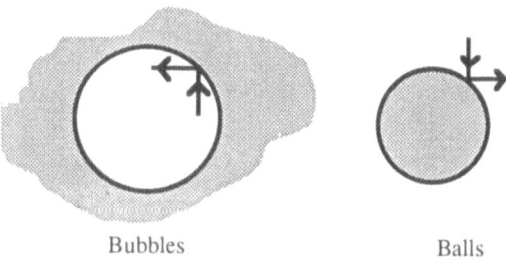

Bubbles   Balls

figure 5 : Bubbles and Balls

Thus the initial principles have been specialized with "physical ball-meshing" as an adaptive structural decomposition of matter. A piece of physical matter will be presented as a set of different sized physical balls.

We have also introduced "agglomerate-compacting". An agglomerate is a group of balls plus a law of interaction between each balls of the set. This law can be attractive, repulsive or more complex (see below).

These two concepts could be written as :

mass + interaction zone = ball
ballS + interaction law = agglomerate

As a consequence, we can now speak of "physical-shaping". The contour of an object can be defined as the physical interaction frontier between several agglomerates.

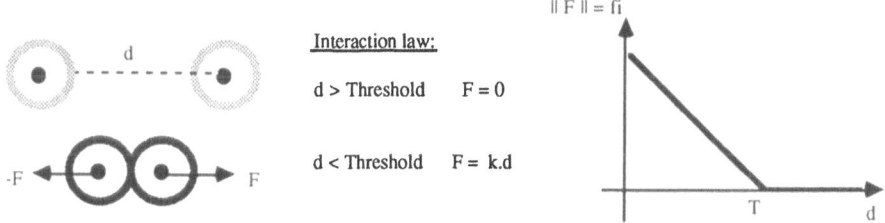

Interaction law:

d > Threshold $F = 0$

d < Threshold $F = k.d$

$\| F \| = f_i$

figure 6 : balls under interaction - the elementary law of interaction

As we said above, agglomerates are composed of a group or set of balls linked together by a specifically <u>unique</u> interaction law. The overall interaction law should be observed as an intrinsic property of the agglomerate.

A $N*(N-1)/2$ liaison module calculates the mutual interactions between the masses (figure 7).

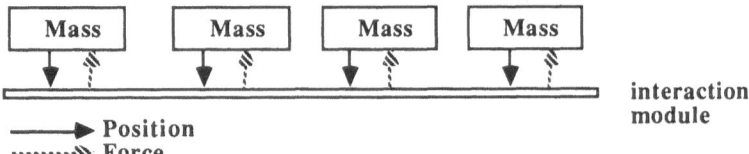

figure 7 : Interaction Module

A particular, and moreover interesting case, is the intermolecular law of liaison (Van der Waals). It enables us to build consistent agglomerates with a centred shape. However, other types of laws are possible.

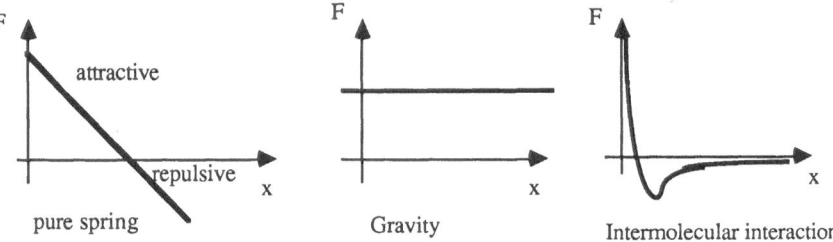

figure 8 : interaction functions

In the case of the agglomerate, the output of the interaction functions depends on only one variable and then, the interaction function can be represented by piecewise linear function (as shown in figure 6 and 8). It is easy to define a generic algorithm to design piecewise linear functions. In addition, because of the formalism of punctual representation, the forces are summed on masses, and thus we can put several interactions in parallel and obtain complex interaction functions from simple linear piecewise functions. Because of this approach, we do not need to have more than two or three pieces in the interaction primitives.

This kind of interaction is an important case of the "conditional link sub-system" implemented in the Cordis-Anima system [Cad 81, Luc 84, Luc 90(1), Luc90(2)] which allows us to describe and simulate general non-linear interactions from "fusible links" as in [Ter 89] to general non-linear multivariable interactions as a bowed string, snow/ski interactions, or track vehicle/non-homogeneous ground interactions, where complex temporal sequences of states occur.

III.2 Agglomerate properties

An agglomerate is an accumulation of undifferentiated balls with a global shape which results from a dynamic process.

<u>The shape does not pre-exist, it is achieved</u>.

It is one state of equilibrium. These states of equilibrium are the peculiar points of a generator process. One characteristic of these particular points is the degree of stability. Thus, an agglomerate can intrinsically break up, without any addition of extra information. A mass violently striking an agglomerate stabilised by Van der Waals, or by gravity, can break it. The agglomerate may not necessarily be able to totally reconstitute itself. It is also possible to define sticky agglomerates so that they cannot be broken apart.

The interaction function and the number of balls define the variety of agglomerate shapes. However, the internal arrangement of the balls depends on dynamic conditions given to the generator process. Two balls could be permuted without any change in the global shape.

In contrast to Cordis-Anima, the position of each ball is not determined when the model is constructed (balls were dropped in quasi-random positions). In fact, it would be useless. Thus, the given model is not really a model of the final object, but an object-making model. The underlying thought process to modelisation work, is a thought mode of movement and temporal processes.

III.3   Objects

An agglomerate is an elementary <u>homogeneous</u> object. In the same way as an agglomerate is a set of balls under interaction, so a complex object can be described by a set of interacting agglomerates. Each couple of agglomerates could be linked by its own interaction law.

$$
\begin{array}{lll}
\text{agglomerateS} & + \text{ P interaction lawS} & = & \text{object} \\
\text{objectS} & + \text{ Q interaction lawS} & = & \text{scene}
\end{array}
$$

To calculate all the interactions between all the balls of two agglomerates, we use an optimized "NxM liaison module". This module corresponds to a unique interaction law distributed over the NxM couples of the cartesian product of two agglomerates.

Unlike the agglomerate, these can be linked together by several different sorts of interaction functions in parallel. It is therefore sufficient to define as many "liaison modules" as required, since the summation of the forces is effected in the balls of the agglomerates.

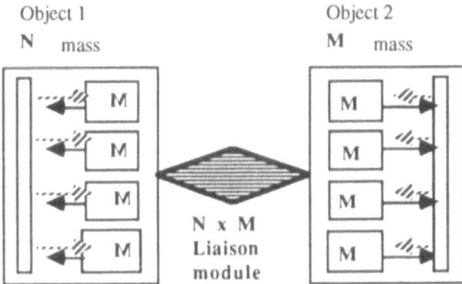

figure 9 : NxM Liaison Module

III.4   A proposition for the construction of malleable objects

The following structure is an operational guide to modelise (more or less rigid) solids by the "physical ball composition" approach. An object can be structured in three relative layers, that are not all necessarily present :

- A deep layer or "**nucleus**" : this represents a centering function that the object organises itself around. The nucleus is either undeformable or only slightly deformable. In the simplest case, it may be reduced to a large attractive or repulsive ball, and is thus indeformable. But this nucleus can also be composed of several masses and springs to define, for example, a cube or any other sort of structured object.

- A **derm** : this will bear the most substantial deformability qualities. Its thickness represents the depth and area of the deformation quite directly.

- An **epiderm**, or "skin" : its role is to reinforce the agglomerate's cohesion. This is where the notion of "surface tension" will be localised.

Each layer is characterised by a specific interaction function between its constituents, that are in complementarity to their neighbouring layers. The object interaction with the exterior varies more or less in depth, depending on the layers concerned.

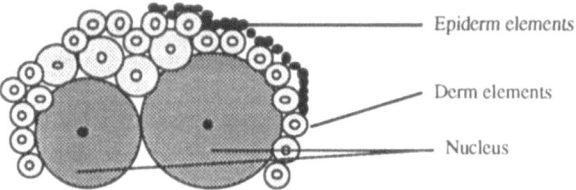

figure 10 : structured object

The main role of this organisation is to structure the interactions between objects, and consequently, to lower their number. For example, in the case where a skin layer exists, it handles the interactions with the outside. In the more extreme case of a scene composed of many objects which can shatter into fragments, and then fall again into new objects, all the layers, including nucleii, must be affected by the outside interactions.

III.5   Simulation examples

1. A multitude of particles in interaction

The water of the cascade (see photograph 1) is modeled as a set of indeformable particles in non-permanent elasto-viscous collision interactions. A big difference between this model and other "particles sytems", is the possibility to obtain pool of water, whirlpool and turbulence - which means that each ball could interact with all the others. This type of effect cannot be obtained with a simple superimposition of independent trajectories.

The principle is similar in the next example : a ball thuds into an heap. Here again, effective interactions are necessary.

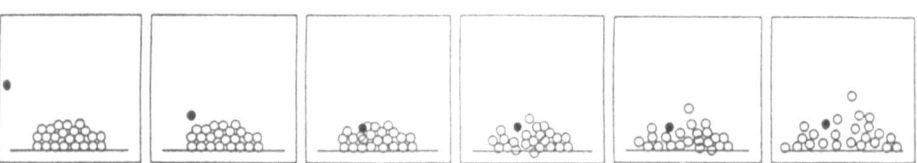

chronogramm 1

2. A simple structured object : the rubber ball

This is a stable, spherical, and slightly deformable object. It is structured in two layers. A nucleus confers the overall shape to the object (a 3D ball or a 2D disc). The derm is composed of a set of inter-repulsive balls. The nucleus/derm interaction law is "intermolecular". The derm balls take up a position of equilbrium by positioning themselves regularly around the nucleus and form a regular crown. When the object runs into a wall, it is slightly crushed, and the derm balls that are in contact with the wall are separated. When the object moves away from the wall, it recovers its initial spherical shape. This model introduces the notions of adaptive meshing and of deformation locality (see photograph 3).

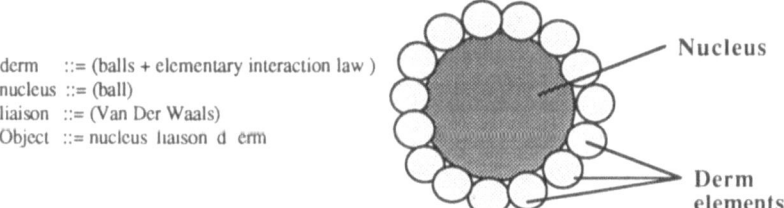

derm   ::= (balls + elementary interaction law)
nucleus ::= (ball)
liaison ::= (Van Der Waals)
Object ::= nucleus liaison d erm

figure 11 : an elementary object (Nucleus-Derm)

3. The rubber ball - separation and then regrouping

This example shows how the previous deformable object is equally transformable without any addition of other functions. Cases of non predefined splitting or of "re-sticking" are entirely taken into consideration. The shape of these objects is not defined as such, but it is made up. It is the free expression of dynamic forces that lead to stable forms. This also illustrates that the first level of complexity, - i.e. the dynamic modification of the structure in the object - is allowed for in the agglomerate. The object can shatter into elementary fragments.

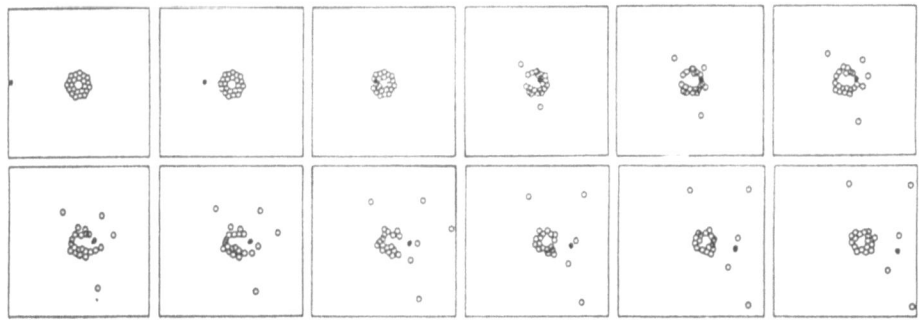

chronogramm 2

4. The rubber ball - sliding without rolling, rolling without sliding

During the contact with a flat floor - that is formed by little adjacent balls - the rubber ball may present a sliding movement without rolling. It occurs when the size of the floor balls is smaller than those of the derm, or when the floor is locally extra flat (simulated by a very large ball).

If the derm of the rubber ball is very thick and the nucleus very small, it has a large depth of deformation. Placed on a flight of stairs - that is obtained also by "ball-meshing" (figure 12) - it tears down the stairs, hugging the steps' shape. It rolls, but it does not slide (see photograph 4).

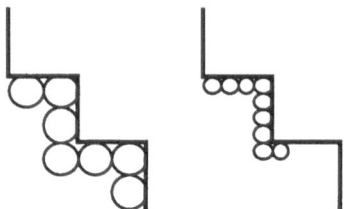

figure 12 : "ball-meshing" stairs

5 Mouldable object

The photograph 5 show a piece of plasticine which is mouldable by the operator in real time. The model of this plastic object is obtained by an agglomerate composed about 30 balls linked by a repulsive-attractive interaction function. The attractive zone is chosen to be lower than a 2 ball radius. The object has the shape that the operator gives it. The plasticine can broken up and then re-stuck together according to the manipulation. We can easily knead the paste, tear and recompact it, and this in real time.

6. A file model example

The model below describes a sort of rattle composed of a tetrahedron enclosed inside a hollow sphere. The sphere can rebound on a flat floor and the tetrahedron inside the sphere. This model is not a program but just the description of elementary objects, and interaction laws between them. In this simple example, movements merely result from gravity and internal interactions effects - five lines more were needed to enable real-time manipulation with force-feedback gestual transducers.

Each line is composed of a keyword, an identification name (if needed) and a set of parameters. It should be noted that "DEFMASS" (as DEFFI) is just used to associate name to numerical values - whereas "DEFMOB" is used to allocate N balls descriptors, to specificy their mass (named), the topology of the internal interaction law (AGGLOmerate), plus the interaction law itself (named). For example, "DEFMOB foo 10 n_m AGGLO n_intl" means : allocate an agglomerate descriptor named "foo", composed of 10 balls (each ball foo1, foo2, .. has a mass "n_m") with an interaction law named "n_intl".

```
VISCOSITY 0.01                                 overall viscosity of the milieu
GRAVITY    9.8                                 Earth's gravity
DEFMASS m_rattle    10e-3                       the rattle masses will weigh 10 g
DEFMASS m_sphere   100e-3                       the sphere mass will weigh 100 g
DEFFI   fi_in_rattle           1 (-1,0) [.05]
DEFFI   fi_rattle_sphere       2 (-1,0) (1,.1) [.1]
DEFFI   fi_sphere_floor        2 (-1,0) (1,100) [100]
# allocations  of  elementary  agglomerates
DEFMOB    rattle 4             m_rattle  AGGLO  fi_in_rattle
DEFMOB    sphere 1             m_sphere
DEFFIX    floor 1
# interactions  between  couples  of  agglomerates
LINKGRP  rattle  sphere        fi_rattle_sphere
LINKGRP  sphere  floor         fi_sphere_floor
# no interaction between rattle and floor
# initial  positions
POSITAROUND    rattle    (0,0,0)   [.1,.1,.1]   quasi-random positions
POSIT          sphere  (0,0,0)
POSIT          floor   (0,100,0)
```

The initial positions of the material points of the rattle are selected in <u>random fashion</u> . Four material points linked together by springs of a given length (5cm, see fi_in_rattle) will spontaneously organise themselves into a tetrahedral shape, whatever their initial configuration. Moreover, the sphere will "swallow" or absorb the tetrahedron even if the latter is initially on the outside. The initial status of the rattle is not determinant here since only one stable structure exists (the rattle masses organised into a tetrahedral, the tetrahedron inside the sphere, and the sphere above the floor)

The ground is a hollow sphere with a 100 m radius. Its center is fixed rigidly at an altitude of 100 m. It therefore behaves like a quasi-flat floor surface. We often use such methods to reduce the effective number of balls ; in some case, ball-meshing can be avoided.

III.6   Optimisation, parallelisation, vectorisation

1. Physical meshing

Our decomposition of physical matter is : <u>adaptive, punctual and isotropic</u>. It therefore offers a considerable gain in calculations compared to the more classical approaches that employ geometric meshing of solids.

Physical Meshing is adaptive : there is no unique best model for a given object. Structural variations could be used exactly as parameter adjustments to obtain very precise effects. The meshing accommodates the shape specificities of the object as well as the deformation-transformation locality (figure 13).

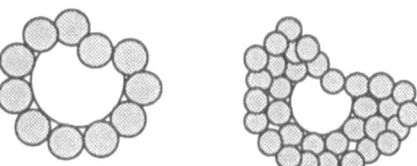

figure 13 : Two meshing examples

Physical Meshing is punctual : as the calculations are based on particle physics they never bring in rotations, projections, vectorial products and so on. The ball has only three degrees of liberty. Its calculation is <u>linear</u>. The equations are only a sum of products. It is the same for each of the 3 degrees of liberty, and for all the balls of all the agglomerates. If the complete scene has N balls, we can easily vectorise the calculation of all these equations.

Physical Meshing is isotropic : there is no integration of any potential function.. The interaction functions are centered. The calculation only involves the distance (or relative speed), which is calculated once for each sampling step. These functions can be represented by linear piecewise functions. These may be expressed in algebraic form, with certain approximations.

We shall only provide two major examples to illustrate the efficiency of this calculation : the first is an example of interaction calculation (intermolecular) ; the second shows how an elementary solid is obtained from punctual masses.

2. Intermolecular interaction calculation

Physics proposes a potential energy model (Lennard-Jones model) which enables definition of a potential family expressed as : $Vn = (S/d)2n - 2 * (S/d)n$ where the threshold S represents the zone of minimum potential. The force family derived from these potentials is written as :

$$Fn = -grad\ Vn = -(\partial Vn/\partial x, \partial Vn/\partial y, \partial Vn/\partial z) \quad \text{which produces } Fn = Fi(d) * Dp$$

where $Dp = (dx,dy,dz)$ is the "distance vector" of norm d
the Fi functions are expressed in the form (figure 14) : $Fi(d) = 2*n*(S^{2n}/d^{2n+2} - S^n/d^{n+2})$

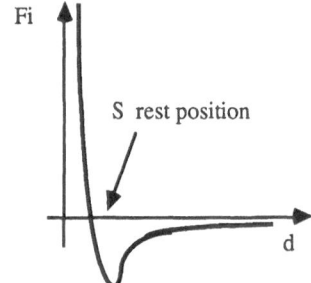

figure 14 : Lennard-Jones Interaction

Below is an example of this type of function approximated by a three piecewise linear function (fig.15) :

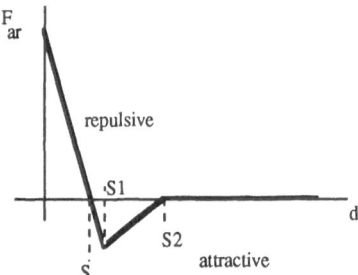

figure 15 : attractive/repulsive interaction fonction

Which, in the same way as any linear approximation, can be expressed as a sum of absolute linear term values (here in three terms) :

$$Far(d) = A_0 * |d| + A_2 * |d - S_1| + A_3 * |d - S_2| + C$$

where A_0, A_1, A_2, C are real constants which depend on S, S_1, S_2.

Concerning the complexity of the interaction function - in this case, the number of pieces - we can make two remarks : in the major cases, three pieces are sufficient ; we can also increase this number by superimposing several functions in parallel.

3. *Construction of an elementary solid (6 DOFs) by ball composition*

A primary challenge for this type of modelisation is to be able to simulate a solid, with 6 degrees of freedom with the previous 3D components. Photograph 2 shows an elementary solid composed of 4 balls which form a tetrahedron, enclosed inside a rectangular compound, and stabilized by the interaction function described above. This object is stable, strikes the walls, bounce, and displaces itself in translation and in rotation after the impacts. The chronogram below shows a similar solid, which is flat and composed of 3 balls (a 4 DOF object composed of two 2 DOF balls).

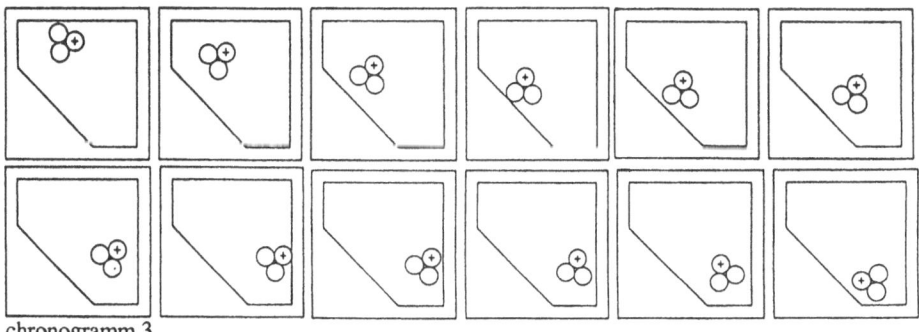

chronogramm 3

V. THE CONTOUR

"Contour" is a rich, multiform and complex notion, that cannot be reduced to the current methods in image synthesis (boundary representation : parametric surfaces and faceting). Our type of modelisation enables frequent or far-reaching structure modifications, so the generation of the contour demands thorough prior definition of the notion.

The contour is what establishes the unity of the object in its relation with the outside, and what implicitly distinguishes an interior (the object) from an exterior (the environment). It characterises the object as an individuated shape. It is a "membrane", "a threshold", and its materiality is sometimes highly partial, as, for example, in the case of a candle flame. It sustains the interactions with the exterior, and these interactions are of a very varied nature, which is why it is sometimes more the coherence between phenomena that allows us to establish the existence of a contour. In short, the object is seen, manipulated, and interacts through its contour.

When a model object includes an epiderm, there is no doubt that the latter conveys the outside shape of the object. Figure 16 gives an example of an epiderm model. The material skin, that is composed of visco-elastic Mass-Liaison bipole elements [Cad 79, Luc 81] plays the role of cohesion for the object like an elastic membrane, and because of this very fact (setting the border between the object and its environment) it is the contour.

Material skin

figure 16 : material skin

The next chronogramm shows an example of material skin.

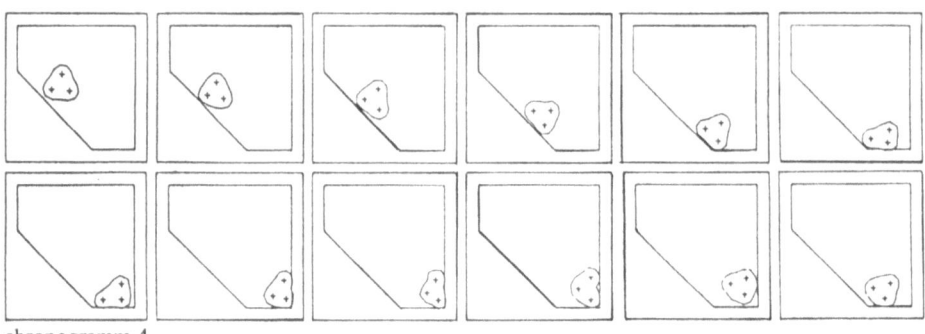

chronogramm 4

On occasions, objects have a weaker internal cohesion, and where the model does not require an "epiderm" layer. For example, this could be said of a more or less viscous fluid - such as a drop of oil or of mercury, or materials that are capable of being broken up or stuck back together - such as modelling clays. In this instance the contour can no longer be sustained by a structurally stable material skin. It should be noticed that in the commonest instance, the contour, when it exists, is a special feature, as a discontinuity or a zero-level, of the interaction function between the object and its environment.

Thus, for an agglomerate as we have just described, it is relatively easy to define a global interaction law, as the sum of the interactions which would be produced by each ball, in a point x,y,z of the empty space. We can then determine the main discontinuities of this 3D interaction field. Finally, we must detect this frontier in order to display it.

For that, we might use systematic or adaptive scanning techniques but the cost of the operation is inacceptable for a simulation that has to take place at a minimum of 25 Hz.

So, we have focussed on a technique that could be called "dynamic scanning". This means running a free mass with an initial speed over the object border. This mass is influenced by the global force field Fp, derivated from the intertaction fied. The successive positions of the mass, defines an approximation of the object envelope (figure 17).

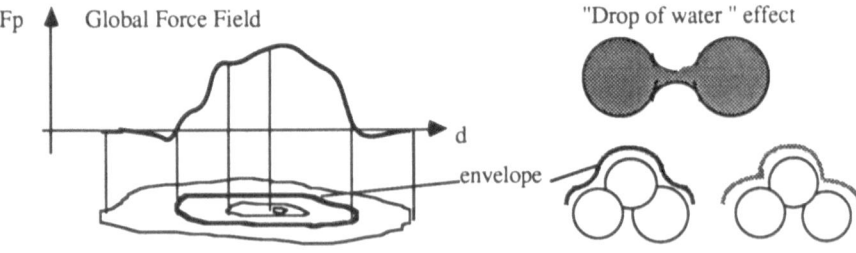

figure 17 : "dynamic scanning"

VI. PHOTOGRAPHS

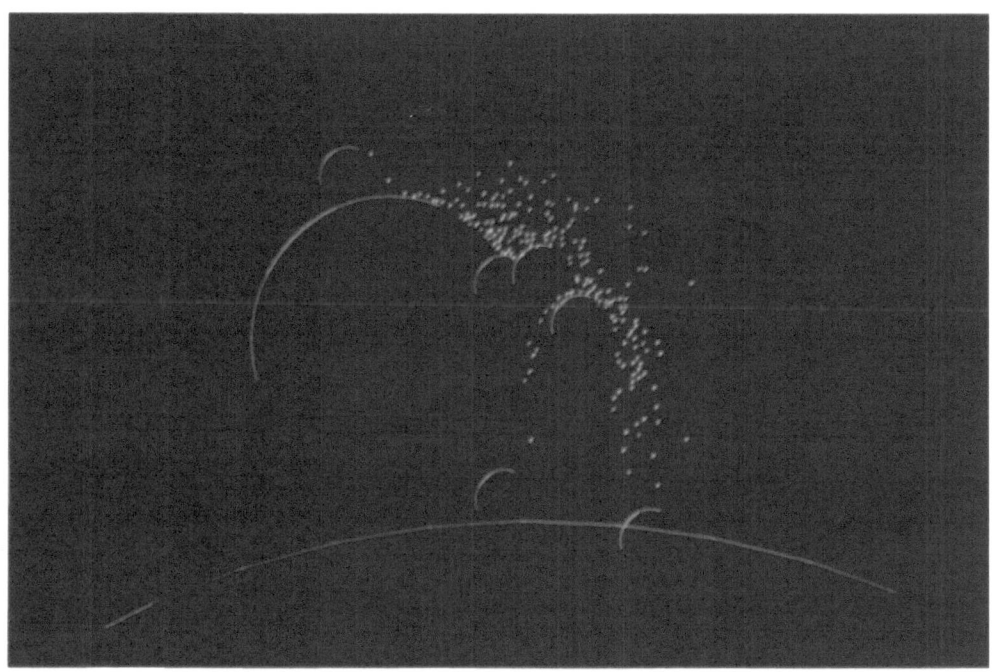

Photograph 1 : The Cascade

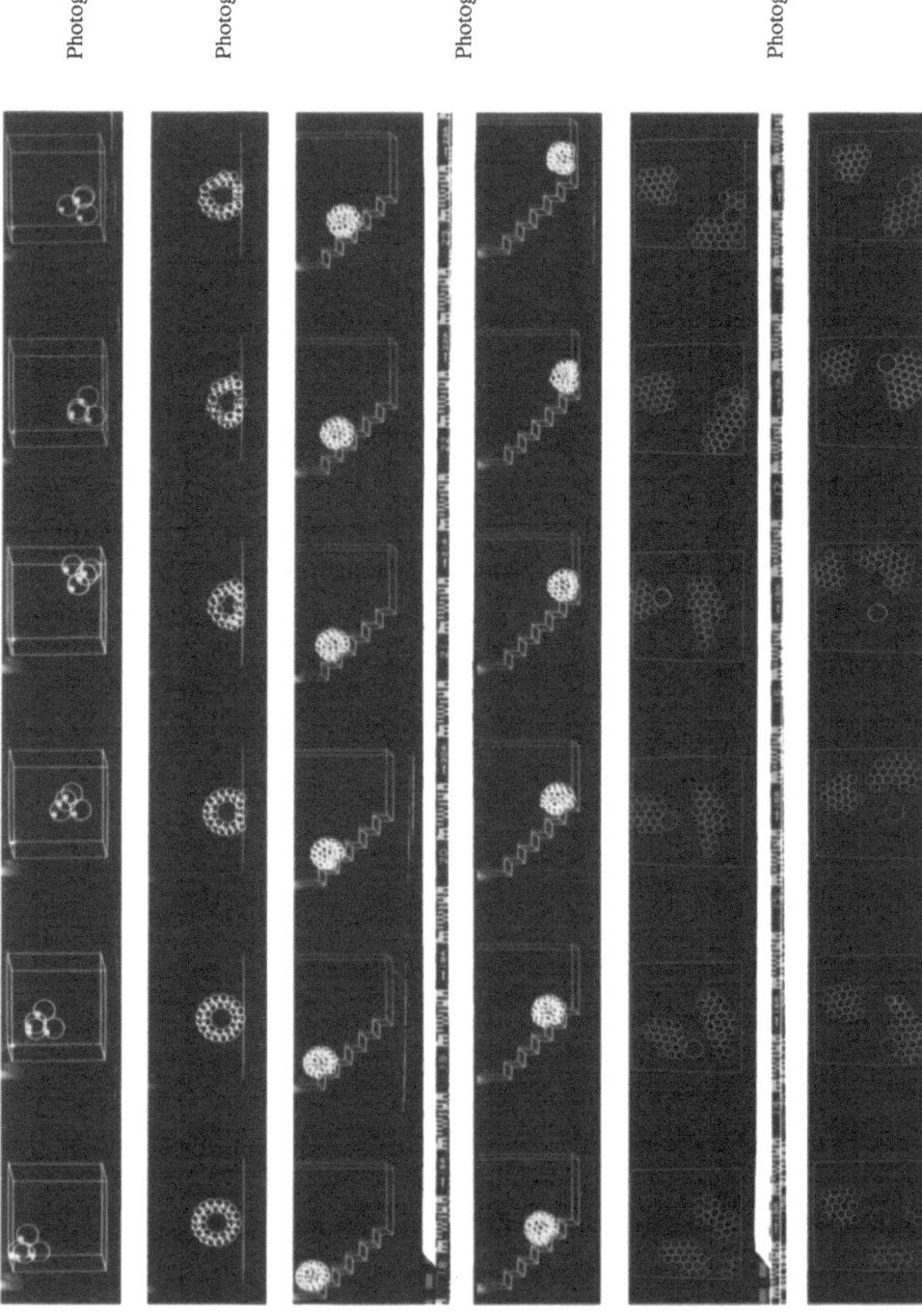

Photograph 2

Photograph 3

Photograph 4

Photograph 5

VII. REFERENCES :

[Cad 79]   C. CADOZ - " Synthèse sonore par simulation de mécanismes vibratoires" - Thèse Doctorat Electronique - INP - Grenoble - 1979

[Cad 81]   C. CADOZ, J.L. FLORENS, A. LUCIANI - " Synthèse musicale par simulation de mécanismes instrumentaux" - Transducteurs gestuels retroactifs" - Revue d'acoustique - N°59 - 1981

[Luc 81]   A. LUCIANI - "Anima, un outil de création d'images animées par modèles physiques" - DEA Electronique - Grenoble - 1981

[Reev 83]   W.T. REEVES - "Particle systems - A technique for modelling a class of fuzzy objects" - SIGGRAPH 83 proc 359-376

[Cad 84]   C. CADOZ, A. LUCIANI, J.L. FLORENS -"Responsive input devices and sound synthesis by simulation of instrumental mechanisms : the Cordis system" - Computer Music Journal - N°3 - 1984 - reprint in "Music Machine" - MIT Press

[Luc 84]   A. LUCIANI - "Modélisation et animation gestuelle d'objets : le système Anima" - 1er colloque Image Cesta - France - 1984

[Sch 84]   M.K. SCHWEPPE - "Motion in computer Graphics" - 1er Colloque Image - Cesta - France - 1984

[Luc 85]   A. LUCIANI - " Un outil informatique d'images animées - modèle d'objets, langage, contrôle gestuel en temps réel" - Thèse Doctorat Informatique - INP - Grenoble - 1985

[Flo 86]   J.L. FLORENS - " Optimized real time simulation of objects for musical synthesis and animated image synthesis" - Proceedings International Computer Music Conference - 1986

[Raz 86]   A. RAZAFINDRAKOTO - "Langage d'objets pour l'animation, implantation temps réel" - Thèse d'Université - Grenoble - 1986

[Reyn 87]   C.W. REYNOLDS - "Flocks, Herds and Schools : A distributed behavorial model" - SIGGRAPH 87 proc 25-34

[Ter 87]   D. TERZOPOULOS - " Elastically Deformable Models" - Proceedings SIGGRAPH 1987

[Arn 88]   B. ARNALDI - "Conception d'un noyau d'un système d'animation tri-dimensionnelles intégrant les lois de la mécanique" - PhD thesis, Rennes I, juillet 88.

[Bar 88]   R. BARZEL, A.H.BARR - "A modeling system based on dynamics constraints" - Proceedings SIGGRAPH 1988

[Hah 88]   J. K. HAHN - " Realistic animation of rigid body" - Proceedings SIGGRAPH 1988

[Mil 88]   G. MILLER - "The motion dynamics of snakes and worms" - Proceedings SIGGRAPH 1988

[Pla 88]   J.C. PLATT, A.H. BARR - "Constraint methods for flexible models" - Proceedings SIGGRAPH 1988

[Ter 88] D. TERZOPOULOS - " Modeling inelastic deformation" - Proceedings SIGGRAPH 1988

[Cad 89]   C. CADOZ, J.L. FLORENS - "Le modèle Physique - Référence et Artifice dans la création musicale par ordinateur", in - MIT Press - 1989 - à paraitre

[DAH 89] G. DUMONT, B. ARNALDI, G. HEGRON - Mechanics of solids for computer animation" - Proc. Pixim 89 p.293-308 - Paris - octobre 89.

[Flo 89]   J.L. FLORENS, C. CADOZ - "Le Modèle Physique - Simulation de l'univers instrumental" - in " - MIT Press - 1989 - à paraitre

[Gas 89]   M.P. GASCUEL - OSEA - "Un nouveau modèle de matière pour traiter les collisions entre objets déformables" - Pixim 89.

[GV 89]   M.P. GASCUEL, A. VERROUST - "Animation à l'aide de la dynamique : état de l'art" - Rapport LIENS - ENS Paris - Mai 89.

[Jim 89]   S. JIMENEZ - "Modelisation et simulation d'objets volumiques déformables complexes" - DEA Informatique - INP - Grenoble - 1989

[Ter 89]   D. TERZOPOULOS, J PLATT, A. BARR, and K. FLEISCHER - " Heating and melting deformable models (from goop to glop)." - Proceedings SIGGRAPH 1988

[Dum 90] G. DUMONT - "Animation de scènes tri-dimensionnelles : la mécanique des solides comme modèle de synthèse du mouvement" - PhD thesis, Rennes I, mai 90.

[GVP 90] M.P. GASCUEL, A. VERROUST, C. PUECH - "Animation with collisions of deformable articulated bodies" - In EUROGRAPHICS Workshop on Animation and Simulation - September 90.

[Gas 90]   M.P. GASCUEL- "Déformations de surfaces complexes : Techniques de haut niveau pour la modélisation et l'animation" - PhD Thesis, Paris-Orsay, octobre 90.

[Luc 90(1)] A. LUCIANI - "Modèles comportementaux : vers une approche instrumentale de la synthèse d'image"- GROPLAN 89 - revue BIGRE + GLOBULE - 1er trimestre 90.

[Luc 90(2)] A. LUCIANI - "Physical models in animation : Towards a modular and intrumental approach" - In EUROGRAPHICS Workshop on Animation and Simulation - September 90.

A.C.R.O.E., Ministère de la Culture, Laboratoire d'Informatique Fondamentale et d'Intelligence Artificielle-IMAG-CNRS, 38000 Grenoble, France

Chapter 3

Geometric Modeling

A NURBS Representation for Cyclides

XIAOLIN ZHOU and WOLFGANG STRABER

Abstract

Cyclides have attracted the interest of researchers in recent years. This family of surfaces includes all the surfaces conventionally used in computer aided design of mechanical parts. They have been found very useful in defining blends and support naturally a piecewise approach to surface design. To make these properties available in an interactive design environment, a NURBS (Non Uniform Rational B–Splines) representation for cyclides has been developed, enlarging in a consistent way the capabilities of our NURBS modeler.

Keywords: Computer aided design, geometric modeling, cyclides, rational B–splines, blossoming

1 Introduction

NURBS are used as a basis in many modelers due to a number of superior properties compared to other traditional representations [Tiller '86, Dokken '89]. They allow us to represent free–form curves and surfaces as well as a wide class of analytical objects used in practice, especially conic curves and surfaces. Here we are mainly concerned with the NURBS representation of cyclides and their interactive properties, i.e. the control points to be specified and manipulated by the designer. The analytical properties of cyclides are reported elsewhere [Martin'82, de Pont'84, Sharrock'85, Pratt'89, Boehm'90].

The paper is organized as follows: Chapter 2 surveys very shortly the properties of cyclides and their use in CAD. In chapter 3 we give a rough idea of the blossoming principle, which is used in chapter 4 to find the control points of a NURBS representation for cyclides. Chapter 5 explains some useful properties concerning piecewise definition and offset surfaces. In Chapter 6 we give some examples to demonstrate the capabilities of the developed NURBS representation. In the last chapter we summarize the results and indicate directions for future work. In general, we stress the applicability of cyclides more than the mathematical foundations.

2   Cyclides and their use in CAD

Recent works [Martin'82, de Pont'84, Sharrock'85, Pratt'89, Boehm'90] describe the useful properties of cyclides for cyclide patches design and blending tasks as well as inclusion of conventional surfaces such as the natural quadrics (plane, cylinder, cone, sphere) and torus in the design. From this it is obvious that cyclides could cover a broad and important range of CAD tasks in case that a user–friendly, transparent definition like a Bézier net of controlpoints could be found.

Forsyth [Forsyth'12] has given the following description for a cyclide in a standard location (see Fig.1):

Two implicit forms:

$$(x^2 + y^2 + z^2 - \mu^2 + b^2)^2 \;\; = \;\; 4(ax - c\mu)^2 + 4b^2 y^2$$

$$(x^2 + y^2 + z^2 - \mu^2 - b^2)^2 \;\; = \;\; 4(cx - a\mu)^2 + 4b^2 z^2 \tag{1}$$

and a parametric form :

$$x \;\; = \;\; \frac{\mu(c - a\cos\theta\cos\psi) + b^2\cos\theta}{a - c\cos\theta\cos\psi}$$

$$y \;\; = \;\; \frac{b\sin\theta(a - \mu\cos\psi)}{a - c\cos\theta\cos\psi}$$

$$z \;\; = \;\; \frac{b\sin\psi(c\cos\theta - \mu)}{a - c\cos\theta\cos\psi} \tag{2}$$

with the following conditions for a, b, c

$(x/a)^2 + (y/b)^2 = 1 \quad$ for $z = 0$
$(x/c)^2 - (z/b)^2 = 1 \quad$ for $y = 0$

and

$c^2 = a^2 - b^2$

θ and ψ are parameters in the range $0 - 2\pi$.

Fig.1 illustrates the cross–sections of a cyclide defined by Forsyth in the $x - z$ and $x - y$ planes respectively.

In the following we consider only the parametric form, for which we try to find a proper NURBS representation.

3   NURBS and the blossoming principle

Since the introduction of polar forms and blossoming in computer graphics and CAD by de Casteljau [de Casteljau '85,'86] and Ramshaw [Ramshaw '86, '87], many researchers have exploited these ideas

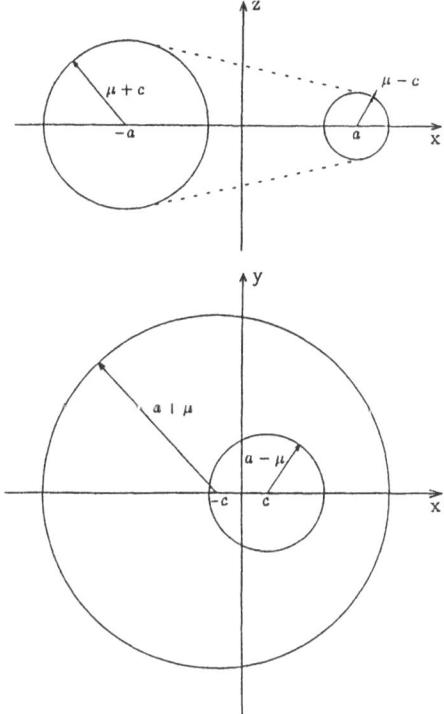

Figure 1: Cross–sections of a cyclide in its planes of symmetry [Pratt '89a]

to develop known results in a more elegant way and to achieve new results in the area of interactive curve and surface design [Boehm '88, Goldmann '89, Seidel '89a, '89b].

This new approch is based on the well known fact that polynomials of degree n and symmetric n-affine mappings are equivalent to each other.

Let F be a nth-degree polynomial of variable u. Then $f = f(u_1, ..., u_n)$ is called polarform or blossom of $F(u)$, if the following conditions are fulfilled:

- f is affine in each variable (n-affine).
- f does not change its value under any permutation of its variables (symmetry).
- $f(u, ..., u) = F(u)$

The following examples illustrate these definitions:

Example 1:

The blossom of the polynomial function

$$F(u) = a_0 + a_1 u + a_2 u^2 + a_3 u^3$$

is given by the symmetric 3-affine map

$$f(u_1, u_2, u_3) = a_0 + \frac{a_1}{3}(u_1 + u_2 + u_3) + \frac{a_2}{3}(u_1 u_2 + u_1 u_3 + u_2 u_3)$$
$$+ a_3 u_1 u_2 u_3$$

Example 2:

The blossom of the bivariate polynomial function

$$F(u, v) = a_{00} + a_{10} u + a_{01} v + a_{11} uv + a_{20} u^2 + a_{02} v^2$$
$$+ a_{21} u^2 v + a_{12} uv^2 + a_{22} u^2 v^2$$

is given by:

$$f(u_1, u_2; v_1, v_2) = a_{00} + \frac{a_{10}}{2}(u_1 + u_2) + \frac{a_{01}}{2}(v_1 + v_2) + \frac{a_{11}}{2 \cdot 2}(u_1 + u_2)(v_1 + v_2)$$
$$+ a_{20} u_1 u_2 + a_{02} v_1 v_2 + \frac{a_{21}}{2} u_1 u_2 (v_1 + v_2)$$
$$+ \frac{a_{12}}{2}(u_1 + u_2) v_1 v_2 + a_{22} u_1 u_2 v_1 v_2$$

A B–Spline curve is defined as

$$F(u) = \sum_{i=0}^{m} d_i \cdot N_i^n(u) \qquad n \leq m \tag{3}$$

where $N(u)$ is the normalized basis function of degree n over the knot vector $T = (t_0, ..., t_{m+n+1}), t_i \leq t_{i+1}$. We know from [Seidel '89a] that the de Boor points (also called control points) d_i of the B-Spline curve can be expressed in terms of blossoming. Let F_j be the restriction of F to the interval $I_j := [t_j, t_j + 1)$ and f_j be the blossom of F_j. The de Boor points d_l are given by the formula [Seidel '89a]

$$d_l = f_j(t_{l+1}, ..., t_{l+n}) \tag{4}$$

where $j - n \leq l \leq j$.

Figure 2 illustrates the relation between the de Boor points of a cubic B–spline and its blossom. The same property is valid for NURBS as well [Zhou '89]. We consider here only the case of NURBS surfaces.

Let $F(u, v)$ be a NURBS surface which is defined as:

$$F(u, v) = \sum_{i=0}^{m} \sum_{j=0}^{q} R_{i,j}^{n,p} \cdot d_{ij} = \sum_{i=0}^{m} \sum_{j=0}^{q} \frac{N_i^n N_j^p(u, v) \cdot w_{ij} \cdot d_{ij}}{\sum_{i=0}^{m} \sum_{j=0}^{q} N_i^p N_j^n(u, v) w_{ij}} \tag{5}$$

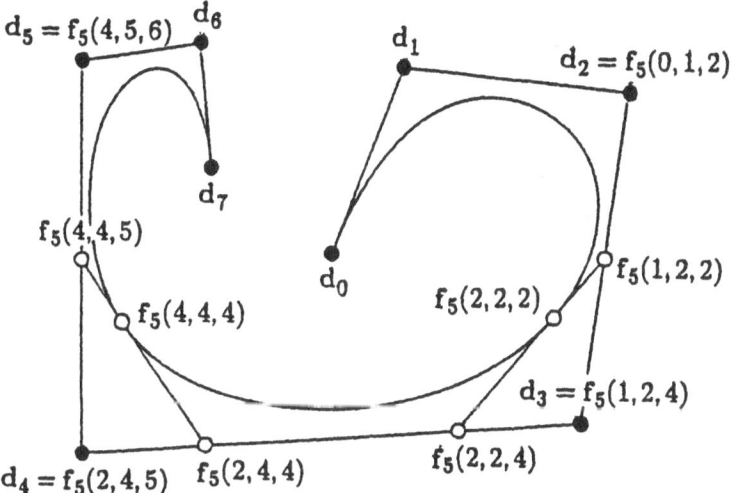

Figure 2: A cubic B-spline over $T = (0,0,0,0,1,2,4,5,6,6,6,6)$. Depicted are the de Boor points $d_0, ..., d_7$ and the Bézier points $b_0 = f_5(2,2,2)$, $b_1 = f_5(2,2,4)$, $b_2 = f_5(2,4,4)$ and $b_3 = f_5(4,4,4)$ of F_5 to the segment $I_6 = [2,4)$ [Seidel '89a]

where R is the bivariate basis function of degree $(n+p)$ over the knot vectors $T = (t_0, ..., t_{m+n+1})$ in the u-direction and $S = (s_0, ..., s_{q+p+1})$ in the v-direction respectively. w_{ij} are the weights.

Let F_{ij} be the restriction of F on the area of $[t_i, t_{i+1}) \times [s_j, s_{j+1})$ and f_{ij} the blossom of F_{ij}. The de Boor points d_{hr} can be computed by the following formula [zhou '89]:

$$d_{hr} = f_{ij}(t_{h+1}, \ldots, t_{h+n}; s_{r+1}, \ldots, s_{r+p}) \qquad (6)$$

where $i - n \le h \le i$, $j - p \le r \le j$ with $t_i \le t_{i+1}, s_j \le s_{j+1}$.

From the above results it can be seen that the de Boor points of a polynomial F can be computed from its blossom f and by this we can get the NURBS representation of F.

4   Representing the cyclide through NURBS

In this chapter we show how to obtain the NURBS representation of the cyclide. The method can be shortly summarized as follows: we begin with the parametric form (2) of the cyclide and reparameterize the angles $\theta \in [0, 2\pi]$ and $\phi \in [0, 2\pi]$ through $u \in [-1, 1]$ and $v \in [-1, 1]$ respectively; then we choose the appropriate knot vectors. With the help of the blossom the de Boor points will be computed and finally we can get the NURBS representation of the cyclide.

Let

$$
u = \begin{cases}
\frac{-1}{\tan\frac{\theta}{2}+1} & \text{for } 0 \leq \theta < \pi \\[2mm]
0 & \text{for } \theta = \pi \\[2mm]
\frac{-1}{\tan\frac{\theta}{2}-1} & \text{for } \pi < \theta \leq 2\pi
\end{cases}
$$

(7)

and analogously:

$$
v = \begin{cases}
\frac{-1}{\tan\frac{\psi}{2}+1} & \text{for } 0 \leq \psi < \pi \\[2mm]
0 & \text{for } \psi = \pi \\[2mm]
\frac{-1}{\tan\frac{\psi}{2}-1} & \text{for } \pi < \psi \leq 2\pi
\end{cases}
$$

(8)

This reparameterization maps the interval $[0, 2\pi]$ onto $[-1, 1]$.

From (7), (8) we get:

$$\cos\theta = \frac{-2u-1}{2u^2+2u+1}, \quad \sin\theta = \frac{-2u(u+1)}{2u^2+2u+1} \quad \text{for } u \in [-1, 0]$$

$$\cos\theta = \frac{2u-1}{2u^2-2u+1}, \quad \sin\theta = \frac{2u(u-1)}{2u^2-2u+1} \quad \text{for } u \in [0, 1]$$

and

$$\cos\psi = \frac{-2v-1}{2v^2+2v+1}, \quad \sin\psi = \frac{-2v(v+1)}{2v^2+2v+1} \quad \text{for } v \in [-1, 0]$$

$$\cos\psi = \frac{2v-1}{2v^2-2v+1}, \quad \sin\psi = \frac{2v(v-1)}{2v^2-2v+1} \quad \text{for } v \in [0, 1]$$

Now we can represent the parametric form (2) through u and v:

for $u \in [-1, 0]$, $v \in [-1, 0]$:

$$x(u,v) \;=\; \frac{\mu\left(c-a\cdot\frac{-2u-1}{2u^2+2u+1}\cdot\frac{-2v-1}{2v^2+2v+1}+b^2\cdot\frac{-2u-1}{2u^2+2u+1}\right)}{a-c\cdot\frac{-2u-1}{2u^2+2u+1}\cdot\frac{-2v-1}{2v^2+2v+1}}$$

$$=\; \frac{4c\mu u^2 v^2+4c\mu u^2 v+4(c\mu-b^2)uv^2+2c\mu u^2+2(c\mu-b^2)v^2+4(c\mu-a\mu-b^2)uv+2(c\mu-a\mu-b^2)(u+v)+c\mu-a\mu-b^2}{4au^2v^2+4au^2v+4auv^2+2au^2+2av^2+4(a-c)uv+2(a-c)(u+v)+a-c}$$

$$y(u,v) \;=\; \frac{b\cdot\frac{-2u(u+1)}{2u^2+2u+1}\cdot\left(a-\mu\cdot\frac{-2v-1}{2v^2+2v+1}\right)}{a-c\cdot\frac{-2u-1}{2u^2+2u+1}\cdot\frac{-2v-1}{2v^2+2v+1}}$$

$$=\; \frac{-4abu^2v^2-4b(a+\mu)u^2v-4abuv^2-2b(a+\mu)u^2-4b(a+\mu)uv-2b(a+\mu)u}{4au^2v^2+4au^2v+4auv^2+2au^2+2av^2+4(a-c)uv+2(a-c)(u+v)+a-c}$$

$$z(u,v) \;=\; \frac{b\cdot\frac{-2v(v+1)}{2v^2+2v+1}\cdot\left(c\cdot\frac{-2u-1}{2u^2+2u+1}-\mu\right)}{a-c\cdot\frac{-2u-1}{2u^2+2u+1}\cdot\frac{-2v-1}{2v^2+2v+1}}$$

$$=\; \frac{4b\mu u^2v^2+4b(\mu+c)v^2u+2b(\mu+c)v^2+4b\mu u^2v+4b(\mu+c)uv+2b(c+\mu)v}{4au^2v^2+4au^2v+4auv^2+2au^2+2av^2+4(a-c)uv+2(a-c)(u+v)+a-c}$$

The corresponding homogeneous representations are given by:

for $u \in [-1,0], \; v \in [-1,0]$:

$$\begin{aligned}
x(u,v) \;=\;& 4c\mu u^2 v^2+4c\mu u^2 v+4(c\mu-b^2)uv^2+2c\mu u^2+2(c\mu-b^2)v^2\\
&+4(c\mu-a\mu-b^2)uv+2(c\mu-a\mu-b^2)(u+v)+c\mu-a\mu-b^2
\end{aligned}$$

$$\begin{aligned}
y(u,v) \;=\;& -4abu^2v^2-4b(a+\mu)u^2v-4abuv^2-2b(a+\mu)u^2-4b(a+\mu)uv\\
&-2b(a+\mu)u
\end{aligned}$$

$$\begin{aligned}
z(u,v) \;=\;& 4b\mu u^2v^2+4b\mu u^2v+4b(\mu+c)v^2u+2b(\mu+c)v^2+4b(\mu+c)uv\\
&+2b(c+\mu)v
\end{aligned}$$

$$\begin{aligned}
h(u,v) \;=\;& 4au^2v^2+4au^2v+4auv^2+2au^2+2av^2+4(a-c)uv\\
&+2(a-c)(u+v)+a-c
\end{aligned}$$

In an analog manner we get:

for $u \in [0,1], \; v \in [-1,0]$:

$$\begin{aligned}
x(u,v) \;=\;& 4c\mu u^2 v^2+4c\mu u^2 v-4(c\mu-b^2)uv^2+2c\mu u^2+2(c\mu-b^2)v^2\\
&-4(c\mu-a\mu-b^2)uv-2(c\mu-a\mu-b^2)(u-v)+c\mu-a\mu-b^2
\end{aligned}$$

$$\begin{aligned}
y(u,v) \;=\;& 4abu^2v^2+4b(a+\mu)u^2v-4abuv^2+2b(a+\mu)u^2-4b(a+\mu)uv\\
&-2b(a+\mu)u
\end{aligned}$$

$$z(u,v) = 4b\mu u^2 v^2 + 4b\mu u^2 v - 4b(\mu + c)v^2 u + 2b(\mu + c)v^2$$
$$-4b(\mu + c)uv + 2b(c + \mu)v$$

$$h(u,v) = 4au^2 v^2 + 4au^2 v - 4auv^2 + 2au^2 + 2av^2 - 4(a - c)uv$$
$$-2(a - c)(u - v) + a - c$$

for $u \in [-1, 0]$, $v \in [0, 1]$:

$$x(u,v) = 4c\mu\, u^2 v^2 - 4c\mu u^2 v + 4(c\mu - b^2)uv^2 + 2c\mu u^2 + 2(c\mu - b^2)v^2$$
$$-4(c\mu - a\mu - b^2)uv + 2(c\mu - a\mu - b^2)(u - v) + c\mu - a\mu - b^2$$

$$y(u,v) = -4abu^2 v^2 + 4b(a + \mu)u^2 v - 4abuv^2 - 2b(a + \mu)u^2$$
$$+4b(a + \mu)uv - 2b(a + \mu)u$$

$$z(u,v) = -4b\mu u^2 v^2 + 4b\mu u^2 v - 4b(\mu + c)v^2 u - 2b(\mu + c)v^2$$
$$+4b(\mu + c)uv + 2b(c + \mu)v$$

$$h(u,v) = 4au^2 v^2 - 4au^2 v + 4auv^2 + 2au^2 + 2av^2$$
$$-4(a - c)uv + 2(a - c)(u - v) + a - c$$

for $u \in [0, 1]$, $v \in [0, 1]$:

$$x(u,v) = 4c\mu u^2 v^2 - 4c\mu u^2 v - 4(c\mu - b^2)uv^2 + 2c\mu u^2 + 2(c\mu - b^2)v^2$$
$$+4(c\mu - a\mu - b^2)uv - 2(c\mu - a\mu - b^2)(u + v) + c\mu - a\mu - b^2$$

$$y(u,v) = 4abu^2 v^2 - 4b(a + \mu)u^2 v - 4abuv^2 + 2b(a + \mu)u^2$$
$$+4b(a + \mu)uv - 2b(a + \mu)u$$

$$z(u,v) = -4b\mu u^2 v^2 + 4b\mu u^2 v + 4b(\mu + c)v^2 u - 2b(\mu + c)v^2$$
$$-4b(\mu + c)uv + 2b(c + \mu)v$$

$$h(u,v) = 4au^2 v^2 - 4au^2 v - 4auv^2 + 2au^2 + 2av^2 + 4(a - c)uv$$
$$-2(a - c)(u + v) + a - c$$

From the homogeneous representations we can obtain the blossoms directly. The blossom of $x(u,v)$ is given:

$$f_x(u_1, u_2; v_1, v_2) = \begin{cases} \text{for } u \in [-1,0],\ v \in [-1,0]: \\[4pt] \begin{aligned} &4c\mu u_1 u_2 v_1 v_2 + 2c\mu u_1 u_2 (v_1 + v_2) \\ &+2(c\mu - b^2)(u_1 + u_2)v_1 v_2 \\ &+2c\mu u_1 u_2 + 2(c\mu - b^2)v_1 v_2 \\ &+(c\mu - a\mu - b^2)(u_1 + u_2)(v_1 + v_2) \\ &+(c\mu - a\mu - b^2)((u_1 + u_2) + (v_1 + v_2)) + c\mu - a\mu - b^2 \end{aligned} \\[10pt] \text{for } u \in [0,1],\ v \in [-1,0]: \\[4pt] \begin{aligned} &4c\mu u_1 u_2 v_1 v_2 + 2c\mu u_1 u_2 (v_1 + v_2) \\ &-2(c\mu - b^2)(u_1 + u_2)v_1 v_2 \\ &+2c\mu u_1 u_2 + 2(c\mu - b^2)v_1 v_2 \\ &-(c\mu - a\mu - b^2)(u_1 + u_2)(v_1 + v_2) \\ &-(c\mu - a\mu - b^2)((u_1 + u_2) - (v_1 + v_2)) + c\mu - a\mu - b^2 \end{aligned} \\[10pt] \text{for } u \in [-1,0],\ v \in [0,1]: \\[4pt] \begin{aligned} &4c\mu u_1 u_2 v_1 v_2 - 2c\mu u_1 u_2 (v_1 + v_2) \\ &+2(c\mu - b^2)(u_1 + u_2)v_1 v_2 \\ &+2c\mu u_1 u_2 + 2(c\mu - b^2)v_1 v_2 \\ &-(c\mu - a\mu - b^2)(u_1 + u_2)(v_1 + v_2) \\ &+(c\mu - a\mu - b^2)((u_1 + u_2) - (v_1 + v_2)) + c\mu - a\mu - b^2 \end{aligned} \\[10pt] \text{for } u \in [0,1],\ v \in [0,1]: \\[4pt] \begin{aligned} &4c\mu u_1 u_2 v_1 v_2 - 2c\mu u_1 u_2 (v_1 + v_2) \\ &-2(c\mu - b^2)(u_1 + u_2)v_1 v_2 \\ &+2c\mu u_1 u_2 + 2(c\mu - b^2)v_1 v_2 \\ &+(c\mu - a\mu - b^2)(u_1 + u_2)(v_1 + v_2) \\ &-(c\mu - a\mu - b^2)((u_1 + u_2) + (v_1 + v_2)) + c\mu - a\mu - b^2 \end{aligned} \end{cases}$$

With the same method we can also get the blossoms of $y(u,v)$, $z(u,v)$ and $h(u,v)$.

Let $d_{ij} = (x_{ij}, y_{ij}, z_{ij}, h_{ij})$ be the de Boor points in homogeneous coordinates. By the use of the simple knot vector $T = (-1,-1,-1,0,0,1,1,1)$ in the u–direction and $S = (-1,-1,-1,0,0,1,1,1)$ in the v–direction the de Boor points(here identical with the Bézier points) can be computed as follows:

for $-1 \leq u \leq 0$, $-1 \leq v \leq 0$:

$$\begin{aligned} x_{00} &= f_x(-1,-1;-1,-1) = b^2 - a\mu + c\mu \\ x_{10} &= f_x(-1,0;-1,-1) = 0 \\ x_{20} &= f_x(0,0;-1,-1) = -b^2 + a\mu + c\mu \\ x_{01} &= f_x(-1,-1;-1,0) = 0 \\ x_{11} &= f_x(-1,0;-1,0) = 0 \\ x_{21} &= f_x(0,0;-1,0) = 0 \end{aligned}$$

$$x_{02} = f_x(-1,-1;0,0) = b^2 + a\mu + c\mu$$
$$x_{12} = f_x(-1,0;0,0) = 0$$
$$x_{22} = f_x(0,0;0,0) = -b^2 - a\mu + c\mu$$

for $0 < u \leq 1$, $-1 \leq v \leq 0$:

$$x_{30} = f_x(0,1;-1,-1) = 0$$
$$x_{40} = f_x(1,1;-1,-1) = b^2 - a\mu + c\mu$$
$$x_{31} = f_x(0,1;-1,0) = 0$$
$$x_{41} = f_x(1,1;-1,0) = 0$$
$$x_{32} = f_x(0,1;0,0) = 0$$
$$x_{40} = f_x(1,1;0,0) = b^2 + a\mu + c\mu$$

for $-1 \leq u \leq 0$, $0 < v \leq 1$:

$$x_{03} = f_x(-1,-1;0,1) = 0$$
$$x_{13} = f_x(-1,0;0,1) = 0$$
$$x_{23} = f_x(0,0;0,1) = 0$$
$$x_{04} = f_x(-1,-1;1,1) = b^2 - a\mu + c\mu$$
$$x_{14} = f_x(-1,0;1,1) = 0$$
$$x_{24} = f_x(0,0;1,1) = -b^2 + a\mu + c\mu$$

for $0 < u \leq 1$, $0 < v \leq 1$:

$$x_{33} = f_x(0,1;0,1) = 0$$
$$x_{43} = f_x(1,1;0,1) = 0$$
$$x_{34} = f_x(0,1;1,1) = 0$$
$$x_{44} = f_x(1,1;1,1) = b^2 - a\mu + c\mu$$

Blosoming applied analogously on $y(u,v)$, $z(u,v)$ and $h(u,v)$ yields the following results (see Fig.3): With the knot vectors T and S chosen above as well as the control net in Fig.3 we have obtained a NURBS formulation which represents exactly the cyclide. This formulation consists of 4 rational Bézier patches. For instance, for the quarter $[-1,0] \times [0,1]$ we have the same result as the rational Bézier representation given in [Boehm '90].

5   Some Practical Considerations

Rational polynomial functions have two main advantages compared to the nonrational ones, namely: the extra degrees of freedom gained from the weights which can be nicely used to design free-forms;

$d_{04} =$ $(b^2 + c\mu - a\mu, 0, 0, a - c)$	$d_{14} =$ $(0, b(a - \mu), 0, 0)$	$d_{24} =$ $(-b^2 + c\mu + a\mu, 0, 0, a + c)$	$d_{34} =$ $(0, b(\mu - a), 0, 0)$	$d_{44} =$ $(b^2 + c\mu - a\mu, 0, 0, a - c)$
$d_{03} =$ $(0, 0, b(\mu - c), 0)$	$d_{13} =$ $(0,0,0,0)$	$d_{23} =$ $(0, 0, b(\mu + c), 0)$	$d_{33} =$ $(0,0,0,0)$	$d_{43} =$ $(0, 0, b(\mu - c), 0)$
$d_{02} =$ $(b^2 + c\mu + a\mu, 0, 0, a + c)$	$d_{12} =$ $(0, b(\mu + a), 0, 0)$	$d_{22} =$ $(-b^2 + c\mu - a\mu, 0, 0, a - c)$	$d_{32} =$ $(0, -b(a + \mu), 0, 0)$	$d_{42} =$ $(b^2 + c\mu + a\mu, 0, 0, a + c)$
$d_{01} =$ $(0, 0, b(c - \mu), 0, 0)$	$d_{11} =$ $(0,0,0,0)$	$d_{21} =$ $(0, 0, -b(c + \mu), 0)$	$d_{31} =$ $(0,0,0,0)$	$d_{41} =$ $(0, 0, b(c - \mu), 0)$
$d_{00} =$ $(b^2 + c\mu - a\mu, 0, 0, a - c)$	$d_{10} =$ $(0, b(a - \mu), 0, 0)$	$d_{20} =$ $(-b^2 + c\mu + a\mu, 0, 0, a + c)$	$d_{30} =$ $(0, b(\mu - a), 0, 0)$	$d_{40} =$ $(b^2 + c\mu - a\mu, 0, 0, a - c)$

Figure 3: The control net of the NURBS representation of a cyclide

the definition of some curves and surfaces through the control points at infinity. A point at infinity can be represented in homogeneous coordinates through $d = (x, y, z, 0)$, where x, y, z are not all zero. In this case, the point d has a map in $\mathbb{R}^3$ which is represented through a pure direction vector. If d is a control point at infinity, its magnitude determines the bulge of the curve or the surface in this direction. The use of the control points at infinity can strongly reduce the number of the control points required to define some curves and surfaces compared to the case in which no infinite control points are used [Piegl '87]. This is also true for the cyclide. In the representation derived above there are some control points at infinity. Fig.4 shows a cyclide with its control net. It is easy to manipulate the control net through knot insertion so that the cyclide can be defined without infinite control points if needed. Another remark is that the representation given in Fig.3 is based on the standard location shown in Fig.1. In a practical application appropriate transformations are necessary. Because of the property of projection invariance of NURBS the transformations need to be carried out only on the control net. The surface can then be computed.

Using the same method as above one can easily get the NURBS representation of any part of the cyclide surface bounded by parametric lines. Suppose a part of the surface is bounded through the parameters θ_0, θ_1 and ψ_0, ψ_1. It is simple to replace θ_0, θ_1 and ψ_0, ψ_1 through u_0, u_1 and v_0, v_1 respectively, as shown in the chapter 4. Then the knot vector in the u-direction can be chosen as follows (the same is also valid for the knot vector S in the v-direction):

if $-1 \le u_0 \le 0, 0 \le u_1 \le 1$:

$$T = (u_0, u_0, u_0, 0, 0, u_1, u_1, u_1)$$

if $-1 \leq u_0 \leq u_1 \leq 0$ or if $0 \leq u_0 \leq u_1 \leq 1$:

$$T = (u_0, u_0, u_0, u_1, u_1, u_1)$$

Fig.5 – Fig.7 show some examples of cyclide patches as NURBS surfaces.

A very useful property of the cyclide is that its offset surfaces are surfaces of the same type. If we fix the parameters a and c and let μ vary in the interval $c < \mu < a$, then the patches generated form a family of offset surfaces of each other.

6 The NURBS Representations of the Family of Cyclide Surfaces

In practice it is important that the internal representation of surfaces in a modeler is kept compact and uniform. As already mentioned above, the family of cyclide surfaces includes some often used object types. We show here some variations generated through the manipulation of the parameters and control points given in Fig.3.

Choosing $c = 0$ and $a > \mu$ yields a torus.

For $c = 0$ and $\mu = 0$, a circle with radius a will be generated.

If d $(d \neq 0)$ is assigned to z_{00}, z_{20}, z_{40} and $-d$ is assigned to z_{04}, z_{24}, z_{44}, then the representation yields a cylinder. The height of the cylinder depends on the size of d . Fig.9 shows some objects. They are often used in applications and can be easily generated through the manipulation of the NURBS representation. In an interactive design environment it is advisable to build a user–friendly interface and let the modeler perform the manipulation.

We have used the NURBS formulation of the cyclide as a basis for the representation of surfaces in our modeler. Using the same method we have represented the algebraic surfaces of degree 2 through NURBS and obtained a uniform NURBS representation for conicoids.[Zhou'89]. Together with the representation developed above we are able to generate and model most object types conventionally used in computer aided design of mechanical parts.

7 Conclusion

We have developed a method to obtain a NURBS representation of cyclides, in which the technique of the control points at infinity is used to keep the representation compact and uniform. We are able to generate and model some very useful objects through the manipulation of the control points of the cyclide. This representation has been implemented as a basis in our NURBS modeler for testing. The well–known algorithms for the manipulation and evaluation of NURBS can be directly integrated with this representation. One of the important properties of a cyclide surface is that all of its lines of curvature are circular arcs (see Fig.8). Patches with this property are called cyclidal patches. The main advantage of such patches is that their curvatures can be easily controlled. On going work currently includes how to construct cyclidal patches under the consideration of their curvatures using NURBS representation and the use of cyclides as blending surface from the NURBS point of view in order to get more flexible and userfriendly blends; the investigation of cyclides and cyclidal patches as piecewise algebraic surfaces as well as the integration of algebraic and parametric surfaces into a modeler.

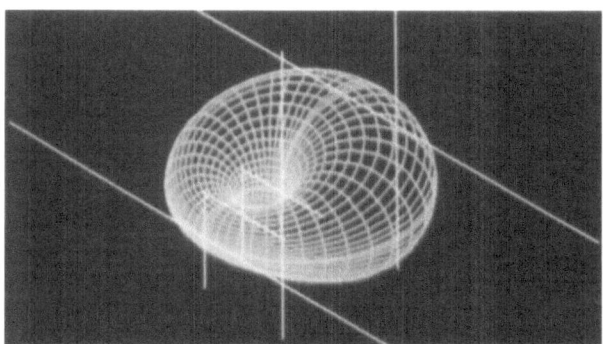

Figure 4: NURBS representation of a cyclide with its control net.

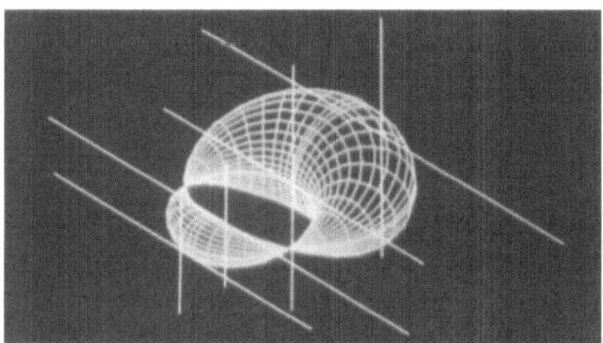

Figure 5: A horned cyclide with its control net.

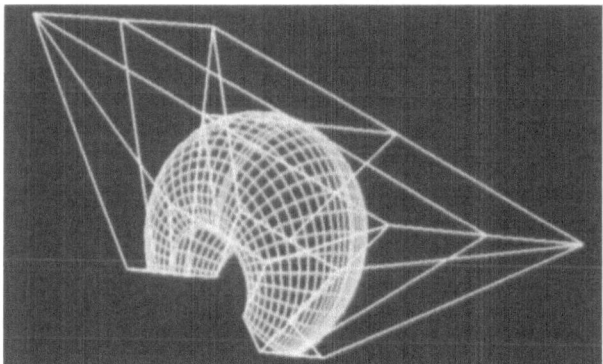

Figure 6: Cyclide patch with the knot vector
$T = (u_0, u_0, u_0, 0, 0, u_1, u_1, u_1)$
$S = (v_0, v_0, v_0, 0, 0, v_1, v_1, v_1)$.

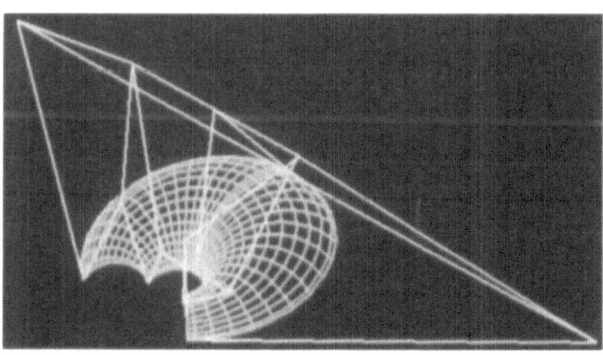

Figure 7: Cyclide patch with the kont vector
$T = (u_0, u_0, u_0, 0, 0, u_1, u_1, u_1)$
$S = (v_0, v_0, v_0, v_1, v_1, v_1)$.

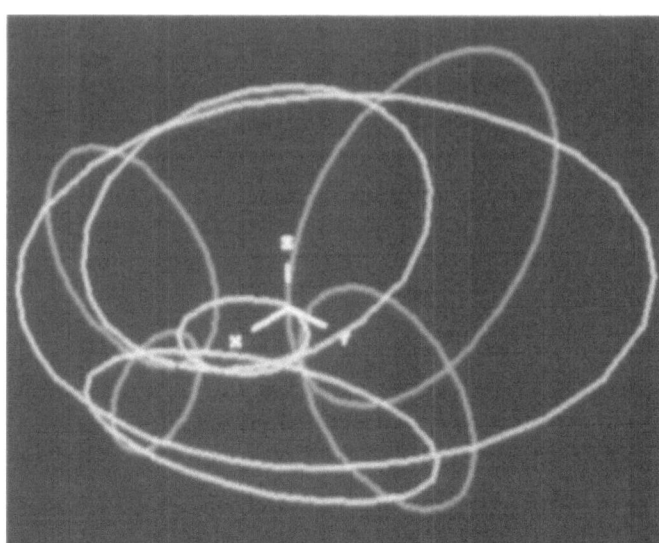

Figure 8: Some lines of curvature of a cyclide. Each line is a circle.

Figure 9: Tablet with bowl and glasses modelled completely with the NURBS representation of cyclide.

8 Acknowledgements

The authors wish to express their thanks to R. Klein for his helpful comments to this paper. This work has been partly supported by the German Academic Exchange Service (DAAD) Grant Nr. 324-306-034-5

9 Literatur

[Boehm'88] W. Boehm 'On the de Boor–like algorithms and blossoming', Computer Aided Geometric Design 5, 1988, 71-79

[Boehm'89] W. Boehm 'Some Remarks on Cyclides in Solid Modeling', in W. Straßer and H-P. Seidel (eds.), Theory and Practice of Geometric Modeling, Springer, 1989

[Boehm'90] W. Boehm 'On cyclides in geometric modeling', Computer Aided Geometric Design 7, 1990

[de Casteljau'85] P. de Casteljau, 'Formes à pôles', Hermes, Paris 1985

[de Casteljau'86] P. de Casteljau, 'Shape Mathematics and CAD', Kogan Page Ltd, London, 1986

[de Pont'84] J. de Pont, 'Essays on the Cyclide Patch', PhD thesis, Cambrige University, 1984

[Dokken'89] T. Dokken, A. M. Ytrehus, V. Skytt 'The Role Of NURBS in Geometric Modeling and CAD/CAM', International Symposium on Advanced Geometric Modeling For Engineering Applications, Berlin(West), Nov. 1989

[Farin'88] G. Farin, 'Curves and Surfaces for Computer Aided Geometric Design', A Practical Guide', Academic Press, 1988

[Forsyth'12] A. R. Forsyth, 'Lectures on Differential Geometry of Curves and Surfaces', Cambridge University press, 1912

[Goldman'89] R.N. Goldman, 'Blossoming and Knot insertion algorithms for B–Spline curves', to appear in Computer Aided Geometric Design

[Martin'82] R. R. Martin, 'Principle Patches for Computational Geometry', PhD thesis, Cambridge Unvisity, 1982

[Piegl'87a] L. Piegl, W. Tiller, 'Curve and Surface Construction for CAD using NURBS', CAD 19, 1987, 485-498

[Piegl'87b] L. Piegl, 'On the use of infinite control points in CAGD', Computer Aided Geometric Design 4, 1987, 155-166

[Pratt'89a] M. J. Pratt 'Cyclide Blending in Solid Modeling', in W. Straßer and H-P. Seidel (eds.), Theory and Practice of Geometric Modeling, Springer, 1989

[Pratt'89b] M. J. Pratt 'Applications of Cyclide Surfaces in Geometric Modeling', in D. C. Handscomb (ed.) The Mathematics of surfaces III, Oxford, 1989

[Ramshaw'87] L. Ramshaw, 'Blossoming: A connect-the-dots approach to splines', Digital Systems Research Center, Palo Alto, 1987

[Ramshaw'88] L. Ramshaw, 'Béziers and B-splines as multiaffine maps', in 'Theoretical Foundations of Computer Graphics and CAD', Springer, 1988, 757-776

[**Ramshaw'89**] L. Ramshaw, 'Blossoms a polar forms', Computer Aided Geometric Design 6, 1989, 323–358

[Seidel'89a] H-P Seidel, 'A new multiaffine approach to B-Splines', Computer Aided Geometric Design 6, 1989, 23–32

[Seidel'89b] H-P Seidel, 'Computing B-spline control points', in W. Straßer and H-P. Seidel (eds.), Theory and Practice of Geometric Modeling, Springer, 1989

[Sharrock'85] T. J. Sharrock, 'Surface Design with Cyclide Patches', PhD thesis, Cambridge University, 1985

[Tiller'83] W. Tiller, 'Rational B-Splines for Curve and Surface Representation', IEEE Computer Graphics Application 3, 61-69, Sept 1983

[Tiller'86] W. Tiller, 'Geometric Modeling using Non-Uniform Rational B-splines: Mathematical Techniques', Siggraph 86 Tutorial Presentation

[Zhou'89] X. Zhou, 'Parametrisierung der Flächen zweiten Grades und Konvertierung in die NURBS–TensorProduktdarstellung', Technical Report, WSI 89–1, Universität Tübingen

Wilhelm-Schickard Institut für Informatik, University of Tübingen, 7400 Tübingen, Germany

B-rep of Plane Regions: Pristine Problems in Computational Geometry and Topology

GERARDO LEÓN LASTRA and J. SERGIO SANTANA-SEPÚLVEDA

Abstract

This paper describes the computation of topological representations of plane partitions induced by finite collections of plane parametric curves. The computation of this arrangement is described through the solutions of six different simpler problems. The final output obtained is a data structure called an *rp-tree*. An rp-tree captures contention, incidence, connection and bounding relations between 2D open regions, contours defined by oriented parametric curves and points. It is shown how to label the nodes of an rp-tree which results from boolean operations between plane regions; this labeling reflects the precise "history" of output regions as a function of the names of regions in an arbitrary finite boolean expression.

Keywords: Geometric Modeling, Topology, Algorithms, Data Structures, Boolean Operations.

1. INTRODUCTION

Many different representation schemes of plane regions have been devised for different computer graphics applications. Among these there are two important categories: the vector data format and the raster data format [SAMET 88]. In this paper we concentrate on a data structure as an extension or generalization of the vector data format to include curved edges.

One vector data format described in [SAMET 88] is supported by Baumgart's winged-edge [BAUM-GART 75]. The application of this data structure to 2D region modeling was first proposed by [WEILER 80], and will be called a planar winged-edge in this introduction. The geometric description of edges in this data structure may be done by assigning coordinates of points to the vertices. This is a fair approach for the representation of polygonal regions bounded by a small number of straight segments, but would be very wastefull to represent regions bounded by polylines. In other words, if two polygonal regions share two or more consecutive edges meeting at vertices of degree two, there is no need to record the explicit representation of these vertices. Therefore, space optimization may be achieved by assigning polylines as a geometric description for the edges. This strategy may also be applied when curved edges should be represented since curves may be approximated by polylines. When the geometry of bounding curved edges is provided through parametric curves, polyline approximations may be stored in half the space by replacing its 2D coordinates by their corresponding 1D parametric values. Taking one final step, when parametric values for polyline approximations are computed by a rule which reproduces the same parametric values, the geometric description of winged-edges can be reduced to parametric descriptions of its vertices with a reference to a procedure which reproduces intermediary parametric values and their mapped image in the plane. The incurred penalty in computing time may or may not be acceptable for different applications and environments, and so we will not discuss space/time trade-offs.

This parametric description of planar winged-edges raises problems of robustness of geometric computations [HOFFMANN 89]. Fortunately, fundamental interesting results have been found recently [MILENKOVIC 89, EDELSBRUNNER 90] and are directly applicable to 2D region modeling. A solution has been already addressed in the context of 2D drawing applications by [GANGNET 89]. In their paper, Gangnet *et al* describe a clever technique to obtain consistent topological relations from intersecting Bezier curves in their derived *planar map*. The planar map and our *rp-tree* capture similar topological and geometric relations. Gangnet's *et al* planar map computation is described in an incremental way to support interactive sketching and therefore it does not addresses the problem of supporting boolean operations between 2D regions with *contour history* computation as attempted – but not succeeding – in [WEILER 80].

The paper is organized as follows, section two formaly states the simpler problem of computing the regions into which a single parametric curve divides the plane. Our final task of computing the history of regions resulting from boolean operations will be simplified by several properties of the output provided by the solution of this simpler problem. The data structures and the algorithmic solution to the single curve problem are detailed in sections three and four. The output resulting from the single curve problem is a *one-component region-pseudograph* with references to information providing its embedding in the plane. A one-component region-pseudograph may be viewed as a collection of contours in the [WEILER 80] sense, and it captures a **remarkable property which characterizes one and only one contour without requiring any analysis of contour orientation**. This characterization is so remarkable that we call it the Jordan's contour characterization. Section five defines the *mixture operation* as a binary operation between region-pseudographs and shows how to compute it. Section 6 generalizes the mixture operation to n-component region-pseudographs. Section 7 reviews the definition of contour history and partially solves its computation. Section 8 introduces the rp-tree and section 9 completes the contour history computation with the aid of the rp-tree. Section 10 briefly explains applications of the rp-tree, and section 11 draws some conclusions and points at further research directions.

2. FUNDAMENTAL PROBLEM

Geometric data unambiguously determines topological data, while the same topological data may be invariant for different geometric models. This obvious statement motivates our fundamental problem. Denote by $[a, z]$ a closed interval in the Euclidean line and by E^2 the Euclidean plane, and define *region* as an open and connected subset of E^2.

PROBLEM 1. Given a plane curve of finite length described by a continuously differentiable parametric function $c : [a, z] \longrightarrow E^2$, describe an algorithm and data structures to represent the different regions into which the given curve divides E^2.

In the solution to this problem, the resulting regions will be naturaly classified by recording their boundaries as ordered, connected and cyclic sequences of *oriented* pieces of the input curve. These boundaries are called *contours* and in the output no pair of distinct contours cross each other. By convention the the traversal of a contour with its orientation will be so that the region it bounds always lies to the left. Figure 1 illustrates the solution to the problem, but before we explain it, we define our data structures.

a) STEP 1

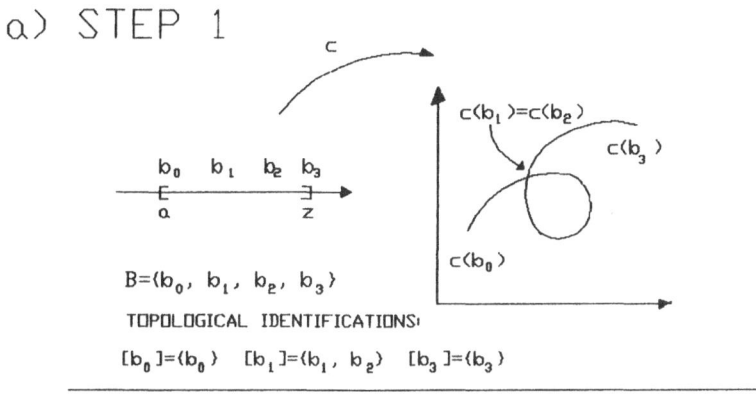

$B = \{b_0, b_1, b_2, b_3\}$

TOPOLOGICAL IDENTIFICATIONS:

$[b_0] = \{b_0\}$ $[b_1] = \{b_1, b_2\}$ $[b_3] = \{b_3\}$

b) STEP 2

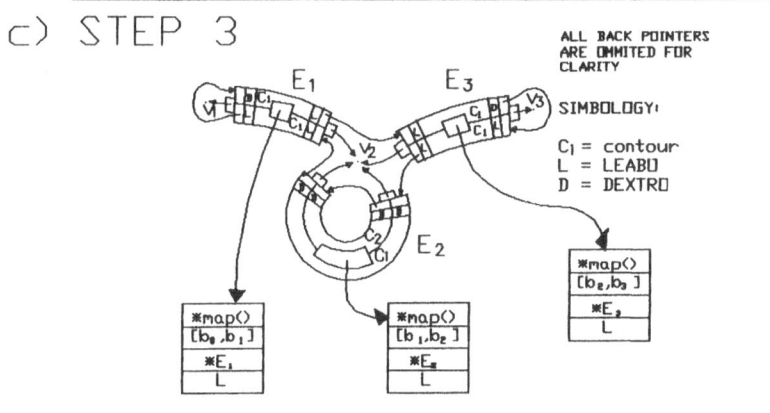

c) STEP 3

d) STEP 4

ENTRY POINTS TO CONTOURS: (E_1, LEABO), (E_2, DEXTRO)

Figure 1. Overview of Algorithm 1.

3. DATA STRUCTURES

Our basic data structure is another "offspring" from Baumgart's winged-edge [BAUMGART 75, WEILER 85], close in organization to the half-edge in [MANTYLA 88] and associates geometrical or *embedding* information in parametric form through a pointer to executable code. Figure 2 diagrams the basic data structure for an edge record and establishes a visual analog with the winged-edge. In this section we explain the C definitions of data structures in figure 3.

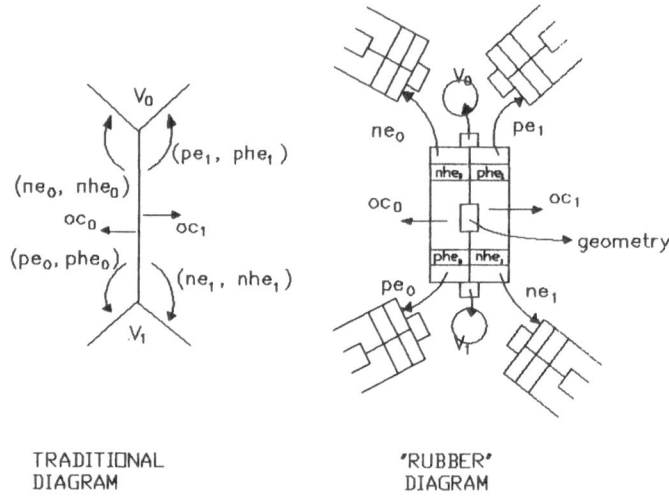

TRADITIONAL
DIAGRAM

'RUBBER'
DIAGRAM

Figure 2. Edge–Record representations.

As usual, the edge record separates topological and geometric information. Through the executable code which provides geometric information, it should be possible to obtain coordinates and tangent vectors to the curve at any specific parameter value where the curve is defined. The **parameters** pointer for an edge, references one **geometry** structure, which provides access to embedding code through the **map** reference. The real numbers **inf** and **sup** are the boundaries of the interval where the parametrization is defined. On input this parametrizes the whole curve, on output one or more edge records will be obtained with its corresponding parameter subinterval for edge embedding.

A topological edge is divided into two oppositely oriented *half-edges* [MANTYLA 88] with parametric descriptions. The parametric description of the curve has a natural orientation corresponding to increasing parameter values. On output, this orientation will be assigned to the half-edge indicated by the **e** pointer and the half-edge index **heindx** in a **struct geometry**.

Any half-edge belongs only to one contour. The whole sequence of half-eges of a contour can be traversed following **ne** pointers indexed by its corresponding **nhe** index within any of the contour half-edges. Thus, if **e** points to an edge and the half-edge index i, is either 0 or 1, the C expressions e->h_e[i].ne->h_e[e->h_e[i].nhe] and e->h_e[i].pe->h_e[e->h_e[i].phe] are valid semantic expressions to access the next and previous half-edges within a contour. These expressions constitute the so called **next-half()** and **previous-half()** operators. The edge also holds two pointers to vertices, whose coordinates may be obtained when the **inf** and **sup** parameter values are provided as arguments to the executable code comprising the edge embedding.

```
typedef struct edge                     EDGE;
typedef struct half_edge                HALF_EDGE;
typedef struct vertex                   VERTEX;
typedef struct contour                  CONTOUR;
typedef struct geometry                 GEOMETRY;


struct edge {
        HALF_EDGE h_e[2];
        VERTEX *v[2];
        GEOMETRY *parameters;
};


struct half_edge {
        EDGE  *ne;    /* next edge */
        EDGE  *pe;    /* previous edge */
        char  nhe;    /* index for next half-edge in ne */
        char  phe;    /* index for previous half-edge in pe */
        CONTOUR *oc; /* owner contour back pointer */
};


struct vertex {
        /* data to enter the spin-orbit around this vertex */
        EDGE *e;
        char he; /* half-edge index towards the vertex */
};


struct contour {
        EDGE    *ee; /* entry to contour of half-edges aided by hee */
        char    hee; /* index for half-edge of ee in this contour */
        CONTOUR  *son;     /* rp-tree pointer */
        CONTOUR  *sibling; /* rp-tree pointer */
        CONTOUR  *parent;  /* rp-tree pointer */
};


struct geometry {
        2DPOINT *(*map)(); /* functional description for edge embedding */
        double inf;        /* interval lower bound */
        double sup;        /* interval upper bound */
        EDGE *e;           /* back pointer to edge */
        char heindx;       /* half-edge of *e oriented by
};                             encreasing parameter values */
```

Figure 3. Basic data structures for a region-pseudograph and its rp-tree.

The record pointed to by oc in a **half_edge** contains an identification of the contour it belongs to. Data serving as entry to the contour and pointers used to link all contours in a hierarchical organization called an *rp-tree*, will be defined later.

4. ALGORITHM 1

The algorithm starts building the topological data structure representing a line segment and transforms it into the data structure depicted in figure 1.c for the particular case illustrated[1].

The algorithm description follows:

STEP 1) Compute the set B of parameter values at which the curve $c([a, z])$ intersects with itself. Concurrent to this computation, the set B must be partitioned into equivalence classes, where two different parameter values $b_i, b_j \in B$ belong to the same equivalence class whenever $c(b_i) = c(b_j)$. The set B is said to be partitioned by *topological identifications* under the curve mapping.

After computing the set B and its partitions, B must be examined and if either interval boundary value a or z is missed, it must be added to B as a new equivalence class with a single element. Assign subindexes $B = \{b_0, b_1, ..., b_n\}$ so that $i < j$ iff $b_i < b_j$; then, $b_0 = a$ and $b_n = z$. See figure 1.a.

STEP 2) Now build the family of subintervals $D = \{[b_0, b_1], [b_1, b_2], ..., [b_{n-1}, b_n]\}$ bounded by the parameter values recorded in B, i.e. $[a, z] = [b_0, b_1] \cup [b_1, b_2] \cup ... \cup [b_{n-1}, b_n]$, where $b_0 = a$ and $b_n = z$. Since each $b_i \in B$ stands for a parameter value where the curve c intersects with itself – except possibly at b_0 and b_n where there may not be an intersection – this intervals family constitutes a decomposition of $c(x)$ into a set of arcs $c([b_i, b_{i+1}])$, where each of these is now either a non-self-intersecting arc or a closed Jordan curve. Hereafter, every element in this decomposition will be refered to by *arc*.

Since in the final output every arc corresponds to a topological edge, now it is possible to derive all the topological edge records required, each corresponding to an interval in the family D. Therefore, all the topological edge records should be created and linked in a "linear" order (figure 1.b). Associated to each edge, there must be a record holding its geometric description in terms of its parametric domain $[b_i, b_{i+1}]$, its embedding function pointer and the indicator **heindx** set for the half-edge oriented for increasing parameter values. We use the symbolic constant LEABO for this first settig of **heindx**.

STEP 3) Rearrange linking pointers of half-edges to build the planar pseudograph[2] which records the adjacency relations between points, arcs and regions. Details for this task follow.

Recall two important permutations in an embedded half-edge structure [MANTYLA 88]: the **next-half()** operator, defined previously, and the **other-side()** operator which for an input half-edge returns the oppositely oriented half-edge that assembles a complete edge. The concatenation of these operators **other-side(next-half())** returns a half-edge which is oriented towards the same vertex as its input operand. Repeated applications of the **other-side(next-half())** operator on its output, yields a finite and ordered cycle of half-edges oriented towards a fixed topological vertex. This cycle spins around the vertex in clockwise sense and will be called a *positive spin-orbit* of a vertex. The *negative spin-orbit*

---

[1]This idea arose from the fact that every finite extent analytic curve is *homotopic* to a line segment in the plane [GUILLEMIN 74].

[2]Our data structures and algorithms admit multiple edges with different embeddings and *loops* in the graph theoretic sense [HARARY 72]. To avoid confusions, we employ Weiler's term *contour* to refer to what many authors of solid modeling literature call a loop.

corresponds to the counterclockwise cycle of half-edges oriented away from its fixed vertex and can be obtained through the permutation other-side(previous-half()). In the rest of this paper we will refer to the positive spin-orbit of a vertex simply by *spin-orbit*.

All the edges meeting a vertex are obtainable through its topological identification of parametric values recorded as a partition of the set B. And the spin-orbit for a vertex is determined geometrically by the angle with which its half-edges meet the vertex, i.e. by the tangents of its half-edges at the vertex, or by curvature when curves meet tangentially at the vertex. Therefore, the determination of the correct linking of half-edges at any fixed vertex can be done sorting by decreasing angle a list of references to members of the spin-orbit, and afterward traversing the sorted list arranging half-edge linkages on the fly [3].

For $0 < i < n$, the current *linear* linkage of edge records (figure 1.b) is such that each parameter value $b_i \in B$ will contribute with four half-edges incident at the vertex with coordinates $c(b_i)$. Two of these half-edges belong to the spin-orbit, one with LEABO index and tangent $c'(b_i)$, and the other with DEXTRO index and tangent $-c'(b_i)$. For the parametric value b_n, its contribution to its spin-orbit consists of one DEXTRO half-edge, and the contribution of b_n is one LEABO half-edge. An alternate way to think of the linkage arrangement process at a vertex is as a merge of different spin-orbits, one spin-orbit per parametric value recorded under the same topological identification of a vertex. The result is shown in figure 1.c.

STEP 4) CONTOURS IDENTIFICATION. The identification of contours may be done with a *maze-traversal* algorithm, as described in [WILSON 85]. Another simpler and elegant recursive algorithm is given in the C pseudocode of figure 4.

The procedure assumes that an edge is created in step 2 with NULL assigned as owner contour pointer (oc field) to both of its half-edges. The first call to the contour recognition procedure should be done providing as actual parameters any half-edge (i.e. any edge pointer and either DEXTRO or LEABO as half-edge index) and NULL as last argument.

Thus we have finaly and successfuly derived the topological relations from the geometric description, i.e. topology was determined from geometry. This ends the description of algorithm 1 as a solution to problem 1.

The planar pseudograph obtained as output from algorithm 1 is a special case of what in this article will be refered to as a *region-pseudograph*. The following are properties of a region-pseudograph: each edge references a finite extent parametric curve as its embedding in Euclidean plane. The regions into which the embedded pseudograph partitions the plane are represented by its oriented boundaries called contours. There is always one region of infinite extent and a finite number – possibly zero – of bounded regions. Every pair of regions is disjoint, and the union of all closed regions is the plane. Each contour is defined as a closed walk of arcs and points. Arcs correspond to oriented embeddings of edges, and points correspond to embeddings of vertices.

Algorithm 1 always produces region-pseudographs in which its underlying pseudograph is connected – or equivalently, always has a single component in the graph-theoretic sense [HARARY 72]. One practical representation of a one-component region-pseudograph is as a list of entry points for its contours, where the first contour in the list always bounds the infinite region. Therefore, we have problem 2.

PROBLEM 2. Given a one-component region-pseudograph, find an algorithm to identify the contour which bounds the infinite plane region.

---

[3]This arrangement should establish both "next" and "previous" linkages between members of the two oppositely oriented spin-orbits.

```
#define          LEABO          0
#define          DEXTRO         1
#define          other_side(he) ((he) == DEXTRO ? LEABO : DEXTRO)

get_contours(e, he, previous_he_contour)
EDGE *e;
char he;
CONTOUR *previous_he_contour;
{
        CONTOUR *create_contour_entry();

        if(e->h_e[he].oc == NULL) {
                if(previous_he_contour == NULL)
                        e->h_e[he].oc = create_contour_entry(e,he);
                else
                        e->h_e[he].oc = previous_he_contour;
                get_contours(e->h_e[he].ne, e->h_e[he].nhe, e->h_e[he].oc);
        }
        if(e->h_e[other_side(he)].oc == NULL)
                get_contours(e, other_side(he), NULL);
}
```
Figure 4. Recursive function to create contour identifiers.

There is a solution to this problem which uses contour orientations [WEILER 80], however we want to present a characterization of the sought contour based on a remarkable property which is independent of its orientation.

ALGORITHM 2: (Jordan's contour characterization).

Given a contour examine it as follows: select a point on one of its half-edges different from any of its vertices. Based on this point, select a ray towards the interior of the region bounded by the contour which avoids all vertices of the contour. If the number of intersections of the ray with all the half-edges *of the contour being examined* is zero or even, the contour bounds the infinite region, otherwise the contour bounds a finite region. We are done.

A proof of the correctness of this algorithm can be obtained by joining loose ends with non self-intersecting arcs and applying the Jordan curve theorem.

5. MIXTURE OF REGION-PSEUDOGRAPHS

In this section we present different conceptual and algorithmic developments for *single component region-pseudographs*. The reader should be carefull with the expressions *single-component*, one-component region-pseudograph and *connected region-pseudograph* all of them meaning that the underlying pseudograph of the region-pseudograph is connected. These terms should be distinguished from the expression *connected region*. For example, the region-pseudograph in figure 1.c is connected since its pseudograph has only one component, but this region-pseudograph has two disjoint regions, one which is finite and *simply connected*, and one which is infinite and *not simply connected*.

Definition.- The **mixture** of two region-pseudographs G1 and G2, is defined as the region-pseudograph in which every contour bounds a region of the form Ri ∩ Rj, where Ri is a region of G1 and Rj is a region of G2.

We first describe the computation of the mixture of two single-component region-pseudographs. Under this situation the resulting region-pseudograph will either be connected or have two components depending if the the underlying pseudographs of the given arguments touch or not.

PROBLEM 3. Given two one-component region-pseudographs G1 and G2, describe an algorithm to obtain their mixture assuming that their corresponding embeddings touch.

ALGORITHM 3: The algorithmic solution to this problem is an extension to the solution of the equivalent problem for straight edges described in [WEILER 80]. This extension should take into consideration the techniques described in ALGORITHM 1: record of topological identifications through references to parameter values and vertices, edge splitting together with interval cutting, spin-orbits merge and unique entry point assignment to newly formed contours.

PROBLEM 4. Given two single-component region-pseudographs G1 and G2, if their underlying pseudographs do not touch, provide an algorithm which will signal the actual spatial relation out of the three possible situations (see figure 5):

A) the pseudograph of G1 lies within the infinite region of G2 and the pseudograph of G2 lies within the infinite region of G1.

B) the pseudograph of G2 lies within a finite region of G1 and the pseudograph of G1 lies in the infinite region of G2.

C) the pseudograph of G1 lies within a finite region of G2 and the pseudograph of G2 lies in the infinite region of G1.

The algorithm 4, emerges as a simple application of the Jordan's contour characterization to this problem in the following way:

ALGORITHM 4:

1. Select any point *on* the pseudograph of G1, and fire a ray in any direction which does not intersects G2 at a vertex of its contour bounding the infinite region.

2. If the number of intersections with the contour of G2 which bounds the infinite region is odd, then this is situation C, we are done. Otherwise, proceed with step 3.

3. Since the number computed in step 2 is zero or even, we know that the pseudograph of G1 lies in the infinite region of G2. Now perform the symmetric test, i.e. do the same as in step 1 interchanging the roles of G1 and G2. If the number of intersections with the contour of G1 which bounds the infinite region is odd, then this is situation B, otherwise, the situation is A. We are done.

PROBLEM 5. Once the above algorithm has been executed, when the resulting situation is C (or B), we may ask which bounding contour for a finite region in G2 (or G1) contains the pseudograph of G1 (or G2). Therefore we have:

ALGORITHM 5: Suppose the pseudograph of G1 lies in a finite region of G2. To determine which finite region of G2 contains the pseudograph of G1, select a point on the pseudograph of G1, this point lies in the interior of the region bounded by the seeked contour. For every contour of G2,

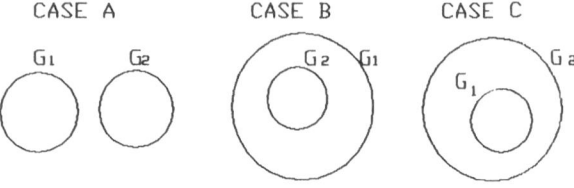

Figure 5. Possible spatial relation for a
2-Component Region-pseudograph.

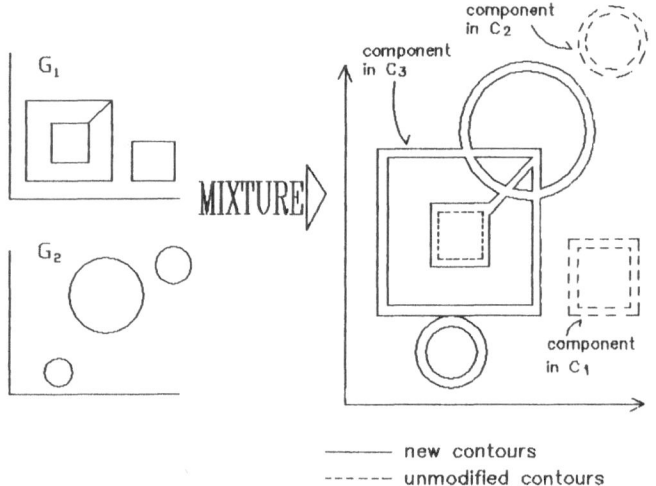

——— new contours
－－－－－ unmodified contours

Figure 6. Characterization of contours for
their labeling.

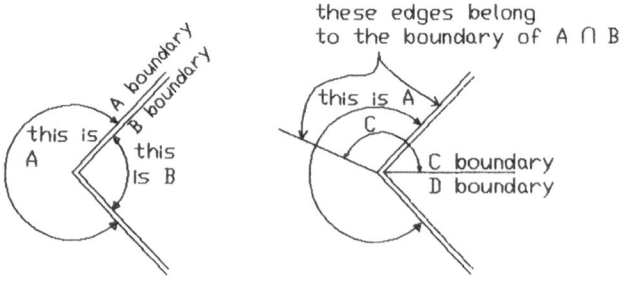

Figure 7. Identifying pairs for regions
at a vertex.

compute the number of intersections of a ray with the contour (the ray is based on the selected point of G1 and avoids all vertices of the contour of G2 being compared). The number of intersections will be odd for exactly two contours of G2, namely the contour which bounds the infinite region of G2 and the contour being seeked. We are done.

6. n-COMPONENT REGION-PSEUDOGRAPHS

PROBLEM 6. Given two region-pseudographs, each with a finite number of components, compute their mixture.

The mixture of multiple-component region-pseudographs complicates since the resulting number of components may be less than those provided as input (see figure 6). We only hint on how to obtain the output components and leave aside the details for a complete implementation which may be done combining the results presented in this paper.

ALGORITHM VI.

1. Let G1 and G2 denote the two input region-pseudographs. Before the computation starts, arrange three sets for component identifiers: C1 for the set of component identifiers belonging to G1, C2 for the component identifiers of G2, and C3 an empty set of component identifiers.

2. Concurrent to edge comparisions to find intersections, if any component from G1 touches a component from G2, the corresponding component's identifiers must be removed from C1 and C2 and placed in a list of identifier pairs.

3. After the comparision of edges has been finished, the resulting list of pairs should be examined to obtain a unique identifier for each component which resulted from the combination of several input components. Every resulting identifier should be placed in the set C3.

When the algorithm terminates, the output identifiers are stored in the set C1∪C2∪C3. This completes the discussion on the mixture of two multiple-component region-pseudographs.

7. LABELING REGION-PSEUDOGRAPHS

Since resulting regions from the mixture operation are always obtained from the intersection of input regions, it is obvious that each point in a resulting region belongs to two, and only two, different input regions. An explanation follows to label the bounding contours of each resulting connected-region – or equivalently, to label each connected-region in the output – with the names of the two input regions from which they are derived. This labeling was first refered to in [WEILER 80] as the "contour history".

To reach this aim, each contour in an input region-pseudograph to the mixture operation should be labeled with a unique identifier. To facilitate our work, a contour identifier should be built as an ordered pair in a preprocessing for the mixture operation. Let G1 stand for the first argument and G2 for the second argument to the mixture operation, and let c1 be a contour of G1 and c2 a contour of G2. The input preprocessing will assign (c1, NULL) to identify c1, and (NULL, c2) for c2. All output identifiers will be of the form (c1, c2).

In the output from the mixture operation we distinguish two types of contours: those which were present on the input and were unmodified on output, and those that are new or change in some way its topological structure. More precisely, we define as *unmodified contour* any output contour which has exactly the same set of input vertices and half-edges with all of them unaffected on output. All other output contours will be called *new contours* (figure 6).

We now describe a two stage procedure as extensions of the mixture operation to obtain the identifiers of output contours. This procedure relies on the partition of output components obtained from algorithm VI: the set C3 which holds components having at least one new contour and an arbitrary number (including zero) of unmodified contours. And those components in sets C1 and C2 which consist solely of unmodified contours. The first stage will be based on a local analysis done on components in C3, and the second stage on a global analysis on components in the set C1∪C2.

The first stage of the procedure will assign an identifier to every new contour. The identifying pair assigned to new contours is easily obtained merging different spin-orbits in the mixture operation [WEILER 80]. This is illustrated in figure 7. However, this procedure is unable to complete an identifying pair for unmodified contours which can come out in components of the C3 output set (see figure 6). These contour identifiers may be completed by propagating through the component the information in new contours to unmodified contours [LAIDLAW 86]. This concludes the first stage of the labeling procedure for contours in components of C3.

The second stage to derive identifiers for the contours in the sets C1 and C2 will perform a global analysis of spatial relations between all the resulting components of algorithm VI. The components in sets C1 and C2 have only unmodified contours, and their corresponding identifiers are still in the form (c1, NULL) and (NULL, c2). If for each of these components we find the complete identifier of the region where the component lies, then it is a trivial task to complete the identifier for the contours of the component. To facilitate the current task of identifying pair completion, let us now divert momentarely the discussion to introduce a new data structure as a better device than the hierarchy proposed in [WEILER 80].

8. THE RP-TREE

Consider figure 8 which shows three different output possibilities of the mixture operation. In each of the three examples there are four contours. However, in example (c) there are four regions, and in examples (a) and (b) there are three regions. In all the examples, there is a single infinite region. In example (a) there is one region (the infinite one) with two non-connected bounding contours, and in example (b) there is also one region (a finite one) with two non-connected bounding contours. All other regions in all examples are bounded by a single (connected) contour.

Each tree of figure 9 encodes all the mentioned relationships for the region-pseudograph of figure 8 labeled with the same letter. The meaning of figure 9 will become clear with the following definition.

Definition.- The *rp-tree* of a region-pseudograph is a non-empty finite tree and a one to one relation between non-root nodes of the tree and contours of the region-pseudograph which satisfies the following properties:

- the level 0 or root-node corresponds to the abstract "contour" at infinity.

- The contours corresponding to even levels are called black nodes, and those corresponding to odd levels are called white nodes.

- Every white node bounds by itself an infinite region and every black node (except the root) bounds a finite region.

- Every connected component of the underlying pseudograph is represented either by a two-level subtree rooted at a non-leaf white node or by a white-leaf.

- Every region of the region-pseudograph is represented either by a two-level subtree rooted at a non-leaf black node or by a black-leaf.

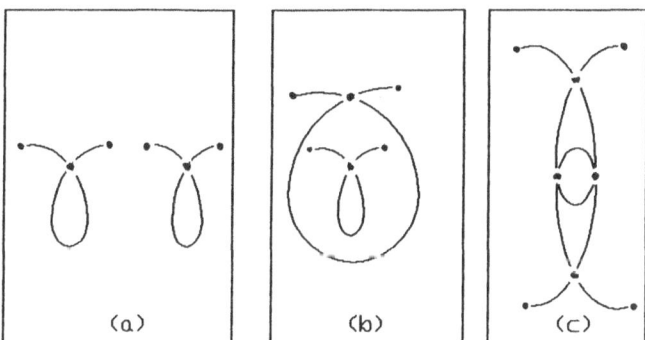

Figure 8. Typical outputs from the mixture of two single—component region—pseudographs.

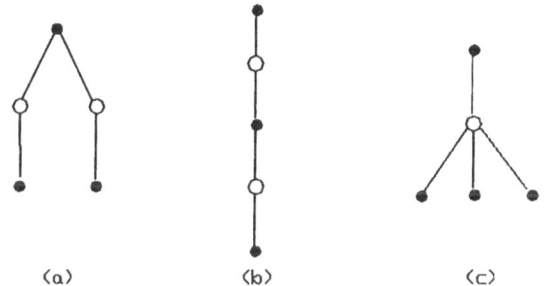

Figure 9. Rp—trees corresponding to region—pseudographs in Fig. 8.

The name rp-tree stands for region-pseudograph-tree. Note that the definition of an rp-tree permits white-leaf nodes which correspond either to isolated points or to non self-intersecting continuous curves; i.e. a single white-leaf corresponds to the boundary of an infinite region whose regularized topological closure is the whole plane. From now on the identifier of a node in an rp-tree will be used to refer either to its associated contour or to the region which the contour bounds; context will clear out the distinction.

Definition.- An *unrooted rp-tree* is defined as the rp-tree of a *single component* region-pseudograph without its root.

Given an arbitrary n-component region-pseudograph (in fact, given the output C1 ∪ C2 ∪ C3 of algorithm VI) it is also an easy task to build its associated rp-tree. First build a list which records all the components of the region-pseudograph as unrooted rp-trees. Starting with the minimal rp-tree – which stands for E^2 – for every unrooted rp-tree invoke the recursive algorithm described in the pseudocode in figure 10. This algorithm takes as first argument an unrooted rp-tree and as second argument the root of an rp-tree whose pseudograph does not touch the pseudograph of its first arument. On output a new rp-tree will be obtained which holds all the input components, and therefore all the contours, in its correct place.

```
insert (component, black_node_in_tree) {
        for (each white_son of black_node_in_tree) {
                case = algorithm4(component, white_son);
                switch(case) {
                    case 'situation C of PROBLEM 4':
                        find_black_grandson(component, white_son);
                        return();
                    case 'situation B of PROBLEM 4':
                        unlink white_son;
                        find_black_grandson(white_son, component);
                }
        }
        link(black_node_in_tree,component);
}

find_black_grandson(component, white_node)
{
        for (each black_son of white_node) {
                if( contained(black_son, component)) {
                        insert(component, black_son);
                        return();
                }
        }
}
```

Figure 10. Recursive insert of a component into an rp-tree.

In the pseudocode of the **insert**() procedure, the invocation of the function **algorithm4**() stands for an implementation of ALGORITHM 4 which returns the actual spatial relation between its arguments. Refer to the description of PROBLEM 4 with **component** as G1 and **white_son** as G2, the quoted strings in the body of the switch statement in figure 10 explain the meaning of the returned values by **algorithm4**(). Situation A of PROBLEM 4 is considered until the end of the **for**() statement when situation A has been checked for all the white-sons of the black-node that becomes the parent of the inserted component.

The pseudocode for **find_black_son**() is a customized implementation of ALGORITHM 5. On its second argument it searches for the black son which contains the pseudograph of its first argument. When it finds it, does a recursive invocation of the **insert**() procedure with the subtree rooted at the black son found. This ends the discussion on the construction of rp-trees.

9. LABELING REGION-PSEUDOGRAPHS WITH RP-TREES

Going back to the discussion under section 7, about the second stage to label output contours of a mixture operation, what we will now describe is a procedure based on an rp-tree to derive the missing identifiers in the component sets C1 and C2 coming out of the mixture operation.

After completing identifiers for C3, build the rp-tree from the components in the three sets C1, C2 and C3. It is obviously correct to assign the pair (∞,∞) as identifier for the root and all white nodes at level 1 of the resulting rp-tree. Let x and y stand for identifying elements from an input regions. Descend one level at any node, now, at level 2 any identifier of the form (x, NULL) should be set to (x, ∞), and symmetrically any (NULL, y) set to (∞, y). Therefore, we are able to complete identifiers at level 2.

At level 3, for the sons of a level 2 node identified as (c1, c2), any identifier of the form (x, NULL) should be set to (x, c2) and symmetrically any (NULL, y) set to (c1, y). So, we were able to complete the identifiers at level 3. This same procedure should be applied to complete node identifiers while descending to traverse the rp-tree either in depth-first or breath-first. The proof of the correctness of this and the rp-tree construction algorithm may be done by induction on the number of components.

10. APPLICATIONS

The implementation of boolean operations of regions bounded by differentiable curve segments is immediate with the mixture of rp-trees and the aid of conjuctive forms. The familiar expressions for boolean operations may be replaced by their equivalent conjunctive forms:

Boolean Expression	Conjunctive Form Employed	Output
A ∩ B	A ∩ B	Conjunctive form.
A ∪ B	$A^c \cap B^c$	Complement of conjunctive form.
A − B	$A \cap B^c$	Conjunctive form.

Different enhancements of the user interface of CAD systems may be achieved through the rp-tree. Since the user may refer to regions by means of a pointing device. Locating the region where the input point lies may rapidly be done with a simple modification of the algorithm explained in section 8 for the inclusion of a 1-component region-pseudograph into an rp-tree. The modification should return the black node visited at deepest level; the returned black node with all its white sons constitutes the boundary of the pointed region.

Another possible enhancement for the user interface of a CAD/CAM system is related to the validity of physicaly realizable solids. Note that each individual contour may or may not constitute an implicit representation of a closed orientable 1D-manifold in the plane, however it is a trivial task to classify any contour as a member of this class or not. A contour belongs to the class of closed orientable 1D-manifolds if and only if its stored representation satisfies two simple tests: 1) the set of its half-edges does not include the two half-edges of the same edge, and 2) for every vertex in the contour exactly one half-edge of the contour occurs in any of its two associated spin-orbits.

Our research was originaly motivated by the problem of describing trimmed-surface patch domains [LASTRA 89]. The results presented may be used to model the preimages of intersection curves described by degree one B-spline curves. A one bit field in rp-tree nodes is sufficient to indicate if the region associated to different contours is or is not in use by a model. It is possible to trim a patch by pointing into a region of the displayed patch domain. If the geometric entities associated with an rp-tree are swept in space, the rp-tree structure serves as an aid to derive a correct radial-edge [WEILER 87] structure of the resulting object.

11. CONCLUSIONS AND FUTURE RESEARCH

Algorithms and data structures were described to derive correct topological and geometrical relations of the plane partition induced by a set of finite length differentiable parametric curves. The obtained rp-tree constitutes a hierarchical data structure of references to contours, and each individual contour always bounds a non-empty open set of the plane. Contours are also associated to a planar pseudo-graph which is one more "offspring" of Baumgart's winged-edge. A characterization of the contour facing towards infinity in a single component region-pseudograph which is independent of its orientation was explained and employed to build the hierarchical structure of the rp-tree, this characterization is based on an "homotopycal limiting case" of a closed Jordan curve and the differiantiability of input curves.

The generalization to higher dimensions of the techniques employed has not been possible due to robustness problems of geometric computations. In particular, we have not been able to obtain correct and consistent topological descriptions in 3D resulting from patch triangulation intersections. The authors believe that the double precision geometry technique of Victor Milenkovic [MILENKOVIC 89] is generalizable to higher dimensions.

12. Acknowledgements

This research work was partialy supported by the National Council of Science and Technology of México (CONACYT). We also want to sincerely thank Wu Shing Ting from FhG-AGD, Darmstadt, Germany, who patiently reviewed an older version of this paper and provided us sharp helpful comments. Finally, we want to sincerely thank the authorities at IIE, México, for their patient support to this work.

13. References

[**BAUMGART 75**] B.G. Baumgart, *A Polyhedron Representation for Computer Vision,* National Computer Conference, AFIPS Proceedings, Vol. 44, 1975, pp 589-596.

[**EDELSBRUNNER 90**] H. Edelsbrunner, E.P. Mücke, *Simulation of Simplicity: A Technique to Cope with Degenerate Cases in Geometric Algorithms,* ACM Transactions on Graphics, Vol. 9, No. 1, Jan. 1990, pp 66-104.

[**GANGNET 89**] M. Gangnet, J.C. Hervé, T. Pudet and J.M. Van Thong, *Incremental Computation of Planar Maps,* SIGGRAPH'89 Proceedings, Computer Graphics, Vol. 23, No. 3, Jul. 1989, pp 345-354.

[**GUILLEMIN 74**] V. Guillemin and A. Pollack, *Differential Topology,* Prentice Hall Inc., Englewood Cliffs, N.J., 1974.

[**HARARY 72**] F. Harary, *Graph Theory,* Addison-Wesley Publishing Co., Reading, Mass., 1972.

[**HOFFMANN 89**] C.M. Hoffman, *The Problems of Accuracy and Robustness in Geometric Computation,* IEEE Computer Society, Computer, Vol. 22, No. 3, Mar. 1989, pp 31-41.

[**LASTRA 89**] G.L. Lastra, J.S. Santana, M.F. Angeles, *The Four-wings-edge for Solid Boolean Operations with Trimmed Surface Patches,* in Lastra, Encarnação, Requicha (Editors), Proceedings of the IFIP TC5 Conference on CAD/CAM Technology Transfer: Applications of Computers to Engineering Design, Manufacturing and Management, (August 1988, Mexico City) Elsevier Science Publishers B.V., The Netherlands, 1989, pp 51-64.

[**LAIDLAW 86**] D.H. Laidlaw, W.B. Trumbore and J.F. Hughes, *Constructive Solid Geometry for Polyhedral Objects,* ACM SIGGRAPH '86 Proceedings, Computer Graphics, Vol. 20, No. 4, Aug. 1986, pp 161-170.

[**MANTYLA 89**] M. Mäntylä, M. O'Connor and J. Rossignac, *Advanced Topics in Solid Modeling,* tutorial course notes distributed at EUROGRAPHICS 89, Hamburg, F.R.G., Sept. 1989.

[**MILENKOVIC 89**] V. Milenkovic, *Double Precision Geometry: A General Technique for Calculating Line and Segment Intersections Using Rounded Arithmetic*, IEEE Computer Society, 30th. Annual Symposium on Foundations of Computer Science Proceedings, Oct.-Nov. 1989, pp 500-505.

[**SAMET 88**] H. Samet and R.E. Webber, *Hierarchical Data Structures and Algorithms for Computer Graphics*, IEEE CG&A, Vol. 8, No. 3, May. 1988, pp 48-68.

[**WEILER 80**] K. Weiler, *Polygon comparision using Graph Representation*, ACM SIGGRAPH '80 Proceedings, Computer Graphics, Vol. 14, No. 3, July 1980, pp 10-18.

[**WEILER 85**] K. Weiler, *Edge-Based Data Structures for Solid Modeling in Curved-Surface Environments*, IEEE CG&A, Vol. 5, No. 1, Jan. 1985, pp 21-40.

[**WEILER 87**] K. Weiler, *Non-manifold Geometric Boundary Modeling*, Draft Prepared for SIGGRAPH'87 Advanced Solid Modeling Tutorial, ACM, 1987. (General Electric, Corporate Research and Development, Schenectady, NY 12301).

[**WILSON 85**] Wilson, P.R., *Euler Formulas and Geometric Modeling*, IEEE CG&A, Vol. 5, No. 8, August 1988, pp 25-36.

Instituto de Investigaciones Eléctricas, Unidad de Cómputo, Cuernavaca, 62000 Mexico

Geometric Modeling System GEMS and its Application

ZESHENG TANG and JIAGUANG SUN

ABSTRACT

The technical features of a Geometric Modeling System (GEMS) developed by CAD Center of Tsinghua University are introduced. An approach to improve the robustness of Boolean operation, which is the key step of geometric modeling system is presented. Some test results showing the improvement of robustness are given. Two application examples of GEMS are introduced briefly in the last section.

Keywords: Geometric Modeling System,   Application

1. INTRODUCTION

The technology for representing, creating and manipulating 3D models with computer is referred to as geometric modeling technology which is the kernel of CAD/CAM. Using geometric modeling technology, the design, analysis and simulation of 3D complex objects may be implemented with computer instead of practical models. It will remarkably reduce the cost, shorten the design period and improve the quality of products. This is the reason why geometric modeling technology has got such a rapid development since the early 1970s.

In recent years, there are some commercial geometric modeling systems available in the market, such as, I-DEAS(SDRC), CATIA, I/EMS (INTERGRAPH), ROMULUS and others. While these systems may be imported and used in CAD/CAM in China, they are very expensive and difficult to be localized and adapted for the special requirement of Chinese users. Under such circumstances, a GEometric Modeling System--GEMS has been developed by CAD Center of Tsinghua University in Beijing.

2. TECHNICAL FEATURES OF GEMS [5]

GEMS includes three modules: define/input, Boolean operations and transformation/output. The compatible data formats are used for communication among these modules. The working flowchart of GEMS is shown in Fig.1

1). Define And Input Of Solid Models

Constructive Solid Geometry(CSG) is used to define and input solid models. CSG representations are trees whose internal nodes represent regularized Boolean operators and rigid motions and whose leaves represent instances of primitive solids. The primitives used in GEMS are shown in Fig.2. Each node in a CSG tree represents some intermediate objects. Thus, the tree itself actually represents an entire hierarchy of objects.

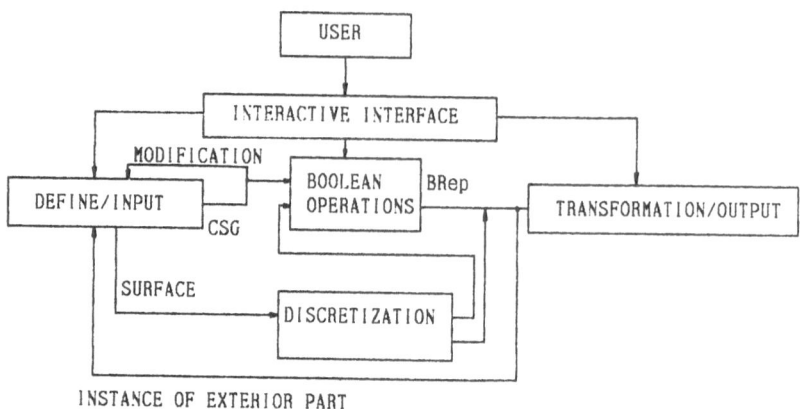

Fig.1 Working Flowchart of GEMS

Some solid models may also be generated by sweeping method. A 2D contour moving along
or rotating around a straight line generates a 3D objects. This method is proved to be
practical and efficient for modeling constant cross section objects.

2). Define and Input of Surface Models

In GEMS, sculptured surface is parameterized and represented by Bezier surface, which
may be inputted by the following approaches:
(1) input control points to generate surface;
(2) input sample points to generate control points inversely;
(3) a 2D curve moving along a trajectory which is a straight line or a curve;
(4) skining the surface on the skeleton which are closed or unclosed curves. The Bezier
    surfaces may be approximated with planar facets by discretization for display in the
    transformation/output module or doing set operations with solid models.

3). User Interface

Graphics Interface Management Environment (GIME) which consists of the Menu Description
Transfer(MDT), Interface Controller Driven by Menu(ICDM) and Macro Definitions (Gshell)
are used for developing the interactive interface of GEMS. GEMS mediates the interactions
between the end user of an application and the application program and validates the
sentences for correct syntax and semantics. MDT is also used to determine how information
is to be displayed to the end user and for partially verifying the syntax of any input
(from the end user) before passing it to the interactive actions. ICDM is responsible
for processing the events of refresh, keyboard, locator, picker, and macro and handling
the interactive actions of the end users. The refresh event serves for multi_windows and
moving, poping, and zooming windows. Gshell is implemented by the end user to define,
design and combine the new interactive functions and systems.

Using GIME leads to a number of advantages. An interface can be quickly modified
without changes to the application program, application program can also be modified
more quickly and maintained more easily. There can be more consistent interfaces among
different applications. Application programs become highly portable between different
installations.

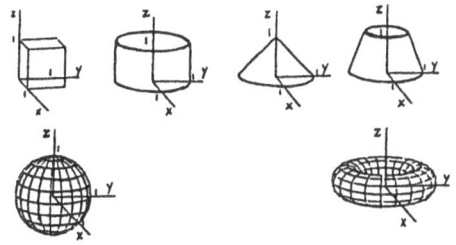 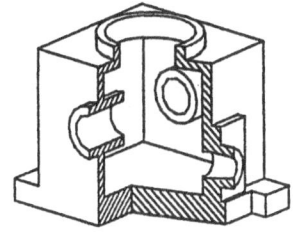

Fig.2 Primitives used in GEMS   Fig.3 Example of divide and section

4). Boolean Operations

The well known Boolean operations, e.g. union, intersection and difference, provide a
useful method for constructing complex objects form simpler ones. The Boolean operations
are usually "regularized" in some way to guarantee that valid input will always produce
valid output. This prevents the creation from unrealistic features such as dangling faces
and edges.

In GEMS, after discretization, the primitives and all other objects modeled from
define/input module are represented by planar facets and may be operated by the following
regularized Boolean operations:

(1) Union (+):   Combine two objects together;
(2) Intersection(^): Find the object that is common to both objects A and B;
(3) Difference (-): Subtract one object from another;
(4) Put (&):   Associate disjoint bodies into one object;
(5) Plane cut: Divide and section an object with one or two planes in arbitrary
                     angle, the example is shown in Fig.3.

Let A and B be two regularized objects, S = A<op>B, here <op> is one of the regularized
Boolean operators. The set operation algorithm used in GEMS is described as follows.

Step1: Classify the old boundary edges of A into three parts; edges in B(EA_IN_B),
edges out of B(EA_out_B), and edges on the boundary of B(EA_ON_B). Similarily, classify
the old boundary edges of B into (EB_in_A),(EB_out_A), and (EB_on_A).

Step2: Classify the edges (Enew) generated by A intersecting B into groups, one on the
boundary of S (Enew_on_S) and the other not on the boundary of S (Enew_not_on_S).

Step3: Let the boundary edge set of S be (E_on_S),then
   A: when<op> = +, (E_on_S) =(Enew_on_S)+(EA_out_B)+(EB_out_A);
   B: when<op> = ^, (E_on_S) =(Enew_on_S)+(EA_in_B)+(EB_in_A);
   C: when<op> = -, (E_on_S) =(Enew_on_S)+(EA_out_B)+(EB_IN_A);

Step4: When <op> = ^, remove all dangling edges from (E_on_S), and dangling faces from
(F_on_S).

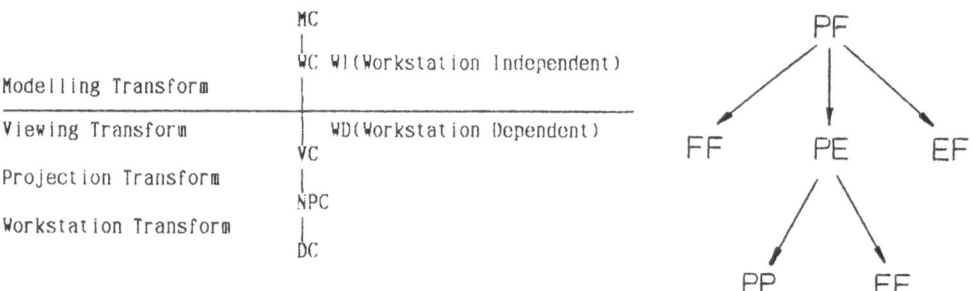

Fig.4 Transformation Pipeline in GEMS

Fig.5 Deduction of on/on relationships

5). Transformation Pipeline

The transformation pipeline of GEMS is identical with PHIGS. GEMS has five coordinate systems: modeling coordinates(MC), world coordinates(WC), viewing coordinates(VC), normalized projection coordinates(NPC), and device coordinates(DC). The transformation pipeline in GEMS is shown in Fig.4

One example generated by GEMS is shown with color picture in FiG.12.

3. IMPROVE THE ROBUSTNESS OF BOOLEAN OPERATIONS[3]

Improve the robustness of Boolean operation is one of the most important modifications in the newest GEMS version (GEMS 3.0). Most commercial geometric modeling systems as well as old versions of GEMS (GEMS 2.0) have robustness limitations which are evident to everyday users. As R. H. Johnson said in [2], all of the systems he had seen in commercial use can be made break and most have sets of pathological conditions where robustness is uncertain. Boolean operation robustness refers to the robustness of algorithm or software to implement Boolean operations. It is defined as to probability of algorithm or software working normally and output correct results under variant conditions of input. The correct results of solid Boolean opereration refer to valid solids which are consistent in the aspects of topology and geometry[4].

In GEMS, Boolean operations are implemented between a pair of polyhedra approximating the input primitives. In some special cases for polyhedra, Boolean operation is unable to output valid solids. For example, it is difficult to decide exactly whether a polygon intersects another or the two polygons are on one plane when they are nearly co_planar; whether a point is on a plane or not when the point is nearly on the plane and so forth. In Fig.7, A is a unit cube centered at origin of coordinate system and B is same as A except rotated around X, Y and Z axes by a small degree x respectively. The characteristics is that the boundaries of two cubes are nearly co_planar, co_linear and co_vertex. Geomod 3.9 (marketed by SDRC) prints error message when it calculates A U B with 0.3. GEMS 2.0 can not output correct results of A U B with 0.5 .

1) Analysis of Boolean Operation Robustness

In Boolean operation algorithm, it needs to make many decisions to determine set membership classifications[6]. Owing to the calculation error inherent in the computer, the results of set membership classification are dependent on the tolerance adopted. For example, let ε be the computing error of distance square $dist^2$ of two points in floating-point system.

The common used method to determine point/point classification is considering the two points coincident when $dist^2$ is less than or equal to an adopted tolerance, or apart from one another when $dist^2$ is greater than that tolerance. Once the tolerance is chosen, the point/point classification is then determined. The classification will change as the tolerance is changed.

The set membership classifications in whole Boolean operation process are interrelated, one of which is determined by and determines the others. For example, if two polygons are co-plannar, all vertices of one polygon should be on the plane of another polygon. This shows that the point/face classification are consistent with face/face classification. All analogous consistences kept by classification can be deduced from primary geometry. It is certain to keep consistence for all classifications in real number system. But in floating-point number system, the interrelated classifications may not keep this consistence and may conflict with each other since the classification are related to adopted tolerance. The conflict among interrelated classifications generated from the computing error is the main factor to reduce the Boolean operation robustness.

2) Improve The Boolean Operation Robustness

In order to improve Boolean operation robustness, we consider results of classifications as two relationships: on/on and $\overline{on/on}$. For example, the point on plane is an on/on relationship of the point/face classification, while both point at positive side of plane and point at negative side of plane are $\overline{on/on}$ relationships of the point/face classification. We believe that if there was no possibility for classifications to be on/on, the classifications would become exact. For example, when we know that a point is not on a plane we certainly consider the point is at the negative side of the plane if the distance of the point to the plane is less than 0. Otherwise the point is at the positive side of the plane. Although there exists error to compute the distance of the point to the plane, it is useless to choose a tolerance for decision.

We set a preprocessor before Boolean operation procedures. In the preprocessor, we first determine on/on relationships of basic classifications required in Boolean operation procedure, and then check if on/on relationships of interelated classifications conflict with each other. If there are any conflicts found, a reasoning technique will be used to correct the classifications which are not correspondent with the actual situation.

The algorithm to compute a new polyhedron $S = A \langle op \rangle B$ is composed of three main stages as follows:

Stage 1. Determine on/on relationships of basic classifications between two polyhedra A and B, and remove conflicts using reasoning technique if there are any conflicts between basic classifications;

Stage 2. Determine edge/polyhedron classifications:
Determine the classifications of edges of polyhedron A with respect to polyhedron B, and determine the classifications of edges of polyhedron B with respect to polyhedron A.

Stage 3. Form edges and polygons on the boundary of new polyhedron S.

The first stage of the algorithm is called the preprocessor of Boolean operation. Boolean operation procedure consists of the second and the last stages.

3). Preprocessor Of Boolean Operation

Basic classifications between two polyhedra refer to point/face, point/line, point/point, edge/face, line/line, and face/face classifications. On/on relationships of basic classifications refer to point on plane, point on line of edge, coincidence of two points, edge on plane, two edges on one line, and two polygons on one plane, which are represented by symbols PF, PE, PP, EF, EE, and FF, respectively.

The preprocessor determines on/on relationships of basic classifications as shown in Fig.6 which is a complex reasoning procedure. In this procedure we first determine the PF relationships of point/face classifications according to numerical calculations and adopted tolerance. Given coordinates (x_0, y_0, z_0) of a point p and plane equation

$$ax + by + cz + d = 0$$

of a plane F, the distance of the point p to the plane F is

$$dist = ax_0 + by_0 + cz_0 + d.$$

Let ε be the error of computing the distance dist and t be the thickness of plane F[3], then there is PF of point p with respect to plane F if

$$|dist| \leqslant |\varepsilon| + t,$$

there is a $\overline{PF}$ of point p with respect to plane F if

$$|dist| > |\varepsilon| + t.$$

Here $|\varepsilon| + t$ is a tolerance chosen for the point/face classification.

We then deduce FF, PE, and EF from PF, and deduce PP and EE from PE as shown in Fig.5. For instance, there is a FF between two polygons G1 and G2 if there are PFs for all vertices of polygon G1 with respect to polygon G2 and for all vertices of polygon G2 with respect to polygon G1.

Since PFs are related to adopted tolerance, some FF, PP and EE relationships can not be deduced. For example, we can not deduce EE or EE from PE when there are PEs for two endpoints of edge e1 with respect to edge e2 and there is PE only for one of two endpoints of edge e2 with respect to edge e1.

For such an undetermined classification, we have two hypotheses, either on/on or $\overline{on/on}$. In order to cause reasoning procedure to choose a more reasonable hypothesis, we use numerical calculations again to determine the classification. For example, when the FF or FF relationship of two polygons G1 and G2 can not be deduced, we use dot product of normal vectors of G1 and G2 as a heuristic function to determine the relationship of G1 and G2 to be FF or not. After all un-deduced classifications are determined by numerical calculations, we will modify PFs according to consistence of interrelated classifications, and then re-deduce all other relationships from the modified PFs.

Re-deducing other relationships will cause two probable results. One is that the relationships of all classifications are determined, which is expected. In this case the reasoning procedure will complete successfully. Another one is that new undetermined on/on relationships occur. In this case, we have different hypotheses according to the different ways to determine the original relationships of these classifications. If a classification is determined by numerical calculation and changed to undetermined now, we will set the relationship of the classification opposite to the original value. If the classification is deduced from PFs, we will use numerical calculation again to determine its value.

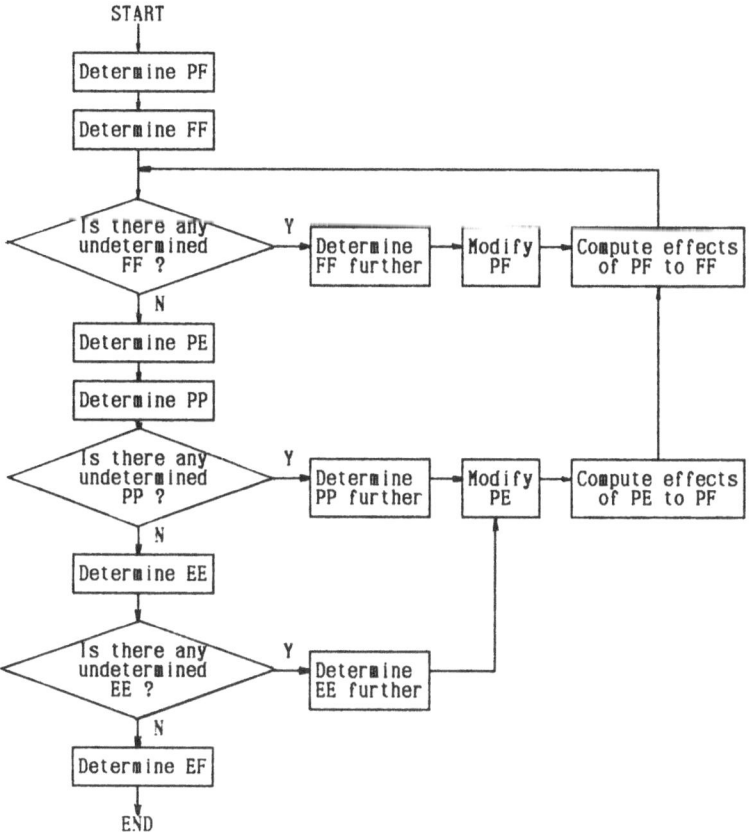

FIG.6 Flow chart of preprocessor

The algorithm will go to next stage to do Boolean operation when reasoning procedure completes successfully. It will notify users of reason for algorithm failure before it returns as soon as reasoning procedure fails. Reasoning procedure failure means that for all probable hypotheses, the determined on/on relationships can not be deduced. For each of the hypotheses, there are two relationships R1 and R2 where R1 will directly or indirectly change to an undetermined one after R2 is determined, while R2 will directly or indirectly change to an undetermined one after R1 is determined. The detailed desciption of boolean operation procedure will be ignored in this paper, please see[3].

Fig.7 to Fig.10 are some sxamples used to test the robustness of GEMS 3.0 using the reliable Boolean operation algorithm mentioned above. We also take these examples to test I/EMS and Geomod 3.9. Table 1 is the comparison of the test results for the three modelling systems, where R refers to correct result, E error result, F system failure, and N system stopping normally without any result. Note that the newest GEMS version (GEMS 3.0) will always stop normally and notify users the reason when it can not calculate the results of Boolean operations. It can be said from comparison that robustness of GEMS 3.0 is higher than the others.

The first test is A ∪ B as shown in Fig.7 described in section 1. The smaller the absolute of α is, the more difficult it is to determine basic classifications. Table 1 gives the smallest α under which the modelling systems can work correctly and output valid results.

The second test is A ∪ B as shown in Fig.8, where A is a cylinder with 100 in length of diameter, center of top circle located at (0,0,100), and center of bottom circle located at (0,0,0). B is same as A except its center of top circle is located at (0,0,50), and center of bottom circle is located at (0,y,-50). The smaller the |y| is, the closer the side surfaces of two cylinders set. Table 1 gives the smallest |y| under which the modelling systems can work correctly and output valid results.

The third test is A ∪ B as shown in Fig.9, where A is a truncated cone with 50 and r in length of radii of top and bottom circles respectively. B is also a truncated cone with 50 and r in length of radii of bottom and top circles respectively. The centers of top and bottom circles of A are located at (0,0,100) and (0,0,0) respectively. The centers of top and bottom circles of B are located at (0,0,50) and (0,0,-50) respectively. As the radius r is changed larger, the difference |d| of radii of top circle from bottom circle will become smaller and the side surfaces of two truncated cones will become near to co-planar. Table 1 gives the smallest |d| under which the modelling systems can work correctly and output valid results.

The fourth test is A-B1-B2-B3 as shown in Fig.10, where A is a cube, and B1, B2, and B3 are cylinders located at three axes, respectively. All base circles of cylinders are co-planar with the side faces of cube.

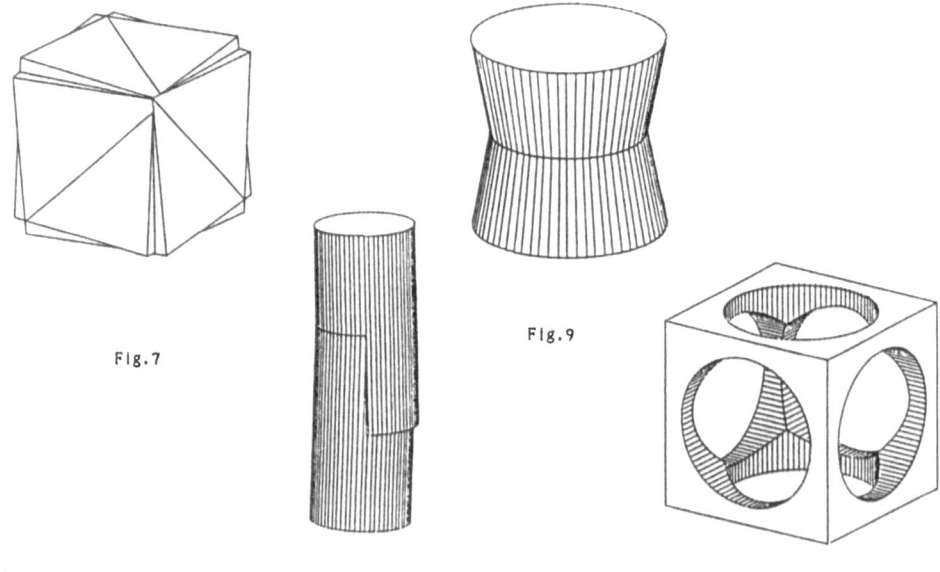

Fig.7

Fig.8

Fig.9

Fig.10

TABLE 1

	FIG.7	FIG.8	FIG.9	FIG.10
GEMS 3.0	0.1°	5E-3	R	R
SDRC 3.9	0.3°	0.05	R	R
I/EMS	0.6°	0.15	1E-3	F

4. APPLICATION OF GEOMETRIC MODELING SYSTEM GEMS

GEMS has found some applications in China. Two examples are shown as follows.

1) A 3D Numerical Simulation System FTSolver has been developed based on GEMS.[1]

The numerical simulation of solidification has become a hot topic for more than 20 years. Many researchers and users pointed out that the numerical sinumlation must be based on the solid geometric modeller. But a very few simulation software could solve the problems concerned about the gap between the geometry inputting and calculation.

A 3D numerical simulation system FTsolver has been developed based on GEMS by the Depart-ment of Mechanical Engineering of Tsinghua University. FTSolver includes five modules: Solid Modeller (GEMS), Mesh Generatar, Numerical Simulatar, Post Processor and a Data Base. Its working flow chart is shown in Fig.11.

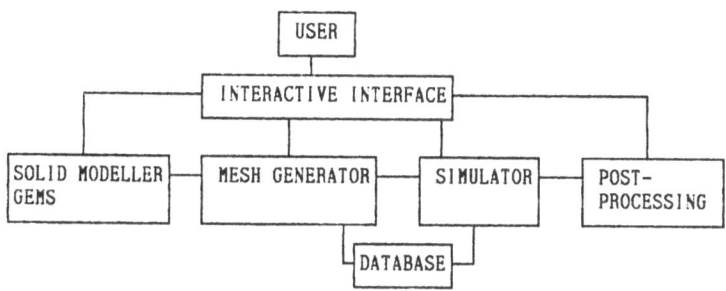

Fig.11 Working Flowchart of FTsolver

In FTsolver, GEMS is used to creat 3D solid modeller. Then, the solid model may be divided into equal sized cubes by the Mesh Generator according to the user's requirement. The location of each cube with its material index may be stored. It is available for users to check whether the mesh is satisfied or not with the help of post_processor. If it is satisfied, the numerical calculation will start without any interrupt of users and the results of calculation may be displayed with color pictures, such as temperature history of any selected points, two dimensional temperature contour lines and color temperature field display, three dimensional color thermal shaded plots and etc. The thermal properties of materials and other related data may be read from a small data base freely. Some results of the numerical simulation system FTSlover are shown in Fig.13.

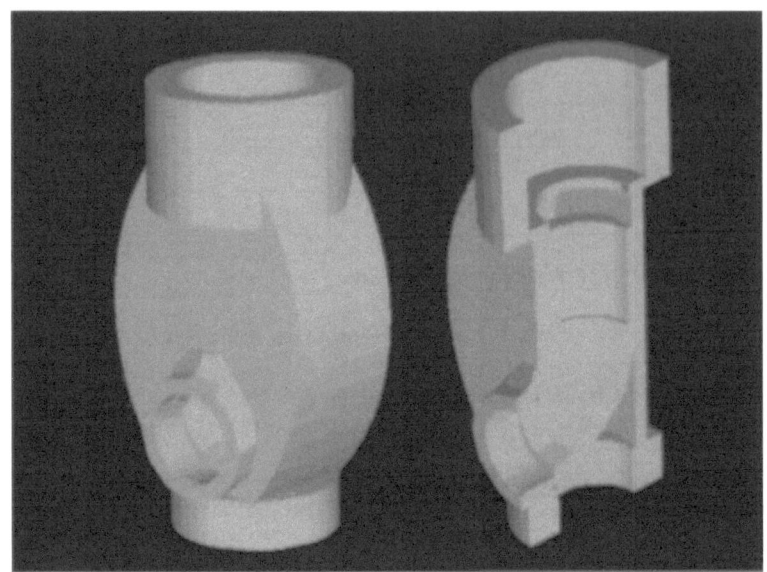

Fig. 12

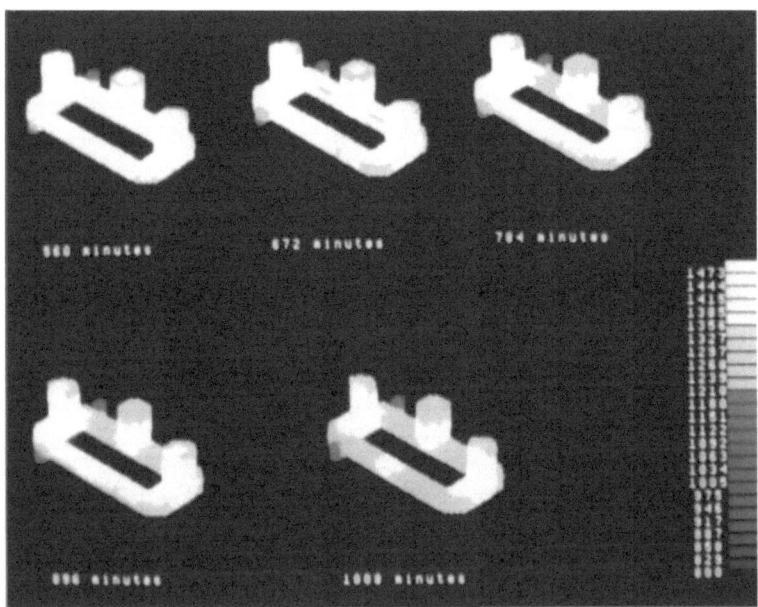

Fig. 13

2) Using Geometric Modeling System (GEMS) to Design Traditional Chinese Garden.

Traditional Chinese Garden is an art combining the architeture, trees, mountains, lakes and etc. Conventionally, pictures of perspective view or human-made physical model are used to show the scenery of Chinese Garden designed. But, the perspective view is dependent on the location of view point. It must be changed when the location of view point is changed. The human-made physical model can only be used to take a bird's eye view rather than an internal view of the garden.

In order to display the design of traditional Chinese Garden realistically and easily, the CAD Laboratory, Instifute of Computing Technology, Academic Sinica, has used GEMS to design it and show it on the screen. The traditional Chinese Garden consists of architecture, bridge, pavilion, porch, stone, rockery, tree, bamboo and etc. Now, only some architectures with chinese style have been designed based on a 3D basic parts graphics database.

References

1. Hao S, Liu B, Niyama E, Huang Z, Sun J (1990)
   "Development of 3D Numerical Simulation System-- FTSolver" (to be published)
2. Johnson RH (1988)
   "Solid Modeling Tutorial Notes", SIGGRAPH 88 Course notes, SM88-1
3. Li X, Sun J, Tang Z (1990)
   "An Approach to Improve the Reliability of Boolean Operation on a Pair of Polyhedra"
   Proceedings of Eurographics'90: pp225--236, Montrex, Swizerland. Sept. 1990
4. Requicha AAG, Voelcker HB (1983)
   "Solid Modeling: Current Status and Research Directions", IEEE CG&A, Vol.3, No.7, pp25--37
5. Sun J, Gu K, Guo Y, Tang Z (1989)
   "Technical Summaries of GEMS", Journal of Computer Science & Technology,
   Vol.4, No.4: PP.374-382
6. Tilove RB (1980)
   "Set Membership Classification: A Unified Approach to Geometric
   Intersection Problems", IEEE Trans on Computers, Vol. C-29, N0.10: pp874--883

Department of Computer Science and Technology, Tsinghua University, Beijing, 100084 China

Chapter 4

Solid Modeling

Hybrid Representation of Feature-Based Models

B. Falcidieno, F. Giannini, C. Porzia, and M. Spagnuolo

ABSTRACT

A double description of a feature-based model is proposed which should be equally efficient both for design with feature systems and automatic recognition of instances of standard or user defined features. This description consists of a primary representation in terms of generic form features (*neutral description*) and a set of viewpoint dependent feature-based representations (*secondary descriptions*) which are created by transformations that are viewpoint specific and apply to the neutral object description.

KEYWORDS: Feature-based Modeling, Geometric Modeling, Topological Modeling, CAD/CAM.

1. INTRODUCTION

The geometry representation requirements to support the automation of design, analysis and manufacturing processes has given rise to the development of Geometric Modeling theory and techniques in research and industry for over twenty years.

After the progress of representation methods, the main characteristics of a product model are clearly identified. It is important to have a simple description of the product and at the same time to distinguish between information on design and data generated during the course of analysis. The final model should include a shape description for each component of the object, and representation should conform as close as possible to the designer's mental model of the object. The model should store a description of the assembly structure of a product, including references to constitute sub-assemblies and components, including dimensions, datums, and tolerances. It is necessary to insert product attributes, constraints and relationships in the model plus information about surface finish to have a more complete description of the product.

Although the product model corresponds to the result of the designer's efforts, it does not represent a complete description of the product in all its possible states, but rather a complex set of instructions to work with in the application process.

The early objective of modeler developers was the representation of the shape of an object accurately and reliably as a computer understandable information. Several different representation schemes have been employed, ranging from the early use of curves and surfaces to the more recent volumetric representations.

The two most commonly used representations for solid models are the volume based form model (Constructive Solid Geometry) and the boundary based form model (Boundary representation). A boundary model is a low level representation in terms of the individual surfaces, curves and points defining the boundary of an enclosed volume and the adjacencies (topology) of the geometric entities (Mantyla 1988).

In CSG modelers, an object is described as a binary tree whose leaf nodes are the primitive volumes used to define the object, and whose interior nodes are the boolean operators used for combining these volumes in order to obtain the final shape (Requicha 1980).

On the basis of such traditional models, several CAD systems were developed and widely used in industry. However, their use up until now has been limited to drafting purposes since, while functionality is a prime concern of designers, present CAD systems do not support adequate means for dealing with functionality.

Furthermore, in detailing the object geometry in terms of low level entities, the overall meaning of the object is hidden. Geometric models only represent the final shape of the product and, the meaning of the shape, which may represent the functionality in the application context, is not maintained in the model. Moreover, a description of the nominal geometry is not sufficient in many application contexts, and tolerances and other constraints must be represented.

In order to develop more intelligent design systems and define a link between design and application, it is necessary to achieve a model able to capture and use the design objectives related to function and manufacturability. For this reason, at present, considerable attention is being focused on the potential of features that are seen as an effective mean to provide a more abstract product model than geometry alone.

Feature is a concept which can be defined in terms of generic shape and engineering semantics. A feature is a physical constituent of a part which synthesized a particular functional meaning in some parts of the productive process. Therefore, feature is a concept which relates form and function, even if a mathematical rigourous definition is still missing. For example, Dixon and Libardi (1990) assert that "A *feature is any named entity with attributes of both form and function*", while our definition is "A *feature is a group of geometric and topological entities which have a functional meaning in a given context*" (Falcidieno, Giannini 1989).

One important aspect of form feature is that they provide a median level of information in the model between the very high level (volumetric primitives) and very low level (individual topological entities). This intermediate level appears to be precisely the level at which information is required by automated application programs.

In this sense, form features may therefore hold the key to the integration of geometric modeling systems and application programs.

The aim of this paper is to explore the appropriate representation schemes to make this information useful in a CAD system.

First of all, since every application views the same object in a different way and requires a different representation, a general purpose feature-based model must be very flexible and suitable for different purposes, such as design, manufacturing and inspection.

A second important issue to be solved is the geometric representation for a feature-based model. It should support direct access to evaluated entities for locating features and assigning tolerances and attributes, and at the same time it should provide a high level description of the object, for example as a hierarchy of feature volumes such as CSG representation.

The advantages and disadvantages of using CSG and B-rep models in feature-based models are somewhat complementary. The CSG model is more useful for operations such as storage, global editing and tolerance processing, whereas the B-rep model has more flexibility for processing, local editing, tolerance storage and assembly modeling.

Several researches have led to dual or hybrid representations for grouping the advantages of the two pure representations. A dual representation solid modeler (that is, a special case of a multiple representation system) maintains the two models CSG and B-rep of a solid object and should ensure consistency and equivalence between the two models. A hybrid solid model is characterized by a hybrid data structure in which a main representation, named *master representation*, is chosen. This reference model is generally the hierarchical volumetric model which maintains the boundary representation at different design levels (Gossard 1988, Wilson 1988, Falcidieno Giannini 1990).

In order to define a feature representation suitable for a general purpose modeler, other requirements should be satisfied. For example, it should be possible to represent and manipulate additional data that do not appear in a resultant shape, such as datum reference frames or construction entities like centre lines or interior faces. Occasionally, a non-manifold intermediate shape may occur even though the final result is manifold, for example while performing boolean operations. Cellular objects should be represented by maintaining their internal structure and not being described as conventional manifold objects.

Thus, the range of representable objects should be enlarged and, in order to cover the complete design spectrum efficiently, a representational scheme able to handle wireframe, surface and solid entities in a unified manner is required. These issues gave rise to researches in the field of non-manifold topology first developed by Weiler (1986). Thus, since in a non-manifold data structure objects can be manipulated as wireframes, surfaces or solids in the same architecture, a non-manifold model can be seen as a more general hybrid representation.

This paper describes a new geometric modeling scheme which may form a basis for the implementation of a next generation feature-based modeling system.
Based on the idea that, while feature meaning is strictly dependent on the context, the shape is more general, we propose a double description of a feature-based model: a primary representation in terms of generic form features, and a set of viewpoint dependent feature-based representations which are created by transformations that are viewpoint specific and that apply to the neutral object description. The proposed representation falls in the category of hybrid models with non-manifold extensions.

2. THE SYSTEM ARCHITECTURE

Two approaches have been considered by researchers in order to obtain a feature-based representation: *design with features* and *feature extraction*.
The first approach, sometimes called implicit or procedural definition, is primarily suited for a top-down design approach due to the ability of features to represent high level abstractions such as functionality and design purpose. The main disadvantage of this method is that it produces context dependent models that cannot be shared between different functional viewpoints.

The second approach, also called explicit or enumerative definition, is more suited for a bottom-up approach in which design information is associated with primitive components of a solid model of the object, such as faces and edges. Feature recognition can be adapted to different application contexts, though it has not yet been proven to work for all kinds of features.
For reason of flexibility and convenience, a complete feature-based system should support a combination of the two approaches in an integrated system.

Figure 1 shows the architecture of the proposed feature-based modeling system.
In this architecture both approaches, design with features and feature recognition, are considered.
The user interacts with the system in three ways. The Feature Definition Interface is a powerful and convenient utility that allows the system to construct feature descriptions from examples (i.e. feature instances on an existing geometric model). In this way, the user creates a consistent library of features that can be used both in design with features and in feature recognition approach.

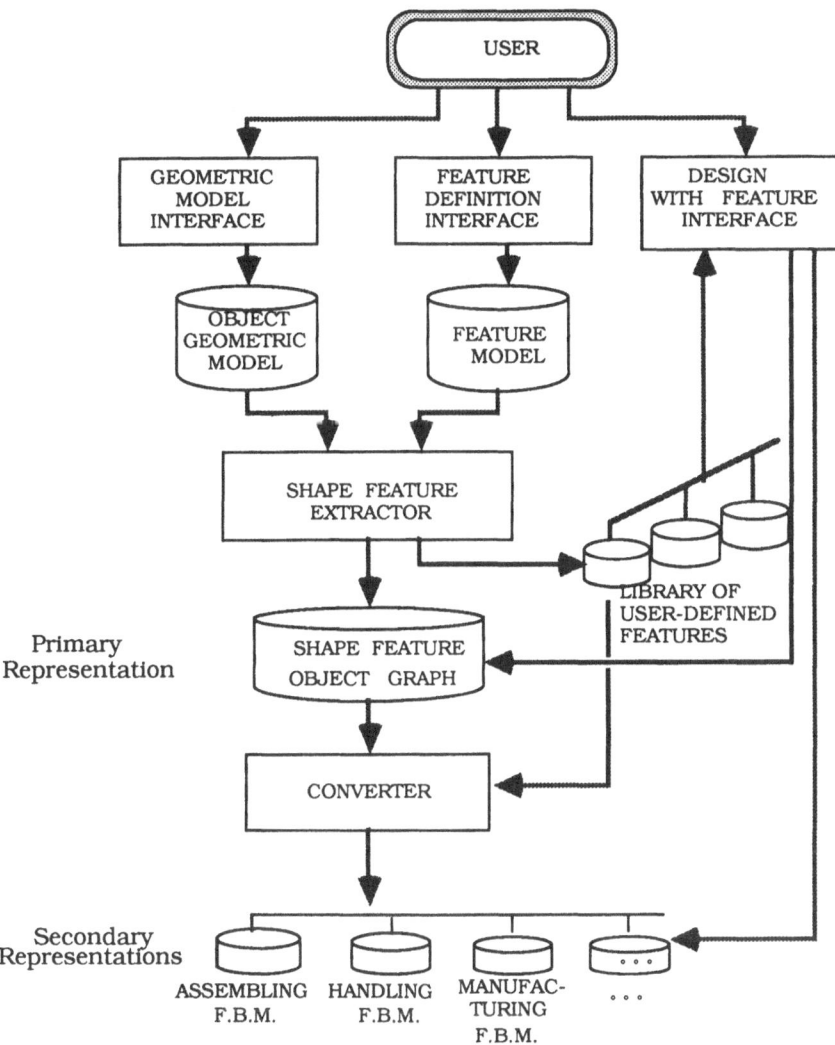

Fig. 1: The system architecture

In the Geometric Model Interface the user defines a traditional boundary model of the object, which is the input for the Shape Feature Extractor module. The neutral model is created by the recognition process and then converted into a specific viewpoint representation using the system library of features created by the user.

If we consider that the number of application contexts (manufacturing, handling, assembling, analysis control, etc.) is multiplied by the fact that different engineering organizations define their own classes of features, this neutral form technique has a clear advantage. This stratagem requires N converters to be written for all possible transfer between N different contexts, as opposed to N(N-1) specialized translators when all possible transformations between the N different application dependent models are performed directly without the use of a neutral format.

The Design with Features Interface allows the user to directly create a feature-based model for a given context. In this case the designer has the library of feature descriptions created with the Feature Definition Interface available.

In order to make this step consistent with the recognition approach the result of a design with feature interaction is a double description: a SFOG representation of the object created and the specific feature-based model.

3. THE PRIMARY REPRESENTATION

In our system, the primary description of a feature-based model is constructed on top of the object feature volumes which are organized in a hierarchical graph.

Graph representations are useful for feature organization as they make the topological and geometric relationships between features explicit. Moreover, some applications may need to have information regarding the surrounding volumes, and a knowledge of feature neighbours may be useful in a design with feature approach for handling features that share one or more common topological entities (faces, edges, vertices).

Our feature graph, called *Shape Feature Object Graph* (SFOG) is a hybrid model (Boundary/Volumetric) that can be considered a neutral format description of a feature-based model, since it is form feature oriented even though independent from a specific application context.

The Shape Feature Object Graph representation consists of a graph where the root nodes correspond to the volumes of the main shape of the object, while the other nodes correspond to the exact volumes of the features as they occur in the part model. Each node in this hierarchical model is described by an evaluated boundary representation. The adopted boundary model is called *Face Adjacency Hypergraph* (FAH) (Falcidieno, Giannini 1989) and is a face based graph model in which the nodes describe the object faces, whereas the arcs and hyperarcs represent the relationships between faces induced by the set of edges and vertices of the object. This reflects the intrinsic hierarchy in the geometric data, in which surfaces are considered as primary defining entities, and curves and points are derived.

Thus, the SFOG graph can be classified as a hybrid boundary-based solid model.

The nodes of the graph corresponding to shape feature volumes are characterized by their type: external or protrusion (P-features) and internal or depression (D-feature).

Links between nodes correspond to the geometric adjacencies between shape feature components.

Any arc joining two nodes expresses a parent-child relationship and is identified by a set of faces which belong to both components. These faces are called *connection faces* in the parent component and *dummy faces* in the child component. In the object, connection faces correspond to those faces to which a feature is attached, while dummy faces represent the closure faces added to the feature.

An attribute is associated to each arc depending on the type of topological entities defining the closure faces (existing, new):

1) *type df:* dummy faces bounded by existing edges and vertices;
2) *type dfe:* dummy faces with new edges in the boundary definition;
3) *type dfev:* dummy faces with new edges and vertices in the boundary definition;
4) *type dfev*:* the same as dfev with the difference that new vertices lie   on existing faces.

In Fig.2 some examples of the different relationship types are shown.

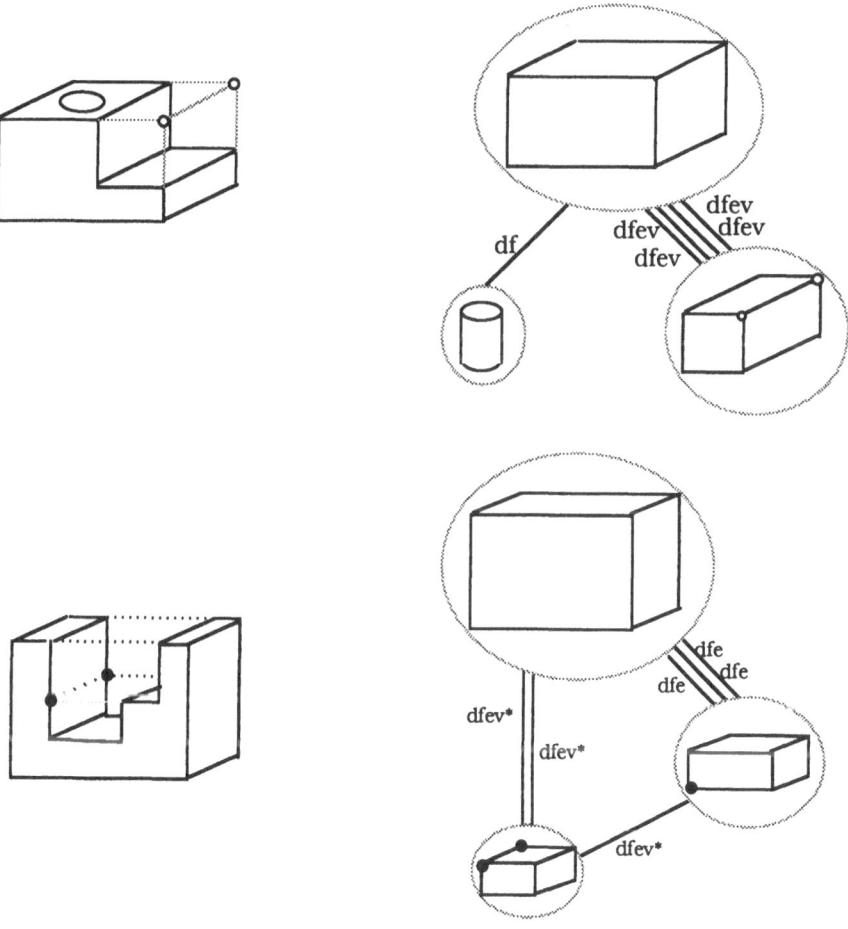

Fig. 2   Examples of attributed relationships between SFOG components.

In formal terms, if SF is the set of shape features of an object S, the Shape Feature Object Graph can be defined as a quadruple $g^* = (N,A,T,D)$, such that:

i) for every shape feature sf in SF, a unique node in N corresponding to it exists, labeled sf;

ii) for every pair of shape features sf_i and sf_k, such that a set of dummy faces $fd_j, j = 1....n$ exists, belonging to sf_i and attached to the connection faces in sf_k, a set of arcs in A labeled fd_j $j = 1....n$, exists, joining the two nodes sf_i and sf_k;

iii) an attribute t in T = { *Main Shape, D-feature, P-feature* } is associated to each node in N;

iv) an attribute d in D = { df, dfe, $dfev$, $dfev^*$ } is associated to each arc in A.

The SFOG primary description can be formed automatically by the system or directly defined in a design with features approach.

The first approach, which we have principally developed, is organized as a shape feature recognizer and extractor which analyses the CAD model of the part and identifies features by considering only their geometric and topological aspects. The feature recognizer works on the FAH representation of a solid object, while the feature extractor separates recognized form features from the main shape of the object, representing them as FAH components. The extracted features are arranged into a hierarchical feature graph which corresponds to the SFOG representation (Falcidieno, Giannini 1990).

In the design with feature approach, a set of feature libraries is given to the user containing a procedural description of standard features. The user can choose the desired features, specifying their dimensions, location and tolerance constraints. Boundary representations of the feature volumes are automatically produced, for example as FAH models. The way these features are combined with the main object shape defines the hierarchical relationships between the components, which are then stored in the SFOG model.

Tolerance constraints can be seen as relationships between object faces belonging either to the main shape or to the boundary of some features. Thus, tolerance constraints may be handled using a relational model defined as a structure, transverse to the SFOG model, which may connect different components (Falcidieno, Fossati 1989).

Such a solution is suitable for both directly linking tolerances to the boundary entities and for having direct access to these constraints from volumetric components in the analysis processes.

The same information regarding tolerances can be inherited by the SFOG model during the feature extraction, if it is already present in the input CAD model.

To enhance the SFOG neutral description, special structures called *wires* are associated to each component. These are used to represent the profile that a shape feature identifies in the parent component connection faces.

Wires consist of a sequence of existing edges and vertices. They can be: *closed,* as in the case of a feature attached to its parent component by an inner loop (see Fig. 3a), or *open* as in the L-shaped depression of Fig. 3.b, formed by one *connected* sequence of edges (Fig. 3.a, 3.b) or by a set of *disconnected* sequences (Fig. 3.c).

Moreover, another structure called *faceset* can be associated to the SFOG. A faceset is a collection of faces having geometrical relationships, such as faces lying on the same surface or parallel faces.

Both wires and facesets are explicitly represented in the SFOG structure to make the conversion of the SFOG into a context dependent feature-based model easier, even if the same information is implicitly stored as non dummy edges in the dummy faces relating to a connection face for the wires and in the boundary object description for facesets.

Thus, the SFOG representation can be regarded as a hybrid CSG/Boundary model with some non-manifold extensions (*wires, facesets*) and the introduction of additional data not present in the object shape (*dummy entities*).

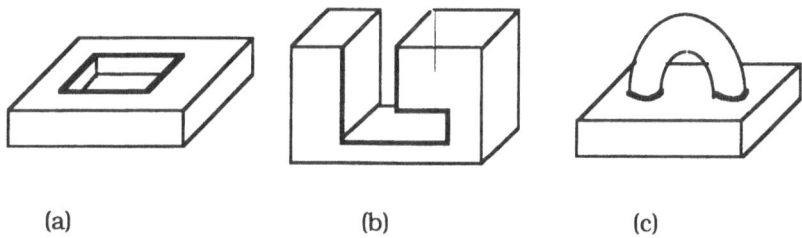

(a)   (b)   (c)

Fig. 3 Examples of wires.

4. THE SECONDARY REPRESENTATIONS

The Shape Feature Object Graph representation is created by taking into account geometric and topological arrangements of faces, edges and vertices, and is independent from the application context. To convert this representation into a context dependent feature-based model it is necessary to interpret the shape feature information present in the SFOG structure according to user defined rules.

Feature used in engineering applications may not in general correspond to single volumes in the SFOG representation. Thus, in our system, features are classified as *simple* or *compound* : simple if they correspond to a unique component in the hierarchical representation, and compound if they are represented by a set of components.

It is important to capture the relationships between features in a compound definition. There appears to be at least two possible types of relationships in compound features. One is where the compound feature geometry is contiguous, such as in a multidiameter-hole, and the other is where the compound feature geometry is disjoint, such as in a hole pattern. In this case, there is an implicit geometric relationship between feature components or there is no geometric relationship at all.

Therefore, there are three possible situations with regard to relationships in compound features:

    1) an explicit geometric relationship;

    2) an implicit geometric relationship;

    3) no geometric relationship.

An example of the type 1 feature (called *compound set features*) is the T-slot feature (Fig. 5.a) where the three components describing it, in our representation, are face adjacent. Note that a compound set feature is bounded by a unique set of connected faces identifying a shell.

Type 2 features include features which have implicit geometric relationships in the hierarchical representation. An example is the set of holes in a circular pattern depicted in Fig. 4.a. In this case, each hole is represented by a single component connected to the same pair of faces of the parent component. These features are called *compound pattern features* as in general the geometric relationship can be parametrized such as with the gear teeth.

A type 3 relationship can correspond to any set of features which are related only by their functionality in the application context. These compound features are labeled *compound group features*. The case of two holes depicted in Fig. 4.b is an example of a compound group feature, since the two holes are attached to different pairs of faces in the parent components and define a single "passage" feature.

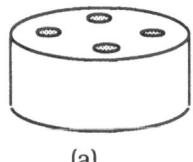 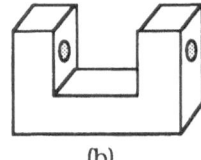

        (a)   (b)

Fig. 4: A circular-patterned-hole-feature (a) and a passage-feature (b)

The converter is implemented as a recursive process which recognizes features according to a set of rules constituting the data base characterizing the application context.

The user defines the features of his application context using the Geometric Modeling Interface, and the system automatically derives the rules describing the functional features in terms of the relationships stored in the SFOG representation.

Then, the converter analyses the SFOG representation of the object in order to identify sub-components complying with the rules derived from the user-defined features.

Simple features are recognized by checking the type (P or D) of the volumes and the attributes which characterize the relationships between their SFOG components and the parent components.

Compound features, which are defined by adjacent SFOG components, are recognized by matching pattern feature graphs with the SFOG representation sub-graphs.

Once the functional feature recognizer has identified the components forming compound features, the conversion of the SFOG into a context dependent feature-based model is performed.

The components recognized as belonging to compound features are grouped in structures called *macro-components*. These define a viewpoint dependent description of the SFOG model without altering its hierarchical organization. However, for compound set features, the possibility of substituting the components representing the feature with a unique boundary structure by applying a refinement operation to the sub-graph nodes, is offered to the user.

It is also possible to apply the same refinement operation to all those components not belonging to any recognized compound feature, thus merging all such nodes into the main shape.

For the second and third classes of compound features the system does not apply a refinement transformation to the components constituting the recognized features, since their union does not form a connected volume.

In Fig. 5.c the resulting feature-based model for a T-slot feature representation is shown. The functional feature recognizer has identified the three SFOG components forming this compound set feature (Fig. 5.b) and has applied a refinement transformation (Fig. 5.c).

In Fig. 6 another example is shown. The shape feature recognizer has produced the SFOG representation (Fig. 6.b) of the part (Fig. 6.a). The conversion algorithm has defined a feature-based model suitable for manufacturing (Fig. 6.c), handling (Fig. 6.d) and assembling (Fig. 6.e) by performing a refinement operation on the main shape.

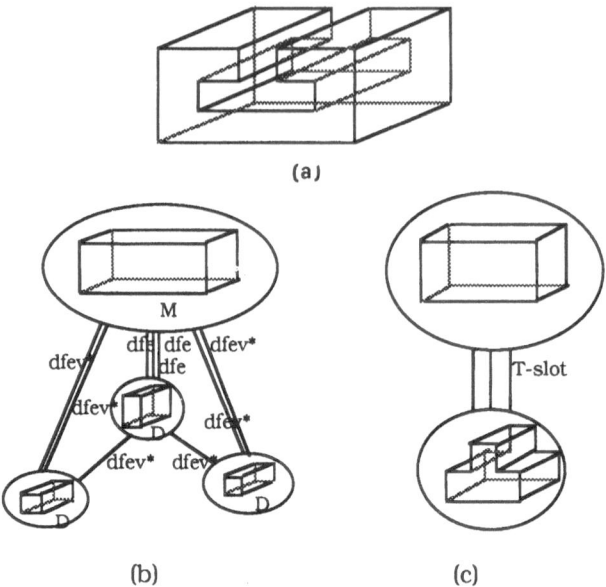

Fig. 5: A T-slot feature (a), its SFOG representation resulting from the Shape Feature
Recognition (b) and its re-arranged SFOG representation (c)

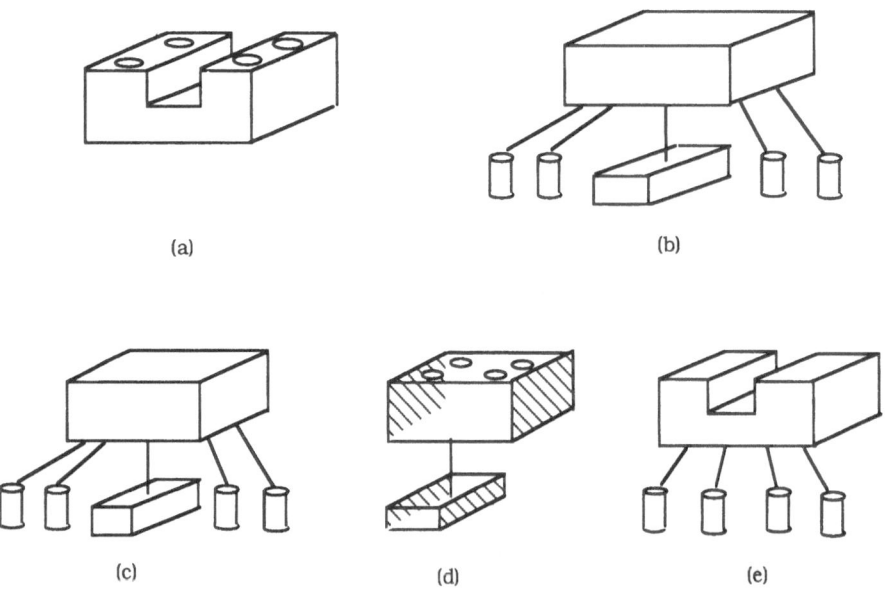

Fig. 6: The SFOG representation resulting from the shape feature recognition (b)
applied to (a) and its re-arranged SFOG representation in manufacturing (c),
handling (d) and assembling (e) contexts.

5. CONCLUDING REMARKS

The hybrid representation described in this paper is the kernel model of an integrated feature-based system designed for different application contexts: manufacturing, handling and assembling (Falcidieno Giannini 1990, Cugini Falcidieno Mussio 1988).

In Fig. 7, an example of the Shape Feature Extractor is shown. An object with two pockets, a T-slot, three blind holes and a protrusion is depicted in the top left window. In the top right window the picture of the last recognized feature, while the SFOG graph and the volumes corresponding to its nodes are shown in the bottom window.

In Fig. 8 and 9 the conversion into a context dependent feature-based model is depicted (De Martino Falcidieno 1990). In Fig. 8 a T-slot feature with its SFOG representation is recognized in the object depicted in the right hand half of the screen. In Fig. 9 the result of the recognition operation with the introduction of the macro-component after the refinement step is shown.

6. ACKNOWLEDGEMENTS

This work has been partially supported by the Progetto Finalizzato Robotica, Sottoprogetto PRORA 2.2.2 and by the I.M.A.-C.N.R.-Italcad agreement.

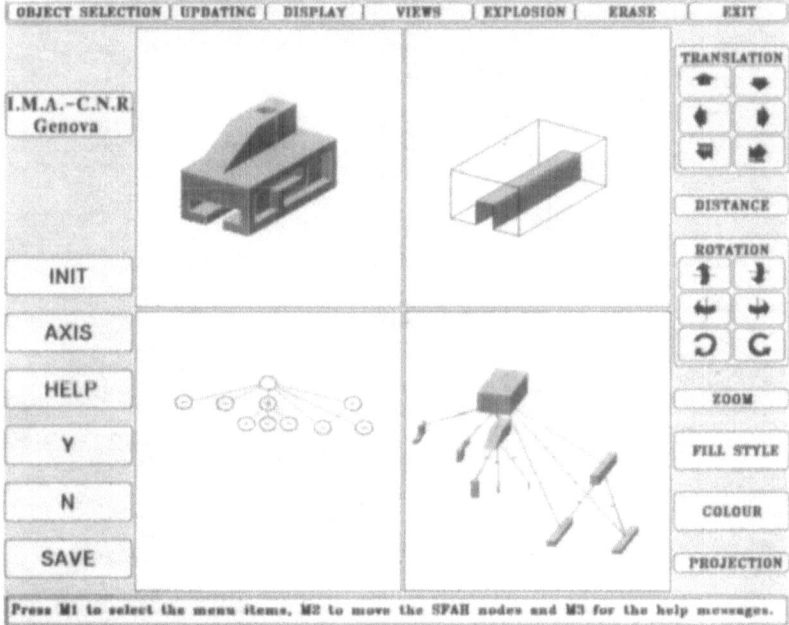

Fig. 7: Feature Recognition example with the SFOG representation of the object

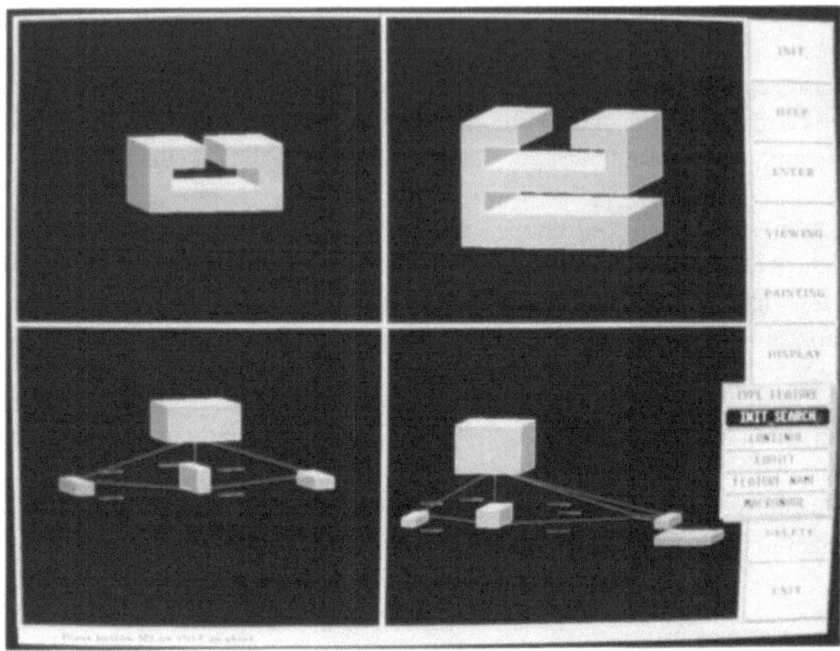

Fig. 8: Functional recognition of the T-slot feature in an object

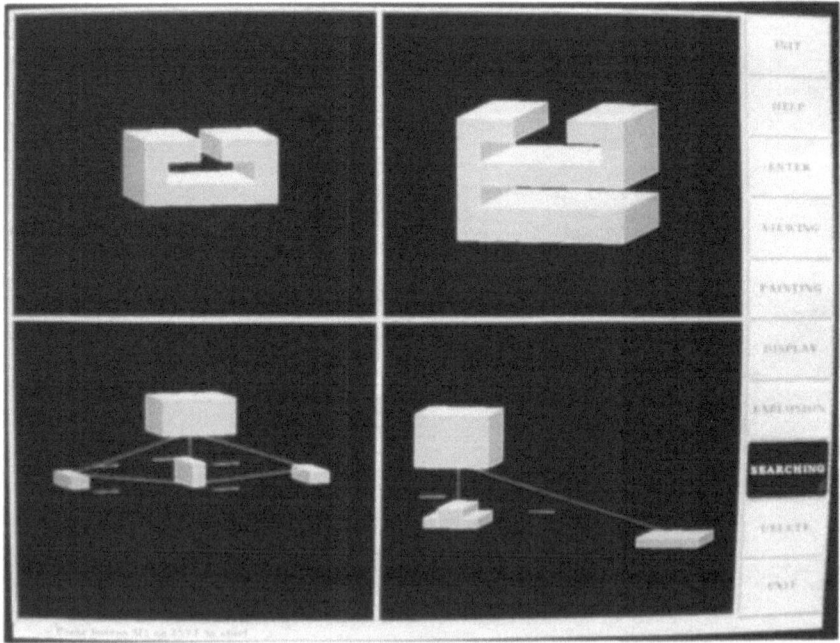

Fig. 9: The feature defined by the user is recognized in the object

Bibliography

Cugini U, Falcidieno B, Mussio P (1988) Exploiting Knowledge in a CAD/CAM architecture. In: Intelligent CAD II, North Holland, Amsterdam

De Martino T, Falcidieno B (1990) Extraction of User-defined Features from a Hybrid Geometric Model. Technical Report N° 16/90, Istituto per la Matematica Applicata del C.N.R., Genova

Dixon JR, Libardi EC (1990) Unresolved Research Issues in Development of Design with Features Systems. In: Geometric Modeling for Product Engineering, North Holland, IFIP 1990: 183-196

Falcidieno B, Fossati B (1989) Representing Tolerance Information in a Feature-based Solid Modeling. In: Eurographics 1989, Hamburg 1989, North Holland: 463-476

Falcidieno B, Giannini F (1989) Automatic Recognition and Representation of Shape-based Features in Geometric Modeling System. Computer Vision, Graphics and Image Processing 48 1989: 93-123

Falcidieno B, Giannini F (1990) A System for Extracting and Representing Feature Information Driven by the Application Context. In: Proceedings IEEE Int. Conf. on Robotics & Automation, Cincinnati, May, 3: 1672-1678

Gossard DC, Zuffante RP, Sakurai RK (1988) Representing Dimensions, Tolerances and Features in a MCAE Systems. IEEE Computer Graphics and Applications, 8,2, March: 51-59

Mantyla M (1988) An Introduction to Solid Modeling. Computer Science Press, Maryland

Requicha AAG (1980) Representations for Rigid Solids: Theory, Methods and Systems. ACM Computer Surveys 12 (4): 437-464

Weiler KJ (1986) Topological Structures for Geometric Modeling. PhD Thesis, Rensselear Polytechnic Institute, August

Wilson PR (1988) Multiple Representations of Solid Models. In: Geometric Modeling for Product Engineering, North Holland, IFIP: 99-113

Consiglio Nazionale delle Ricerche, Istituto per la Mathematica Applicata del C.N.A., 16132 Genoa, Italy

Boolean Operations on Solids Bounded by a Variety of Surfaces

T. Satoh, T. Takamura, H. Toriya[1], and H. Chiyokura[2]

Abstract

In the CAD/CAM/CAE field, it is important that solid modeling systems support and handle characteristics of many different types of surfaces. This paper describes a Boolean operations algorithm for such solid modeling systems. The algorithm works for solids with a wide range of surfaces. There are two main problems in Boolean operations on solids with various types of surface. The first problem is that the curves calculated by the intersection of two surfaces are given in a very complicated form, and therefore must be represented approximately. The algorithm avoids the accumulation of approximation errors by using the three-surface intersection calculation method. The second problem is the speed of intersection calculations and also the range of surfaces supported by the Boolean operation algorithm. The algorithm uses two intersection calculation methods depending on the type of surface. This means that Boolean operations can be applied to a wide range of surfaces, and also that the speed and reliability of the Boolean operations increase due to the selection of the most suitable algorithm.

Key words: Boolean operations, trimmed surface, marching method, geometric method

1   INTRODUCTION

Solid modeling systems are widely used and play an important role in the CAD/CAM/CAE field. In CAD/CAM/CAE, many types of surfaces are used. Quadric, Bézier, Coons, Gregory[5,9], and NURBS (non-uniform rational B-spline)[21] surfaces are examples. These surfaces have their own characteristics, and solid modeling systems need to manipulate those characteristics to model shapes flexibly. Moreover, since solid modeling systems are the nucleus of CAD/CAM/CAE systems, it is important that they be able to handle various types of surface data from other systems.

There are two approaches to support various surfaces in a solid modeling system[12]. In one approach, the solid modeling system supports a surface that can represent various surfaces in one form. NURBS is the most popular example[14,20]. It is known that the NURBS surface can represent many types of surface exactly, for example, quadric surfaces. However, some surfaces are difficult to represent in NURBS exactly[19]. Another problem is that it is impossible to use the characteristics of surfaces other than NURBS. The other approach is the parametric evaluator approach[11]. A surface is interpreted as a black box that only returns coordinates and the normal vector of any given point on the surface. Since this approach never exploits the surface information, efficiency is a problem. The surface characteristics also cannot be utilized with this approach.

We have been developing the solid modeling system DESIGNBASE[4], which supports various types of surface using a general surface data structure. The general surface is represented by a data structure which contains plane, quadric surfaces and general parametric surfaces. When we need to add a new surface type to the solid modeling system, it is easy to add it to the data structure. The advantage, as compared to the parametric evaluator approach, is that an application program can distinguish the surface type. If there is a suitable algorithm for a surface, that algorithm can be utilized. However, if an application program is not concerned with the surface type, the general surface can be regarded as a black box as in the parametric evaluator approach.

To implement Boolean operations on solids with general surfaces, there are two main problems that have to be solved. The first is the representation and manipulation of the intersection curves. In general, intersection curves between two general surfaces are given in a very complicated form and since the representation and manipulation is not very practical, the curves must be represented approximately. The Boolean operations algorithm finds exact intersection points from approximately represented intersection edges using a three-surface intersection calculation method. The second problem is the speed of intersection calculations and also the range of surfaces supported by the Boolean operation algorithm. In the Boolean operations, two intersection calculation methods, a marching method[1] and a geometric method[13,18], are used depending on the type of surface. As a marching method is used, intersection calculations can be applied to many types of surface. A geometric method can be only applied to plane and quadric surfaces, but since these surfaces are more widely used in geometric modeling, intersections of solids can be calculated more quickly than by using just the marching method. By using both approaches, the Boolean operations are reliable, fast and can be applied to solids with various types of surface.

In this paper, the Boolean operations algorithm is described as follows:

- Section 2: Problems of Boolean operations on solids with free-form surfaces.

- Section 3: A general surface structure and an overview of the Boolean operations algorithm.

- Section 4: Manipulation of intersection curves in the algorithm and the three-surface intersection calculation method.

- Section 5: Surface-surface intersection calculations.

- Section 6: Some examples of modeled objects using the Boolean operations.

- Section 7: Conclusion.

2 BACKGROUND

Some researchers have shown the complete Boolean operations algorithm for polyhedral solids [10,22], and in some practical solid modeling systems, Boolean operations for polyhedral solids have been implemented. However, there are still problems with Boolean operations for solids with free-form surfaces. There are two main reasons why Boolean operations on solids with free-form surfaces are difficult. The first reason is that intersection curves between free-form surfaces are very complicated, and the second one is that it is difficult to calculate the intersections between free-form surfaces accurately, stably and quickly to accomplish the practical use of Boolean operations.

2.1 Intersection Curves

The Boolean operations algorithm first needs to calculate the intersections between two solids, and then the intersection curves must be generated as edges of the solids. However, if the intersection curves between free-form surfaces are calculated exactly, they are represented in a very complicated curve form. Consider the example of the intersection between two bicubic parametric surfaces. The bicubic parametric surface is converted to an implicit surface of degree 18[16]. Intersection curves between two bicubic surfaces are given by the solution of two 18th degree simultaneous equations. Accordingly, the intersection curves are degree $324(= 18 \times 18)$. A very large amount of computer memory is needed just to store these high degree equations. Furthermore, other application programs cannot use these high degree curves directly. Consequently, representation of exact intersection curves is not very practical. The intersection curves must be represented approximately. This means that the intersection curves do not lie on the surfaces exactly. Howerer, if Boolean operations are applied several times to the solids with intersection curves containing approximation error, intersections may not be calculated accurately because of the accumulated errors.

Since intersection curves define the new boundary of the surface, a method that generates new surfaces using the new boundary curves is proposed[15,23]. This method is called repatching. Using the repatching method, intersection curves are always on the surfaces. However, the problem with this method is that the shapes of surfaces are changed, because the surfaces generated by the method are approximations of the original surface. This means that repetition of Boolean operations greatly changes the shape of surfaces. And if very complicated boundary curves are generated, it may be impossible to interpolate the new surfaces. In this case, the surface is lost.

Another approach to the problem of intersection curves is to represent an intersecting surface by a trimmed surface, which consists of two kinds of data: geometrical data and boundary curve data. An intersection curve is represented by the boundary curve data of the trimmed surface.

To represent the intersection curve, the following two methods are available:

1. As a curve in the parametric space of a surface

2. As a curve in the 3D Euclidean space

If the intersection curve is defined in the parametric space, it always lies exactly on the surface. In this method, however, there are two demerits. One is that the intersection curve is defined on each intersecting surface and they are slightly different because each intersection curve is approximately calculated and they are not exactly coincident. The other demerit is that this representation method can only apply to the parametric surface, so that much difficulty remains for the system that can operate a variety of surfaces.

If the 3D Euclidean space is used to represent the curve, dual representation of intersection curves is avoided and this representation method can apply to non-parametric surfaces. However, the curve does not necessarily lie on the surface exactly.

Problems remain to be solved in both of the above methods because the precise intersection curves are not always obtained.

2.2 Intersection Calculations Between Surfaces

The second problem with Boolean operations on solids with free-form surfaces is the difficulty of the intersection calculations between two surfaces. There has been much research on the intersection calculation problem. The calculation methods can be classified as follows:

1. Recursive subdivision[2]

2. Marching[1]

3. Algebraic[16]

4. Geometric[13]

A recursive subdivision method divides surfaces until small parts of the surface are regarded as planes. It then calculates the intersection between them. This method can find all branches of intersection curves, but it is necessary that the surfaces be divided recursively. If a surface with an unknown subdivision algorithm is given, this method cannot be applied. Efficient execution is difficult for a surface whose subdivision cost is high. Another problem is that this method may not find intersections at points that just touch[11].

A marching method finds an intersection point of two surfaces at first, then traces the intersection curves from the point. This method can be applied to any type of surface that can calculate coordinates and normal vector from any parametric point on the surface. The marching method requires that all starting points be given for the tracing. If some starting points are not found, some intersection curves cannot be found. However, algorithms to find all starting points exist[3,11,17]. Computational efficiency is better than by the recursive subdivision method[7].

By an algebraic method, intersection curves are obtained by solving the simultaneous equations of two surfaces' implicit formula. This method can get exact intersection curves, but the calculation is not efficient because high degree equations must be solved. In particular for parametric surfaces, their implicit forms are usually given by high degree equations, and it is difficult to solve them efficiently and stably.

A geometric method finds the intersection curves by classifying the intersection of two surfaces geometrically. This method can only be applied to surfaces whose characteristics are well-known, like plane or quadric surfaces. For free-form surfaces, it cannot be applied. However, an advantage of this method is that it can calculate intersections quickly and precisely.

3 AN OVERVIEW OF THE BOOLEAN OPERATIONS

3.1 General Surface Structure

A general surface is represented by the data structure shown in Figure 1(a). Each element of the structure points to the real structure of each surface. The degree of each parametric surface is $n \times m$ and high degree surfaces can be represented easily. Figure 1(b) is the Bézier surface data structure, which is one of the surfaces contained in the general surface structure.

Using this general surface data structure, many types of surface can be supported in a solid modeling system. Moreover, since application programs can check the type of a surface, if there is an algorithm to manipulate a particular surface efficiently, that algorithm can be added to the solid modeling system.

For example, Figure 2 shows the calculation of the normal vector from a point on a surface. For plane, sphere, cylinder, and cone surfaces, by using their geometric features, the normal vector can be calculated easily, fast and accurately. For parametric surfaces which are represented by two parameters u and v, the normal vector is calculated by the outer product of two tangent vectors in the u and v direction at the given point.

```
struct general_surface {
    int     type;                     /* surface type */
    union   surface_data   *sf;  /* surface data */
    struct  boundary_curve *bd;  /* boundary curve data */
};

union surface_data {
    struct Plane      pl;   /* plane */
    struct Sphere     sp;   /* sphere */
    struct Cylinder   cy;   /* cylinder */
    struct Cone       co;   /* cone */
    struct Bezier     bp;   /* Bezier */
    struct RBezier    rbp;  /* rational Bezier */
    struct Gregory    gp;   /* Gregory */
    struct RGregory   rgp;  /* rational Gregory */
    struct BSpline    bs;   /* B-Spline */
    struct RBSpline   rbs;  /* NURBS */
};
```

(a) Data Structure of General Surface

```
struct Bezier {
    int                  m, n;    /* degree of surface */
    struct coordinates  *ctlp;   /* control points */
};
```

(b) Data Structure of Bezier Surface

Figure 1: General Surface Structure

3.2   Approaches to the Problems

As mentioned in section 2, there are two main problems in Boolean operations.

For the intersection curve representation method, we use the trimmed surface approach, and define the boundary curves of the trimmed surface in 3D Euclidian space. Using the trimmed surface representation, surfaces are represented without any approximation error. To solve the problem that the boundary curves of a trimmed surface do not lie exactly on the surface, we propose the three-surface intersection calculation method. When a surface and a boundary curve which is represented approximately intersect, the intersection point is re-calculated by the three-surface intersection calculation method. This method is explained in section 4.

```
get_normal(sf, pnt, nrml)
    struct general_surface *sf;
    struct coordinates *pnt;
    struct vector *nrml;
{
    switch (sf->type) {
    case PLANE:
        get_plane_normal(sf, pnt, nrml);
        break;
    case SPHERE:
        get_sphere_normal(sf, pnt, nrml);
        break;
    case CYLINDER:
        get_cylinder_normal(sf, pnt, nrml);
        break;
    case CONE:
        get_cone_normal(sf, pnt, nrml);
        break;
    case BEZIER:
    case R_BEZIER:
    case GREGORY:
    case R_GREGORY:
    case BSPLINE:
    case RBSPLINE:
        get_parametric_normal(sf, pnt, nrml);
        break;
    default:
        /* type error */
    }
}
```

Figure 2: An Example of the Calculation of the Normal Vector From a Point

There are several methods to calculate the intersections between two surfaces. Each method has both merits and demerits. Therefore, we use two calculation methods: a marching method and a geometric method, depending on the type of the intersection surfaces. For parametric surfaces, the marching method is used; for plane and quadric surfaces, the geometric method is used. Boolean operations can be applied to a wide range of surfaces because of the marching method. Moreover, since plane and quadric surfaces are widely used in geometric modeling, the speed of Boolean operations is faster than by using the marching method alone.

3.3　An Overview of The Boolean Operations

The Boolean operations algorithm gets only the union of two solids. There are three Boolean operations: union, intersection, and subtraction. But by De Morgan's law, intersection and subtraction are realized using the union operation and the negative operation (operation reversing a solid). So it is sufficient that only the union operation be implemented.

There are the following six steps in the Boolean operations algorithm:

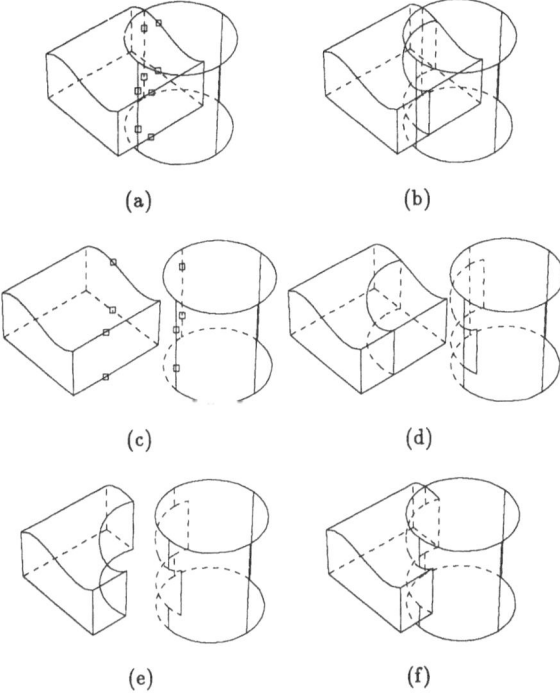

Figure 3: An Overview of The Boolean Operation Algorithm

1. Intersection calculations between edges and surfaces (Figure 3(a))

2. Intersection calculations between surfaces (Figure 3(b))

3. Generation of vertices at intersection points (Figure 3(c))

4. Generation of edges along the intersection curves (Figure 3(d))

5. Detection and removal of included parts of solids (Figure 3(e))

6. Joining two solids (Figure 3(f))

In step 1, all combinations of edges and surfaces of two solids are checked for intersections. If they intersect, the intersection points are calculated. An edge that is generated by the intersection of two surfaces often contains approximation error. Such an edge is called an approximation edge. If an approximation edge intersects with a surface, the intersection points are not accurate. The coordinates of each intersection point are refined by the three-surface intersection calculation method, described in section 4.

In step 2, all combinations of surfaces of two solids are checked for intersections, and intersection curves are calculated if any surfaces intersect. The marching method and the geometric method are used depending on the types of intersecting surfaces for the calculations. If the marching method is invoked, intersection points found in step 1 are used as the start points; if the geometric method is invoked, these intersection points are used as the end points of curves to be generated. If the curves are approximately represented, an approximation flag remains. Details of the surface-surface intersection algorithm are described in section 5.

In step 3, vertices are generated at the intersection points found in step 1, and in step 4 intersection edges are generated along the intersection curves obtained in step 2. In steps 3 and 4, the topological structure is generated in the solids. During the generation of each intersection edge, if the intersection curve that the edge is derived from is approximately represented, approximation flags are given to those edges.

When step 4 has been completed, intersection edges have been generated on each solid. Parts of a solid that penetrate the boundary of another solid are called included parts. In step 5, such included parts are detected and removed. As a result of removing the included parts, the two solids meet at their intersection edges. In step 6, the two solids are joined. Details of steps 5 and 6 are almost the same as in the method described by Toriya et al.[22].

4 TRIMMED SURFACE AND THREE-SURFACE INTERSECTION CALCULATIONS

In general, when the intersection of two free-form surfaces is calculated exactly, the form of the intersection curves is very complicated. If exact intersection curves are given, a lot of computer memory is needed just to store them. Therefore, the intersection curves between two surfaces should be represented approximately as mentioned in section 2.

We represent an intersection edge with approximation error and give an approximation flag to it. If an approximation edge intersects a surface, the intersection points are found with approximation error. For example, consider the Boolean operation shown in Figure 4. Solid A in Figure 4 has the approximation edge E. The edge E is generated by the intersection of two surfaces F1 and F2. However, E does not lie exactly on F1 and F2. If the Boolean operation shown in Figure 4 is carried out, the intersection point between the surface F3 and the edge E is on F3 but not on F1 and F2.

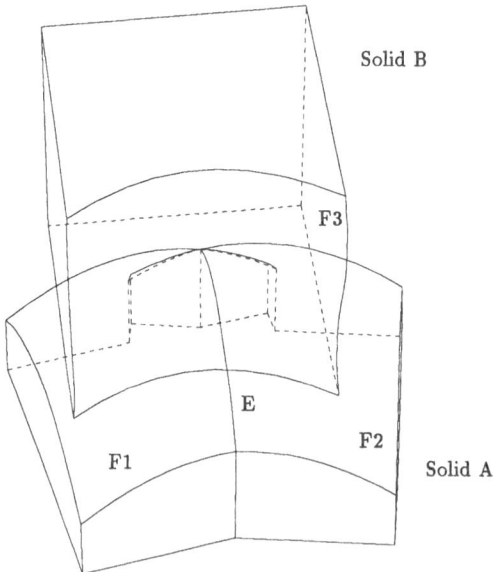

Figure 4: Three-Surface Intersection Calculations

A real intersection point between a surface and an approximated edge is the intersection point between the surface and both the two side surfaces of the edge. Therefore, in this example, the real intersection point between the edge E and the surface F3 is obtained by the calculation of the intersection point among the three surfaces F1, F2 and F3. This method is named the three-surface intersection method. Using this method, the real intersection point is always calculated by reference to both side surfaces of the intersection edge.

5 SURFACE-SURFACE INTERSECTION

5.1 Intersection Calculation Method

Since the Boolean operations are applied to solids containing many types of surfaces, so must the intersection calculation method. As mentioned in section 2, a method that can be applied to various surfaces is the marching method, and that is the method we use to calculate intersections between parametric surfaces.

Considering the modeling of mechanical parts, most of their surfaces are formed by plane and quadric surfaces. Because of that fact, we use the geometric method to calculate intersections between planes, between plane and quadric surfaces, and between quadric surfaces. Calculation by the geometric method is much faster than that by the marching method and it can obtain intersection curves more accurately.

The geometric method and the marching method are used depending on the combination of surfaces shown below:

Type	plane, quadric	parametric surfaces
plane, quadric	*geometric*	*marching*
parametric surfaces	*marching*	*marching*

5.2 Representation of Intersection Curves

Exact calculation of intersection curves between surfaces is difficult and time-consuming. Therefore, intersection curves are represented approximately. In our system, they must satisfy the following conditions:

- The distance between the intersection surface and the end points on the curve must be ε or less.

- The distance between the intersection surface and any other points on the curve must be δ or less.

ε is a constant and if the distance between two points is ε or less, they are considered to be the same point. δ is a constant that satisfies $\varepsilon < \delta$. In our implementation, ε is 10^{-6} and δ is 10^{-3}. δ means the allowance of approximation error.

If the distance between the intersecting surface and some points on the intersection curve is ε or less, the curve is accurate. If the distance between the surface and some points on the curve is over ε, the curve is an approximate curve. Since δ is defined as being much larger than ε, intersection calculation cost is reduced.

5.3 Intersection Calculations

The Boolean operations use two intersection calculation methods: the marching method and the geometric method.

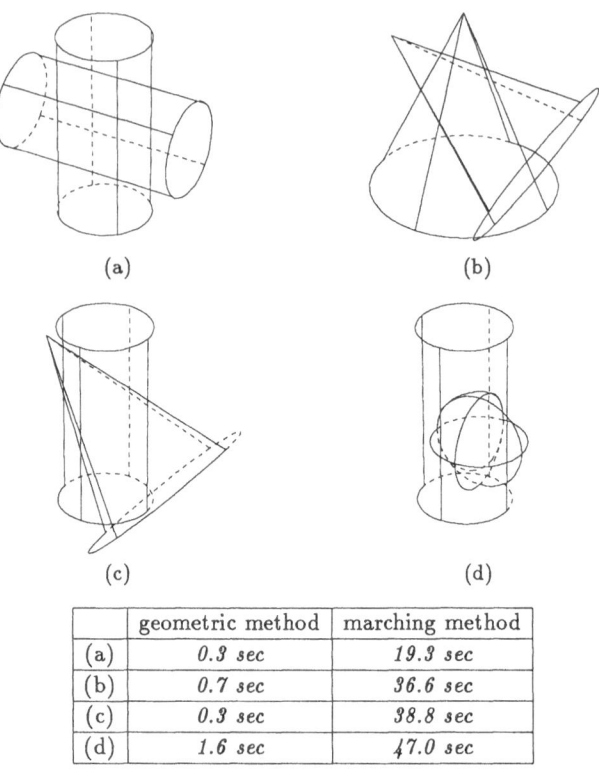

	geometric method	marching method
(a)	0.3 sec	19.3 sec
(b)	0.7 sec	36.6 sec
(c)	0.3 sec	38.8 sec
(d)	1.6 sec	47.0 sec

Calculation times (on a SPARC station 1)

Figure 5: Calculation times of Surface-Surface Intersections

The marching method calculates the intersection curves of two surfaces by tracing from the given start point that was calculated previously. In the Boolean operation algorithm, all intersection points between a surface and the boundary edges of a surface are calculated before the surface-surface intersection routine is invoked. Using these points, intersection curves are traced. If the two surfaces intersect, but not at any boundary, an interior intersecting point is calculated as the starting point.

The geometric method for quadric surfaces is discussed by Miller[13]. At first, intersection curves are found by classification of the position and the type of surface. Then, using the intersection points data between the surface and the boundary edges, unnecessary parts of the curves are trimmed[18].

The intersection between two quadric surfaces can also be calculated by the marching method. However, as the marching method is a Newton type algorithm, computation cost is high. We show some examples of improvement of speed by using the geometric method. Figure 5 shows examples of Boolean operations and the computation time by the geometric method and by the marching method. As this result shows, the geometric method improves the speed of Boolean operations greatly.

There is another merit in using the geometric method. By this method, the quality of intersection curves is better than by the marching method. For example, when two spheres intersect, the geometric method gives a circle, but the marching method gives only coordinates and tangent vectors at some points on the intersection curve. By the marching method, only an approximation circle is generated.

Since both methods have merits and demerits, the marching method and the geometric method are used depending on the types of surfaces. By using the marching method, the Boolean operations can support a wide range of surfaces and by using the geometric method, the speed of the Boolean operations increases.

6 Examples

The color plates show examples of solids generated using the Boolean operations. Color plate 1 shows a caterpillar tractor piston. It consists of many cylinder surfaces. Color plate 2 shows intersecting pipes. The curved parts of each pipe consist of Rational Boundary Gregory surfaces[6]. Color plate 3 shows an example of a solid designed for a bench mark test for CAM-I[8]. Color plate 4 shows a vacuum cleaner.

7 Conclusion

It is important that a solid modeling system supports many types of surfaces because each surface has its own characteristics. A user of a solid modeling system uses the characteristics to model various shapes. We have discussed an algorithm for Boolean operations on solids with general surfaces. Since Boolean operations can be applied to solids with various surfaces, the intersection curves can become very complicated. Because the algorithm uses the three-surface intersection calculation method, intersection points are always calculated accurately from intersection edges that contain approximation error. And since approximation representation of intersection curves is allowed, the calculation is done faster. Moreover in the algorithm, two intersection calculation methods are used depending on the type of surface. For parametric surfaces, the marching method is used; for plane and quadric surfaces, the geometric method is used. Consequently, intersection calculations can be applied to a wide range of surfaces, and since plane and quadric surfaces appear quite frequently in geometric modeling, the speed of Boolean operations increases. The algorithm has been implemented in DESIGNBASE.

8 ACKNOWLEDGEMENTS

We would like to thank Fumihiko Kimura, a professor of the University of Tokyo, for his valuable suggestions; Hideko S. Kunii, general manager of Ricoh's Software Research Center, for her support in our research; and Aidan O'Neill of Ricoh Co. and Hiromi Yaguchi of I.C.C.S. for their assistance with the text.

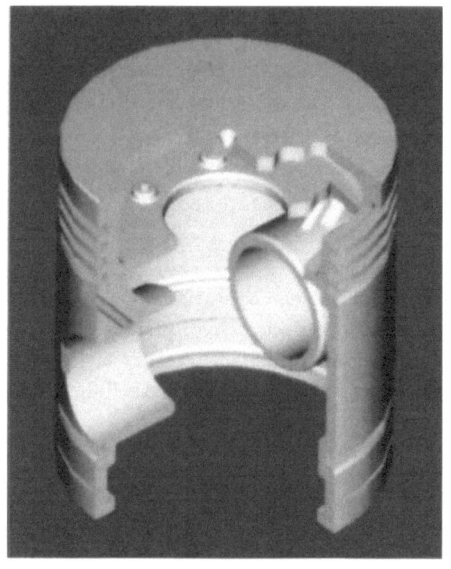

Color plate 1: A Caterpillar Tractor Piston

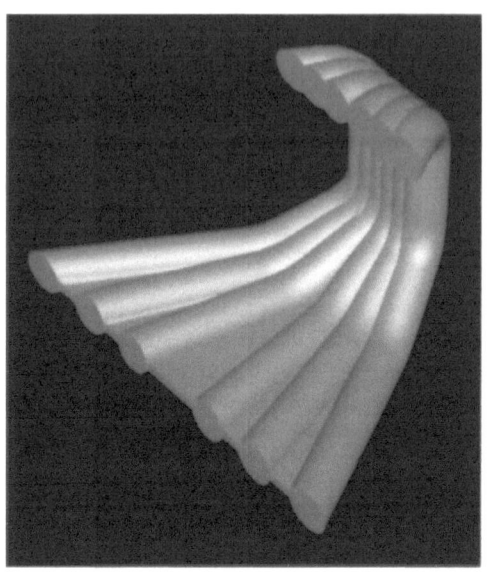

Color plate 2: Intersecting Pipes

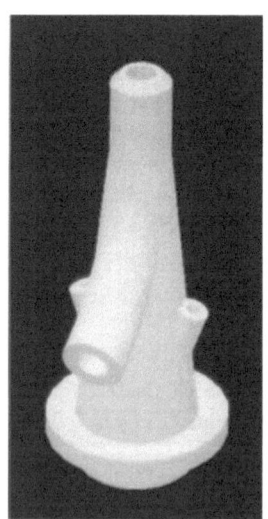

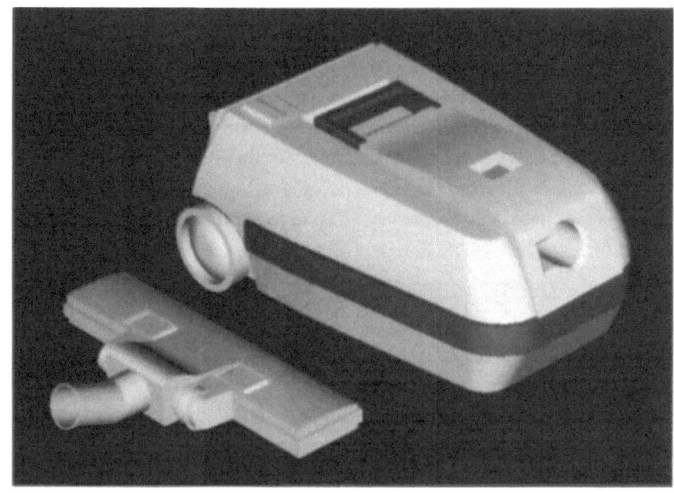

Color plate 4: A Vacuum Cleaner

Color plate 3:

A Benchmark Test for CAM-I

References

[1] R. E. Barnhill, G. Farin, M. Jordan, and B. R. Piper. Surface/surface intersection. *Computer Aided Geometric Design*, 4(1–3):3–16, 1987.

[2] W. E. Carlson. An algorithm and data structure for 3D object synthesis using surface patch intersection. *Computer Graphics*, 16(3), 1982.

[3] K. -P. Cheng. Using plane vector fields to obtain all the intersection curves of two general surfaces. In W. Strasser and H. -P. Seidel, editors, *Theory and Practice of Geometric Modeling*, Springer-Verlag, Berlin, 1989.

[4] H. Chiyokura. *Solid Modelling with DESIGNBASE*. Addison-Wesley, 1988.

[5] H. Chiyokura and F. Kimura. Design of solids with free-form surfaces. *Computer Graphics*, 17(3):289–298, 1983.

[6] H. Chiyokura, T. Takamura, K. Konno, and T. Harada. G^1 surface interpolation over irregular meshes with rational curves. In G. Farin, editor, *Fromtiers in Geometric Modeling*, SIAM, Philadelphia, 1990. to appear.

[7] T. Dokken, V. Skytt, and A. -M. Ytrehus. Recursive subdivision and iteration in intersections and related problems. In T. Lyche and L. L. Schumaker, editors, *Mathematical Methods in Computer Aided Geometric Design*, Academic Press, New York, 1989.

[8] I. D. Faux, editor. *Geometric Modeling: User Experience, System Development and Benchmark Tests*. CAM-I, 1984.

[9] J. A. Gregory. Smooth interpolation without twist constraints. In R. E. Barnhill and R. F. Riesenfeld, editors, *Computer Aided Geometric Design*, Academic Press, New York, 1974.

[10] M. Mäntylä. *An Introduction to Solid Modeling*. Computer Science Press, Maryland, 1988.

[11] R. P. Markot and R. L. Magedson. Solutions of tangential surface and curve intersections. *Computer Aided Design*, 7(21), 1989.

[12] J. R. Miller. Architectual issues in solid modelers. *IEEE Computer Graphics and Applications*, 9(5), 1989.

[13] J. R. Miller. Geometric approaches to nonplanar quadric surface intersection curves. *Transactions on Graphics*, 6(4), 1987.

[14] R. F. Riesenfeld. Design tools for shaping spline models. In T. Lyche and L. L. Schumaker, editors, *Mathematical Methods in Computer Aided Geometric Design*, Academic Press, Boston, 1989.

[15] R. F. Sarraga and W. C. Waters. Free-form surfaces in GMSolid: goals and issues. In Mary S. Pickett and John W. Boyse, editors, *Solid Modeling by Computers from Theory to Applications*, Plenum Press, New York, 1984.

[16] T. W. Sederberg. *Implicit and Parametric Curves and Surfaces for Computer Aided Geometric Design*. PhD thesis, Purdue Univ., 1983.

[17] T. W. Sederberg, H. N. Christiansen, and S. Katz. Inproved test for closed loops in surface intersections. *Computer Aided Design*, 21(8), 1989.

[18] J. S. Snoeyink. Intersecting trimmed quadric surface patches: a geometric method using parametric functions. 1990. unpublished.

[19] T. Takamura, M. Ohta, H. Toriya, and H. Chiyokura. A method to convert a Gregory Patch and a Rational Boundary Gregory Patch to a Rational Bezier Patch and its application. In *Proceedings of Computer Graphics International '90*, 1990.

[20] S. W. Thomas. The Alpha-1 computer-aided geometric design system in the UNIX environment. *;login:*, 10(4), 1985.

[21] W. Tiller. Rational B-Splines for curve and surface representation. *IEEE Computer Graphics and Applications*, 3(6), 1983.

[22] H. Toriya, T. Satoh, K. Ueda, and H. Chiyokura. Undo and redo operations for solid modeling. *IEEE Computer Graphics and Applications*, 6(4), 1986.

[23] H. Toriya, T. Takamura, T. Satoh, and H. Chiyokura. Boolean operations of solids with free-form surfaces through polyhedral approximation. In R. A. Earnshaw and B. Wyvill, editors, *New Advances in Computer Graphics*, Springer-Verlag, Tokyo, 1989.

---

[1]Software Research Center, Ricoh Co. Ltd., Bunkyo-ku, Tokyo, 113 Japan
[2]Faculty of Environmental Information, Keio University, Fujisawa, 252 Japan

Chapter 5

Animation Modeling

A Knowledge-Based Approach to the Synthesis of Human Motion

ROBERTO MAIOCCHI

Abstract

In several current realizations of human figure animation systems, motion control is achieved through physical models of human movement dynamics of various degrees of complexity. Although realistic motions can be produced in this way, the computational time required to solve the equations characterizing such models is considerably high and reduces the possibility of real-time interaction between the animator and the motion control system. Recently, several proposals on the way to build models that require management of complex physical systems have appeared in the field of qualitative modeling. The main assumption of such proposals is that it is possible to obtain convincing simulations of physical phenomena through specification and use of common sense knowledge of the world.

In this paper we present a knowledge-based approach to the synthesis of human motion in computer animation. The challenge of the proposal is to verify the possibility of controlling the movement of the human figure by developing a qualitative model of human motor behavior that avoids the significant calculations necessary if complex mathematical models are adopted. The most relevant characteristic of the system is that knowledge about the human figure and its motor behavior is composed dynamically to fit the task at hand. Task execution can be varied to account for the flexibility and adaptation shown by humans through the control of modeling assumptions expressing common sense knowledge about human motor behavior. Three examples of motor skills implemented according to such assumptions are presented in detail: sitting, stepping upwards, and level walking.

Key words: human figure animation, qualitative modeling, motor knowledge, motion recording

1. INTRODUCTION

Every person must organize his or her movement in relation to constraints of a mechanical nature. Like every object on earth, animate or inanimate, the human body is continuously acted upon by forces and the way in which it moves depends on the magnitude and direction of these forces (Watkins 1983).

Mechanics of human movement, i.e., the study of the conditions under which the human body moves or stays at rest, has provided a basis for the development of several motor control systems for computer animation developed in the last few years (Armstrong and Green 1985; Arnaldi et al. 1989; Girard and Maciejewski 1985; Isaacs and Cohen 1987; Wilhelms 1987). If the human body is considered to be an articulated rigid object, its movement can be quite naturally described in terms of complex laws of dynamics and indeed realistic animations have been produced adopting this modeling approach.

Whether the animation system is based only on a dynamic model or it combines kinematic and dynamic aspects, several drawbacks can in fact arise from its use. Due to the large number of degrees of freedom in the human figure, the computational time required to solve the motion equations is considerably high and reduces the possibility of real-time interaction between the animator and the motor control system. Furthermore, an animator does not conceive the control of the motion of the human character in terms of forces and torques, but rather specifies the desired movement performance by defining task-level commands, positional constraints, and some qualitative aspects of the motion such as the effort in carrying it out.

In order to improve motion control, higher level systems categorized as *task-level systems* in Zeltzer (1985) have been developed in which the animator specifies the broad outlines of a particular movement and the animation system computes the details of the motion (Badler et al. 1985; Badler 1989; Bruderlin and Calvert 1989; Zeltzer 1982). For instance, in Bruderlin and Calvert (1989) a range of gaits for walking can be generated by the animator by simply specifying forward velocity, step length and step frequency.

Two goals are pursued in the development of task-level systems: *parametrization* and *adaptation*. Parametrization consists of choosing the parameters that the animator can control to produce the expected motor performance. On the other hand, adaptation is a property of a system which uses information about the environment and the human figure to automatically generate different motor performances as the scene varies, i.e., the human model executes a motion adjusting its form according to knowledge about environmental conditions.

Although parametrization and adaptation allow to obtain a wide range of instances of the same motor skill, computational time and motion control remain a problem. Task-level systems proposed so far in literature in fact just hide the underlying model of motion computation to the user, but are still based on laws of motion dynamics, at most tailored and simplified to reproduce a specific movement. Convincing visual simulation requires an account for the flexibility and adaptability shown by humans in performing a task. For this reason, it is necessary that the animator can naturally determine various aspects of the movement to make it as expressive and natural as possible. This goal can be better achieved by a model of motor behavior that allows to control the movement of the human figure in the same way as we understand its characteristics.

In this paper we discuss the modeling assumptions of PINOCCHIO, a motion control system for computer animation based on a qualitative description of human motor behavior. As in task-level animation systems, PINOCCHIO is given general knowledge about which parts of the body are moved in performing a task and how they are moved to determine automatically the details of the motion. The distinctive approach proposed in PINOCCHIO is that task execution is controlled by a set of rules expressing common sense knowledge about how motions are performed, i.e., the laws of dynamics governing the mechanics of human movement are implemented by specifying qualitative rules of motor behavior. Such rules are responsible, for example, for keeping the balance of the human body model during the motion and for controlling the muscular effort and the speed during the phases of motion execution. Being closer to the way in which humans express and understand knowledge about motor behaviors the system allows the animator to define various aspects of the desired instance of motion that satisfy particular expressional or environmental constraints. Furthermore, the system gives real-time responses speeding up the animation process.

The paper is organized as follows. In Section 2., we discuss in detail the four steps of the methodology adopted in PINOCCHIO for the development of the knowledge-based model of human motor behavior. In Section 3., three examples of motor skills implemented in PINOCCHIO are given: sitting, stepping upwards, and level walking. Parametrization and adaptation are demonstrated showing how it is possible to obtain a wide range of performances of the same motor skill by controlling variables having a logical correspondent in human knowledge. Finally, in Section 4., we conclude discussing the results achieved in PINOCCHIO and envisioning future developments.

2. A METHODOLOGY FOR THE DEVELOPMENT OF A QUALITATIVE MODEL OF HUMAN MOTION

The model of human motor behavior underlying PINOCCHIO has been obtained through the application of a methodology which is composed of four phases (Fig. 1). The need of a complete methodology stems from the complexity of the phenomenon under study. The first step of the methodology relies on the direct *observation* of human motor skills by means of Elite, a 3D digital vision system developed for biomedical applications at the Centro di Bioingegneria, Fdn. Pro Juventute, Politecnico di Milano, Italy. Kinematic and qualitative dynamic aspects of motor behavior have been abstracted through *analysis* of the motor skills digitized using Elite and used for the *synthesis* of the corresponding classes of motions. Finally, *validation* of the synthetic motions against observational data is carried out, possibly providing a feedback loop to the phase of analysis if the model is not satisfactory. In the rest of this section, we discuss in some detail each of the four phases of the methodology.

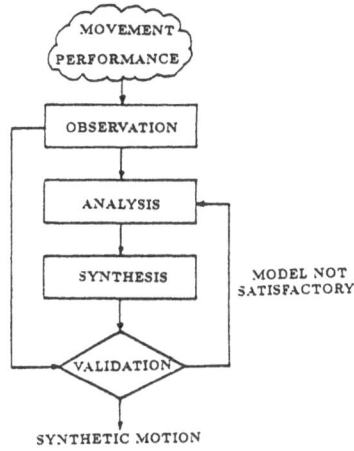

Fig. 1 - Methodological steps in PINOCCHIO

2.1 Observation

The first step of the methodology adopted in PINOCCHIO consists of the direct observation and digitization of the movements performed by real actors. The tool we use for such a purpose is Elite (Ferrigno and Pedotti 1985), a 3D vision system aiming at the support of human movement analysis in biomedical applications. The analysis is performed by marking the joints of real actors with passive markers and following their trajectories during body movements. The markers are pieces of reflective paper that are recognized by Elite simply on the basis of their shape.

Depending on the particular observation to be made, a specific stick model of the parts of the body to be analyzed is first to be chosen by placing markers at the joints. Being interested in movements of the total body, we have positioned the markers on the human subjects as shown in Fig. 2. Elite is able to reconstruct and record the positions assumed in time by each marker during the performance of a motion. Movements are then represented as sequences of 3D coordinates of the joints of the stick figure.

The Elite system employs a two-level hierarchical structure to recover the 3D coordinates from images received from a set of TV cameras. The first level of this structure is contained in the system hardware which processes the data using a Single Instruction Multiple Data approach. This allows in fact an unlimited numbers of markers to be detected in each frame, at up to 100 frames per second. The second level of the structure is contained in the system software installed in a general purpose personal computer. This level performs several tasks: corrects image distortions; establishes marker identities; carries out the required tracking, space resection and intersection; and filters the data stream. The overall accuracy of the 3D system is estimated to be 1 part in 2800 over the field of view.

In this way, a rich source of observational data is provided, and details of the recorded motions can be analyzed. In addition, through the collection of data from different subjects, patterns of the variation of angles at the joints and their statistical attributes can be derived and used for comparison with the patterns obtained by movement synthesis in the validation phase. The creation and organization of a movement database relying on data collected with Elite has been presented in Maiocchi and Pernici (1990).

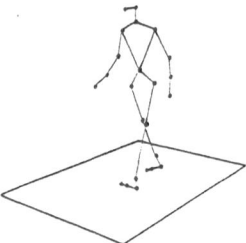

Fig. 2 - The stick figure used for movement observation

2.2 Analysis

The second step of the methodology consists of the analysis of the motions digitized using Elite in order to create a model of human motor behavior that is easy to control and that accounts for the flexibility and adaptability shown by humans in performing a certain skill. For this reason, we tackled the problem of modeling human motion by developing a knowledge-base that contains the core knowledge that humans apply in understanding and expressing their motor behavior.

As for the systems developed in the field of qualitative modeling (Barr et al. 1989; Bobrow and Hayes 1984; Clancey 1989; Fishwick 1988), our goal is to provide a convincing simulation of a physical phenomenon like human motion by reducing the amount of computation required if a complex mathematical model is adopted. The distinctive standpoint of our approach consists indeed of identifying a general set of kinematic and dynamic rules applied by humans to control their movements and to model such rules through the definition and manipulation of variables and parameters that have a logical meaning in human knowledge terms.

Due to the large amount of knowledge required for modeling human motor behavior, various modeling assumptions have been introduced in the system to simplify motion control. In the literature on qualitative physics, the importance of using assumptions to decompose complex domains into simpler ones and to make such modeling assumptions explicit has been acknowledged by various researchers (deKleer and Brown 1984; Falkenhainer and Forbus 1988). In this section, we provide a detailed description of the modeling assumptions that have been adopted in PINOCCHIO and we discuss the kind of knowledge that we have specified in the phase of analysis.

Three kinds of knowledge are required to build a model of the human figure: *structural knowledge*, *functional knowledge*, and *behavioral knowledge* (Cohen 1988).

Structural knowledge refers to the way in which the human figure is articulated and to the proportion of the various body parts. *Functional knowledge* is the legal range of movement at each articulation. To introduce these first two kinds of knowledge into the system, anthropometric data have been taken from Winter (1979). Limb lengths and masses have been expressed as fractions of total body height and of total body mass respectively in order to obtain a higher degree of parametrization. Body segments are considered symmetric. Feasible ranges for angles at joints have also been specified. The choice of introducing this knowledge from data taken from the literature rather than from direct observation with Elite is due to the large sample of measurements required to obtain high accuracy in the definition of the proportions between body parts. The specification of a precise anthropometric model is anyway out of the aims of our current investigation.

Behavioral knowledge specifies how the human figure moves in the performance of a particular motor task. In defining behavioral knowledge we are particularly concerned with parametrization and adaptation. The sequence of movements characterizing a motor skill may indeed be executed in many different ways depending on the circumstances at hand. For this reason, general behavioral rules have been abstracted from several observations of performances of the same task. We distinguish between two kinds of behavioral knowledge, which we specify through *kinematic rules* and *qualitative dynamics rules*.

Kinematic rules give a description of which parts of the body are moved and how they are moved to perform a task, e.g., the coordination of the leg motion during the gait in walking. Kinematic rules depend on the physiological structure of the human body (Morton and Fuller 1952); by themselves, they provide the general characteristics of a wide class of motion performances. Kinematic rules are given in PINOCCHIO in terms of relative timing between the phases of the motion, positional constraints, specification of trajectories of some of the joints and limbs, and relationships of the human figure with objects in the environment. Kinematic rules apply in the calculations of the linear and angular displacement, velocity, and acceleration of the body joints required for the solution of *direct* and *inverse kinematic problems*. For instance, the position of a free hand is determined given the joint angles at the shoulder, elbow, and wrist (direct kinematic problem); on the other hand, given the position of the foot and the hip of the same leg, the joint angles at the ankle, knee, and hip are computed automatically by the system as a solution of the inverse kinematic problem. Examples of kinematic rules for the motor skills implemented in PINOCCHIO are given in the next section of the paper.

Qualitative dynamics rules express knowledge of the dynamic aspects of human motion and are used by the system to compute the details of the motion once the kinematic constraints are given. Although qualitative dynamics rules are responsible for the final form of the performance of a motion, they cannot change the general characteristics of the motion stated by the kinematic rules. Qualitative dynamics rules are handled in PINOCCHIO as additional constraints to be satisfied in the application of the kinematic rules. For example, in the inverse kinematic problem for the leg described above the position of the pelvis of the human figure must be specified so that constraints of global dynamic equilibrium of the human body are considered. Qualitative dynamics rules are in turn divided into three classes: *balance rules*, *effort rules*, and *inertial rules*. This classification has been introduced with the aim of considering the various aspects of dynamics control separately, even if a strong interdependence among such aspects exists in determining a motor behavior.

2.2.1 Balance rules

For the purpose of controlling the balance of the human figure, we consider the mass of the body being concentrated in one point, which is the *center of gravity* of the body. The vertical line passing through the center of gravity is called the *line of gravity* of the body. For a person to be in a balanced position, the line of gravity of his/her weight must remain within the *base of support*. For instance, if we consider a person standing upright, the base of support is the area between the feet. If the line of gravity passes outside the base of support during a motion, the person will fall over unless a new base of support is established. As the body is moved from one position to another, its weight should then be redistributed for the sake of maintaining stability.

In order to keep the balance of the human figure during motion execution, in PINOCCHIO we control the line of gravity so that it does not fall outside the base of support. Since the line of gravity is related to the center of gravity (approximately located at the lumbar vertebrae), such a control is performed by computing the amount of forward lean of the spine throughout the motion. For movements such as sitting and stepping upwards, we have verified that it is sufficient to control the equilibrium in the sagittal plane. On the other hand, for more complex motions such as walking, where the base of support changes continuously, consideration of transversal components is required.

2.2.2 Effort rules

The control of the balance of the human figure is not sufficient by itself to obtain natural movements. Although some simulations of motor skills resulting from the application of the balance rules alone appear quite convincing, most of the time they do not show total naturalness. This is due to the lack of consideration of the muscular tension in computing the trajectories of the joints. For the purpose of producing more realistic sequences of motion, we have introduced in the system the ability to vary the muscular tension through the specification of *effort rules*.

Whereas balance rules depend only on the resultant force acting vertically downwards on the body as applied in its center of gravity (qualitatively modeled and controlled by means of the line of gravity), effort rules consider instead the action of the weight of the various limbs as separate; namely the hands, the forearms, the upper arms, the upper body (trunk, head, and neck), the thighs, the lower legs, and the feet.

All the forces applying to a body segment determine a moment, or torque, which tends to rotate the body around its center of gravity. The extent of such moment is proportional to the limb weight and to the distance of the direction of this force from the center of gravity of the body. If we take the moment of a limb as a measure of the muscular effort transmitted to the adjacent limbs, we can increase or decrease the tension of a muscle by altering the line of action of the weight limb, i.e., we can obtain a different, more natural performance of the same motion through modification of the limb trajectories computed by simply respecting the balance rules.

In PINOCCHIO, we take limb moments as a qualitative measure of the muscular effort and we control their values by limiting the range of admissibility of the moment of each body segment. Limb moments are computed using structural knowledge about the limb lengths and masses of the human figure and the actual position of the body during the motion. In this way, the system allows an animator to directly control the computations carried out in determining a motion. The interaction is facilitated by the correspondence between the numerical values that must be controlled and their logical meaning, the muscular tension.

2.2.3 Inertial rules

An important aspect of the mechanics of human movement not included in the balance and effort rules is body's inertia. As for any other object on earth, human body's inertia is a measure of its inability to change its state of rest or motion. In comparison with the inertia of an inanimate object that is just proportional to its mechanical attributes (i.e., mass and velocity), the reluctance of a living body to alter its speed and direction of movement depends also on physiological properties. This causes the various phases of a motion to be executed at varying speed and acceleration according to a global planning of biological optimization (Beckett and Chang 1968; Capozzo et al. 1976; Chow and Jacobson 1971; Pedotti 1977; Pedotti et al. 1978).

Whereas balance and effort rules in PINOCCHIO are responsible for the definition of the general form of the motion that satisfies the kinematic rules, *inertial rules* control the speed and acceleration of the body joints along the spatial path throughout motion execution. Given the complexity of the human body, such control represents the refinement of the various phases of a motion and their coordination.

A precise computation of speed and acceleration would require calculating first and second derivative of the motion in space and time. In qualitative dynamics terms we have verified that to obtain satisfactory simulations in a wide category of motions (e.g., sitting and stepping upwards) it is sufficient to control the speed of certain joints so that it describes in time a bell-shaped curve, i.e., velocity of the joint is considered null at the beginning of the motion or any of its sub-phases, it then increases to a maximum halfway through the motion, and finally decreases towards zero at the end of the motion (Pedotti et al. 1989). Analogous considerations have been verified for acceleration. More complex assumptions are required for cyclical motions such as walking, as discussed in the next section of the paper.

2.3 Synthesis

The third phase of the methodology consists of the realization of the knowledge-base presented above and of its application in the simulation of motor skills. The most relevant characteristic of PINOCCHIO is that knowledge about the human figure and its motor behavior is composed dynamically to fit the task at hand. Task execution can be varied to account for the flexibility and adaptation shown by humans by adding kinematic constraints or by modifying the range of admissibility for the value of the variables controlled with the dynamic rules.

Since our goal is graphic simulation, in the phase of synthesis we trade-off physical exactness for convincing motion quality and real-time response. For example, most of the kinematic and dynamics rules are defined only in the sagittal plane. Little motion components in the frontal and transversal planes have been considered in the movements discussed in this paper; this is an assumption made also in robotics in the study of motor behaviors with the introduction of the notion of *plane of motion* (Murthy and Raibert 1986).

In the next section of the paper, we describe in detail three examples of motor skills implemented in PINOCCHIO: sitting, stepping upwards, and level walking. For each motor skill, a detailed description of how we control its simulation is given in pseudo-code English (Fig. 5, Fig. 10, and Fig. 11). In the description, we specify *input parameters* (i.e., the variables that the animator can control to vary motion execution), *modeling assumptions* (i.e., simplifications that we introduced in the computation of the motion), *task execution assumptions* (i.e., specifications of the kinematic rules that determine the particular form of the execution of the skill under study), and *task execution control assumptions* (i.e., how the qualitative dynamic rules apply to the task at hand). Furthermore, we give a general outline of the main task execution control algorithms and functions that implement the kinematic and dynamic rules.

All the motor skills implemented in PINOCCHIO share the following sequence of application of the behavioral rules for motion control purposes:

1. determine the number of frames of the various phases of the motion according to the total execution time and the relative timing of such phases (kinematic rules)

2. for each frame, determine the position of the pelvis of the figure according to its trajectory and velocity (kinematic and inertial rules)

3. for each frame, determine the position of the feet and consequently of the base of support of the figure through the kinematic rules

4. for each frame, refine the position of the pelvis of the figure in order to satisfy the balance rules

5. for each frame, determine the position of the lower body (kinematic rules)

6. for each frame, determine the position of the upper body (kinematic rules)

7. for each frame, refine the position of the figure in order to satisfy the balance and effort rules

The human figure animation model is based on a stick figure model is taken, i.e., a skeleton made up of a collection of body segments and joints arranged as in Fig. 2. Such a model is the same that is used for real movement observation with Elite. For final display we make the skeleton wear a 3D outfit designed following the description of the puppet Pinocchio by the Italian writer Carlo Collodi in the book that gives the name to the system (Collodi 1883). Although the model does not have the appearance of a real human character, it is particularly appropriate for real-time visualization. In Fig. 3, we show Pinocchio performing the three motions discussed in this paper: sitting, stepping upwards, and level walking.

The system has been implemented on a workstation HP9000 model 360 turboSRX using the C programming language, Unix operating system. In addition to the motions described in this paper,

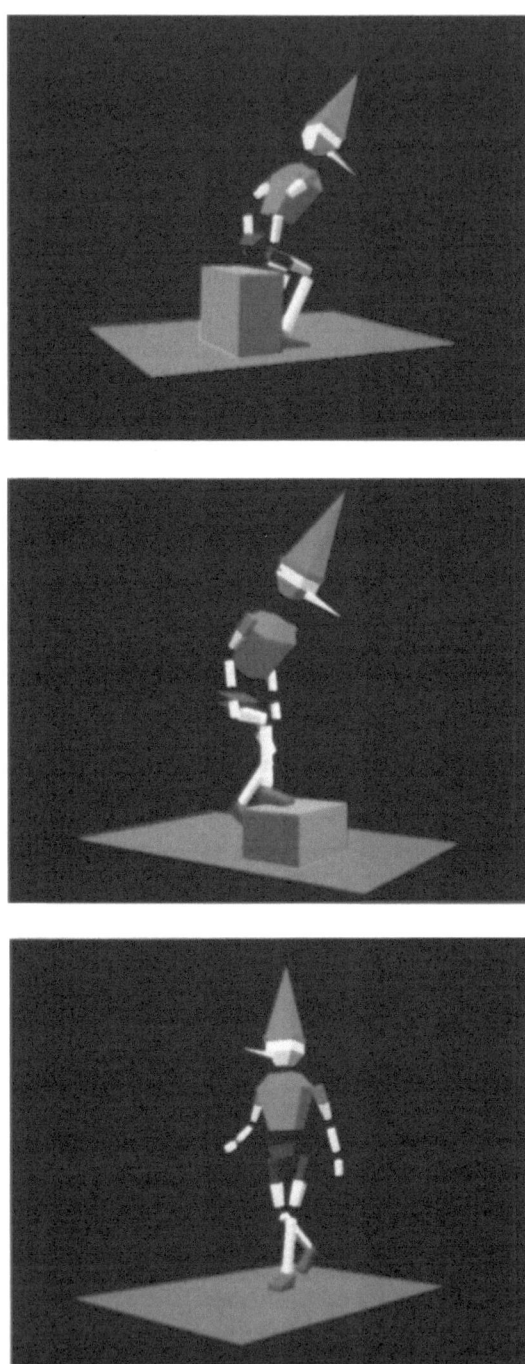

Fig. 3 - The 3D character performing three motions: sitting, stepping upwards, and level walking

the knowledge base of PINOCCHIO has been extended to include other skills among which the motion of a gymnast performing a somersault and the motion of an athlete throwing the discus.

2.4 Validation

The last step of the methodology used in PINOCCHIO for the development of rule-based qualitative motor programs consists of the verification of the synthesized model against observational data. The challenge of our approach is to verify if it is possible to control the movement of the human figure by building a qualitative model of human behavior that avoids the significant calculations necessary for instance for the control of robots and for biomedical applications.

The way in which the motor behavior of the synthetic figure is tested for validity consists of the visual comparison of the direct observations of the movements recorded during the first phase of the methodology against the synthesized performances. In this case, the judgment of the animator is essential, especially if exaggeration of movement characteristics is required for animation purposes. If realistic reproduction of a motion has to be achieved, a more precise validation can be carried out by comparing the patterns of variation of joint angles throughout the motion with the data collected from different subjects with Elite.

More kinematic and dynamic rules can in fact be generated during the phase of validation. Our claim is that the rules we have implemented constitute a minimal core necessary to reproduce and control some human motor skills. Additional rules can be integrated in the system when different motor skills are considered. In addition, specific aspects such as the differences in male vs. female motor behavior (Cutting 1978) can be studied with the available motion recordings and easily introduced in the appropriate knowledge source.

3. EXAMPLES OF MOTOR SKILLS

In this section, we describe three examples of motor skills that we have implemented using the knowledge-base developed through the application of the methodology presented in the foregoing discussion. For each skill, several digitizations of the movements performed by real subjects have been recorded and analyzed to define behavioral knowledge. The synthesized motions have then been validated both by visual comparison with digitized observations and by careful analysis of relevant parameters of each motion.

In the following presentation, we describe how PINOCCHIO generates simulations of normal performances of the implemented skills pointing out how the behavioral rules apply in each case. Parametrization and adaptation are demonstrated showing how it is possible to obtain a wide range of performances of the same motor skill by controlling variables having a logical corresponding in human knowledge.

3.1 Sitting

Among the different ways in which the action of sitting can be performed, we consider the case of a person that stands in front of the chair and then symmetrically sits down keeping his/her hands on the thighs in a fixed position (Fig. 4). Flexion of the hips and knee and forward lean of the spine are the dominant movements. Since for the sake of balance the line of gravity must intersect the base of support throughout the motion, a person must lean forward when bending the knees. The forward lean is produced by flexion in the hips and forward bending of the lumbar spine. When the buttocks reach the chair, the body's supporting area increases accordingly through contact between chair seat and buttocks, and the trunk may be raised to adopt an upright sitting position.

In PINOCCHIO, kinematics rules given to the system to constraint the form of the execution of the sitting task include the position of the feet, which is supposed to be fixed throughout the motion, the distance between the feet and the seat, the position of the hands, fixed at the middle of the thighs, and the trajectory of the center of the pelvis, which is a straight line from the upright position to the middle of the seat. The last assumption is motivated by consideration of minimization of the distance between the initial position and the goal position of the human figure. We also assume that the phase of the motion in which the person approaches the seat last twice as long as the phase in which the person adopts an upright sitting position.

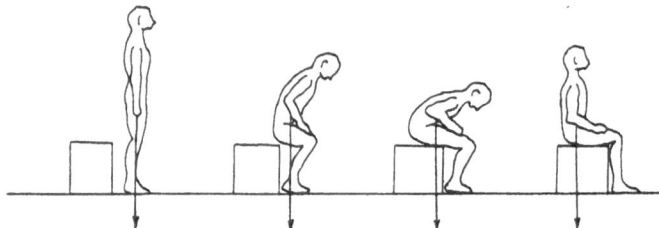

Fig. 4 - Sequence of intermediate positions for sitting

Environmental characteristics such as seat height are then considered as external parameters that the motor control system takes into account in determining a particular motor performance, i.e., a particular instance of sitting. For the particular task at hand (and for a wide class of movements) we can also introduce the following *simplification assumption*: kinematic and dynamic rules control the motion of the human figure only in the sagittal plane. Furthermore, we assume the motion to be symmetric with respect to such a plane.

In Fig. 5, a detailed description of how PINOCCHIO controls the simulation of sitting is given. In the figure, input parameters, modeling assumptions, and task execution assumptions that constraint the outcome of the task execution control algorithm are specified. In the task execution control algorithm, two phases of the action of sitting are considered. In the first phase, the goal is to approach the seat; in the second phase, the position of the legs is fixed and the trunk is raised to assume an upright position. Different execution times are assumed for the two phases: the function *determine-frame-distribution* assigns the proper number of frames to each sub-phase.

The control of the phase in which the seat is being reached by the human body model is carried out as follows. As the pelvis moves towards the seat following the predifined linear trajectory (*determine-midpelvis-position*), the amount of knee bending is determined by feet positions and leg lengths as solution of an inverse kinematic problem (*determine-hip-extension*). Consequently, forward lean of the trunk is derived for the sake of balance: as the pelvis is moved backwards, the upper body must lean forward (*determine-trunk-bend*). Analogously to the way in which knee bending is determined, elbow bending depends on the length of the arms, once hand and shoulder positions have been fixed (*determine-elbow-bend*).

In this first phase, the balance rules are implemented by the function *determine-trunk-bend* that computes the amount of forward lean of the lumbar spine so that the line of gravity falls into the base of support. The base of support is supposed to be fixed in the area between the feet. Normal motion speed as observed from real subjects has then been assumed in determining the way in which the linear trajectory of the mid-pelvis is covered. Such an assumption defines the shape of the bell curve that implements the inertial rules embedded in the function *determine-midpelvis-position*. In Fig. 6 we show the typical pattern of the module of the velocity of the mid-pelvis obtained from an observation carried out with Elite of a subject sitting on a 45cm high seat (velocity is in mm/msec).

In the second phase of the motion, a sitting upright position is reached by simply raising the trunk backwards from the maximum forward lean determined in the first phase. In this case, the balance rules are not used because the balance of the figure is given by the seat; on the other hand, the inertial rules apply in the control of the angle of backward raise for each frame (*assume-sitting-upright-position*). In Fig. 7, the sequence of intermediate positions for sitting as computed only with balance and inertial rules is displayed by the stick figure on the left hand side of each frame.

SITTING

Input parameters
      1. seat-height
      2. motion-speed
      3. initial-body-position: standing upright
      4. final-body-position: sitting upright

Modeling assumptions
      1. all motions are executed in the sagittal plane
      2. all motions are symmetric with respect to the
         sagital plane

Task execution assumptions (kinematic rules)
      1. position of the feet is fixed throughout the motion
      2. hands are kept on the midthighs throughout the motion
      3. midpelvis-to-seat-trajectory
      4. body-seat distance
      5. relative timing between the phases of the motion

Task execution control assumptions (dynamic rules)
      1. position of the midpelvis on its trajectory towards
         the seat (inertial rules)
      2. amount of fwd lean of the trunk (balance and effort
         rules)

Main control algorithm
      determine-frame-distribution (motion-speed)
      approach-seat (phase1-frames, seat-height)
      assume-sitting-upright-position (phase2-frames)

Functions
      approach-seat (phase1-frames, seat-height)
         for each frame
            determine-midpelvis-position (motion-speed,
                      midpelvis-to-seat-trajectory)
            determine-hip-extension (midpelvis, feet-position)
            determine-trunk-bend (midpelvis)
            determine-elbow-bend (hip-extension, shoulder)

      assume-sitting-upright-position (phase2-frames)
         for each frame
            determine-trunk-bend (max-trunk-bend, frame)

      determine-hip-extension (midpelvis, feet-position)
         hip-extension = 0 /* vertical position */
         while (distance(knee, ankle) < lower-leg-length)
            increase-hip-extension

      determine-trunk-bend (midpelvis)
         trunk-bend = 0 /* vertical position */
         while (line-of-gravity outside base-of-support)
            increase-trunk-bend

      determine-trunk-bend-with-effort (midpelvis)
         trunk-bend = 0 /* vertical position */
         while (line-of-gravity outside base-of-support)
            increase-trunk-bend
         determine-trunk-moment (trunk-bend)
         while (MIN-LEG-EFFORT<trunk-moment<MAX-LEG-EFFORT)
            increase/decrease-trunk-bend

Fig. 5 - A detailed description of how PINOCCHIO controls the execution of sitting

The sequences of intermediate positions of the motion of sitting on a chair displayed in Fig. 7 by the stick figure on the right hand side of each frame has been obtained controlling also the muscular effort at the thighs. The maximum and minimum values of such an effort have been fixed before the system automatically determined the amount of forward lean in the lumbar spine required by the balance rules. In the task execution control algorithm, the function *determine-trunk-bend* introduced above has been substituted by the function *determine-trunk-bend-with-effort*. In addition to determining the amount of forward lean of the lumbar spine so that the line of gravity falls in the base of support, such a function modifies the forward lean to keep the value of the moment of the upper body in the range of admissibility given by the animator.

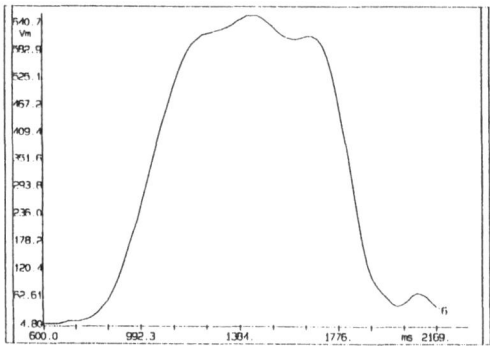

Fig. 6 - Pattern of the module of the velocity of the mid-pelvis in mm/sec as obtained with Elite from a subject sitting on a 45cm high seat

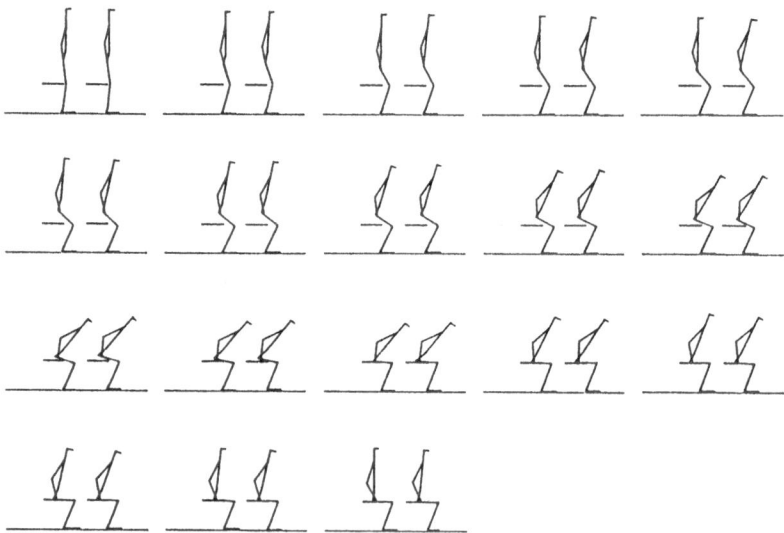

Fig. 7 - Sequence of intermediate positions for sitting as computed with the balance and inertial rules only (left) and with all the behavioral rules (right)

By comparing the positions assumed by the stick figure in the two cases, anticipation of the forward lean can be noticed (frames 2 through 6). Variations in the minimum and maximum values of the moment of the upper body allow an animator to control the form of motion execution within a range corresponding to a person that seats down smoothly to a person that drops himself/herself on the seat. In addition, since seat height is an input parameter, the system is able to generate automatically the sequence of intermediate positions assumed by a person sitting on a seat of variable height through use of the same knowledge.

3.2 Stepping upwards

As for sitting, the dominant movements for stepping upwards are motion of the legs and forward lean of the spine. The main difference between sitting and stepping upwards is that in the latter case the base of support shifts forward from the initial position where the person stands upright in front of the step to the final position where the person stands upon the step (Fig. 8).

The motion can be divided into three phases. In the first phase, the leading leg is placed on the step. Then, the base of support is shifted from the foot on the ground to the foot on the step by forward lean of the spine, so that the line of gravity falls into the new base of support. Finally, extension of the leading leg is carried out. During this last phase of the motion, the amount of forward lean of the spine depends again upon the position of the new base of support. The following leg is consequently extended to reach the final upright position. In Fig. 9, the sequence of intermediate positions for stepping on a 30cm high step as computed by PINOCCHIO is shown by the figure on the left hand side of each frame. In Fig. 10, a detailed description of how such a sequence is generated is given.

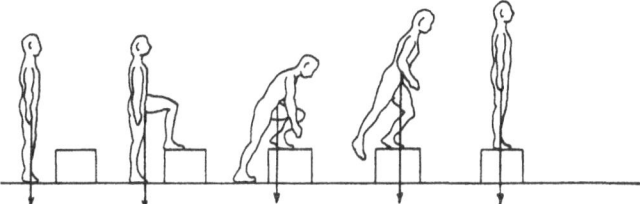

Fig. 8 - Sequence of intermediate positions for stepping upwards

As for sitting, the main kinematic constraint we assumed for stepping upwards is that the mid-pelvis covers a straight line from the position reached at the end of the second phase of the motion to the position in which the person is standing upon the step (function: *determine-midpelvis-position*). The same function controls also the shape of the bell curve that implements the inertial rules. As for sitting, the function *determine-trunk-bend* that implements the balance and effort rules determines the position of the line of gravity as the base of support moves throughout the motion.

Since forward shift of the base of support is obtained by placing the foot of the leading leg on the step first, symmetry in computing the leg motions cannot be applied. In addition, obstacle avoidance in determining leg angle variations throughout the motion has to be considered. Although we did not provide the human model with general knowledge for planning collision-free paths as in Lozano-Perez and Wesley (1979) and Moore and Wilhelms (1988), we control knee and ankle flexion and extension in order to avoid collisions with the step. Flexion of the arms is instead symmetric and proportional to the amount of forward lean of the trunk: this assumption has been expressed as a kinematic rule.

The maximum step height that the figure is able to mount depends on the maximum value of hip flexion that can be performed according to the anthropometric data of the human model. In Fig. 9, the sequence of intermediate positions assumed by the human figure in mounting a 45cm high step is shown by the stick figure on the right hand side of each frame. With respect to the motion determine for the lower step, further forward lean during the shift of the base of support can be noticed (frames 11 through 13). This is due to the increase in muscular effort required to the leading leg in stepping upwards, which is counterbalanced by an increase in the forward lean of the spine. The motion generated for the higher step has been determined automatically by PINOCCHIO without the specification of additional knowledge with respect to the motion determined for the lower step.

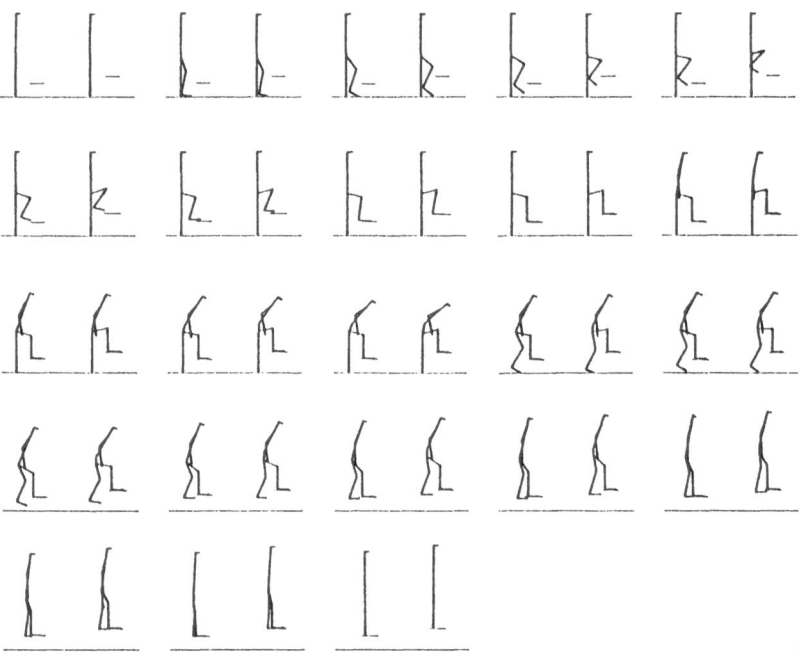

Fig. 9 - Sequence of intermediate positions for stepping upwards as computed with all the behavioral rules for a 30cm high step (left) and a 45cm high step (right)

3.3 Level walking

The complexity of human gait has attracted the interest of various disciplines: robotics (McMahon 1984; Raibert and Sutherland 1983; Raibert 1986), biomechanics (Inman et al. 1981; Murray 1967; Saunders et al. 1953), and psychology (Shapiro et al. 1981; Smith and Wing 1984). Few systems for the control of level walking have been proposed also in computer animation (Boulic et al. 1990; Bruderlin and Calvert 1989; Zeltzer 1982). The distinctive aspect of PINOCCHIO from the previous implementations of the human gait is the use of qualitative dynamics for controlling motion computation. In the following discussion we present how we synthesized human gait as performed at a normal speed (140cm/sec) by a man of normal height (175cm). Higher level control systems for varying speed and other parameters characterizing human gait can then be added on top of this model to account for parametrization (Boulic et al. 1990, Bruderlin and Calvert 1989).

The general description of the algorithm for the control of the execution of this skill is given in Fig. 11. In the following discussion, we do not give the details of the functions that realize the task execution control algorithm, but we outline the main assumptions adopted for its implementation. We first divide the walking cycle into four phases after Shapiro et al. (1981) (Fig. 12). Separation of the four phases makes it easier to calculate and control the entire motion sequence. Heel strike marks the beginning of the phase of *restraint*, as the body weight is supported by the bearing leg. From the moment when the hip joint stands vertically over the ankle joint to the moment when the foot finally leaves the ground, the leg assumes an increasingly backward direction and acts as *propulsion*. Together, the phases of restraint and propulsion constitute the *stance* phase.

```
STEPPING UPWARDS

Input parameters
        1. step height
        2. motion speed
        3. initial position: standing upright in front of the step
        4. final position: standing upright upon the step

Modeling assumptions
        1. all motions are executed in the sagittal plane

Task execution assumptions (kinematic rules)
        1. left-leg leading
        2. arm joint angles are proportional to leg joint angles
        3. midpelvis-to-seat-trajectory
        4. body-step distance
        5. relative timing between the phases of the motion

Task execution control assumptions (dynamic rules)
        1. position of the midpelvis on its trajectory
           (inertial rules)
        2. amount of fwd lean of the trunk (balance and effort
           rules)

Main control algorithm
        determine-frame-distribution (motion-speed)
        place-leading-leg-on-step (phase1-frames, step-height)
        shift-base-of-support-to-leading-leg (phase2-frames,
                leading-leg-position)
        step-upwards (phase3-frames, step-height,
                leading-leg-position, midpelvis-to-seat-trajectory)



Functions
        place-leading-leg-on-step (phase1-frames, step-height)
            determine-max-hip-extension (step-height)
            for each frame
                determine-hip-extension (max-hip-extension,
                                                motion-speed)

        shift-base-of-support-to-leading-leg (phase2-frames,
                        leading-leg-position)
            determine-max-trunk-bend (leading-leg-position)
            for each frame
                determine-trunk-bend (max-trunk-bend, frame)

        step-upwards(phase3-frames,step-height,leading-leg-position)
            for each frame
                determine-midpelvis-position (motion-speed,
                        midpelvis-to-seat-trajectory)
                determine-leading-hip-extension (midpelvis,
                        leading-foot-position)
                determine-trunk-bend-with-effort (midpelvis)
                determine-following-leg-bend (midpelvis, trunk-bend,
                        step-height)
                determine-arm-angles-bend (hip-extension)

        determine-following-leg-bend (midpelvis, trunk-bend,
                        step-height)
            hip-extension = alpha * trunk-bend
            knee-extension = beta * hip-extension
            ankle-extension = gamma * knee-extension
            while (foot-position hits step)
                increase knee-extension
```

Fig. 10 - A detailed description of how PINOCCHIO controls the execution of stepping upwards

The *swing* phase is also divided in two sub-phases. The *flexion* phase begins as the toe leaves the ground and continues until the thigh reaches a perpendicular position; then knee *extension* begins, which terminates when foot contact is made to start the next walking cycle.

```
WALKING

Input parameters
        1. motion-speed
        2. step-lenght
        3. initial-body-position: standing upright
        4. final-body-position: standing upright

Modeling assumptions
        1. all the motions of the legs and the arms
           are executed in the sagittal plane
        2. division of the walking cycle into four phases

Task execution assumptions (kinematic rules)
        1. walking cycle begins at left heel strike
        2. arm joint angles are proportional to leg joint angles
        3. heel-trajectory
        4. relative-timing between the phases of the walking cycle

Task execution control assumptions (dynamic rules)
        1. position of the midpelvis along its trajectory
           (inertial rules)
        2. variation of the position of the center of gravity
           (balance rules)
        3. amount of fwd lean of the trunk (balance and effort
           rules)

Main control algorithm
        determine-frame-distribution (motion-speed, relative-timing)
        determine-compass-gait (step-length)
        for each phase
            for each frame
                determine-hip-position (motion-speed)
                determine-hip-extension(hip-position,heel-trajectory)
                determine-ankle-extension (heel-trajectory)
                determine-pelvis-rotation (hip-positions)
                determine-cog-position (feet-positions, midpelvis)
                determine-trunk-bend (midpelvis)
                determine-shoulder-rotation (pelvis-rotation)
                determine-arm-joint-angles (leg-joint-angles)
```

Fig. 11 - A general description of the control of the execution of walking

Kinematic rules that determine leg motion during the walking cycle have been specified to reproduce the major gait determinants (Saunders et al. 1953). A first approximation of the motion of the hips is computed by assuming step symmetry based on a compass gait; then, pelvic rotation and pelvic tilt are derived by appropriate timing and coordination of the various phases of the motion. Once hip positions have been fixed, knee-joint angle variations are determined by assuming inverted pendulum motion of the thigh (McMahon 1984) and by controlling the behavior of the heel and foot-base joints directly. During the restraint phase, which is initiated at heel strike and terminated when the foot is flat on the ground, it is assumed that the leg rotates around the heel while the foot is always kept flat (Fig. 13).

The propulsion phase starts at the end of the restraint phase by dorsal flexion in the foot base joint, and ends when the toe leaves the ground. Linear increment of the dorsal flexion is assumed during this phase. The ankle is then constrained to follow a previously defined curve during the entire swing phase, from when the foot leaves the ground until the next heel strike. The ankle trajectory is an approximation of the data provided in Murray (1967). The knee is first flexed, and then extended after the thigh reaches the vertical position. During the swing phase, ankle flexion is controlled in such a way that the toes never go under the level of the floor. Complete motion of one leg at natural speed (140cm/sec) for normal height male subjects (175cm) is shown in Fig. 14.

For what concerns the arm swing, it is assumed that the rotations at the shoulder and the elbow depend on the angles in the lower body according to appropriate coordination functions (Murray 1967). Such coordination functions are implemented as kinematic rules in PINOCCHIO.

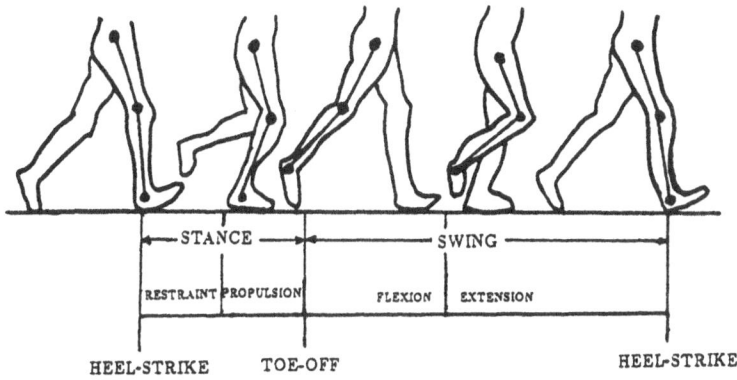

Fig. 12 - Separation of phases of the walking cycle

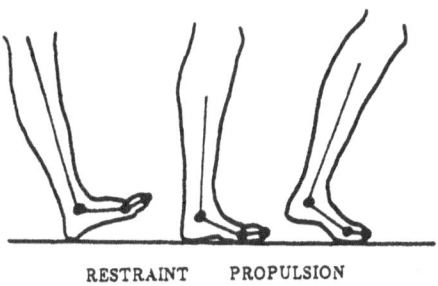

RESTRAINT   PROPULSION

Fig. 13 - Movements at the heel and footbase joints during the stance phase

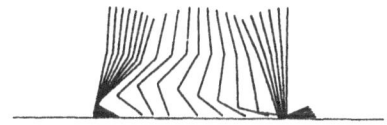

Fig. 14 - Complete motion of one leg during the walking cycle at normal speed (140cm/sec)

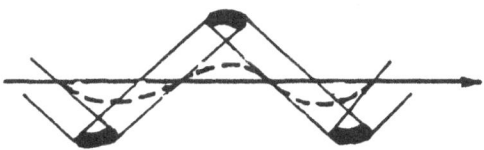

Fig. 15 - Control of the displacement of the center of gravity during the gait

A special task of a computer program synthesizing locomotion is to control the balance of the human figure. Human gait can in fact be seen as a constant play between loss and recovery of equilibrium. When the center of gravity of the forward leg passes beyond the base of support, the balance is lost throughout the entire phase of propulsion of the weight-bearing leg. Only at heel strike of the opposite leg, when a restraining action is exercised, body balance is regained. As for sitting and stepping upwards, the equilibrium of the human body during the walking cycle is controlled through balance rules regarding the behavior of its center of gravity. Similar considerations, implemented by means of dynamic equations, have been applied in robotics in the study of the stability of anthropomorphic systems reproducing bipedal gait (Vukobratovic and Stepanenko 1972).

Two assumptions are made in PINOCCHIO to obtain the rhythmic displacements of the center of gravity in the implementation of the balance rules. The vertical upward and downward displacement is taken to be proportional to the vertical motion of the hips. Wave-like movements in the horizontal plane are then obtained by defining a feasible area of support for the projection of the line of gravity as indicated in Fig. 15. Then, effort rules determine the muscular tension of the lower limbs during the restraint and propulsion phases through control of the forward lean of the upper body, as indicated in the previous section of the paper. For the implementation of the inertial rules, we have just considered the relative timing between the four phases in which we have divided the gait as obtained in Murray (1967) from the observation of several real subjects.

Validation of the curves of joint angle variations during the synthesized gait has been conducted by comparison with the kinematic measurements obtained with Elite. In Fig. 16, we display the leg angles as obtained from a human subject of average height (175cm) walking at a normal walking speed (140 cm/sec) (left) and the corresponding angles computed by applying the rules of PINOCCHIO (right). The walking cycle is considered to start at heel strike. As shown in the figure, the shape of the curves of variations of the angles at the lower limbs is very similar. The main differences are due to the fact that the control of speed and acceleration during the various phases of the walking cycle has been obtained by simply considering their relative timing and by applying linear interpolation of the values of the parameters controlling the motion between such phases. This assumption causes the variation of the angles computed by the system to be smoother than in the real walking subject.

4. CONCLUDING REMARKS

The essential problem of modeling human movement in computer animation is the difficulty to account for the flexibility and adaptability shown by humans in performing a task. In this paper, we have introduced a knowledge-based approach to the synthesis of human motion designed to provide such aspects which is based on a set of rules expressing qualitative knowledge about human motor behavior. The challenge of our proposal is to verify if it is possible to control the movement of the human figure by building a model that avoids the significant calculations necessary for the control of robots and for biomedical applications. Being closer to the way in which we express and understand knowledge about motor behaviors, the system allows also an animator to control easily various aspects of the desired instance of motion.

In the previous section, we have described how PINOCCHIO controls the performance of three motor skills, namely sitting, stepping upwards, and level walking. Normal execution of each skill has been assumed. However, the model is flexible enough to account automatically for variations of the behavioral rules that specify the characteristics of particular instances of the general motor skill. Parametrization of sitting with respect to seat height has been pointed out, and parametrization of stepping upwards with respect to step height has been displayed in Fig. 9. Different instances of human gaits can also obtained with PINOCCHIO. For example, by simple modification of the base of support that is admissible in walking, the system can generate automatically the gait of a person which is carrying a heavy bag. In this case, the line of gravity should fall in an area that is not symmetrical to the sagittal plane as in a normal gait, but that is closer to the side not carrying the weight. Similarly, the line of gravity of a person walking on an inclined plane with a positive gradient falls in an area which is positioned forward with respect to level walking; vice versa if the gradient is negative. Again, additional kinematic rules can constraint the system to simulate the gait of a person which has a limp.

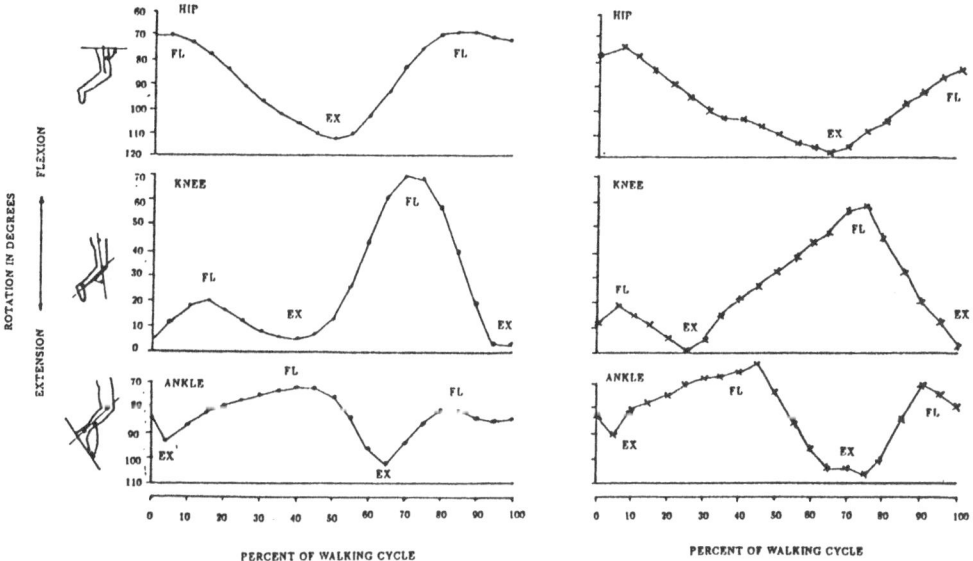

Fig. 16 - Comparison of the variation of the angles at the lower limb as obtained from a walking subject (right) with the angles computed by PINOCCHIO (left)

Future developments of PINOCCHIO will focus on the generalization of the separate motor programs so far implemented into a unique framework that organizes knowledge about human motion for *task planning* (Zeltzer 1986). Given a general task description, the system should be able to divide a global task in a sequence of sub-tasks whose invocation and execution depend on environmental and postural constraints. In turn, the movements composing each task should be controlled dynamically according to general knowledge about the human figure and its motion behavior. Problems such as smoothness in the transition between sequences of motions should then be automatically solved by the system with the possibility of direct control by the animator.

Acknowledgments

I would first like to thank prof. Harold Cohen at University of California, San Diego, for supervising this work during my visit at this school last summer. His guidance and support have been extremely illuminating in achieving the results presented in this paper. I am also grateful to prof. Antonio Pedotti and prof. Alessandro Polistina at Politecnico di Milano for their help in the initial phase of the project and to prof. Barbara Pernici at the same school for her suggestions on the organization of the paper. Finally, I would like to thank prof. Boi Faltings at Ecole Polythecnique Federale de Lausanne for his comments on the aspects of qualitative modeling underlying the approach discussed in the paper.

5. REFERENCES

Armstrong WW, Green MW (1985) The Dynamics of Articulated Rigid Bodies for Purposes of Animation. Visual Computer 1(4):231-240

Arnaldi B, Dumont G, Hegron G, Magnenat-Thalmann N, Thalmann D (1989) Animation Control with Dynamics. In: Magnenat-Thalmann N, Thalmann D (eds) State of the Art in Computer Animation. Springer-Verlag, pp 113-122

Badler NI, Korein JD, Korein JU, Radack GM, Brotman LS (1985) Positioning and Animating Human Figures in a Task-Oriented Environment. Visual Computer 1(4):212-220

Badler NI (1989) Artificial Intelligence, Natural Language, and Simulation for Human Animation. In: Magnenat-Thalmann N, Thalmann D (eds) State of the Art in Computer Animation. Springer-Verlag, pp 19-31

Barr A, Cohen PR, Feigenbaum EA (eds) (1989) Qualitative Physics. In: The Hanbook of Artificial Intelligence IV. Addison-Wesley, pp 323-413

Beckett R, Chang K (1968) An Evaluation of the Kinematics of Gait by Minimum Energy. Journal of Biomechanics 1, pp 147-159

Bobrow DG, Hayes PJ (eds) (1984) Special Volume on Qualitative Reasoning about Physical Systems. Artificial Intelligence 24(1-3)

Boisvert D, Magnenat-Thalmann N, Thalmann D (1989) An Integrated Control View of Synthetic Actors. In: Earnshaw RA, Wyvill B (eds) Proc. of CG International '89. Springer-Verlag, pp 277-287

Boulic R, Magnenat-Thalmann N, Thalmann D (1990) Human Free-Walking Model for a Real-Time Interactive Design of Gaits. In: Magnenat-Thalmann N, Thalmann D (eds) Computer Animation '90. Springer-Verlag, pp 61-79

Bruderlin A, Calvert TW (1989) Goal-Directed, Dynamic Animation of Human Walking. Computer Graphics 23(3):233-242

Capozzo A, Figura F, Marchetti M, Pedotti A (1976) The Interplay of Muscular and External Forces in Human Ambulation. Journal of Biomechanics 9:45-53

Chow CK, Jacobson DH (1971) Studies of Human Locomotion Via Optimal Programming. Mathematical Biosciences 10:239-306

Clancey WJ (1989) Viewing Knowledge Bases as Qualitative Models. IEEE Expert, pp 9-23

Cohen H (1988) How to Draw Three People in a Botanical Garden. Proc. of AAAI '88, pp 846-855

Collodi C (1883) Le avventure di Pinocchio

Cutting JE (1978) Generation of Synthetic Male and Female Walkers through Manipulation of a Biomechanical Invariant. Perception 7, pp 393-405

deKleer J, Brown JS (1984) A Qualitative Physics Based on Confluences. Artificial Intelligence 24(1-3):7-83

Falkenhainer B, Forbus KD (1988) Setting up Large-Scale Qualitative Models. Proc. of AAAI '88, pp 301-306

Ferrigno G, Pedotti A (1985) ELITE: A Digital Dedicated Hardware System for Movement Analysis Via Real-Time TV Signal Processing. IEEE Trans. on Biomedical Engineering BME-32(11):943-949

Fishwick PA (1988) The Role of Process Abstraction in Simulation. IEEE Trans. on Man, Systems, and Cybernetics 18(1):18-39

Girard M, Maciejewski AA (1985) Computational Modeling for the Computer Animation of Legged Figures. Computer Graphics 19(3):263-270

Inman VT, Ralston HJ, Todd F (1981) Human Walking. William & Wilkins

Isaacs PM, Cohen MF (1987) Controlling Dynamic Simulation with Kinematic Constraints, Behavior Functions and Inverse Dynamics. Computer Graphics 21(4):215-224

Lozano-Perez T, Wesley MA (1979) An Algorithm for Planning Collision-Free Paths Among Polyhedral Obstacles. Communications of the ACM 22(10):560-570

Maiocchi R, Pernici B (1990) Directing an Animated Scene with Autonomous Actors. In: Magnenat-Thalmann N, Thalmann D (eds) Computer Animation '90. Springer-Verlag, pp 41-60

McMahon TA (1984) Mechanics of Locomotion. The International Journal of Robotics Research 3(2):4-28

Moore M, Wilhelms J (1988) Collision Detection and Response for Computer Animation. Computer Graphics 22(4):289-298

Morton DJ, Fuller DD (1952) Human Locomotion and Body Form: A Study of Gravity and Man. The Williams & Wilkins Company

Murray P (1967) Gait as a Total Pattern of Movement. American Journal of Physical Medicine 46(1):290-333

Murthy SS, Raibert MH (1986) 3D Balance in Legged Locomotion: Modeling and Simulation for the One-Legged Case. In: Badler NI, Tsotsos JK (eds) Motion: Representation and Perception. Elsevier Science

Pedotti A (1977) A Study of Motor Coordination and Neuromuscolar Activities in Human Locomotion. Biological Cybernetics 26:53-62

A. Pedotti, V.V. Krishnan, and L. Stark L (1978) Optimization of Muscle-Force Sequencing in Human Locomotion. Mathematical Biosciences 38:57-76

Pedotti A, Crenna P, Deat A, Frigo C, Massion J (1989) Postural Synergies in Axial Movements: Short and Long-Term Adaptation. Experimental Brain Research 74:3-10

Raibert MH, Sutherland IE (1983) Machines that Walk. Scientific American 248(1):44-53

Raibert MH (1986) Legged Robots. Communications of the ACM 29(6):499-514

Saunders M, Inman VT, Eberhart H (1953) The Major Determinants in Normal and Pathological Gait. The Journal of Bone and Joint Surgery 35-A(3):543-558

Shapiro DC, Zernicke RF, Gregor RJ, Diestel JD (1981) Evidence for Generalized Motor Programs Using Gait Patterns Analysis. Journal of Motor Behavior 13(1):33-47

Smith MM and Wing AM (eds) (1984) The Psychology of Human Movement. Academic Press

Vukobratovic M and Stepanenko J (1972) On the Stability of Anthropomorphic Systems. Mathematical Biosciences 15:1-37

Watkins J (1983) An Introduction to the Mechanics of Human Movement. MTP Press

Wilhelms J (1987) Using Dynamic Analysis for Realistic Animation of Articulated Bodies. IEEE Computer Graphics and Applications, pp 12-27

Winter D (1979) Biomechanics of Human Movement. John Wiley & Sons

Zeltzer D (1982) Motor Control Techniques for Figure Animation. IEEE Computer Graphics and Applications, pp 53-59

Zeltzer D (1982) Towards an Integrated View of 3-D Computer Animation. Visual Computer 1:249-259

Zeltzer D (1982) Knowledge-Based Animation. In: Badler NI and Tsotsos JK (eds), Motion: Representation and Perception. Elsevier Science, pp 318-323

Dipartimento di Elettronica, Politecnico di Milano, 20133 Milan, Italy

Cloth Animation with Self-Collision Detection

BENOIT LAFLEUR, NADIA MAGNENAT-THALMANN, and DANIEL THALMANN

ABSTRACT

This paper addresses the problem of detecting collisions of very flexible objects, such as clothes with almost rigid bodies, such as human bodies. In our method, collision avoidance consists of creating a very thin force field around the obstacle surface to avoid collisions. This force field acts like a shield rejecting the points. This volume is divided into small contiguous non-overlapped cells which completely surround the surface. As soon as a point enters into a cell, a repulsive force is applied. The direction and the magnitude of this force are dependent on the velocities, the normals and the distance between the point and the surface. Particular cases are discussed with the ways of solving them.

We also briefly present various approaches for simulating flexible objects and the difficulties, due to the numerical methods of solving the differential equations involved. Finally, we briefly describe the implementation of our software for creating and animating clothes.

Keywords: collision, clothes, human animation, flexible objects, self-collision

1. INTRODUCTION

Computer Animation has become more and more interdisciplinary and now uses techniques from very different areas such as art, robotics or cinema. For several years, animators have used models with little consideration for the physical laws which drive the real world. Most of the time, animation sequences have showed geometric and rigid objects moving and changing according to simple or complex predefined transformations. These traditional methods have become tedious and even unable to recreate the simplest realistic effects.

In the last five years, researchers in Computer Animation have proved that only physics-based animation laws may efficiently simulate the laws of nature. Almost all natural phenomena can be modeled with differential equations. Now the question is: how to find suitable models and stable and efficient numerical methods for solving the equations.

The use of these methods not only improves the realism of motion, but also it reduces the work of the animator by introducing automatic motion control. However, the systems are often difficult to control and the constraints which are used tend to make the systems unstable. Moreover, the numerical methods require a lot of CPU time. Fortunately, in Computer Animation we are more interested in the appearance than in a strict simulation of the motion. Consequently, it is possible to accept compromises and heuristic methods can be introduced, which do not change the look of the animation.

For several years, our research has dealt with human animation. In particular, we have introduced operators, called JLD operators (Magnenat Thalmann and Thalmann 1987; Magnenat Thalmann et al. 1988) to automatically adapt the human body to the skeleton. However, clothes were simulated as a part of the body with no autonomous motion. Two separate problems have to be solved for cloth animation: the motion of the cloth without collision detection and the collision detection of the cloth with the body and with itself. The first problem was addressed by Weil (1986) and Terzopoulos et al (1987). Kunii and Gotoda (1990) have solved the problem of garment wrinkle formation.

In this paper, we propose a method of collision detection especially efficient for dynamic models. Particular cases are discussed with ways of solving them. We also briefly present various approaches for simulating flexible objects and discuss the difficulties due to the numerical methods for solving the differential equations involved. Finally, we briefly describe the implementation of our software for creating and animating clothes.

2. COLLISION DETECTION FOR FLEXIBLE OBJECTS

A flexible or deformable object is different from a rigid object because it cannot be computed from a small set of its points. The flexible object must be divided into small parts and each point submitted to a set of local and global constraints. These constraints create forces which prevent the violation of these constraints. Solving the dynamic system requires finding an equilibrium between all these forces. Collision detection adds extra constraints and requires a specific algorithm. For very flexible objects like clothes, it is necessary to solve self-collisions. Moore and Wilhelms (1988) have described a method to solve collision detection for flexible objects composed of polygons. Van Herzen et al. (1990) developed an algorithm to detect geometric collisions betweeb pairs of time-dependent parametric surfaces. Our method is a modification of the Moore-Wilhelms method for processing dynamic cases like clothes on a body during a walking animation. Let us review this method.

Consider two non-parametric objects A and B with triangular facets. We have to detect points of A which come into collision with the facets of B during a certain period of time. The displacement volume of a triangle is limited by the edges and the line segments corresponding to the paths of the three points P_0, P_1 and P_2 in the directions V_0, V_1 and V_2 (see Fig.1). This volume is compared with the path of the point P in the direction V. The intersection is found by solving the equation:

$$P + V*t = P_0 + V_1*t + ((P_1-P_0) + (V_1-V_0)*t)*u + ((P_2-P_0) + (V_2-V_0)*t)*v \quad (1)$$

where the left term is the path of the point A and the right term the displacement volume of the triangle of B. The variables u and v define the triangle surface, and the variable t, the time. Vector equation (1) corresponds to three scalar equations in x, y and z with three unknown u, v and t. There is an intersection when $0 \le t \le t_{max}$, $u \ge 0$, $v \ge 0$ and $u+v \le 1$.

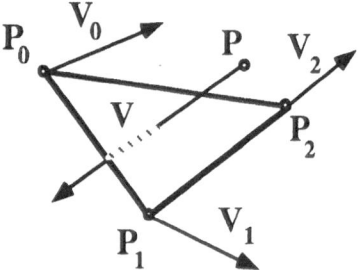

Fig.1 The point P of object A following the direction V and triangle of object B, built with points P_i following the directions V_i

An exact solution of Equation (1) implies that points follow exactly the directions defined by the direction vectors. In a dynamic model, V and V_i correspond to the velocity vectors of points P and P_i. Unfortunately, when the differential equation system is solvec numerically, the velocities at t=0 are not the only parameters involved in the calculation of the new position of the points. Forces modify the velocity direction and magnitudes when t varies from 0 to t_{max}. In this case, a point may go across a triangle without being detected (see Fig.2). One way of solving this problem is to increase the range of u, v and t when an intersection is considered. However, several intersection triangles are obtained for a point and this makes the calculation of the force more complex. Moreover, there are cases where it is not sufficient to circumvent the problem. It would be possible to perform the intersection test after calculation of the new positions and repeat again, taking into account forces until there are no more intersections. This is time-consuming when there are numerous intersections and a infinite loop can even occur if there are a very large number of intersections in a short time. For example, the intersection of a cloth with the human body implies several hundreds of simultaneous collisions.

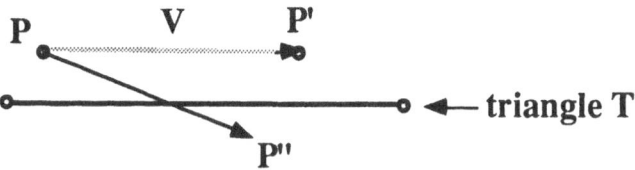

Fig.2 The triangle T is fixed and lies horizontally. The method assumes that the point P moves to P' with a velocity V and no collision is detected. Because of the force F, P moves to P'' and P goes across the triangle T

In order to solve these difficulties, we propose a method of collision avoidance consisting of creating a very thin force field around the obstacle surface to avoid collisions. This force field acts like a shield which rejects the points. This volume is divided into small contiguous non-overlapped cells which completely surround the surface as shown in Fig.3.

As soon as a point enters into a cell, a force is applied. The direction and the magnitude of this force depend on the velocities, the normals and the distance between the point and the surface. The displacement volume is replaced by a cell built from the points P_i of the triangle and the normals N_i at these points. The velocities V and V_i are only present in the calculation of the repulsion forces.

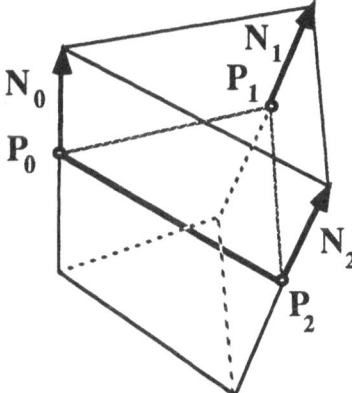

Fig.3 Cell built using a triangle $P_0P_1P_2$ and the normals N_i at points P_i

The intersection is calculated by solving the following equation:

$$P = P_0 + N_0*w + ((P_1-P_0) + (N_1-N_0)*w)*u + ((P_2-P_0) + (N_2-N_0)*w)*v \quad (2)$$

with $0 \le u < 1$

$$0 \le v \le 1 \qquad (3)$$

$u+v \le 1$

$-0.5*w_{min} \le w \le 0.5*w_{min}$

where the parametric variables u, v and w define the cell volume and w_{min} is the length of the smallest edge of the triangle of vertices P_0, P_1 and P_2. The vector equation (2) is a system of three scalar equations in x, y and z with three unknowns u, v and w. By the substitution method, a third degree equation in w is derived which may be solved analytically (Press et al. 1986). The real solution corresponding to the conditions (3) and having the minimum magnitude is then selected. The sign of w determines on which side of the triangle the point P is located.

The repulsion is simulated by temporarily adding a spring between P and a point P_t on the triangle surface. From u and v, the position P_t, the velocity V_t and the normal N_t may be computed:

$$P_t = P_0 + (P_1 - P_0) * u + (P_2 - P_0) * v \qquad (4)$$

$$V_t = V_0 + (V_1 - V_0) * u + (V_2 - V_0) * v$$

$$N_t = sign(w) * (N_0 + (N_1 - N_0) * u + (N_2 - N_0) * v)$$

The repulsion force (see Fig.4) is then calculated as:

$$f_{repulsion} = \left(\frac{k_1}{\parallel P - P_t \parallel} + k_2 * ((V_t - V) \cdot N_t) \right) * N_t \qquad (5)$$

where the first right term is the spring force, the second term is the damping force to decrease oscillations and k_1 and k_2 are constants.

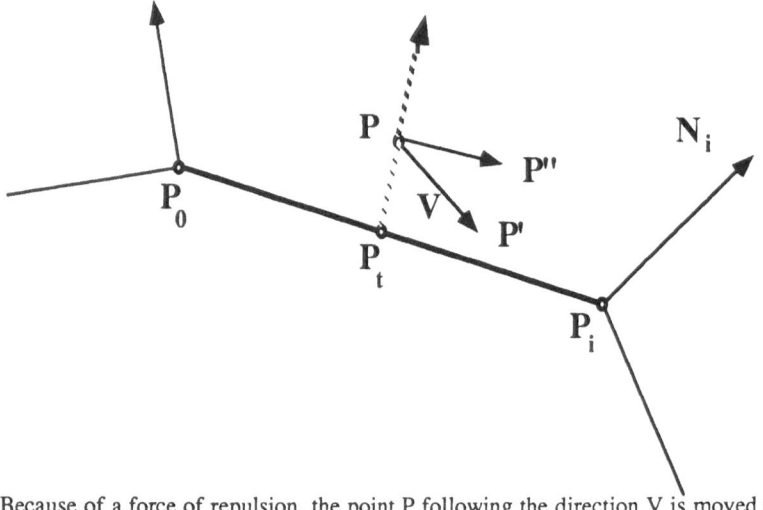

Fig.4 Because of a force of repulsion, the point P following the direction V is moved to P'' instead of P'. The triangle is assumed to be immobile ($V_T = 0$).

This model requires a time interval small enough between intersection calculations in order to avoid that P goes completely across the volume or be detected on the other side of the triangle. Generally, this requirement does not impose a interval smaller than the interval required by the numerical method to assure stability. However, particular cases may cause problems. For example, problems may occur when triangles are degenerate or when the angles between the normals of adjacent triangles tends to 180°. Fortunately, these cases are infrequent and may be avoided by adding local constraints to the dynamic model.

For example, a minimal area may be imposed on a triangle by adding the function gradient as a constraint:

$$f = \frac{k}{||(P_1-P_0) \times (P_2-P_0)||} \qquad (6)$$

or a finite area may be imposed using

$$f = \frac{||(P_1-P_0) \times (P_2-P_0)||^2}{4} - A_t^2 \qquad (7)$$

where k is a constant and A_t the area imposed to the triangle.

The maximal angle between adjacent triangles T_i and T_j is limited by

$$f = \frac{k}{||(N_i) \times (N_j)||} \qquad (8)$$

where N_i and N_j are the normals and k a constant.

In order to avoid the automatic calculation of a third degree equation, each cell is surrounded by a bounding box. The third degree equation is only used when the point belongs to the bounding box of a cell. Other ways of accelerating calculations, like the use of octrees are explained by Moore (1988).

3. DYNAMIC MODELS AND NUMERICAL METHODS

Recent research deals with dynamic models for flexible or deformable objects. In every case, the system is perturbed by external and internal constraints and the solution consists of finding an equilibrium between these forces. Terzopoulos et al. (1987) obtain the elastic force of an object by deriving a potential energy function. The system behaves like a set of points linked together by non-linear springs (Terzopoulos and Witkin 1988). A hybrid model is proposed that takes into account other internal forces and the global behavior. Platt and Barr (1988) use a dual optimization constraint method and a variation of the projected gradient method for solving constrained systems. Gourret et al. (1989) model deformations between the hand and grasped objects using a method based on finite-element theory.

Several of these methods are based on the mechanics equation:

$$m\frac{\partial^2 r}{\partial t^2} + c\frac{\partial r}{\partial t} + \frac{\partial E(r)}{\partial r} = g(r,t) \qquad (9)$$

where r is the position of a point of the object, g is an external force applied at this point, m is the mass, c the damping and E(r) a stiffness function.

In the simplest case, $\frac{\partial E(r)}{\partial r}$ is replaced by $e*r$ (where e is a constant). Because of the second degree term in t, the partial derivative equation (9) becomes a problem of initial value of hyperbolic type. The solution is given initially and is propagated in time and space. Solving Equation (9) implies discretization of the domain of r and t. The following algebraic equations are then obtained:

$$M*\Delta(\Delta R/\Delta t)/\Delta t + C*\Delta R/\Delta t + K*R = F \qquad (10)$$

where R and F are n-vectors and M, C, K are nxn matrices with n the number of points of the discretization of the domain of r.

The system may be solved by explicit or implicit methods. Explicit methods directly calculate a new solution from the previous one. They tend to be unstable and hard to apply to equation (10). Implicit methods iteratively calculate the solution and require more computation. Equation (10) yields linear systems A*R=B which must be solved at each time step. If K depends non-linearly on R, solving the system A(R)*R may become very unstable, because some solutions may cause significant variations for certain values of R and insignificant variation for other values (Rice 1893). Methods for solving stiff ordinary differential equations are described by Thompson (1977).

However, these problems may be controlled when the influence of equation parameters about the stability of the numerical method are known. In the implicit case, stiffness makes the matrix A badly conditioned, but the value of R which satisfies A*R = B is a minimum of the quadratic function

$$f(R) = \frac{Rt*A*R}{2} - Rt*B \qquad (11)$$

It can be proved (Luenberger 1984) that when A is positive definite, f(R) is convex and a local minimum is a global minimum, which means that it is easy to find a solution. It is also possible to prove that a diagonally dominant matrix is positive definite. This allows us to force the effects of the variation of parameters on the convergence.

Among the dynamic models, flexible objects are those which require the most CPU time because of the large number of non-linear equations coming from the discretization. For objects containing tens of points, real-time animation is no always possible on standard graphics workstations. However, in specific cases, the animation requires a very limited control from the animator. In our case, clothes have very little impact on body motion. The animator builds his/her sequence without taking into account the clothes. Once the animation of the actor is defined in a script, clothes may be added easily. Calculation of the equation system may be performed concurrently with the rendering. The sparsity of hollow matrices, typical of structure problems is well-suited to multiprocessing calculations. However, as we use a Silicon Graphics IRIS 4D 240GTX Power workstation with four processors; three processors are used for calculating three frames at the same time; the fourth processor is used for control.

IMPLEMENTATION

Software for designing various clothes has been implemented using the method introduced by Terzopoulos and Fleischer (1988) and our collision algorithm. Animation sequences are created in three steps:

- creation of the cloth by choosing the geometric and dynamic parameters
- application of the cloth on the actor body
- body animation

The geometric step consists of dividing the cloth into simpler pieces. These pieces are semidiscretized using finite-difference approximations on a discrete mesh of nodes. In our system, each point is linked to 16 other points by virtual springs. The various pieces are linked together by additional links. It is essential to avoid any particular case that tends to make the matrix too complex or increase the risk of divergence of the dynamic system. At the same time, tests are performed on small surfaces in order to select good values for dynamic parameters. Two types of parameters have to be considered: internal parameters, such as stretch and curvature and external parameters, such as gravity and wind.

The way of placing the cloth on the body varies depending on the kind of cloth. For example, a skirt must be fixed at the waist. The easiest way of doing this is to impose the position of the border points to coincide with the body. If the points are too distant, the system will diverge. In order to avoid this problem, we temporarily relax system constraints and we add forces to push the points towards the body. Once terminated, constraints are reestablished and the detection of collisions may be activated. The skirt will slowly adhere to the body. Collisions between clothes and rigid objects are detected in the same manner.

Fig. 5. A frame of the film Flashback — flying papers

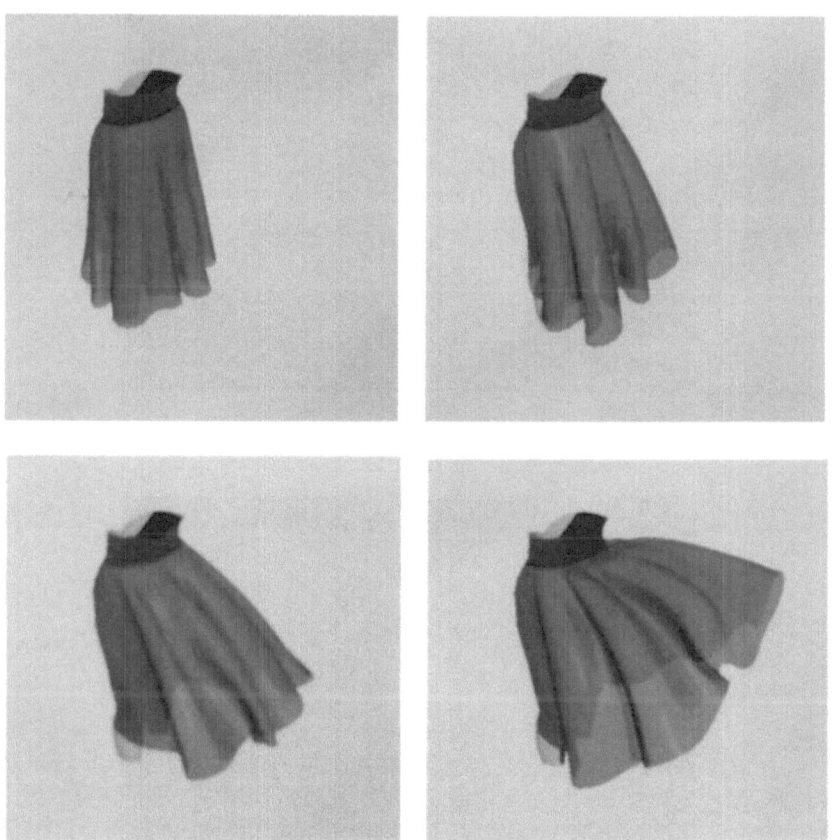

Fig. 6: An animated sequence of a skirt

Fig. 7. A frame of the film "Flashback" with the synthetic actress Marilyn

Fig. 8. A frame of the film "Flashback" with the synthetic actress Marilyn

Fig. 9. A frame of the film "Flashback" with the synthetic actress Marilyn

CONCLUSION

In this paper, we have discussed the problem of detecting collisions of very flexible objects like clothes with almost rigid bodies like human bodies. Collision avoidance consists of creating a very thin force field around the obstacle surface to avoid collisions. Particular cases have been presented with the ways of solving them.

Various approaches for simulating flexible objects have also been discussed as well as the difficulties, due to the numerical methods for solving the differential equations involved. Finally, the implementation of a software for creating and animating clothes has been briefly introduced.

ACKNOWLEDGMENTS

The research was supported by le Fonds National Suisse pour la Recherche Scientifique, the Natural Sciences and Engineering Council of Canada and the FCAR foundation.

REFERENCES

Gourret JP, Magnenat Thalmann N and Thalmann D (1989) Simulation of Object and Human Skin Deformations in a Grasping Task, Proc. SIGGRAPH '89, Computer Graphics, Vol. 23, No. 3, pp. 21-30.
Kunii TL and Gotoba H (1990) Modeling and Animation of Garment Wrinkle Formation Processes, Proc. Computer Animation '90, Springer, Tokyo, pp.131-147.
Luenberger DG (1984) Linear and Nonlinear Programming, Second Edition, Addison-Wesley
Magnenat Thalmann N, Laperrière R and Thalmann D (1988) Joint-Dependent Local Deformations for Hand Animation and Object Grasping, Proc. Graphics Interface '88, Edmonton,
Magnenat Thalmann N, Thalmann D (1987) The Direction of Synthetic Actors in the Film Rendez-vous à Montréal, IEEE Computer Graphics and Applications, Vol.7, No. 12, pp.7-19.
Moore M (1988) A Flexible Object Animation System, MSc Thesis, University of California, Santa Cruz, California
Moore M and Wilhelms J (1988) Collision Detection and Response for Computer Animation, proc. SIGGRAPH '88, Computer Graphics, Vol.22, No4, pp.289-298.
Platt JC and Barr AH (1988) Constraints Methods for Flexible Models, Proc. SIGGRAPH '88, Computer Graphics, Vol. 22, No. 4, pp. 279-288
Press WH, Flannery BP, Teukolsky SA and Vetterling WT (1986), Numerical Recipes in C: The Art of Scientific Computing, Cambridge University Press, Cambridge, UK.
Rice JR (1983) Numerical Methods, Software and Analysis, McGraw-Hill
Terzopoulos D, Platt J, Barr A and Fleischer K (1987) Elastically Deformable Models, Proc. SIGGRAPH '87, Computer Graphics, Vol.21, No 4, pp.205-214.
Terzopoulos D, Fleischer K (1988) Deformable Models, The Visual Computer, Vol.4, No 6, pp.306-331.
Terzopoulos D, Witkin A (1988) Physically-based Models with Rigid and Deformable Components, IEEE Computer Graphics and Applications, Vol.8, No6, pp.41-51.
Thompson S (1977) A Comparison of Available Software for the Numerical Solution of Stiff Ordinary Differential Equations, report No. NPGD-TM-368, Babcock and Wilcox
Von Herzen B, Barr AH, Zatz HR (1990) Geometric Collisions for Time-Dependent Parametric Surfaces, Proc. SIGGRAPH '90, Computer Graphics, Vol. 24, No 4, pp.39-48
Weil J (1986) The Synthesis of Cloth Objects, Proc. SIGGRAPH '86, Computer Graphics, Vol.20, No.4, pp.49-54

Département d'Informatique, Laboratoire d'Infographie, 1015 Lausanne, Switzerland

SMILE: A Multilayered Facial Animation System

Prem Kalra[1], Angelo Mangili, Nadia Magnenat-Thalmann, and Daniel Thalmann[2]

ABSTRACT

This paper describes a methodology for specifying facial animation based on a multi-layered approach. Each successive layer defines entities from a more abstract point of view, starting with phonemes, and working up through words, sentences, expressions, and emotions. Finally, the high level layer allows the manipulation of these entities, ensuring synchronization of the eye motion with emotions and word flow of a sentence.

Keywords: Facial Animation, Speech, Synchronisation

1. INTRODUCTION

1.1   The human facial motion problems

Three dimensional modeling and animation of the human face has been one of the major research fields in human animation. One of the ultimate objectives of this research is to model exactly the human facial anatomy and movements to satisfy both structural and functional aspects. This, however, involves many problems to be solved simultaneously. Some of these are: the geometric representation of the actual facial structure and shape, the modeling of interior facial details such as muscles, bones, and tissues, the incorporation of dynamics for the motion involved in making expressions, and the synchronization of speech and emotions.

This paper addresses the problems associated with facial animation and discusses some methods to solve them using a multi-layered animation system. A language for synchronizing speech, emotions and eye motions is developed to provide a way to naturally specify animation sequences.

1.2   Complexity of the human facial motion

The difficulty of the modeling of human facial motion is mainly due to the complexity of the physical structure of the human face. Not only are there a great number of specific bones, but there is also an interaction between muscles and bones and between the muscles themselves. This complex interaction results in what are commonly called facial expressions. To create a model of these expressions, we must first analyze in more detail the role of the components of the human face: bones, muscles, skin and organs.

Bones in the face may be divided into two main parts: the cranium itself, which surrounds the brain and the eyes, and the lower jaw which is articulated and plays an important role in speech. These bones force a more or less rigid shape to the skin which may only slip on the cranium. The skin covers the bony structure: it is elastic and flexible. There are 40 Muscles which are an intermediate between the skin and the bones. They force the skin to move in a certain direction and in a given way. Face muscles have various shapes: long, flat, wide, thin, etc. In addition to their action, muscles also have volume.

1.3   Basic facial animation

As stated by Ekman (1975), humans are highly sensitive to visual messages sent voluntarily or involuntary by the face. Consequently, facial animation requires specific algorithms able to render with a high degree of realism the natural characteristics of the motion. Research on basic facial animation and modeling has been extensively studied and several models have been proposed.

For example, in the Parke models (1975,1982) the set of facial parameters is based on both observation and the underlying structures that cause facial expression. The animator can create any facial image by specifying the appropriate set of parameter values. Motions are described as a pair of numeric tuples which identify the initial frame, final frame, and interpolation. Pearce et al. (1986) introduced a small set of keywords to extend the Parke model.

Platt and Badler (1981) have designed a model that is based on underlying facial structure. The skin is the outside level, represented by a set of 3D points that define a surface which can be modified. The bones represent an initial level that cannot be moved. Between both levels, muscles are groups of points with elastic arcs.

Waters (1987) represents the action of muscles using primary motivators on a non-specific deformable topology of the face. The muscle actions themselves are tested against FACS (Facial Action Coding System) which employs action units directly to one muscle or a small group of muscles. Two types of muscles are created: linear/parallel muscles that pull and sphincter muscles that squeeze.

Magnenat-Thalmann et al. (1988) defined a model where the action of a muscle is simulated by a procedure, called an Abstract Muscle Action procedure (AMA), which acts on the vertices composing the human face figure. It is possible to animate a human face by manipulating the facial parameters using AMA procedures. By combining the facial parameters obtained by the AMA procedures in different ways, we can construct more complex entities corresponding to the well-known concept of facial expression.

Nahas et al. (1987) propose a method based on the B-spline. They use a digitizing system to obtain position data on the face from which they extract a certain number of points, and organize them in a matrix. This matrix is used as a set of control points for a 5-dimensional bicubic B-spline surface. The model is animated by moving these control points.

1.4   Synchronization between speech, emotions and eye motion

Lip synchronization in computer animation was first studied by Parke (1982) using its parameterized model. Three recent papers report studies of problems in computer animated speech: Hill et al. (1988) introduce an automatic approach to animate speech using speech synthesized by rules; the extra parameters needed to control lips, jaw and facial expression are simply added into the table of parameters needed to control the speech itself. Lewis and Parke (1987) automate the lip synchronization between computer generated imagery and real speech recorded from a real actor. Magnenat-Thalmann et al. (1988) describe a lip synchronization based on AMA procedures.
Previous works on facial animation (Pearce et al. 1986) propose methods where synchronization is manual (e.g. "do action from frame x to y"). However, the parametrization of an emotion is hard to control because once defined it is always played the same way.

Magnenat-Thalmann et al. (1988) used a collection of multiple tracks. A track is a chronological sequence of keyframes for a given facial parameter. Tracks are independent, but they may be mixed in the same way as sound is mixed in a sound studio. With such an approach it is easy to define, for example, an eye movement in an expression corresponding to a phoneme. Although the approach works and was used for the film Rendez-vous à Montréal (Magnenat-Thalmann and Thalmann, 1987), the process of synchronization is manual and must be performed by the animator.

This paper describes a method that can be used to solve the synchronization problem.

2. THE MULTI-LAYERED APPROACH

2.1 The layers

Although all movements may be rendered by muscles, the direct use of a muscle-based model is very difficult. The complexity of the model and our poor knowledge of anatomy makes the results somewhat unpredictable. This suggest that more **abstract entities** should be defined in order to create a system that can be easily manipulated. A multi-layered approach is convenient for this.

The system proposed in this paper is independent of the animation system. The results are specified in terms of perceptible movements (e.g. elevate the eyebrows with an intensity of 70%).

In order to manipulate abstract entities like our representation of the human face (phonemes, words, expressions, emotions), we propose to decompose the problem into several layers. The high level layers arc the most abstract and specify "what to do", the low level layers describe "how to do". Each level is seen as an independent layer with its own input and output. This approach has the following advantages:

- the system is extensible.
- the independence of each layer allows the behavior of an element of the system to be modified without impact on the others.

Five layers are defined in our approach: (Fig. 1)

layer 0: definition of the entity **muscle** or equivalent.
layer 1: definition of the entity **minimal perceptible action**.
layer 2: definition of the entities **phonemes** and **expressions**.
layer 3: definition of the entities **words** and **emotions**.
layer 4: **synchronization** mechanism between emotions, speech and eye motion.

2.2 Layer 0: Abstract muscles

This level correspond to the basic animation system. In our case, the software implementation is currently based on the Abstract Muscle Action procedures as already introduced in a previous work (Thalmann, 1988). These actions are very specific to the various muscles and give the illusion of the presence of a bony structure. More generally, basic facial animation is based on independent facial parameters simulated by specific AMA procedures. A problem with such an approach is that deformations are based on empirical models and not on physical laws.

An interactive and more general model is currently under development. The model consists on a generic representation for the facial components, namely skin, bones, and muscles. The skin is represented as a polygonal mesh. The skull is considered rigid and immobile except the mandible. The muscles are the links between the skin points and the bone. These muscles act as directional vectors for determining the deformations on the skin and their direction can be changed interactively by the designer.

Using region mapping, the designer can interactively map muscles on the model. With another interactive interface the designer can compose the actions of various muscles resulting into an expression. Each muscle has parameters like max, min and value for the amount of contraction. The action units (AUs) of FACS may be used as the guide for constructing the expressions. The deformation of the muscles is based on the simple force equation ($F=kU$). To improve the realism of the simulation, we are currently considering the possibility of using finite elements methods.

192

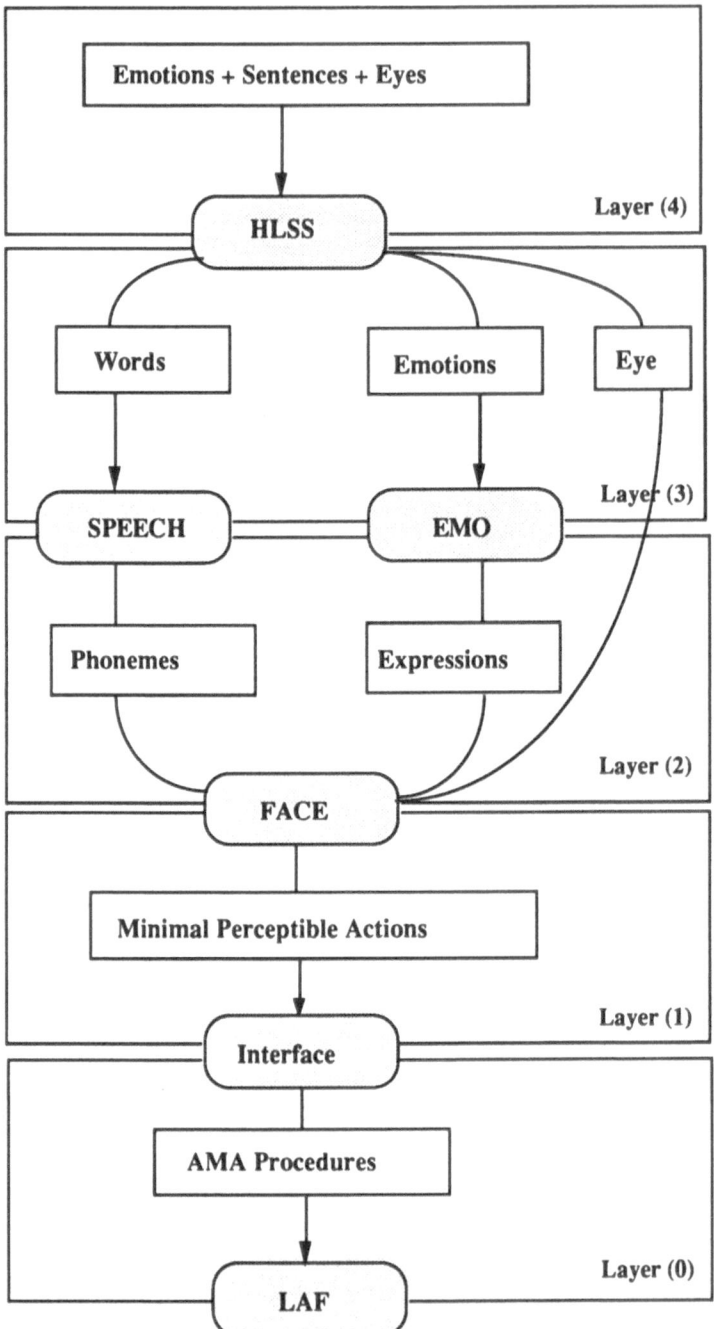

Fig. 1: Entities defoned at each level

2.3   Layer 1:   Minimal Perceptible Action

A minimal perceptible action is a basic facial motion parameter. The range of this motion is normalized between 0% and 100% (e.g. raise the right eyebrow 70%). An instance of the minimal action is of the general form <frame number> <minimal action> <intensity>. The animation is carried out by traditional keyframing.

2.4   Layer 2:   Facial snapshot

A facial snapshot is obtained by specifying the value of each minimal action. Once defined, a snapshot has the form that follows: <frame number> <snapshot> <intensity>. It should be noted that several snapshots may be active at the same time, this allows for example to specify a phoneme and a smile at the same time. (Fig. 2)

2.4.1   Layer 2a: Phonemes

A phoneme snapshot is a particular position of the mouth during a sound emission. It is possible to represent a phoneme instance by a set of minimal actions interacting with the mouth area.
e.g.

```
[ snapshot      pp =>
        [ action            raise_sup_lip   30%]
        [ action            lower_inf_lip   20%]
        [ action            open_jaw        15%]
]
```

Normally, each word of a language has its phonetic representation according to the International Phoneme Alphabet. A representative subset of this is encoded in form of snapshots.

2.4.2   Layer 2b: Expressions

An expression snapshot is a particular position of the face at a given time. This is generated by a set of minimal actions in the same way as phonemes.

Based on Ekman's work on facial expressions (Ekman), several primary expressions may be classified: surprise, fear, disgust, anger, happiness, sadness (Fig. 3-6). Basic expressions and variants may be easy defined using snapshots.

2.5   Layer 3:   Sequences of snapshots

2.5.1   Layer 3a: Words

As already mentioned, a word may be specified by the sequence of component phonemes. However there is no algorithm for automatic decomposition of a word into phonemes (Allen 1987). The solution to this problem is to use a dictionary that may be created using a learning approach: each time an unknown word is detected, the user should enter the decomposition, which is then stored in the dictionary.

Another problem is the adjustment of the duration of each phoneme relative to the average duration of the phoneme and its context in the sentence (previous and next phonemes). Several heuristic methods have been proposed to solve this problem by researchers in the area of speech synthesis from text (Allen 1987). In our case the system is able to generate the correct sequence of phonemes in the given time using a

Fig. 2: Two different snapshots mixed together

Fig 3: Smile (mouth region)

Fig 4: Disgust (mouth region)

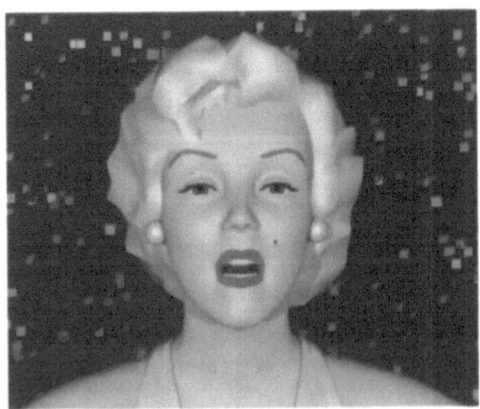

Fig 5: Surprise (mouth region)

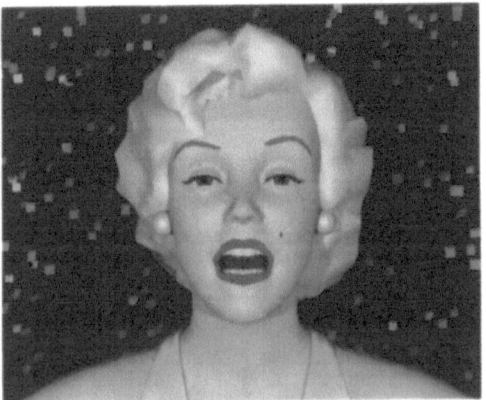

Fig 6: Anger (mouth region)

specification such as "How are you (pause 200 ms) Juliet". Optional commands may act on intensity, duration and emphasis of each word and pauses may be also added in order to control rhythm and intonation of the sentence.

2.5.2 Layer 3b: Emotions

An emotion is defined as the evolution of the human face over time: it is a sequence of expressions with various durations and intensities. The emotion model proposed here is based on the general form of an envelope: signal intensity = f(t) (Ekman 1978b).

An envelope may be defined using 4 stages:

- ATTACK: transition between the absence of signal and the maximum signal.
- DECAY: transition between the maximum signal and the stabilized signal.
- SUSTAIN: duration of the active signal.
- RELEASE: transition to the normal state.

For each stage of an emotion, the average duration of the stage and the sequence of expressions may be specified. One of the major problems is how to parameterize the emotions. To solve this, we introduce the concept of **generic emotion**.

An emotion has a specific average duration, but it is context-sensitive. For example, a smile may have a 5-6 second duration, but it may last 30 seconds in case of a laughable situation. It is also important to note that the duration of each stage of the emotion is not equally sensitive to the time expansion. If you expand the overall duration of the emotion envelope, the ATTACK and RELEASE stages will expand proportionally less than the SUSTAIN stage. To take into account this proportional expansion, we introduce a **sensitivity factor** associated to each stage.

In order to naturally render each emotion, mechanisms based on **statistical distribution** have been introduced. For example, we may define a stage duration of 5 ± 1 seconds according to a uniform distributed law, or an intensity of 0.7± 0.05 according to a Gauss distribution.

These parameterization mechanisms allow the creation of generic emotions. Once a generic emotion is introduced in the emotion dictionary, it is easy to produce an instance by specifying its duration and its magnitude.

2.6 Layer 4: Synchronization mechanism

We already mentioned the needs for synchronizing the various facial actions: emotions, word flow in a sentence and eye motion. In this layer we introduce mechanisms for specifying the **starting time**, the **ending time** and the **duration** of an action. This implies that each action can be executed independently of the current state of the environment, because the synchronization is dependant on time alone.

3. THE HLSS LANGUAGE

HLSS (High Level Script Scheduler) is a formalism for specifying the synchronization and the dependence between the various actions. An action is an entity defined by a starting time and a duration of execution using the general model:

while <duration> **do** <action>.

3.1   Action duration

The action duration may be specified in various ways:

-    no specification (corresponds to *default value*)
     e.g. [**emotion** SMILE]
-    *relative* duration (% of the default value)
     e.g. [**emotion** SMILE **while** 80% **myduration**]
-    *absolute* duration
     e.g. [**emotion** SMILE **while** 30 seconds]
-    *relative to another action*
     e.g. [**emotion** SMILE **while** [**say** "How are you"]]

3.2   Starting time of an action

The starting time of an action may be specified as follows:

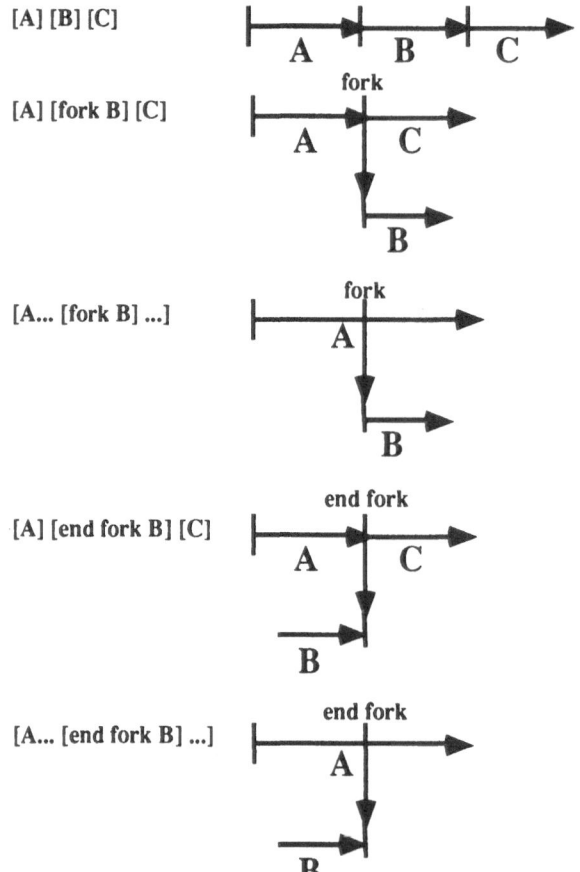

3.3 Action types

3.3.1 Actor synchronization

A mechanism of actor names allows several actors to be synchronized at the same time.

e.g.　[actor JULIET **while**
　　　　　[　　[**say** "What's the time?"]
　　　　　　　[**actor** ROMEO **while**
　　　　　　　　　　[**say** "It's midnight..."]
　　　　　　　]
　　　　　　　[**say** "Oh, it's late..."]
　　　　　]
　　　]

3.3.2 Emotion synchronization

This action generates a facial emotion of an actor; the emotion is assumed to be in the emotion dictionary.

e.g.　[**emotion** FEAR]
　　　[**emotion** ANGER **while**
　　　　　　[**say** "Aghh"]
　　　]

3.3.3 Sentence synchronization

For the purpose of the synchronisation of the word flow with other expressions, each word is considered as an independent action with a starting time and a duration. Therefore, it is possible to execute any action between two words.

e.g.　[**say**　"My name is Juliet"
　　　　　　[**emotion** WINK]
　　　　　　"and your's ?"
　　　]

4. IMPLEMENTATION

This multi-layered facial animation system is part of a new system for the intelligent animation of human characters in their environment, developed in the C language for the IRIS Silicon Graphics Workstations network at the Swiss Federal Institute of Technology in Lausanne and the University of Geneva. Some of the aspects of this system include task-level animation, behavioral walk based on a vision approach, and local deformations of the body.

5. CONCLUSION

The facial animation system described in this paper is based on a multi-layered model. At each level, the degree of abstraction increases. This results in a system where the degree of complexity is relatively low and therefore the animation is simple to specify. Also, the defined entities correspond to intuitive concepts such as phonemes, expressions, words and emotions, which make them natural to manipulate.

We also have introduced a manipulation language HLSS which provides simple synchronization mechanisms. These mechanisms completely hide the time specification. Moreover the mechanisms are general and may be extended to any type of action which may be calculated independently from the actor position and the the environment state.

198

6. ACKNOWLEDGEMENTS

The authors are grateful to Enrico Gobbetti and Russell Turner for the revision of the english text. The research was supported by le Fonds National Suisse pour la Recherche Scientifique, the Natural Sciences and Engineering Council of Canada, and the FCAR foundation.

7. REFERENCES

Allen J. and al. (1987), From Text to Speech: The MITalk System, Cambridge University Press.
Darwin C. (1872), The Expression of Emotion in Man and Animals, Curr. ed: University of Chicago Press, 1965.
Guenter B.(1889), A System for Simulating Human Facial Expression, State-of-the-art in Computer Animation, Springer-Verlag, pp.191-202.
Ekman P. and Friesen WV. (1975), Unmasking the Face: A Guide to Recognizing Emotions from Facial Clues, Prentice-Hall.
Ekman P and Friesen W (1978a) Facial Action Coding System, Consulting Psychologists Press, Palo Alto.
Ekman P., Friesen WV. (1978b), Facial Action Coding System, Investigator's Guide Part 2, Consulting Psychologists Press Inc.
Ekman P. (1980), L'Expression des Emotions, La Recherche, No 117, pp. 1408-1415.
Hill DR, Pearce A and Wyvill B (1988) Animating Speech: an Automated Approach Using Speech Synthesised by Rules, The Visual Computer, Vol.3, No.5
Jonsson A. (1986), A Text to Speech System Using Area Functions and a Dictionary, Göteborg.
Lewis JP, Parke FI (1987) Automated Lip-synch and Speech Synthesis for Character Animation, Proc. CHI '87 and Graphics Interface '87, Toronto, pp.143-147.
Magnenat-Thalmann N, Thalmann D (1987) The Direction of Synthetic Actors in the film Rendez-vous à Montréal, IEEE Computer Graphics and Applications, Vol.7, No.12.
Magnenat-Thalmann N, Primeau E, Thalmann D (1988), Abstract Muscle Action Procedures for Human Face Animation, The Visual Computer, Vol.3, No.5
Nahas M, Huitric H and Saintourens M (1988) Animation of a B-spline Figure, The Visual Computer, Vol.3, No.5.
Parke F.I. (1972) Animation of Faces, Proc. ACM Annual Conf., Vol.1.
Parke F.I. (1974) A Parametric Model for Human Faces, PhD dissertation, University of Utah, department of Computer Science.
Parke FI (1975) A Model for Human Faces that allows Speech Synchronized Animation, Computers and Graphics, pergamon Press, Vol.1, No.1, pp.1-4.
Parke FI (1982) Parameterized Models for Facial Animation, IEEE Computer Graphics and Applications, Vol.2, No.9, pp.61-68.
Pearce A, Wyvill B, Wyvill G and Hill D (1986) Speech and expression: a Computer Solution to Face Animation, Proc. Graphics Interface '86, pp.136-140.
Platt S, Badler N (1981) Animating Facial Expressions, Proc. SIGGRAPH '81, pp.245-252.
Waters K (1987) A Muscle Model for Animating Three-Dimensional Facial Expression, Proc. SIGGRAPH '87, Vol.21, No.4, pp.17-24.

[1]MIRALab, Centre Universitaire d'Informatique, University of Geneva, 1207 Geneva, Switzerland
[2]Département d'Informatique, Laboratoire d'Infographie, 1015 Lausanne, Switzerland

PART 2

Roles of Modeling

Chapter 6

Rendering Models

Non-Linear Perspective Projections

MASA INAKAGE

Abstract

This paper proposes new projection techniques of three dimensional object space to two dimensional screen space. The techniques provide visual effects which break the laws of the traditional linear perspective technique. *The curvilinear projection technique* is shown to be a visual simulation of lens distortions. *The inverse perspective projection technique* is introduced which reverses the effects of perspective technique. We further extend the new projection technique to achieve *the trompe l'oeil* effect using *the 3-D warping techniques*. A wide variety of visual expression become available by the non-linear perspective projection techniques, which enrich the visual work of computer graphics artists and designers.

Keywords: curvilinear projection, inverse-perspective, linear perspective, stretching, squeezing, tromp l'oeuil, 3-D warping, twisting

1. Introduction

Three dimensional computer graphics has achieved photo-realistic rendering, but artists and designers do not always pursue photographic realism. Impressionists paint with colors which are different from photography. They paint with colors that are based on impressions, the way the eyes of artists have seen.

The linear perspective projection technique that is used in computer graphics provides perspective depth cues which is similar to the effect of one point perspective drawing technique that Renaissance artists have invented. Linear perspective projection technique transforms the geometry of three space to two space. Linear perspective projection technique is based on *the planar geometry transformation*, which does not simulate the perceptive vision of the human eyes. This claim can be justified by the changes in the drawing techniques by painters.[15,19] *The perspective technique* in art was once the popular technique during the Renaissance period, but it has become less popular.[10,1] There are many other projection techniques that artists today use. New perspective drawing techniques are tools for artists and designers that provide a wide range of visual expressions.

This paper proposes new techniques to project three dimensional graphics onto two dimensional screens. It provides a variety of visual effects which are useful to computer graphics artists and designers. The techniques exploit the possibilities of visual effects and expressions with three dimensional computer graphics.

To outline the paper, the classic perspective technique is reviewed in section 2.1, and the linear perspective projection technique is reviewed in section 2.2. In section 3, the new non-linear perspective projection techniques are proposed. Examples are shown in section 4, and section 5 concludes and discusses the future research issues.

2. The Classics Reviewed

2.1 The Perspective Technique

Perspective technique is devised to draw three space onto the two dimensional flat plane. It is a technique to systematically draw the appearance of objects which diminish and converge as the distance increases from the viewer. The technique makes assumptions that [5]:

- it relates the viewer, the object, and the drawing plane.
- the viewer is fixed in position, and it is *monocular* (view by one eye).

The horizon is set at an infinite distance where two parallel lines converge. The converging point is called *the vanishing point*. The number of vanishing points determines the characteristics of different types of perspective drawing techniques, one point, two point, and three point perspective technique[5].

A written document on perspective technique in art first appeared by an Italian architect, Alberti around 1436. Many documents followed soon after describing different ways of achieving the illusion of perspective. Leonardo da Vinci decribed three types of visual effect which the perspective drawing should reproduce linear perspective, color perspective, and vanishing perspective.[9] Linear perspective describes the scaling of objects by distance. Color perspective treats the changes in color, and the vanishing perspective treats the levels of detail. Perspective technique became very popular during the Renaissance period, but soon after, artists started to pursue new perspective techniques.

Holbein showed an extended technique called *anamorphosis* which distorts the perspective of an image. A distorted object was painted in his work *The Ambassadors* (1533), which is only properly seen when the painting is viewed from far to the right. Barbaro demonstrated that images can be concealed.[7] In the paintings by Chirico, objects were drawn in one canvas with different types of perspective technique viewed from different angles. Flocon and Escher[2,4] invented *the curvilinear perspective* which provides a fish-eye lens effect. Escher further extended his ideas to obtain the effects called *trompe l'oeil*, visual illusion effects. In oriental paintings, the inverse perspective technique was frequently used.[9,10] It showed the opposite effects of linear perspective. That is, an object becomes bigger as it moves away from the viewer. Such a technique is also adopted by the contemporary artist Francis Bacon. These variations of non-linear perspective techniques consciously broke the rules of linear perspective.[11] Today, linear perspective is still widely used to draw architectural plans and art works.

The linear perspective technique has the following problems and limitations [16,17]:

•It is most effective when the drawing is viewed from the proper angle and distance. Thus, it is difficult to properly reproduce the intention of the artists.

•It does not account for the view from the two eyes. Hence, it does not accurately reproduce the view from human eyes.

2.2 Projections

In computer graphics, *projections* transform geometry from object space to screen space. The class of projections that is used is called the planar geometry projections since the geometry is projected onto a planar surface and it uses straight line projectors.[3,6] In order to obtain *the perspective foreshortening effect* discussed in the previous section on drawings and paintings, *the perspective projection technique* is used in computer graphics.

Figure 1 illustrates the basic mechanism of perspective planar geometry projection

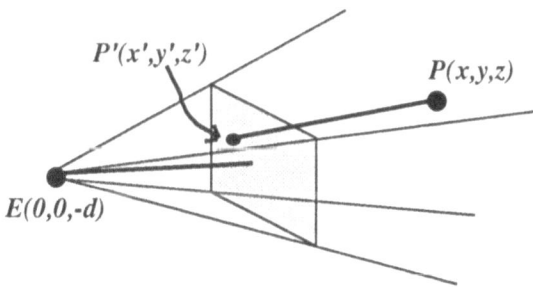

Figure 1 Linear perspective projection.

technique. The purpose of this technique is to transform a point P in the object space to a planar screen viewed from the eyepoint E. The eyepoint E is a monocular eye. To simplify the model, the eyepoint is located at a distance d from the origin of screen along the z-axis, E(0,0,-d). The origin of screen is located at the origin of coordinate system, and it is normal to the z-axis with the up-vector to be parallel to the y-axis. The transformation of point P(x,y,z) to point P'(x', y', z') is [6,14]:

$$x' = x / ((z/d)+1)$$
$$y' = y / ((z/d)+1)$$

or

$$x' = x / ((z+d)/d)$$
$$y' = y / ((z+d)/d)$$

The ratio z/d is the scaling factor of the perspective projection. In order to account for arbitrary viewing, appropriate transformations are applied to the arbitrarily defined viewing so that the eyepoint and the screen satisfy the model previously described. Figure 2 is an example of a ray traced image which uses the standard linear perspective projection technique.

Previous work on non-linear projection techniques can be found in the OMNIMAX films. Max[12] showed the procedure to calculate the oval distortion of an image on film. Miller[13] described the projection technique onto a spherical screen. Projection techniques are similarly used for texture mapping. In Yaeger and Upson[21], a method for non-linear texture mapping is used to concentrate the resolution of the texturing image where it is most needed.

Figure 2 An example of ray traced image illustrating the effect of linear perspective projection.

3. New Methods

Techniques of non-linear perspective projection are presented in this section. The techniques are used in viewing transformations, but the techniques may also be valid for texture mapping transforms.

3.1 Curvilinear Perspective

Curvilinear perspective provides lens distortions. Figure 3 shows the curvilinear perspective. The screen is a curved surface. In order to calculate the perspective foreshortening effect, the distance between the eyepoint and the point which needs to be transformed is calculated. The distance between the eyepoint and the screen is a constant for a spherical screen. The transformation equations are written as:

$$x' = x / (D+d)/d$$
$$y' = y / (D+d)/d$$
$$D = \sqrt{(x2 + y2 + (z+d)2}$$

where D is the distance between the eyepoint E and point P in the object space. When d is set to a constant, the spherical projection is obtained. (D+d)/d acts as the scaling factor for the perspective foreshortening effect.

The generalized curvilinear screen can be achieved by controling the distance d between the eyepoint and the screen. It is expressed as:

$$d = f(q,f)$$

where q and f denotes polar angles in x-axis and y-axis respectively. A similar effect to the distortion of optical lenses can be achieved by this function. The anamorphosis effect can be realized if d is incremented either from left-to-right or right-to-left. This makes the perspective distortion changing in the horizontal direction.

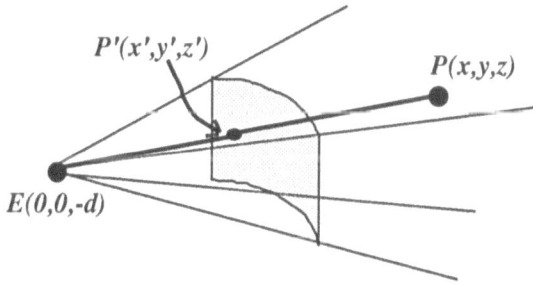

Figure 3 Curvilinear Perspective Projection.

3.2 Inverse Perspective

Inverse perspective is a technique that is often used in oriental paintings. It provides visual effects opposite to linear perspective. As parallel lines extend away from the eye point, they diverge. This effect creates illusion of openess of an space, whereas the linear perspective gives the feeling of finite space. The inverse-perspective effect actually occurs in reality. For example, when the eye is very close to a cigarette box, we see the edges of the cigarette box t diverge.[9] This is due to the fact that we see with two eyes.

To achieve the inverse-perspective effect, the projection equation can be written as:

$$x' = x / (d/(z+d))$$
$$y' = y / (d/(z+d))$$

Note that the scaling factor d/(z+d) creates the zoom effect as the object becomes distant from the eyepoint. Curvilinear functions can also be added to the inverse perspective projection as they are applied to the standard perspective projection.

3.3. 3-D Warping

The non-linear perspective projection techniques discussed in the previous sections have focused on algorithms to calculate the scaling factor for the perspective distortion effects. The distance between the eyepoint and the screen determined the scaling factor for a given point in object space. In this section, we introduce 3-D warping techniques to extend the possibilities of non-linear perspective projection.

3-D warping is similar to the 2-D warping techniques discussed by Smith[18] and Wolberg[20]. The 3-D warping techniques are presented in this paper as methods to manipulate the distance between the eyepoint and a given point in the object space. The unit length in the object space is redefined by the 3-D warping techniques prior to the calculation of the non-linear perspective. Some of the basic 3-D warping techniques include stretching, squashing, and twisting. Stretching and squeezing scales the unit length of object space, and twisting bends the object space.

Figure 4 illustrates 3-D warping. The Cartesian object space is represented by a cube. To apply the 3-D stretch in x-axis, the cube becomes elongated in x-axis. The squash operation in y-axis makes the cube flattened in y-axis. The twisting twists the cube. The 3-D warping is a 3-D to 3-D mapping function.

To render the 3-D warped scene, two methods can be used: a 2-pass technique and a volume tracing technique. The algorithm for 2-pass technique is:

Step 1:   transform the objects to the warped coordinate system by applying the function f.

Step 2:   use the standard renderer to render the scene.

Note that the distance between the eyepoint and a given point in the transformed object space can be calculated by the Pythagorean theorem. We are still in the same Cartesian coordinate system because only the objects are warped by this technique.

The 2-pass technique is difficult to apply for quadric surfaces. Volume tracing [8] is used to solve for the 3-D warped object space containing quadric surfaces. Th ray is actually bent by the function f. In volume tracing, each eye ray is extended incrementally to volume sample the object space until it hits an object or the clipping volume, as shown in figure 5. To bend the ray,

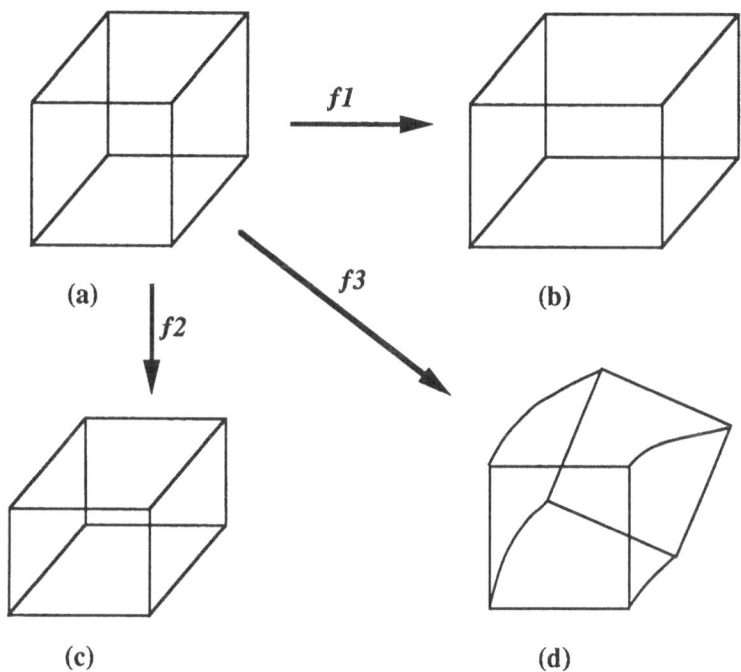

(a)

f1

(b)

f2

f3

(c)

(d)

Figure 4 (a) a cube representing the Cartesian coordinate system, (b) the stretch in x-axis, (c) the squash in y-axis, and (d) the twisting using the z-axis rotation function.

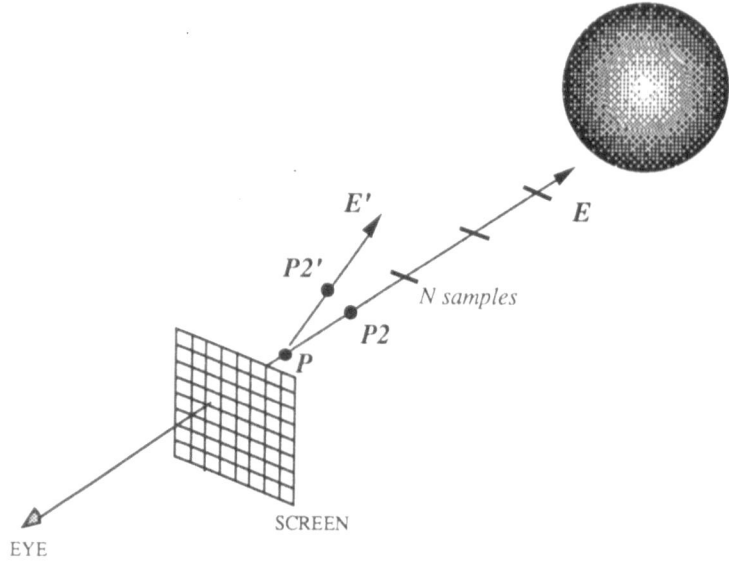

Figure 5 Volume tracing by incrementally extending the eye
ray. Sample point *P2* is transformed to a new point *P2'* by the
warping function *f*.

Step 1:   Calculate the next sample point P2 by extending the ray in the direction
of the current eye vector.
Step 2:   Transform P2 using function *f*.
Step 3:   Repeat steps 1 and 2 until it hits an object.

One of the problems in 3-D warping techniques is the anti-aliasing issue. The 3-D to
3-D mapping does not guarantee a continuous surface. To alleviate the problem, a
higher sampling rate should be chosen for volume tracing.

4. Examples

Figure 6 and 7 show linear perspective and curvilinear perspective respectively. Figure
8a and 8b are examples of linear perspective and inverse perspective. The inverse
perspective produces a visual illusion because human eyes are not trained to see images
of inverse perspective except for the few cases mentioned previously.

Figure 6 Grid plane by linear perspective projection.

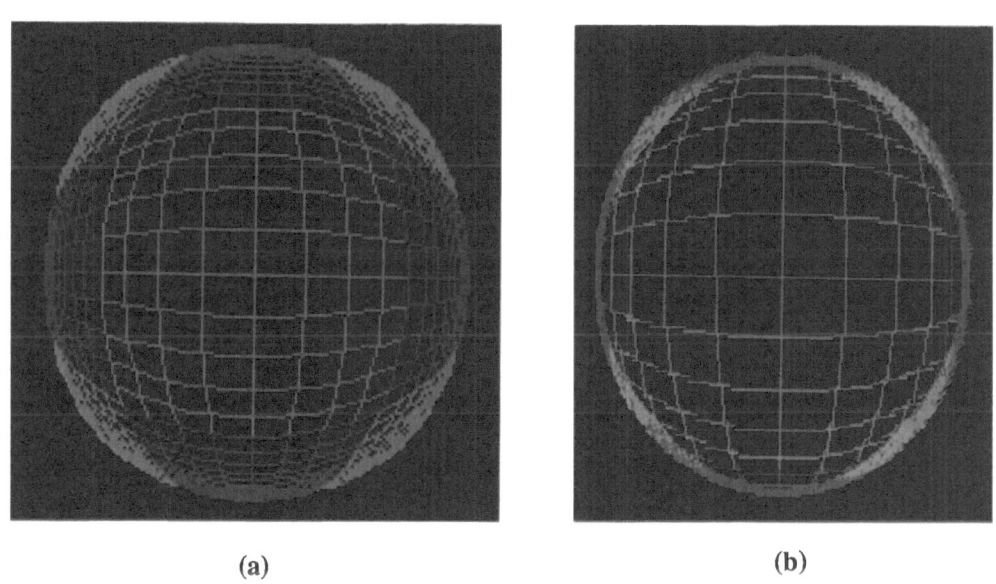

(a)   **(b)**

Figure 7 Curvilinear perspective projection using
(a) spherical lens and (b) cosine lens fucntions.

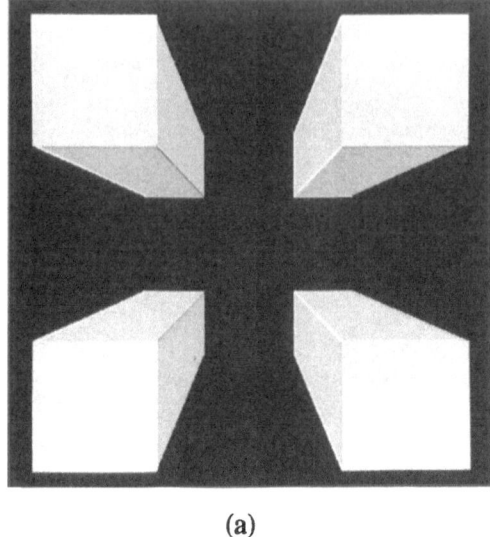

(a)

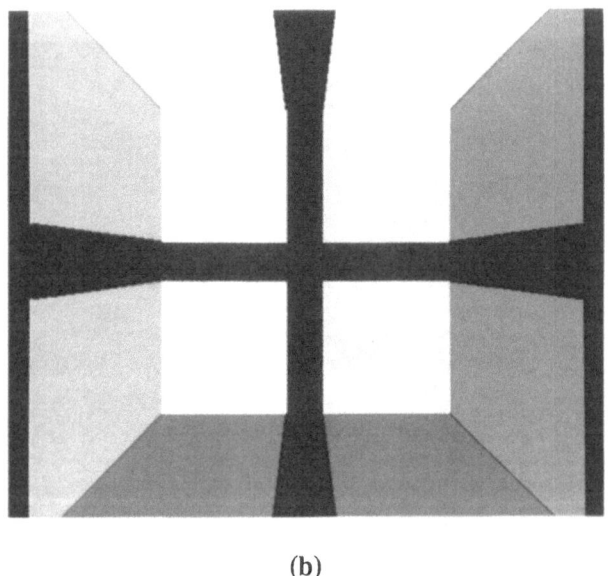

(b)

Figure 8 Comparison of (a) standard linear perspective and (b) inverse perspective

Figure 9a is an example of linear perspective, and figure 9b illustrates a result of the same scene rendered by a sinusoidal screen projection function in which the origin of the function is seeded at the center of the screen. The screen is modulated by the distance from the center of the screen (figure 9c). Figure 9d is an example of anamorphosis function.

Figure 10 ("The Frozen Tension") is an example of 3-D warping technique applied to texture mapped spheres. Volume tracing was used to render the warped spheres. A sinusoidal warping function is applied in x and z axes. The background was composited in post-processing.

5. Summary and Future

In this paper, we have presented non-linear perspective projection techniques: the curvilinear perspective, the inverse perspective, and the generalized functional perspective using 3-D warping. These new techniques provide opportunities to the computer graphics artists and designers for flexibility and variety of visual expressions.

The techniques presented in this paper are transformations from 3-D object space to 2-D screen space. There are many issues yet to be researched. Some of the future research issues include researches on complex examples of the non-linear perspective functions, generalization on 3-D warping techniques, anti-aliasing of the 3-D warping, and the transformation and warping techniques extended to transform higher dimensional geometry.

References

[1]Arnheim, R., Art and Visual Perception, University of California Press, 1954
[2]Bruno, E., Magic Mirror of M.C. Escher, Randomhouse Pub., 1976
[3]Carlbom, I. and Paciorek, J., "Geometric Projection and Viewing Transformations," Computing Surveys, 1, 4, 1978, pp.465-502
[4]Descargues, P., Perspective, Harry N. Abrams Inc., New York 1977
[5]Doblin J., Perspective: A New System for Designers, Whitney Library of Design, New York, 1956
[6]Foley, J.D. and Van Dam, A., Fundamentals of Interactive Computer Graphics, Addision-Wesley, Reading, MA, 1982
[7]Holt, M., Mathematics in Art, Cassell & Collier-Macmillan Pub., 1971
[8]Inakage, M., "Volume Tracing," proceedings of Technical Paper Presentation at NICOGRAPH '89, pp.19-28
[9]Koyama, K., Geometry of Pictorial Space, Bijutsu-Shuppan Pub., Tokyo, 1980 (in Japanese)

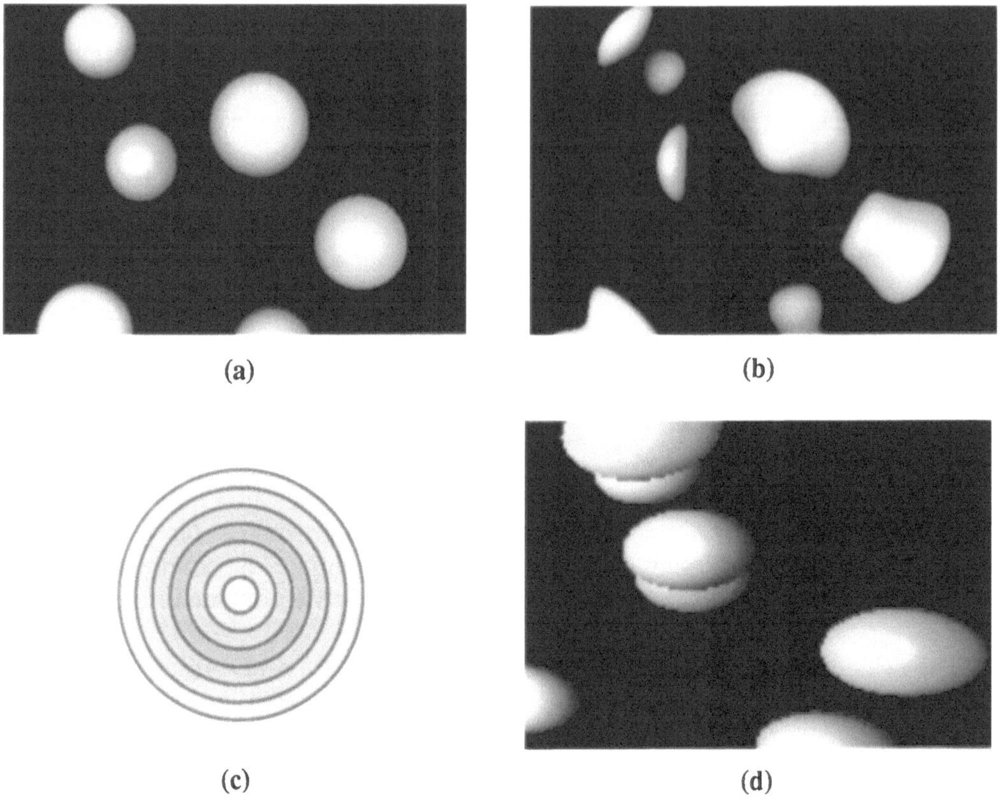

Figure 9 (a) linear pespective, (b) sinusoidal function, (c) illustration of sinusoidal function, and (d) anamorphosis function, to be viewed from far to the right.

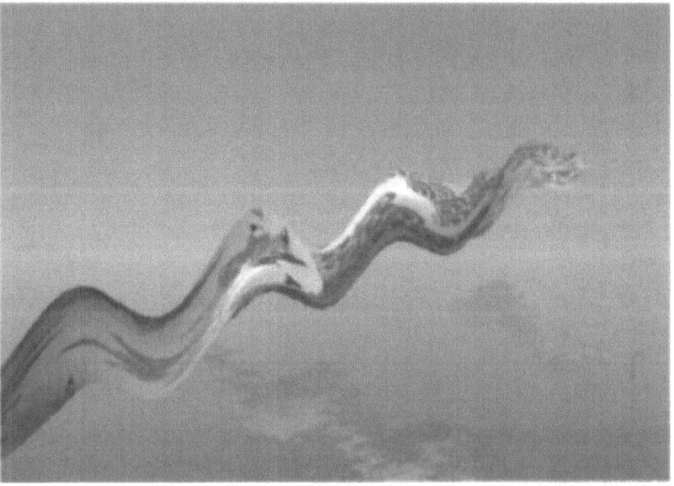

Figure 10 "The Frozen Tension", an example of 3-D warping.

[10]Kuroda, M., Perspective Drawings, Mimatsudo Pub., Tokyo Japan, 1965 (in Japanese)

[11]Luckiesh, M., Visual Illusions, Dover Pub., New York, 1965

[12]Max, N.L., "Computer Graphics Distortion for IMAX and OMNIMAX Projection," proceedings of NICOGRAPH '83, pp.137-159

[13]Miller, G.S.P., "The Definition and Rendering of Terrain Maps," Computer Graphics, 20, 4, 1986, pp.39-48

[14]Rogers, D.F. and Adams, J.A., Mathematical Elements for Computer Graphics, McGraw-Hill, New York, 1976

[15]Seike,K., "On Inverse-Perspective," Proceedings of Japan Architecture Society, Nov. 1950, p.115-118 (in Japanese)

[16]Seike,K., "On Inverse-Perspective (2)," Proceedings of Japan Architecture Society, June1951, p.197-199 (in Japanese)

[17]Seike,K., "On Inverse-Perspective (3)," Proceedings of Japan Architecture Society, Nov. 1951, p.49-52 (in Japanese)

[18]Smith, A.R., "Planar 2-Pass Texture Mapping and Warping," Computer Graphics, 21, 4, 1987, pp.263-272

[19]Thouless, R.H., "Phenomenal Regression to the 'Real' Object," British Journal of Psychology, 22, 1932, pp.1-30

[20]Wolberg, G. and Boult, T.E., "Separable Image Warping with Spatial Lookup Tables," Computer Graphics, 23, 3, 1989, pp.369-378

[21]Yaeger, L. and Upson, C., "Combining Physical and Visual Simulation — Creation of the Planet Jupiter for the Film '2010'," Computer Graphics, 20, 4, 1986, pp.85-93

Media Studio, Meguro-ku, Tokyo, 153 Japan

An Improved Adaptive Ray Casting Algorithm

Renben Shu, Alan Liu, and Kuan-Tsae Huang

Abstract

Ray casting is frequently used as a means of rendering volume data. While this results in realistic images, the computational cost associated with ray casting is high. (Levoy 1990) has proposed a method of performing adaptive ray-casting. In this paper, we propose a relatively straightforward improvement to this algorithm which, under simulation, casts only $\frac{1}{2}$ the rays used in the orignal algorithm on the average.

Keywords: Ray-casting , Visualisation, voxel data.

1. INTRODUCTION

Volume rendering is a relatively new method for visualising information bearing a spatial relationship with one another. It differs from other techniques in its ability to generate images that can selectively display more than one type of data within the volume of 3-dimensional space under consideration. Many volume rendering algorithms and applications in current use impose some form of structure on the **volume of interest**. The volume of interest is that region of 3-space which contain values whose variations are to be studied. For example, in medical imaging applications, this value might be X-ray absorption values. These values would vary according to the spatial coordinates of the sampling point and the object being scanned. We call the X-ray absorption value, or any other values we wish to study within this volume as **densities**. This volume may be structured by dividing the volume of interest with 3 sets of mutually perpendicular planes such that planes within the same set are parallel and equidistant to one another. The space defined by taking two successive planes from each set is called a voxel. This is known as the cuberille model and is widely used (see (Gideon 1985) (Tuy 1984) (Hohne 1990)). The cuberille model effectively partitions the volume of interest into discrete blocks (voxels). Within each voxel, density values are assumed to be constant. Note that this may not be a valid assumption for all applications. However, in some areas like medical visualisation where current medical scanner technology have a resolution in the order of millimeters, this assumption is justified.

If this assumption does not hold, the computational cell model is more suited (Upson 1988). This model assumes that data values do not remain constant at different points within the same voxel but vary according to some function. Such is the case with some forms of simulations. In these cases, the simulations produce data only at specific points in the simulated volume and this data cannot be assumed to be constant in the space between points.

One of the main strengths of volume rendering is its ability to display more than just surface features (Drebin 1988). In (Levoy 1988), a typical approach to volume rendering is described. Essentially, volume rendering algorithms perform two main functions, classification and shading. Classification is the process of determining which of the voxels in the dataset are displayable while shading facilitates the visual identification of displayed values by mapping voxel densities to color values. Classification is usually done by assigning opacity values to each voxel. Voxels containing data values of interest are assigned a high opacity value, thereby making them visible for display. Voxels of no interest are assigned low opacity values, making them transparent.

An image suitable for display on a raster device is created by operating on the classified, shaded dataset. Many approaches adopt some form of ray casting (see (Tuy 1984) (Hohne 1990) (Goodsell 1989) among others). The raster device is assumed to be in the view plane. Rays are cast from each pixel along the view direction. At regular intervals along the ray path, the voxel dataset is sampled. Color and opacity values are accumulated until the opacity reaches 1, where it is assumed that the ray can go no further and is terminated. The accumulated color value is used to set the pixel color.

This approach, combined with appropriate shading and classification transfer functions, can yield highly realistic and detailed images. Unfortunately, ray casting involves many computations and is very costly in terms of processing time. Thus, some way of reducing either the cost of ray casting, or the number of rays that must be cast should be sought. At the same time, image quality should not be compromised.

In (Levoy 1990), Levoy describes a solution to the second approach mentioned above. His algorithm allows less than 1 ray per pixel to be cast, depending on the desired level of image quality and image complexity. The algorithm can be broadly divided into two phases, ray casting and shading interpolation. In the next section, we provide a brief overview of his algorithm. For consistency, notations used in this paper have the same definition as those in (Levoy 1990), unless otherwise specified.

2. LEVOY'S ALGORITHM

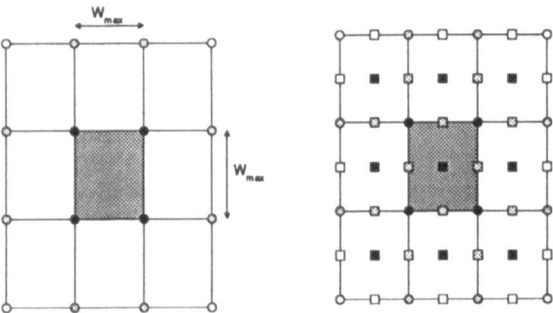

Fig. 1. Subdivision in Levoy's algorithm.

Levoy divides the image plane into square sample regions each of side W_{max}. Rays are cast from the corner pixels of each region. The figure on the left illustrates this process. Consider the region at the centre (shaded region). This region represents a typical region on the view plane. The region is in turn surrounded by other regions. Rays are cast from the corner pixels. These pixels are denoted in black. No further ray casting for the region of required if the color from each corner pixel differs by less than some value (say Epsilon). Otherwise, the region is divided into 4 subregions and more rays are cast. The process is illustrated in the figure on the right. The pixels from which new rays are cast during this step are marked as square dots. The subdivision occurs recursively until either Epsilon is satisifed or the length of the side of the region falls below W_{min}. However, ray casting as described does not determine color values for all pixels. Interpolation is required. Levoy uses a recursive binary interpolation technique which is described in more detail in (Levoy 1990).

This method provides a fast and efficient technique of ray casting when used in volume rendering, since the number of rays fired for a region is determined by image complexity. In addition, it has the capability of progressively displaying images of increasing distinctiveness. Hence, the response time for the initial image to appear can be quite short. However, Levoy's algorithm requires up to 5 additional rays to be cast in order to obtain 4 subsequent subdivisions during the ray casting phase. Again, consider the left diagram of fig. 1. Observe that the pixels in black are shared by up to 4 regions. In this way, the efficiency of the algorithm is improved, since we need only cast the ray related to this pixel once, then use it 4 times. Now consider the figure on the right, which show the additional rays that must be cast as square dots. Consider the region in the middle. We can see that the centre black dot is used by all 4 subdivisions of the central region. Thus, it is clear now that to subdivide a region into 4 subregions, we need to cast a minimum of 1 and up to a maximum of 5 rays. Other regions, particularly those at the edges of the view area, may require more rays to be cast since they do not share the rays with as many neighbors. This is illustrated in fig. 1 above by the color of the dots. White dots are used by only 1 region, grey dots by 2 and black dots by 4. This can be improved upon. In the next section, we propose a technique for achieving this.

3.   FAST RAY CASTING

Our algorithm is described below. To compare the performance of both Levoy's algorithm and our algorithm, we apply both algorithms on a variety of different geometric shapes in a simulated ray-ray casting program and compare their performance. This is then followed by a discussion on predicted difference in image quality between Levoy's algorithm and our improvement

3.1   Triangular Recursion

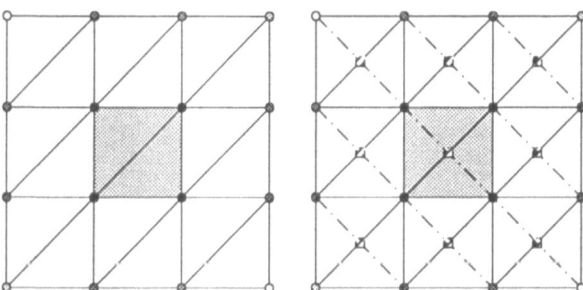

Fig. 2. Dividing the Image Plane.

Consider fig. 2. Unlike Levoy's algorithm, we partition the image plane into right angled isosceles triangles. These triangles are then recursively divided along its hypotenuse.

The color values at each of the triangle's vertice are compared. If their difference is greater than some value (say Epsilon), then the triangle is subdivided into two smaller triangles. The triangle on the left in fig. 3 illustrates this.

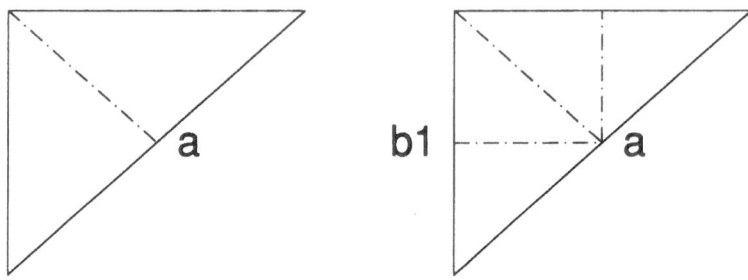

Fig. 3. Triangular Recursion.

Subdivision occurs along the midpoint of the hypotenuse (ie. point a). The triangle on the right in fig. 3 illustrates a further subdivision, in which each subtriangle is in turn subdivided. Such an operation requires only 2 additions and 2 binary right shifts, both of which can be performed quickly.

Note that after the initial partitioning, 4 subtriangles can be generated by casting at most one additional ray. This is possible because we do not perform subdivisions on the side of the region but on its hypotenuse. Since two triangles always share a common hypotenuse, we are guaranteed of getting 4 subregions by casting just 1 additional ray. This is unlike the original algorithm, in which some rays may not be shared by the maximum number of subregions.

4.   SIMULATION

Both Triangular Recursion and Levoy's algorithm are concerned with **controlling** when a ray casting algorithm is applied as a means of reducing the computational expense. Both algorithms perform no ray-casting on their own. As such, we assume that a ray caster has already been developed and can be called by either the Triangular Recursion Algorithm or Levoy's Algorithm to perform ray-casting from a particular pixel location. The purpose of this simulation is hence to determine the number of times the ray caster needs to be called to produce an image of a given quality for the 2 algorithms.

4.1   Termination Criteria

We perform a comparison of the color values returned for each pixel. If their values differ by less than some Epsilon, then the recursion is terminated. This ensures that the image quality from both algorithms are the same. (see analysis in Section 6).

In the paper (Levoy 1990), the actual method to determine when the color differences of ray-cast points exceed the threshold Epsilon is not specified. Accodingly, we have made our own assumptions. Let **MaxDiff** be the maximum color difference between any 2 ray-cast points in the currently considered region. Recall from earlier discussion that in Levoy's Algorithm, this region corresponds to a square (4 points) and a triangle (3 points) in Triangular Recursion. The threshold Epsilon is said to have been exceeded iff MaxDiff > Epsilon.

5.   RESULTS

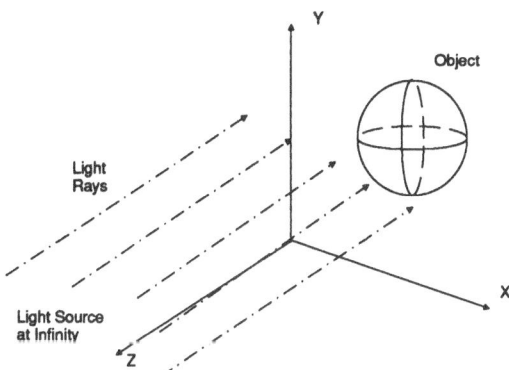

Fig. 4. Lighting Model.

6 figures are ray cast. These are a sphere, a cone, a cylinder, an ellipsoid a torus and a pinched cylinder. Each figure was created on a 240 by 240 pixel view area. **Contour maps** are given for some of these figures. In this context, a contour map gives regions of the image where the color values are the same. Figs. 6 to 8 give the contour maps for a sphere, ellipse and torus. These figures are presented to facilitate understanding on the behaviour of both algorithms. The color values values were generated using a simplified version of Phong shading (Phong 1975) on a number of geometric shapes. The simulation was performed based on the following assumptions;

- □   There is only one light source

- □   The light is locatedat infinity with direction vector L=L'=(c-x,c-y,c-z) where c-x, c-y, c-z are

  constants. in our simulation take 1. (see fig. 4)

- □   The object has uniform texture and opacity =1.

With these assumptions, the color at any pixel should be propotional to the noraml (actually $n(x)+n(y)+n(z)$). The number of rays fired off for each figure is given in figs. 27 to 32 as graphs. The **solid line** gives the performance for Levoy's Algorithm while the **dotted line** shows the performance of Triangular Recursion. Observe that for the range of Epsilon considered, Triangular Recursion requires consistently less ray casting to be performed.

5.1   Pixel Maps

In our context, **a pixel map** gives a pictorial representation of the locations where ray-casting is performed. Figs. 9 to 26 are pixel maps of a sphere, ellipse and pinched cylinder.

Consider the sphere. From the contour map (fig. 6), we see from the close spacing of the bands that regions near the edges of the sphere change color values. Accordingly, both algorithms tend to control ray-casting around the visible edges of the sphere (figs. 9 to 14). However, our algorithm performs less unnecessary ray casting in the sense that the centre of the circle is cast with less rays than with Levoy's algorithm. This tendency becomes quite apparent at Epsilon = 10.

In the case of the ellipse, we vary the color values such that there is a region of high image complexity running from the upper right hand corner to the lower left hand corner. This can be observed on the contour map, in which the specified region contains many closely spaced contour lines, thereby indicating that the color values change rapidly here. Predictably, both algorithms successfully determine that this region requires more rays to be cast. However, Triangular Recursion fires of noticabily less rays.

A similar case occurs with the pinched cylinder. Here, there are 2 patches of low image complexity, 1 in the top left hand corner and the other in the right hand corner. As can be seen from figs. 21 to 26, both algorithms concentrate ray casting on regions of high complexity.

6.   IMAGE QUALITY

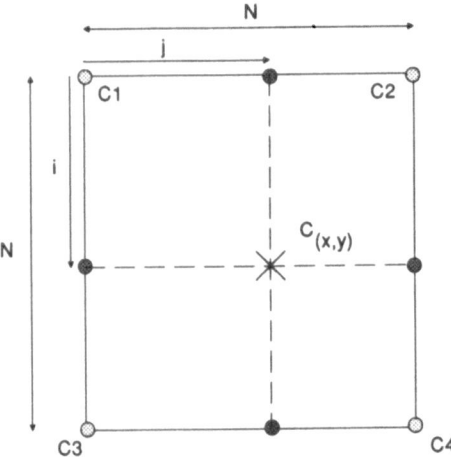

Fig. 5. Bi-linear Interpolation.

Results obtained indicate that Triangular Recursion fires only $\frac{1}{2}$ the number of rays required by Levoy's Algorithm. The difference in image quality between a fully ray cast image and that obtined using either algorithms are essentially in the same order. As Triangular Recursion is employed only to determine the points at which ray casting is to be performed, interpolation of color values is performed in a similar way to Levoy's Algorithm. Levoy's method of performing color interpolation is equivanent to bi-linear inteerpolation. Fig. 5 gives an illustration of bi-linear interpolation. Let C_1, C_2, C_3 and C_4 denote color values of pixels at the vertices of a given square of side N. Let $C_{(i,j)}$ be a pixel whose color value is interpolated from C_1, C_2, C_3 and C_4. Then,

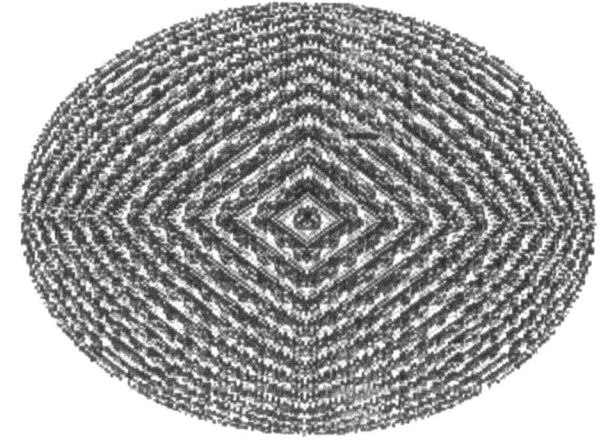

Fig. 6. Gradient Map of Sphere.

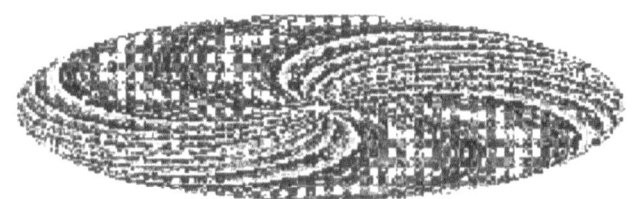

Fig. 7. Gradient Map of Epllisoid.

Fig. 8. Gradient Map of Pinched Cylinder.

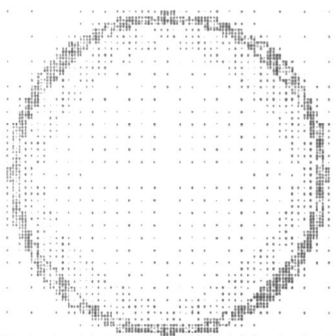

Fig. 9. Sphere with Levoy's Algorithm.
Epsilon = 30

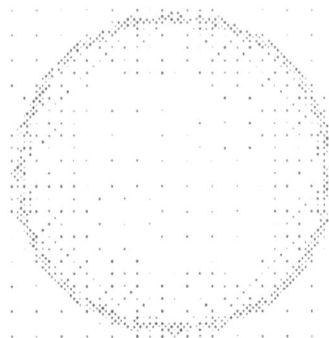

Fig. 10. Sphere with New Algorithm.
Epsilon = 30.

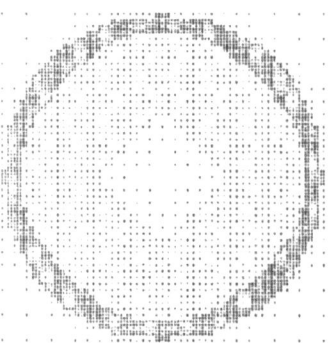

Fig. 11. Sphere with Levoy's Algorithm.
Epsilon = 20.

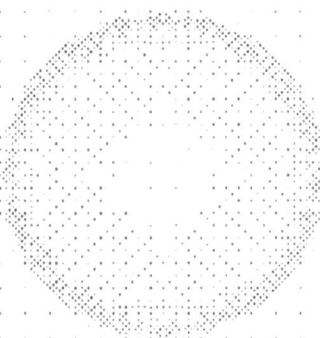

Fig. 12. Sphere with New Algorithm.
Epsilon = 20.

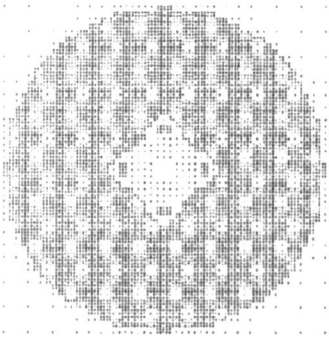

Fig. 13. Sphere with Levoy's Algorithm.
Epsilon = 10.

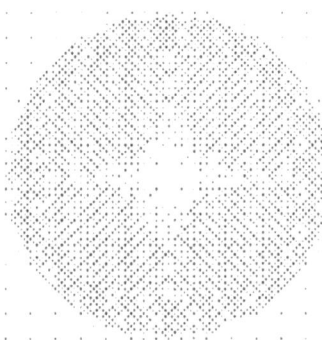

Fig. 14. Sphere with New Algorithm.
Epsilon = 10.

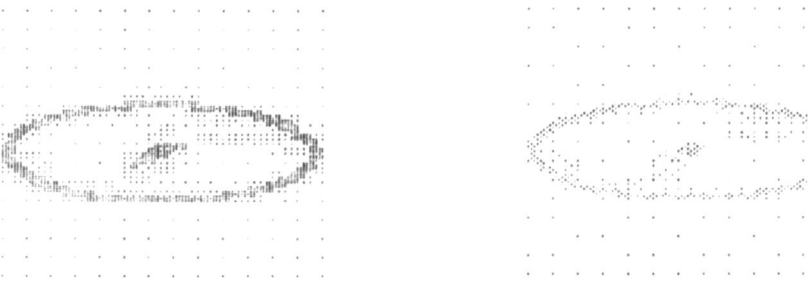
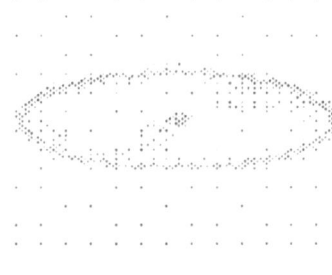

Fig. 15. Ellipse with Levoy's Algorithm.
Epsilon = 30.

Fig. 16. Ellipse with New Algorithm.
Epsilon = 30.

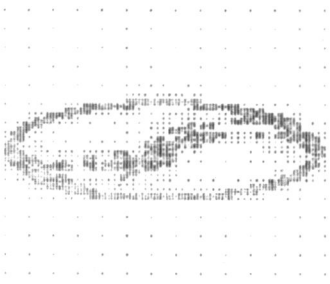
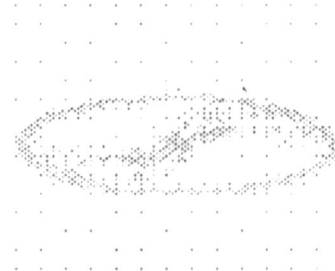

Fig. 17. Ellipse with Levoy's Algorithm.
Epsilon = 20.

Fig. 18. Ellipse with New Algorithm.
Epsilon = 20.

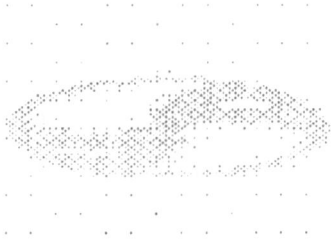

Fig. 19. Ellipse with Levoy's Algorithm.
Epsilon = 10.

Fig. 20. Ellipse with New Algorithm.
Epsilon = 10.

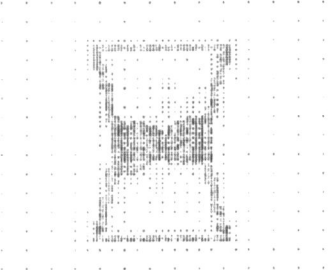

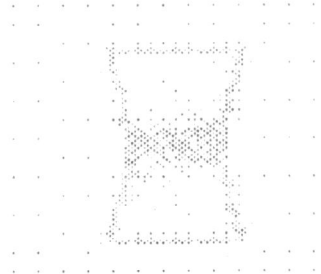

Fig. 21. Pinched Cyl. Levoy's Algorithm.
Epsilon = 30.

Fig. 22. Pinched Cyl. New Algorithm.
Epsilon = 30.

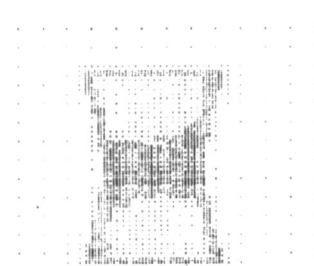

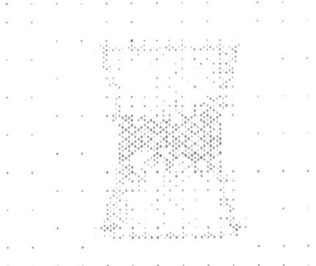

Fig. 23. Pinched Cyl. Levoy's Algorithm.
Epsilon = 20.

Fig. 24. Pinched Cyl. New Algorithm.
Epsilon = 20.

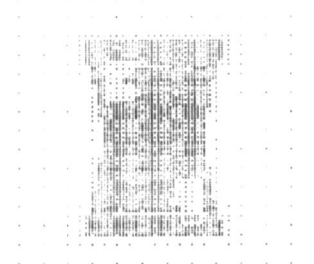

Fig. 25. Pinched Cyl. Levoy's Algorithm.
Epsilon = 10.

Fig. 26. Pinched Cyl. New Algorithm.
Epsilon = 10.

227

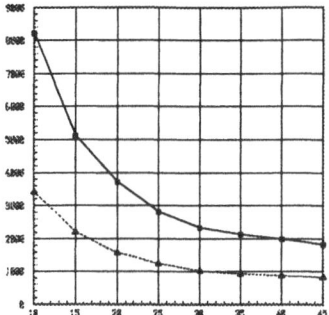

Fig. 27. Rays Traced vs Epsilon for Sphere.

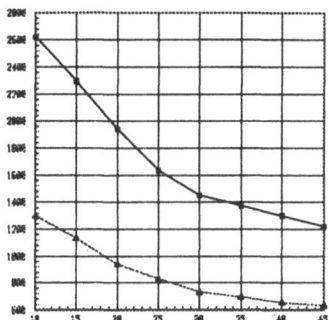

Fig. 30. Rays Traced vs Epsilon for Ellipsoid.

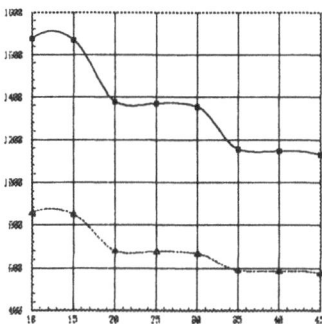

Fig. 28. Rays Traced vs Epsilon for Cone.

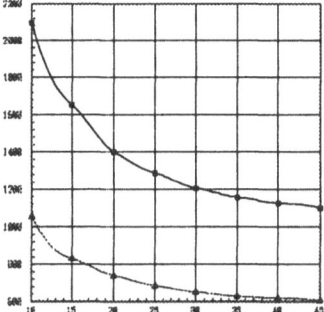

Fig. 31. Rays Traced vs Epsilon for Torus.

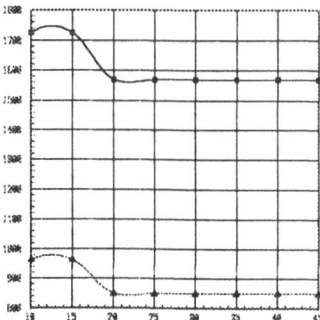

Fig. 29. Rays Traced vs Epsilon for Cylinder.

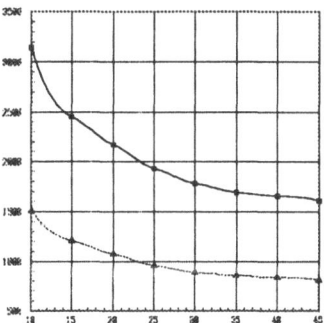

Fig. 32. Rays Traced vs Epsilon for Pinched Cylinder.

$$C_{(i,j)} \quad = \quad (C_1\, C_2\, C_3\, C_4) \times \begin{pmatrix} (n-i)(n-j) \\ i(n-j) \\ (n-i)j \\ ij \end{pmatrix}$$

Now if C_1, C_2, C_3 and C_4 were themselves obtained through interpolation, then if $C'_{(i,j)}$ were the actual color value for point (i,j), we would have

$$|\, C_{(i,j)} - C'_{(i,j)}\,| \quad = \quad (D_1\, D_2\, D_3\, D_4) \times \begin{pmatrix} (n-i)(n-j) \\ i(n-j) \\ (n-i)j \\ ij \end{pmatrix}$$

Where D_i is the absolute value difference between C_i and the actual color value of point i obtained through ray casting, $(1 \le i \le 4)$. ie.

$$D_i \quad = \quad |\, C_i - C'_i\,| \qquad\qquad (C'_i = \text{actual color value})$$

$$< \quad \text{Epsilon} \qquad\qquad (1 \le i \le 4)$$

Since $D_i < \text{Epsilon}$, we may conclude that

$$|\, C_{(i,j)} - C'_{(i,j)}\,| \quad = \quad (D_1\, D_2\, D_3\, D_4) \times \begin{pmatrix} (n-i)(n-j) \\ i(n-j) \\ (n-i)j \\ ij \end{pmatrix}$$

$$< \quad \text{Epsilon}$$

7.   CONCLUSION

We have proposed a simple refinement to the original adaptive algorithm proposed by Levoy.   With this refinement, we have performed simulated ray casting on a number of objects and compared the performance of our algorithm to that of Levoy's. In all the cases, we have consistently observed that our algorithm performed better than the original algorithm. Savings of 50% from the original algorithm can be expected. In addition, the difference in image quality between Levoy's Algorithm and Triangular Recursion with respect to a fully ray cast image is within the same order of each other.

8.   REFERENCES

Drebin R.A., Carpenter L., Hanrahan P. Volume Rendering. Computer Graphics, Vol. 22, No. 4, Aug. 88.

Gideon F., Gordon D., Reynolds R.A. Back-to-Front Display of Voxel-Based Objects. IEEE CG&A January 85. pp 52-60.

Goodsell D.S., Olson A.J. Molecular applications of volume rendering and 3-D texture maps. CH Volume Visualisation Workshop 1989.

Hohne K.H., Bomans M., Pommert A., Riemer M., Schiers C., Tiede U., Wiebecke G. 3D visualisation of tomographic volume data using the generalised voxel model. The Visual Computer (1990) 6:28-36

Levoy M. Display of surfaces from volume data. IEEE Computer Graphics Applications 8(3). pp29-37

Levoy M. Volume rendering by adaptive refinement. The Visual Computer (1990) 6:2-7.

Phong B.T. Illumination for Computer Generated Images. Comm. ACM 18.6 (June 75). pp 311-317.

Tuy H.K., Tuy L.T. Direct 2-D Display of 3-D objects. IEEE CG&A. October 84. pp 29-33.

Upson C., Keeler M. V-Buffer: Visible Volume Rendering. Computer Graphics, Vol. 22. No. 4, Aug. 88.

Institute of System Science, National University of Singapore, Kent Ridge, 0511 Singapore

Chapter 7

Display Algorithms

Pattern Translation in Images Encoded by Linear Quadtree

AMEUR TOUIR and BRIGITTE KERHERVÉ

Abstract:

Linear quadtrees are a method of encoding digitized images which offers a wide range of operations and manipulations. In this paper, we present a new method to significantly reduce the cost of the translation of a pattern in an image encoded with linear quadtrees. We represent images and patterns by a set of prefixes. Each prefixe is composed with string of bits coding homogeneous areas. The translation operation is processed on the set of strings of bits coding the pattern. In this paper, we here propose and analyse an algorithm which reduces the cost of this operation from $nlogn$ to $logn$ in the worst case and to a constant time in several cases.

keywords: quadtree, filtering, translation, binary prefix, pattern, decompositon coefficient, associative searching

1 INTRODUCTION

Nowadays, existing graphics and image systems are oriented towards a variety of applications such as CAD, cartography or multimedia databases. Such systems use different coding techniques and different types of data structures. Each of these data structures is more or less adapted to some applications or others. Here, we are interested in linear quadtrees [SAMET 84] and essentially in the translation of pattern on the images which are encoded by linear quadtree [GARGA82].

The objective of our project [CHEIN 90] is the design and the specification of an Image DataBase Management System, which allows searching according to the contents. Such a system should offer primitives to search images containing a given pattern or form without any specification of this form when inserting the images into the system. The problem is then to define a strategy to access the images without using intermediate information such as the symbolized images or the data dictionary.

Existing systems that deal with Image DataBases offer many possibilities for image storage and manipulation. In [CHANG 88], [ROUSS 85], images are stored as a set of basic objects that have been previously identified and indexed . This approach consists in associating symbolized information- the set of basic objects- to an image whose digitized version is stored elsewhere. Access and manipulation of images are then done through the symbolized information and needs an "a priori" image analysis. This approach allows to manipulate the alphanumerical data associated with these images in using a traditional DBMS. The alphanumerical data associated to an image is defined by the user when the image is inserted.This approach allows to select images according to the properties that are previously defined, but they cannot permit to manipulate images according to their contents.

The representation we adopt is the linear quadtree representation [GARGA 82]. This representation isderived from quadtree which is abundantly described in [SAMET 90a, 90b]. The 2^n x 2^n pixel image is there transformed into a binary tree through a recursive partitioning of the space. Each time an area is not uniform (i-e not completely white or black), it is cut in 4 once again (i-e we break up the area according to the two dimensions) and reconsider. Partitioning is done until we obtain uniform area or until the maximal resolution is reached. The maximum depth of the tree, which corresponds to the deepest partitioning, is equal to 1. In linear quadtrees, pointers storing is avoided : only black nodes are considered. The representation of a black area implicitly encodes the path from the root of the tree to the node associated to the area. The quadrants which compose the image are numbered according to their position in the decomposition process and are coded in a digit string. In a quaternary code, a black area is identified by a digit string containing 4 symbols {0, 1, 2, 3}; with two symbols {0, 1} then we build binary prefix. It is also possible to compact the strings with prefixes when the four values of the digit on the right exist in the image. The binary prefixes have at most 2^n bits, n being the depth of the decomposition, depth corresponds to the desired resolution. Figure 1.a gives the effected order of the image for the numeration of the quadrants. This order corresponds to the Morton order [LAURI 85]. Figure 1.c shows the group of prefixes coding the image of fig1.b with the linear quadtree structure we adopt.

The generated prefixes have different lengths. The size in pixels of an area can be calculated by the length of its prefix. The more a prefix is short, the more the represented area is important. A prefix with 2n bits length represents a pixel.

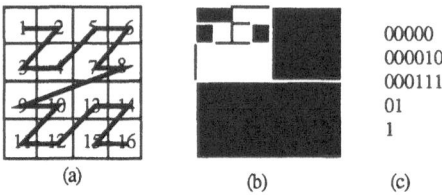

00000
000010
000111
01
1

(a)   (b)   (c)

Fig. 1 coding form of image

In this paper, we are particularly interested in the search of a pattern in an image. Searching a pattern consists in scanning the pattern on the image until we find its best position, otherwise we conclude that this pattern does not exist. The scanning operation is done by successive translations of the pattern in the image and we test if the pattern is found, or not.

The search of a pattern in an image is a very expensive operation. In fact, an important number of translations have to be executed, each translation being itself very expensive. Its complexity varies with the pattern size and the number of areas that compose this one [GARGA 83], so we propose in this paper to introduce a method that reduces the cost of this operation. We will show that the cost of this operation varies only with the number of areas that compose the pattern.

This paper is organized as follows; in section 2, we define the notion of translation vector (VT), and we present the method we propose. In section 3, we study the influence of VT on the decomposition of the pattern; successively, we analyze the translation West-East, then North-South and finally we will generalize to any translation. We will show that our new method has a cost in $\log n$, then we conclude with presenting our future work.

2 IMAGE CODING AND TRANSLATION VECTOR

The system we are designing must offer primitives for associative searching on images. The internal representation of the image should then be adapted to this type of manipulation. In this section, we present the internal structure we have chosen for coding images and patterns and we examine the properties of the translation on this representation.

2.1 Translation Vector

The linear quadtree representation we have chosen allows to store the images as ordered lists of binary prefixes. This representation is adapted to searching according to the contents since it allows to consider the searching as filtering the prefixes list of the image with the prefixes list encoding the pattern . During the searching process , filtering should be executed many times. In fact, pattern searching in an image requires to set this pattern to the North-West (NW) position of the image; then to move it and to filter the image again and that for each new position.

Let's suppose that we wish to make a translation of a given pattern. We should first decompose this pattern in pixels, then process the translation for each pixel and finally group together the areas encoding the pattern after translation. These steps are illustrated in fig3, where we consider an $2^3 \times 2^3$ image , the pattern is composed of 16 pixels encoded by one prefix P=00. These steps are due to the fact that VT is defined with a prefix that has 2n bits length, resulting from the difference between the extremity prefix and the origin prefix of the vector (fig 2). So, it clearly appears in this example that using the pixel notion, to define translation vector, leads to an important complexity due to the prefixes splitting generated by the translation; if we suppose that the pattern to be translated is composed of M prefixes which group m pixels $(m<2^n \times 2^n)$, the complexity of this operation [GARGA 83] is $c_1 \times m \times M + c_2$, where c_1 and c_2 are two constants.

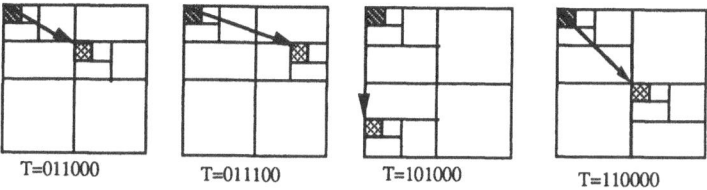

T=011000   T=011100   T=101000   T=110000

Fig. 2 Definition of VT by using the pixel notion

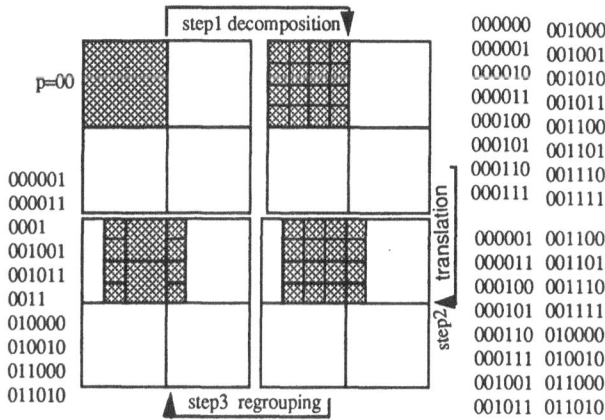

Fig. 3

The disadvantage of this operation is that it is very costly since the prefixes must be splitted, and this corresponds to the decomposition of the pattern. Moreover it is a crucial operation which is necessary to be optimized. In [AHUJ 84], the complexity of this operation is proportional to the product of the resolution of the image and the number of nodes in the target tree; [OSSE 84] report an improvement, but their algorithm has the same complexity as that in [AHUJ84]. [WALS 88] use the binary representation of the translation vector to determine the decomposition of the translated pattern. Our method consists (fig 4) to determine directly the target tree (and so the complexity is carried to M), without using steps presented in fig 3 but in processing a direct translation.

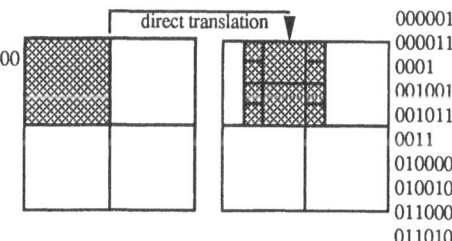

Fig. 4

2.2 The Translation Operation

To avoid the problem of decomposition and the change to the pixel notion, we introduce a new definition of VT. We consider that VT is defined by a variable length prefix, which is obtained from the difference between extremity and origin areas of the vector (fig 5).

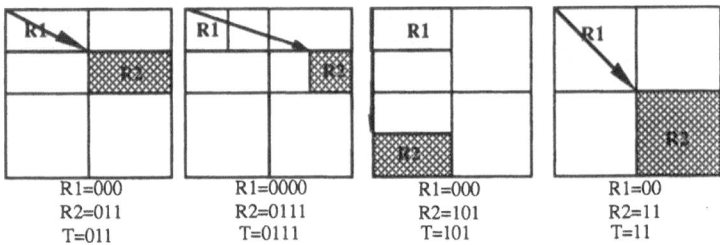

Fig. 5 Definition of VT by using the area notion

This definition of VT is of prime necessity because it allows to determine the complexity of this operation and in certain case to reduce this complexity to a constant cost. Figure 5 shows that prefixes of the vectors have variable lengths whether in fig 3 all the prefixes of the vectors have the same length.

2.3 Variation of the Decomposition

The prefix length of the vector has an important role as we notice in fig 6. Particularly, we note that when the prefix length of the vector is less than or equal to the length of a pattern prefix P, this translation is executed without any decomposition of P. On the contrary, if the length of P is less than that of the vector, the translated pattern P is then a group of prefixes computed using the decomposition.

Let M be the set of a pattern prefixes to be translated, T the vector prefix , the general algorithm of this operation is then:

```
for each P in M do
begin
        if (prefix_length (P)≥prefix_length (T))      then P_image=T+P;
        else decomposition(P,T);
        P= next_prefix(P);
end;
```

where *prefix_length* computes the length of a prefix and *decomposition* computes the translated pattern P. In next section, we analyze this function, in order to executed it as shown in fig 4.

3 ANALYSIS OF THE PATTERN DECOMPOSITION

In this section, we will show that the complexity of the pattern decomposition depends on the vector prefix. First we examine the properties of the data structure, then the behavior of the decomposition for particular translation (West-East and North-South) and finally we expose the general case.

3.1 Structure Properties

We have seen in (§2) that a pattern is composed of a set of areas; each one being represented by a prefix Pz which length is LPz. To process the translation of a pattern, we have to move each area that composes this one. This remark leads us to take patterns that are composed with one area and having the length of their prefixes less than the one of the vector prefix . In next sections, we adopt the following notations:

an image is composed of $2^n \times 2^n$ pixels

Z is an area to be translated, defined by (P,LP) where P is its prefix and LP its length

VT is defined by (T,LT) where T is its prefix and LT its length

NP the size of Z in pixels

N the number of the areas generated by decomposition

x(T), y(T) two prefixes defined as follow:

$x(T)=t_{x1}t_{x2}...t_{xk}$, $y(T)=t_{y1}t_{y2}...t_{yk}$ where t_{xl}, t_{yl} are bits of T, l=1,...k;

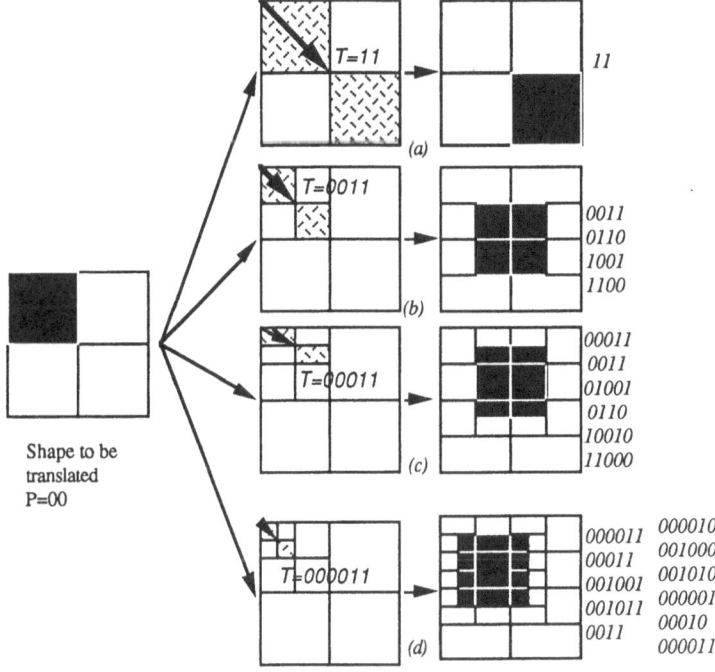

Fig. 6 variation of the complexity of the decomposition with T

The Proofs of the following propositions are exposed at the end of this paper.

P1)- Let Z' be an area defined by (P',LP') having a size NP', such as LP'=LP+k, where k is an integer then $NP'=NP/2^k$

P2)- $NP=2^{(n-LP)}$, moreover if LP is even Z is a square otherwise Z is a rectangular

P3)- Let two areas Z1, Z2 be defined respectively by (P1,LP1) and (P2,LP2), where LP1≥LP2, NP1, NP2 their size then $NP2=NP1*2^{(LP1-LP2)}$

P4)- Let L1,L2 be two integers where L1≤L2, then we can decompose Z on N new areas, where N has one of the following forms (we will show that when area is translated, its decomposition has one of these forms):

$$(1) N=\sum_{k=1}^{L1}2^k+2^{L1}$$

$$(2) N=\sum_{k=0}^{L1-1}2^k+2^{L1-1}$$

$$(3)\ N= \sum_{k=0}^{L1-L2} 2^{(L1-k)} + \sum_{k=(L1-L2)+1}^{L1} (2^{(L1-k)}-1)+2^{L1}+ \sum_{k=1}^{L2-1} (2^{k}-1)+(2^{(L2-1)}-1)$$

$$(4)\ N= \sum_{k=1}^{L1-L2} 2^{(L1-k)} + \sum_{k=(L1-L2)+1}^{L1-1} (2^{(L1-k)}-1)+2^{L1-1}+ \sum_{k=1}^{L2} (2^{k}-1)+(2^{L2}-1)$$

P5)- Let define VT1 by the LP bits left of T and VT2 by the (LT-LP) bits right of T, that we add LP bits null on the left, then these two following assertion are equivalent:

    (a) Z is translated of VT

    (b) Z is translated of VT1, then its image Z1 is translated of VT2

P6)- If $y(T)$ is less than or equal to $x(T)$ then LT is even otherwise LT is odd.

Remarks

R1)- One of the consequences of the decomposition as (P4) is that each term 2^k represents a number of areas having the same size.

R2)- According to (P5), since LP=LT1, the first translation of (b) is done without any splitting.

3.2 Decomposition Coefficient

We have shown with the example of fig 6 that a translated pattern can be presented under various forms. This very variable aspect of the decomposition is due to the difference between LT and LP . We note that if (LT-LP)=0 (fig 6.a) the translation is executed without any decomposition. But when (LT-LP)>0 the decomposition is done. We will treat only the last case because in the first one the translation is a simple 'addition' between P and T.

In this section, we introduce first the decomposition coefficient CD as a prefix defined by the (LT-LP) right bits of T; we note also $x(CD)$ (resp. $y(CD)$) the prefix obtained by concatenation of the even (resp. odd) bits of CD. We have then by noticing t_k the bit of T having a row k :

```
if even(LT-LP) then
        if even(LT) then
                begin
                    y(CD)=t(LT-LP)+1 t(LT-LP)+3 ... tLT-1
                    x(CD)=t(LT-LP)+2 t(LT-LP)+4 ... tL T
                end
        else begin
                    y(CD)=t(LT-LP)+1 t(LT-LP)+3 ... tLT
                    x(CD)=t(LT-LP)+2 t(LT-LP)+4 ... tLT-1
                end
else begin
        if even(LT ) then
        begin
                    y(CD)=t(LT-LP)+2 t(LT-LP)+4 ... tLT-1
                    x(CD)=t(LT-LP)+1 t(LT-LP)+3 ... tLT
        end
        else begin
                    y(CD)=t(LT-LP)+2 t(LT-LP)+4 ... tL T
                    x(CD)=t(LT-LP)+1 t(LT-LP)+3 ... tLT-1
            end
        end
```

As we defined previously (§2) VT as a prefix with a variable length, we adopt the same principle for x(CD) and y(CD) by eliminating the rightest null bits. We call x(CD) (resp.y(CD)) the WE (resp. NS) decomposition coefficient. For example if T=000100110010 and P=00, then CD=0100110010, x(CD)=101 and y(CD)=00101.

3.3 West-East Translation

In this section, we analyze the behavior of W.E. translation and we show that latter is depends entirely on knowledge of x(CD).

3.3.1 The Decomposition Behavior According to x(CD)

In this section, with the help of examples, we examine first the behavior of the decomposition by moving an area several times, then we expose the general case. Let a pattern be defined by (P,LP), we process several translation from the original position, then we analyze the results obtained and show the function played by x(CD).

The example that we analyze (fig 7) is a pattern having prefix P=00. In fig 7.a T=0001 then x(CD)=1. The translated pattern is composed of two identical columns where each column is composed of 2 areas having the same size. On the other hand, the second translation (fig 7.b), where x(CD)=01, the generated areas are distributed in three columns, while the decomposition in fig 7.c (resp. fig 7.d) where x(CD)=001 (resp. x(CD)=0001) the areas are distributed in four (resp.five) columns.

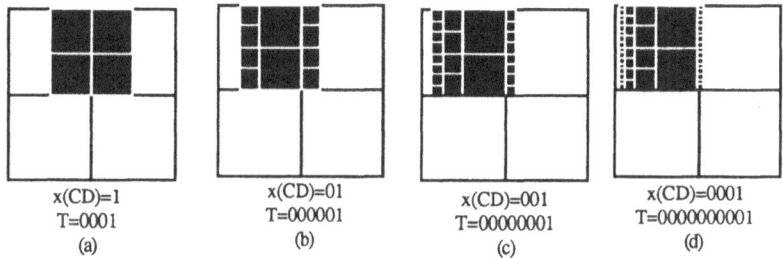

x(CD)=1
T=0001
(a)

x(CD)=01
T=000001
(b)

x(CD)=001
T=00000001
(c)

x(CD)=0001
T=0000000001
(d)

Fig. 7 variation of the complexity of the decomposition with x(CD)

The first notice that we pick out and can define a priori our application rules are:

Proposition 1)- Let Z be defined by (P,LP); Z goes trough a translation which vector is defined by (T,LT); x(CD) the decomposition coefficient having i bits length defined from T and P, then:

a)- the generated areas have a square form and are distributed in (i+1) columns where each column is composed with same size areas.

b)- let k be the row of one column k=2...i; this column is then composed of 2^k areas if LP is even otherwise this one is composed of $2^{(k-1)}$; furthermore, the first and the last columns are identical and composed of 2^i areas.

Proof)- First we apply (P5.b) to Z; let Z1 be the obtained area from the first translation; if LP is even Z1 is decomposed as (P4.1) otherwise it is decomposed as (P4.2)

Second we execute the second translation to the set of areas generated by this decomposition. Since all these generated prefixes have a length less than or equal to LT1 (consequence of the decomposition), this second translation creates the transfer of the first column to the last position and this by propagation of the shifting. Since LT2 is even (according to P6) by applying P4.2 all the prefixes have the same parity that is LT2's one.

b)- let's suppose that i=L1, the number of columns and their composition are then a consequence of (P4.1), (P4.2), (R1), (R2).

Since, each column is composed with identical areas, the recognition of the first prefix of one column allows to fix the remaining prefixes of the areas. The function even_column allows to compute the prefixes of one column.

```
even_column(p:prefix,nb_column,rang:integer)
nb_pref,i:integer;
begin
   nb_pref=2^(nb_column-rang);
   for i:=1 to nb_pref do    displace1(p);
end;
```

We notice finally that the columns generated by the decomposition are distributed in a monotonous manner; in an other word, the size of the areas that compose each column increases from West to East direction. In reality, this monotony is conserved only for well determined x(CD) values, that is x(CD)=00...01.

3.3.2 Decomposition Distribution

In this section, we will show that each bit of x(CD) determines the position of its column and the number of areas that compose it. We will compare the results of examples (fig 7&8), then we give the general case for this type of translation. In these examples, the pattern to be translated has a prefix P=00 and we move it with translation vectors where their prefixes T have 10 bits lengths.

Fig 7.d shows that where x(CD)=0001, we have a monotonous distribution of columns; this characteristic is lost in the examples of fig 8. We note for example that in fig 8.a where x(CD)=0011, the value of the second bit from the right is changed and so its column (the second one from the left) is moved. In fig 8.b where x(CD)=0101 the third bit is changed and so its column (the third one from the left) is moved. Yet in fig 8.c where x(CD)=0111 the second and the third bit are changed and so their columns are moved.

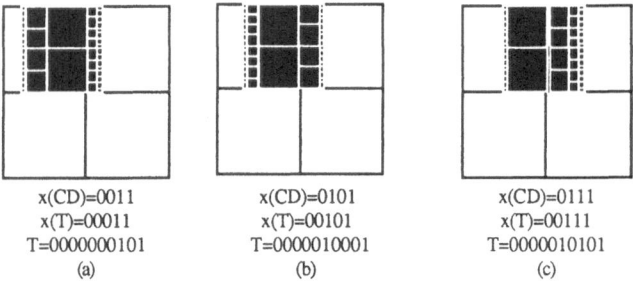

x(CD)=0011	x(CD)=0101	x(CD)=0111
x(T)=00011	x(T)=00101	x(T)=00111
T=0000000101	T=0000010001	T=0000010101
(a)	(b)	(c)

Fig. 8 variation of the decomposition with the bits values of x(CD)

According to the proposition 1 and notes of section 3.3.2 we can describe the general algorithm as follows:

```
translation_WE(T,P:prefix)
XCD:prefix;
i:integer;
begin
     calcul_XCD(T,P,XCD)
     i=prefix_length(XCD);
     LP=prefix_length(P);
     if even(LP) square_area(P,i,XCD)
     else rectangular_area(P,i,XCD);
end;
```
```
square_area(p0:prefix; i:integer; XCD:prefix)
rang: integer ;
```

```
begin
    even_column(p0,i,0);
    displace0(p0);
    for rang:=1 to (i-1) do
            if valeur_bit(XCD,rang)=0 then
            begin
                    even_column(p0,i,rang);
                    displace0(p0);
            end;
    for rang:=(i-1) downto 1 do
            if valeur_bit(XCD,rang)=1 then
            begin
                    even_column(p0,i,rang);
                    displace0(p0);
            end;
    even_column(p0,i,0);
end;
```

the function rectangular_area is analogous to square_area. We express now the operation cost for this type of translation:

Corollary1 a)- let an area be defined by (P,LP), if it is translated by a translation vector (T,LT), such as the length of x(CD) is i; we have then N areas generated where:

$$\text{if LP is even } N=\sum_{k=1}^{i}2^k +2^i, \text{ otherwise } N=\sum_{k=0}^{i-1}2^k+2^{i-1}=2^i+2^{(i-1)}-1.$$

b)- the complexity of this operation depends only on x(CD).

Proof a)- according to (P6) LT is even; we apply then (P4) and proposition1 we have:

$$\text{if LP is even } i=(LT-LP)/2 \text{ and according to (P4.1) } N=\sum_{k=1}^{i}2^k+2^i$$

$$\text{otherwise } i=(LT-LP+1)/2 \text{ and according to (P4.2) } N=\sum_{k=0}^{i-1}2^k+2^{i-1}$$

b)- the principle of the Proof consists of taking 2 areas Z1: (P1,LP1,) and Z2: (P2,LP2) having different sizes where the lengths of their decomposition coefficients x1(CD), x2(CD) are the same and show that the complexity N1 and N2 of their movings is the same.

Let P2 be a prefix defined by the concatenation of P1 and k bits (k is an even number) then size(Z1)=size(Z2)*2^k; since LP1 and LP2 have the same parity, by applying (a) for each area we have N1=N2.

3.4 North-South Translation

In this section we adopt the same steps as the previous ones in order to determine the behavior of the decomposition pattern for the N.S. translation. We first notice that x(T) is null and then x(CD) is also.

3.4.1 The Decomposition Behavior According to y(CD)

In this section,We define the behavior of the decomposition of a pattern by its moving. We begin by describing this behavior by giving examples, then we establish the rule of decomposition.

We suppose that the prefix of the area that we translate, is P=01. The examples of fig 9 show that if y(CD)=1 (fig 9.a), the pattern after translation is composed of two rectangular areas distributed in two identical rows; but where y(CD)=01 (fig 9.b), the generated areas are distributed in three rows; yet in fig 9.c (resp fig 9.d) where y(CD)=001 (resp. y(CD)=0001) we obtained four (resp. five) rows.

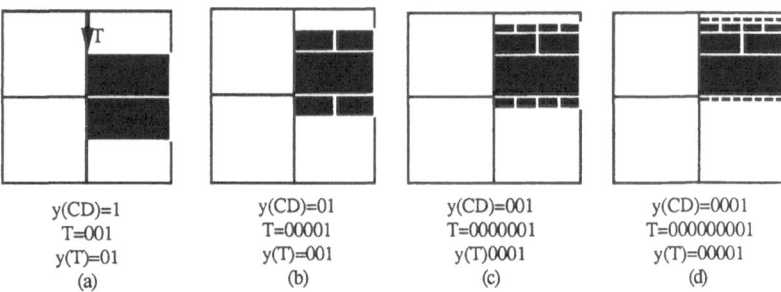

$$
\begin{array}{cccc}
y(CD)=1 & y(CD)=01 & y(CD)=001 & y(CD)=0001 \\
T=001 & T=00001 & T=0000001 & T=000000001 \\
y(T)=01 & y(T)=001 & y(T)0001 & y(T)=00001 \\
(a) & (b) & (c) & (d)
\end{array}
$$

Fig. 9 Variation of the decomposition with y(CD)

Proposition 2)- Let Z be an area defined by (P,LP) going through a decomposition characterized by VT defined by (T,LT) such that x(CD) is null and the length of y(CD) is j then :

a)- the generated areas have a rectangular form and are distributed in rows, where each row is composed of areas having the same size. The kth row (from the top) where k=0...j-1 is composed with 2^k areas; the last row j is identical to the first one (k=0).

b)- if LP is even we have j rows otherwise we have (j-1) rows.

Proof a)- the principle of the Proof is the same as (a) of proposition1:

first we apply (P5.b) to Z; let Z1 be the area obtained from the first translation; if LP is even, we put L1=(LT-LP)/2-1 and we apply (P.4.2) to Z1; otherwise we put L1=(LT-LP+1)/2-1 and we apply (P.4.1) to Z1, then we apply the second translation for these generated areas. Since all these length prefixes of these areas are less than or equal to LT2 (decomposition consequence),where LT2 is the length of the second vector; this one is obtained without any decomposition. Since, according to this decomposition, we have two identical rows that are composed of prefixes having LT2 bits length; the execution of the second translation generates the transfer of the first row to the last position. Since LT2 is odd, according to (P4), all the generated areas have prefixes with odd length, so their form are rectangular.

b)- if we put j=L1, the number of rows and their composition are then a consequence of (P4.1), (P4.2) and (R2).

We present here the function even_line that computes all the areas of a row linked to a bit k:

```
even_line(p:prefix; nb_row,k:integer)
nb_pref,i:integer;
begin
    nb_pref=2^(nb_row+k-1);
    for i:=1 to nb_pref do      displace0(p);
end;
```

3.4.2 Decomposition Distribution

We showed that the length of y(CD) determines the number of rows generated by the decomposition. In this section, we show that the values of the bits of y(CD) determine the exact distribution of the rows; in another words each row is directly linked to a bit of y(CD). Let analyze the decomposition on examples (fig 9& 10). We suppose that the pattern to be translated has a prefix P=01.

In fig 9.d, y(CD) =0001, rows are distributed in a monotonous manner; this characteristic is lost in examples of fig 10. Since for y(CD)= 0011 (fig 10.a), the second right bit of y(CD) has changed and the second row is moved; where y(CD)=0111 (fig 10.c), the second and the third ones are changed so the second and the third row are moved.

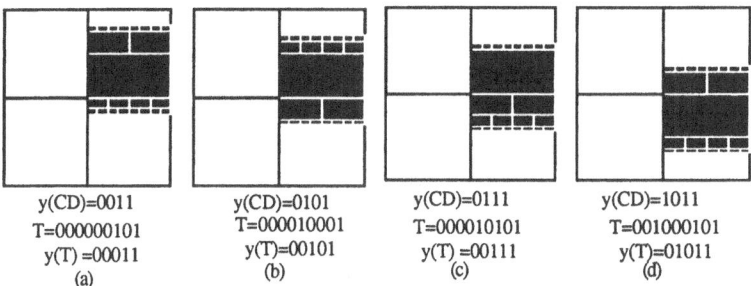

y(CD)=0011	y(CD)=0101	y(CD)=0111	y(CD)=1011
T=000000101	T=000010001	T=000010101	T=001000101
y(T) =00011	y(T)=00101	y(T) =00111	y(T)=01011
(a)	(b)	(c)	(d)

Fig. 10 variation of the decomposition with the bits values of y(CD)

corollary2 a)- let a pattern be defined by (P,LP), that is translated by a vector defined by (T,LT), such as the y(CD) length is j; then this translation generates N areas where :

$$\text{if LP is even } N=\sum_{k=0}^{j-1}2^k+2^{(j-1)}, \quad \text{otherwise } N=\sum_{k=1}^{j-1}2^k+2^{(j-1)}$$

b)- the complexity of this operation depends only on y(CD).

Proof : the same as of corollary1.

3.5 General case of Translation

In this section we show that the decomposition and the complexity vary with x(CD) and y(CD).

3.5.1 Decomposition The Behavior

In this section, we first analyze examples of fig 11 and fig 12 -where we take a pattern having a prefix P=00- and define conditions in order to determine the exact behavior of the decomposition. These examples show that the generated areas vary with x(CD) and y(CD).

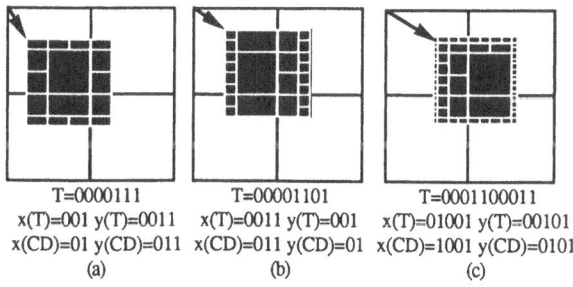

T=0000111	T=00001101	T=0001100011
x(T)=001 y(T)=0011	x(T)=0011 y(T)=001	x(T)=01001 y(T)=00101
x(CD)=01 y(CD)=011	x(CD)=011 y(CD)=01	x(CD)=1001 y(CD)=0101
(a)	(b)	(c)

Fig. 11 complexity of the decomposition with x(CD) and y(CD)

In fact, where x(CD)=01 and y(CD)=001 (fig 11.a), we have three rows and three columns; yet in fig 11.b, where x(CD)=001 and y(CD)=01, we have two rows and four columns; we note that the same rules are verified in fig 12 too.

Finally, we notice that

*- Let the length of x(CD) and y(CD) be respectively i and j, the distribution is then composed with (i+1) columns and j rows.

*- the bits values of x(CD) and y(CD) determine the position of each column and row as in §3.3 and §3.4.

*- the number of areas that compose each column and row do not verify rules exposed in §3.3 and §3.4.

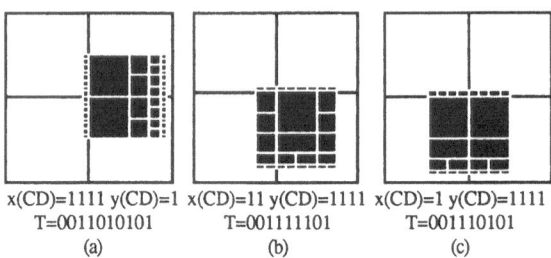

x(CD)=1111 y(CD)=1   x(CD)=11 y(CD)=1111   x(CD)=1 y(CD)=1111
T=0011010101   T=001111101   T=001110101
(a)   (b)   (c)

Fig. 12 various behaviors of the decomposition

3.5.2 Analyse of the Decomposition Complexity

we show here how the behavior of the decomposition varies with the length i of x(CD) and j of y(CD). We first treat the case where i≥j then the case j>i.

3.5.2.1 the Case i≥j

In this section, we start to analyze the decomposition behavior, and we give the rules of the general case. The example of fig 11.b (resp.fig 11.c) shows that for i=3 and j=2 , where i-j=1 (resp.i=4 and j=4, i-j=0), we have 3 columns (resp. two columns) that reach the limit of the pattern; since in the fig 12.a where (i-j)=3, we have 5 columns that reach the limits. We note that in this case, we obtain always (i-j+2) columns that reach the limit. In another word there are (i-j+2) columns composed of an even number of areas; the other ones are composed of an odd number of areas. Each row is composed of $2^{(j-k)}-1$ areas where k=2, ..., j-1 and 2 rows composed by $2^{(j-1)}-1$ areas.

Corollary3 a)- let a pattern be defined with (P,LP), that is translated by a vector defined by (T,LT), such as the length of x(CD) and y(CD) are i and j where i≥j; then this translation generates N areas where :

$$\text{if LP is even } N==\sum_{k=0}^{i-j}2^{(i-k)}+\sum_{k=i-j+1}^{i}(2^{(i-k)}-1)+2^{i}+\sum_{k=1}^{j-1}(2^{k}-1)+(2^{(j-1)}-1)$$

$$\text{otherwise } N=\sum_{k=1}^{i-j}2^{(i-k)}+\sum_{k=i-j+1}^{i-1}(2^{(i-k)}-1)+2^{i-1}+\sum_{k=1}^{j}(2^{k}-1)+(2^{j}-1)$$

Proof) - Since i≥j then LT is even (according to P6).

if LP is even i=(LT-LP)/2; we replace then L1 by i and L2 by j and we apply (P.4.3);

otherwise i=(LT-LP+1)/2; we replace then L1 by i and L2 by j and we apply (P.4.4);

3.5.2.2 the Case j>i

In this section, We show that in contrary to (§3.5.2.1), the rows reach the limit and none column reach it. Figure 11.a (resp. fig12.b) where i=2 and j=3 (resp. i=2 and j=4), we have 2 (resp. 3) rows that reach the limit. Yet, where (j-i)=3 (fig12.c), we have 4 rows. We note that we obtain (j-i+1) rows reaching the limit. Each row k is composed of $2^{(j-k)}$ rectangular areas, where k=2,...,j-i+1; we have 2 rows composed of $2^{(j-1)}$ and having the same form. The others rows are composed of $2^{(j-k)}$-1 k=j-i+2,...,j-1. None of the columns reaches the limit, each column k is composed of $2^{(i-k+1)}$-1 square areas, where k=1,...,i.

corollary4)- Let Z be an area defined by (P,LP), VT defined by (T,LT), such as j>i, then the image of Z is composed of a group of N areas where :

if LP is even $N = \sum_{k=1}^{j-i} 2^{(j-k)} + \sum_{k=j-i+1}^{j-1} (2^{(j-k)}-1)+2^{j-1} + \sum_{k=1}^{i} (2^k-1)+(2^i-1)$

otherwise $N = \sum_{k=0}^{j-i} 2^{(j-k)} + \sum_{k=j-i+1}^{j} (2^{(j-k)}-1)+2^{j} + \sum_{k=1}^{i-1} (2^k-1)+(2^{(i-1)}-1)$

Proof)- Since j>i, LT is odd number (according to P6), then:

if LP is even j=(LT-LP+1)/2, we put L1=j L2=i and we apply (P4.4);

otherwise j=(LT-LP)/2, we put L1=j L2=i and we apply (P4.3).

4- PERFORMANCE EVALUATION AND COST OF THE OPERATION

In this section,we express, the cost of this operation; first, we evaluate the performance of the previously studied cases; then we compare the cost of our method to that one of which the translation vector is defined from pixel notion.

We showed that the complexity of this operation depends only on the length i and j of the decomposition coefficient. So the principle that we adopt for this evaluation consists of computing the number of generated areas with i and j, for each type of translation. We note finally that for $2^n \times 2^n$ image, the worst case is presented when i=n and j=n-1; that means that the area is defined by (P,LP=1) and VT is defined by (T,LT=2n). We consider the case (a) of the corollaries 1, 2, 3 and 4 as the cost functions and we name them by F(i) where j=0, F(j) where i=0 and F(i,j) in the general case.

Fig13, where we consider n=10, shows the evolution of the decomposition for each type of translation. Yet in fig14, we translate patterns defined by (P1,LP1=14), (P2,15), (P3,16) and (P4,17) then we compare the two methods by computing the number of areas that are generated. We name our curve F(i,j) and the other ones LP.

The complexity of the method that uses pixel to define the VT increases with the size of the area; let C be this complexity and the area be defined by (P,LP) then $C=N*2^{(2n-LP)}$, where N is the number of the generated areas after translation. Yet the complexity of our method is C=N. We finally note, that the factor of comparison is about the size (in pixels) of the pattern to be translated.

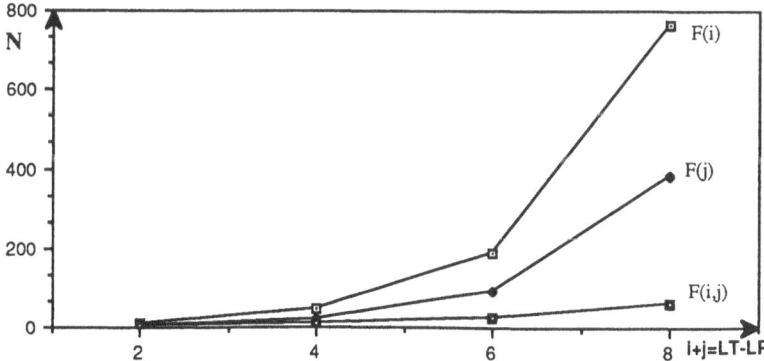

Fig. 13 comparison of the 3 types of translation

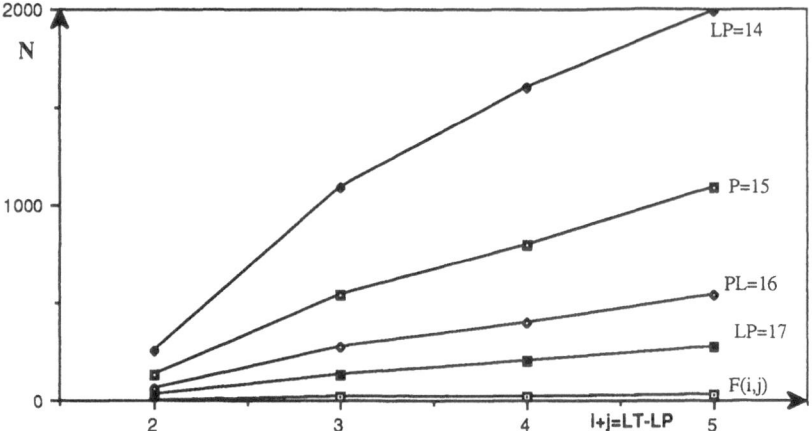

Fig. 14 evaluation and comparison of the two methods

5- CONCLUSION

In this paper, we have got interested in optimizing the search of a pattern in an image, we have proposed an efficient method for executing the operation of translation on the linear binary quadtree, we have introduced a new definition of the translation vector that reduces considerably the complexity of this operation. This result then allows us to accomplish the search of a pattern in an image in a reasonable time. We are currently implementing this method in the team which works to the design of the Images DBMS ZENOBIE.

6. REFERENCES

[AHUJ84]   AHUJA N. and NASH C. (1984) Octree Representation of Moving Object, Computer Vision, Graphics and Image Processing 26.2 pp 2O7-216 Vol A.6.5.3

[CHANG88]   CHANG S.K., YAN C.W., DIMITROFF D.C., ARNDT T. (1988) An Intelligent Database System", IEEE Transactions on Software Engineering, Vol 14, N°5

[CHEIN90]   CHEINEY J.P., KERHERVE B. (1990) Image Data Storage and Manipulations for Multimedia Database Systems Proc. of 4th Int. Conf. on Spatial Data Handling, Zurich

[GARGA82]   GARGANTINI I. (1982) An Efficient Way to Represent Quadtrees, Communications of the ACM, Vol 25, N° 12 .

[GARGA83]   GARGANTINI I. (1983) Translation, Rotation and Superposition of Linear Quadtrees, Int. Juornal of Man-Machine Studies, Vol 18, N°3 .

[LAURI85]   LAURINI R. (1985) Graphics DataBases builts on Peano space-filling curves, Proc. EUROGRAPHICS conf, NICE

[OSSE84]   OSSE W. and AHUJA N. (1984) Efficient Octree Representation of Moving Object, Proceeding of Seventh International Conference on Pattern Recognition pp 821-823 Vol A.6.5.3

[ROUSS85]   ROUSSOPOULOS N., LEIFKER D. (1985) "Direct Spacial Search on Pictorial Database using Packed R-trees", proc. of ACM SIGMOD

[SAMET84]   SAMET H. (1984) The Quadtree and Related Hierarchical Data Structures, Computing Survey, Vol 16, N°2, pp 187-260

[SAMET90a]   SAMET H. (1990) The Design and Analysis of Spatial DAta Structures, Addison-Wesley

[SAMET90b]   SAMET H. (1990) Applications of Spatial Data Structures, Computer Graphics, Image Processing, and GIS, Addison-Wesley

[WALS88]   WALSH T.R. (1988) Efficient Axis-Translation of Binary Digital Pictures by Blocks in Linear Quadtree Representation, Computer Vision, Graphics and Images Processing 41 pp 282-292 Vol A.6.5.3

Proofs

D1:   Since for each bit of P, its area is reduced half then if we add k bits, its area is divided by 2^k.

D2:   consequence of (P1).

D3:(recurrence)   LP=0 ==> the area is equal to the image then $NP=2^{n-0}x2^{n-0}$

LP=1 ==> P is then composed with one bit; if P=0, its area is set in the upper half of the image; if P=1 it is set in the lower half and then $NP=2^n x 2^{n-1}$.

Let suppose that (P3) be true for a row LP let's demonstrate that it is true for (LP+1).

If LP is even (a) is then verified, then let's show that (b) is true for a prefix having (LP+1) bits length; according to (a), Z is composed of $NP=2^{(n-LP/2)} x2^{(n-LP/2)}$ pixels; if we add one bit to P, then according to (P1), the new area represented by this new prefix having LP+1 length, is set in the half of Z then it is composed by NP/2 pixels, where $NP/2=2^{(n-(LP+1)/2)} x2^{(n-(LP+1)/2)}/2 =2^{(n-(LP-1)/2)} x2^{(n-(LP+1)/2)}$.

Let's suppose that LP is odd then (b) is verified, we demonstrate that (a) is true for one prefix having LP+1 length; according to (b), $NP=2^{(n-(LP-1)/2)} x2^{(n-(LP+1)/2)}$; if we add one bit to P, the area represented by this new prefix, is set in then the half of Z then it is composed of NP/2 pixels;

where $NP/2=2^{(n-((LP+1)-1)/2)} x2^{(n-((LP+1)+1)/2)}/2 =2^{(n-LP/2)} x2^{(n-LP/2)}$.

D4: (recurrence)

(1) : If L1 =0 N=1; no decomposition

L1=1, we add then two bits to P, so we have four prefixes generated P1=P00, P2=P01, P3=P10, P4=P11 then N verifies (P4.1).In the following, we mean by adding k bits to P having LP bits lengt, the decomposition of its areas to $2^{(LP+k)}$ new areas where each one having a prefix with (LP+k) bits length.

Let's suppose (P4.1) be true until a row (L1-1) let's demonstrate that it is true for L1.

we have $N= \sum_{k=1}^{L1-1} 2^k + 2^{L1-1}$. If we add two bits to each of the 2^{L1-1} prefixes of N, we obtain $4*2^{L1-1}$ new prefixes;

then $N= \sum_{k=1}^{L1-1} 2^k + 4*2^{L1-1} = \sum_{k=1}^{L1} 2^k + 2^{L1}$

(2) : We show now that N verifies (2) on using a new form of subdivision. For L1 =1, we add one bit to P, we obtain then two prefixes; (2) is then verified. Let's suppose that (2) is true until a row (L1-1) we, then show that it is true for the row L1.

Since (2) is true until a row (L1-1) then $N= \sum_{k=0}^{(L1-1)-1} 2^k + 2^{(L1-1)-1}$. If we add two bits to each of the $2^{(L1-1)-1}$ prefixes of N, we obtain $4*2^{(L1-1)-1}$ new prefixes; then $N= \sum_{k=0}^{(L1-1)-1} 2^k + 4*2^{(L1-1)-1} = \sum_{k=0}^{L1-1} 2^k + 2^{L1-1}$.

(3) : We note that (1) is a particular case of (3) if we put L2=1; Then for L2=1 (3) is true.

It is also true for L2=2, if we add first one bit to one of the N prefixes where N verifies (1), then new decomposition generates $N= \sum_{k=2}^{L1} 2^k + 2^{L1} +1+2$ prefixes that we can write by putting L2=2 as follows:

$$N= \sum_{k=0}^{L1-2} 2^{(L1-k)} + \sum_{k=(L1-2)+1}^{L1} (2^{(L1-k)}-1)+2^{L1} + \sum_{k=1}^{2-1} (2^k-1)+(2^{(2-1)}-1).$$

Let's suppose now that (3) is true until the row (L1,L2-1) and let's show that it is true for the row (L1,L2); Since (3) is true for (L1,L2-1) then we can write N as follows:

$$N= \sum_{k=0}^{L1-(L2-1)} 2^{(L1-k)} + \sum_{k=(L1-(L2-1))+1}^{L1} (2^{(L1-k)}-1)+2^{L1} + \sum_{k=1}^{(L2-1)-1} (2^k-1)+(2^{((L2-1)-1)}-1).$$

If we add two bits to the $(2^{((L2-1)-1)}-1)$ prefixes and one bit to one of the $2^{(L1-(L1-(L2-1)))})$ prefixes; we obtain then :

$$N= \sum_{k=0}^{L1-(L2-1)-1}2^{(L1-k)}+2+(2^{(L1-(L1-(L2-1)))}-1)+ \sum_{k=L1-(L2-1)+1}^{L1}(2^{(L1-k)}-1)+2^{L1}+ \sum_{k=1}^{(L2-1)-1}(2^k-1)+4*(2^{((L2-1)-1)}-1);$$

where $N= \sum_{k=0}^{L1-L2}2^{(L1-k)}+ \sum_{k=(L1-L2)+1}^{L1}(2^{(L1-k)}-1)+2^{L1}+\sum_{k=1}^{L2-1}(2^k-1)+(2^{(L2-1)}-1);$

(4) : To demonstrate that Z is decomposable on N areas where N verifies (4), we follow the same steps than (D3) . We subdivide Z according to (2) and for the generated areas we do an other form of decomposition.

Let's add first one bit to one of the N prefixes, This new decomposition is then $N=1+1+ \sum_{k=1}^{L1-1}2^k+2^{L1-1}$; if we put

L2=1 we can write N as follows:

$$N= \sum_{k=1}^{L1-1}2^{(L1-k)}+ \sum_{k=(L1-1)+1}^{L1-1}(2^{(L1-k)}-1)+2^{L1-1}+\sum_{k=1}^{1}(2^k-1)+(2^1-1)$$

Let's suppose that (4) is true until a row (L1,L2-1) and let's show it is true for (L1,L2);

$$N= \sum_{k=1}^{L1-(L2-1)}2^{(L1-k)}+ \sum_{k=(L1-(L2-1))+1}^{L1-1}(2^{(L1-k)}-1)+2^{L1-1}+\sum_{k=1}^{L2-1}(2^k-1)+(2^{L2-1}-1)$$

if we add first one bit to one of the $2^{(L2-1)}$ prefixes; then we have

$$N= \sum_{k=1}^{L1-(L2-1)-1}2^{(L1-k)}+2+(2^{(L2-1)}-1)+ \sum_{k=(L1-(L2-1))+1}^{L1-1}(2^{(L1-k)}-1)+2^{L1-1}+\sum_{k=1}^{L2-1}(2^k-1)+(2^{L2-1}-1)$$

and second we add two bits to $(2^{L2-1}-1)$ prefixes, we obtain then :

$$N= \sum_{k=1}^{L1-L2}2^{(L1-k)}+ \sum_{k=L1-L2+1}^{L1-1}(2^{(L1-k)}-1)+2^{L1-1}+\sum_{k=1}^{L2-1}(2^k-1)+4*(2^{L2-1}-1)+2$$

then $N= \sum_{k=1}^{L1-L2}2^{(L1-k)}+ \sum_{k=L1-L2+1}^{L1-1}(2^{(L1-k)}-1)+2^{L1-1}+\sum_{k=1}^{L2}(2^k-1)+(2^{L2}-1)$

_D5)-_ We have just to note that T is the sum of T1 and T2.

_D6)-_ According to the definition of VT, the rightest bit of T is not null, moreover the bits of x(T) (resp.y(T)) are set in the bits in the even(resp. odd) row of T; (we suppose that the first bit is the most left one); if the length of y(T) is less than the x(T) one, then the rightest bit of T is a x(T) one LT is even otherwise LT is odd.

Département INF, Ecole Nationale Supérieure des Télécommunications, 75013 Paris, France

A CSG Scanline Algorithm for Quadrics

REINIER VAN KLEIJ and RONALD ROUSSOU

Abstract

CSG (Constructive Solid Geometry) is a method for defining complex solid objects as a combination of simple primitives. This paper presents a new and efficient scanline display algorithm for CSG models with quadric primitives. Efficiency is gained by making use of silhouette curves, and by splitting the scanplane sections into monotonic pieces, which allows efficient testing for intersections on spans and avoids the calculation of depth-values of the faces at every pixel. We also give a procedure for the selective skipping of spans, which in complex cases leads to a substantial reduction of the number of spans to be processed, and gives an increase of the average length of the spans.

Keywords: Display algorithms, constructive solid geometry, scanline algorithms

1. Introduction

Constructive solid geometry (CSG) is a powerful technique for modelling complex mechanical parts (Requicha 1980). With CSG, simple parametrized objects, also called primitives, are positioned in space using geometric transformations. After positioning, the primitives are combined into a composite object by applying the volumetric set operations, union, intersection and difference. About 85% of the mechanical parts can be described as a combination of blocks, cones, cylinders and spheres, the so-called natural quadrics (Hakala et al. 1983).

CSG models can be displayed in two ways. One approach is to convert the CSG model into a boundary representation (Brep) and to apply a standard visible-surface algorithm. This method has the disadvantage that the conversion of the CSG model into a Brep is a time-consuming and numerically sensitive process. Moreover this conversion must be done before display each time the model is changed, which happens frequently during the design of a part. Another approach is to take the CSG model as input for a direct display algorithm, which during display determines by traversing the CSG tree whether a face of a primitive is on the boundary of the composite object; this process is called the classification of faces (Bronsvoort 1988). Well-known direct display algorithms are the CSG ray casting algorithm (Roth 1982) and the CSG scanline algorithm (Atherton 1983).

Atherton (1983) describes a CSG scanline algorithm for primitives with faces approximated by polygons. This is an efficient display algorithm, but it has a disadvantage: although the faces can be made to look smooth by Gouraud or Phong shading, the silhouette and the intersection curves still look jagged. This can be avoided by using many polygons for approximation, but this leads to a large number of spans. It is therefore worthwhile to look for techniques for displaying quadrics directly. In the last decade, several papers have been written on displaying CSG models with quadrics. Chung (1984) describes a scanline-based ray-tracer for quadrics that uses silhouette curves, span coherence and scanline coherence to gain efficiency. The method described by Pueyo and Mendoza (1987) performs a classification of all intersection curves of the scanplane and the primitives, i.e. the scanplane sections, before determining visibility on a scanline. Goldfeather and Fuchs (1986) present a special-purpose hardware platform for fast CSG display of quadrics.

Our goal was to develop an algorithm for general-purpose hardware to efficiently display CSG models composed of quadrics. The developed algorithm is based on the CSG scanline algorithm for polyhedral objects described by Atherton (1983), and uses the notion of subdividing the scanplane sections into monotonic pieces (Pueyo and Mendoza 1987). The mixture of these two concepts gives a new, efficient algorithm. It differs from the algorithm of Pueyo and Mendoza (1987), in that only the faces up to and including the visible surface of the composite object are classified. In contrast to the algorithm of Chung (1984), the depths of the faces are computed only at the span boundaries, and explicitly calculating c-polygons (Chung 1984) is not necessary.

To improve efficiency in displaying complex models even more, we have developed an efficient span selection procedure to reduce the number of spans to be processed.

Section 2 briefly describes the CSG scanline algorithm for polyhedral objects. Section 3 discusses the adaptation of this algorithm for the correct display of CSG models with quadrics, and the efficient span selection procedure. In section 4 measurements for different versions of the algorithm are presented. Section 5 concludes this paper with some conclusions on the algorithm.

2. The polyhedral CSG scanline algorithm

Atherton (1983) describes an elegant algorithm for displaying polyhedral CSG models, which is based on the standard scanline visible-surface algorithm for polyhedral objects. The algorithm consists of two parts: preprocessing and display. In the preprocessing part, the primitives in the CSG model are transformed to image space (see Figure 1a), and their edges are sorted on minimal Y-value into the edge-buckets. An edge-bucket is a linked list of edges that occur for the first time at the scanline the bucket belongs to (see Figure 1b).

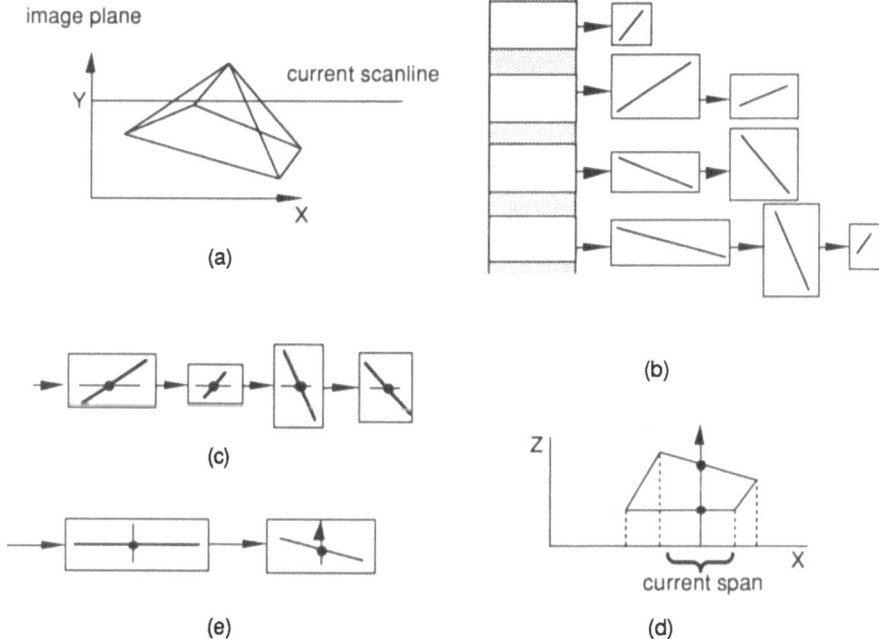

Figure 1. (a) A pyramid projected on the image plane.
(b) Edge-buckets and the edge records in linked lists.
(c) Active edge list on the current scanline.
(d) The scanplane section of the pyramid.
(e) Active face list on the current span.

The display part draws the image scanline by scanline, from the bottom of the screen to the top. A scanline is drawn from left to right. Two important data structures are used in the display part:

- The Active Edge List (AEL): a list of all edges intersecting the current scanline, sorted on increasing x-value of the edges on the scanline (see Figure 1c). Two adjacent edges determine a span (see Figure 1d)

- The Active Face List (AFL): the list of all faces that might be visible on the current span (see Figure 1e).

The AEL is updated when the next scanline is to be drawn: edges in the AEL not intersecting the next scanline are removed from the list, the intersections of the remaining edges with the next scanline are computed incrementally, and finally edges in the bucket of the next scanline are merged into the AEL. Figure 2 gives a pseudo-code version of the algorithm.

```
perform viewing transformation;
sort all edges on minimal Y-value in edge-bucket;
for each scanline do
begin
  update the AEL;
  while AEL is not processed do
  begin
    get edge from the AEL;
    remove face(s) left of edge from the AFL;
    insert face(s) right of edge into the AFL;
    handlespan (X-value of edge, X-value of next edge in AEL);
  end;
end;
```

Figure 2. Basic scanline algorithm.

The handlespan procedure (see Figure 3) determines the visible face as follows: the faces in the AFL are sorted on increasing depth-value at the left side of the span, and, starting from the first face in the AFL, the faces are classified until either a face is classified as being on the composite object, which is then the visible face, or all faces have been classified, in which case there is no visible face. So only the faces in front of and including the visible face are classified. The same is done for the right side of the span. When the depth-order of the faces up to and including the visible face is equal on both sides of the span, the span can be drawn with the colour of the visible face. When the depth-order is not the same, there are at least two intersecting faces, and the intersection of the first two different faces is computed. The span is then subdivided into two subspans, which are recursively handled by the handlespan procedure. Figure 3 gives the pseudo code of the handlespan procedure.

```
procedure handlespan_for_polyhedral_objects ( left, right );
{left:      X-value of left span boundary }
{right:     X-value of right span boundary}
begin
  sort faces at left and determine visible face;
  sort faces at right and determine visible face;
  if the order of the faces is the same up to and
      including visible face at left and right then
    if there is a visible face then
      colour the span with the colour of the visible face;
    else
      colour the span with the background colour;
  else
  begin
    determine the intersection point ip of the first pair of
    different faces;
    handlespan_for_polyhedral_objects (left, ip);
    handlespan_for_polyhedral_objects (ip, right);
  end;
end; {handlespan_for_polyhedral_objects}
```

Figure 3. The handlespan procedure for polyhedral objects.

The CSG scanline algorithm is efficient by exploiting several kinds of coherence:

- coherence between scanlines: the x-value of edges on a scanline can be computed incrementally on successive scanlines

- coherence between spans: the depth order of the faces on two successive spans will vary slowly, so the active face list can be sorted efficiently with a bubble sort

- coherence on a span: mostly the same face will be visible at the left and right side of a span, so subdivisions will rarely occur, and the span can be drawn with one call to the handlespan procedure.

Bronsvoort (1986) gives a number of improvements on the CSG classification, which include pruning of the CSG tree, bottom-up classification with a status tree, and the notion that at the right side of the span the faces need only be sorted to detect whether the span must be subdivided.

3. A CSG scanline algorithm for quadrics

In the previous section we discussed the Atherton scanline algorithm, which displays CSG models with polygonal primitives correctly and serves as a basis for our algorithm. In order to display CSG models with quadrics correctly, both the preprocessing part and the display part of this algorithm need to be adjusted. The preprocessing part must be able to transform quadrics to image space. The fact that a quadric might already be active at the left of its edges (see Figure 4a), is handled by computing its silhouette edge, which is the locus of the points for which the Z-component of the normal is zero. The silhouette edge is calculated by intersecting the quadric with the polar plane of the quadric and the eyepoint (Blinn 1984). A silhouette edge splits the quadric into a front- and a backface. The silhouette edges are sorted into the edge-buckets.

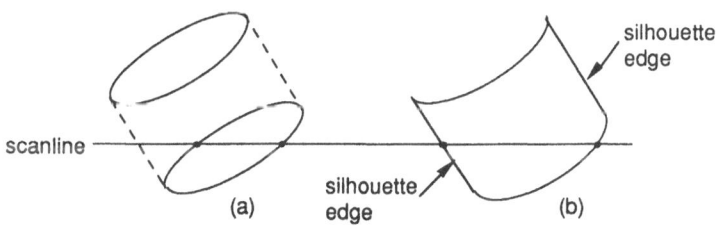

Figure 4.   (a) Quadric active at the left of the edges.
            (b) Quadric active at the right of silhouette edge.

Another problem is the fact that a quadratic edge bounding a quadric may intersect the scanline twice, which hinders efficient processing of the AEL (see Figure 5a). The solution for this is to split the edge at the y-extreme(s) into monotonic pieces, which intersect the scanline at most once (see Figure 5b). These monotonic pieces are sorted into the edge-buckets. With the edges split into monotonic pieces, the exact range of the scanlines of a primitive on the screen is simply found by determining the minimal and maximal Y-coordinate of the endpoints of all edges of the primitive.

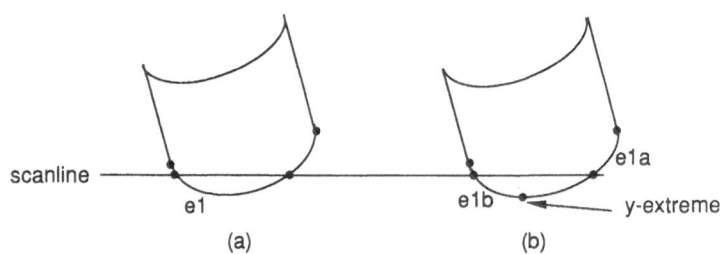

Figure 5.   *(a) Quadratic edge intersects scanline twice.*
(b) Monotonic edges intersect scanline only once.

Even in case of an equal order of faces on the span boundaries, intersection points can still occur (see Figure 6a). In this situation intersection points must be calculated between every pair of faces in the AFL. This problem can be solved by sorting the X-silhouettes into the edge-buckets. A X-silhouette is defined as the locus of the points where the X-component of the normal is zero, and is calculated by intersecting the quadric with the polar plane of the quadric and the point at infinity on the X-axis of the image space. The silhouette and the X-silhouette divide the scanplane section of a quadric into monotonic pieces (see Figure 6b) (Pueyo and Mendoza 1987).

An important property of monotonic scanplane sections is that intersection points between two faces can only occur when there is overlap in depth between these faces (see Figure 7). Consequently, it is not necessary to calculate the depths of all the faces for each pixel on the span to determine whether there are intersections on a span: the depths of the faces at both sides of the span are computed, and only when depth-overlap of two faces up to and including the visible face occurs, the two faces have to be tested for intersection points by the method described below.

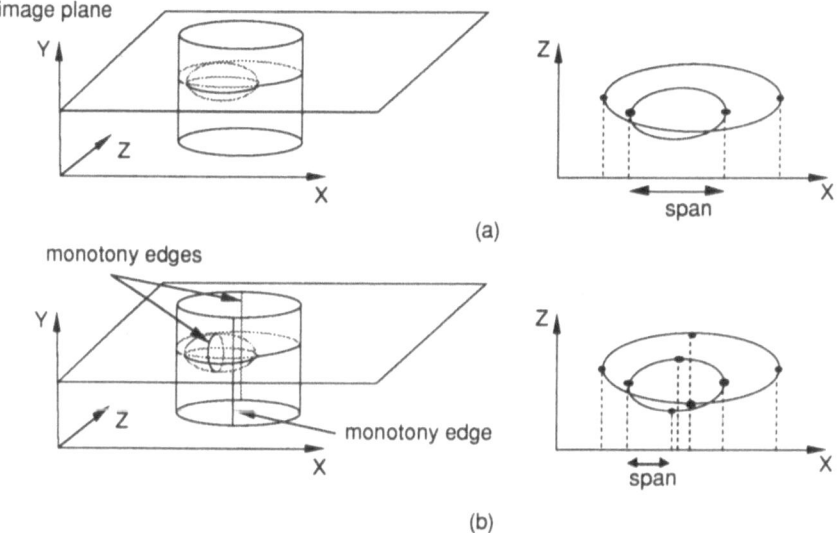

Figure 6.   (a) Intersection points occur on a span with the same order
on both sides.
(b) The silhouette and X-silhouette give monotonic scanplane
sections.

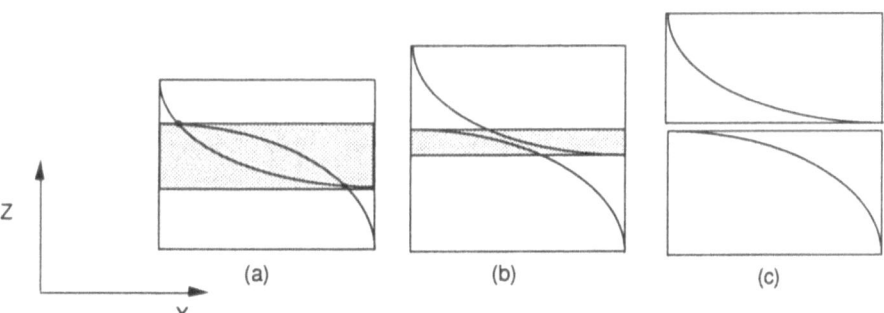

Figure 7.   (a) Depth-overlap with two intersection points.
(b) Depth-overlap without intersection points.
(c) No depth-overlap means no intersection points.

Note that the intersection of two monotonic, quadratic faces can lead to two
intersection points (see Figure 7a). So the handlespan procedure needs to be able
to handle two intersection points on a span. Figure 8 gives the handlespan
procedure for quadrics.

Testing for intersections in case of depth-overlap
When two faces have equal depth-order at both sides of the span, and depth-
overlap on the span, a test for intersection points is required. This is done by
splitting the span into two subspans, and again testing whether the faces have

```
procedure handlespan_for_quadric_objects ( left, right );
{left:      X-value of left span boundary              }
{right:     X-value of right span boundary             }
{equal:     Boolean indicating whether order of faces is }
{           equal at left and right                    }
begin
  determine the visible face on left span boundary;
  determine the visible face on right span boundary;
  equal := true if the order of the faces is the same
              on the spanbounds and false otherwise;
  if equal and the AFL contains quadric faces then
  begin
    test each face in the AFL against all faces that have
    depth-overlap with this face for intersection points;
    equal := false if there are intersection points,
                true otherwise;
  end;
  if equal then
    if there is a visible face then
      colour the span with the colour of the visible face;
    else
      colour the span with the background colour;
  else
  begin
    {there are intersections}
    calculate intersection points;
    case number of intersection points of
      1 :
        handlespan_for_quadric_objects (left, ip);
        handlespan_for_quadric_objects (ip, right);
      2 :
        {two intersection points, ip1 and ip2, ip1 < ip2 }
        handlespan_for_quadric_objects (left, ip1);
        handlespan_for_quadric_objects (ip1, ip2);
        handlespan_for_quadric_objects (ip2, right);
  end;
end;{handlespan_for_quadric_objects}
```

Figure 8. Handlespan for quadric objects.

different depth-order on both sides of a subspan. If they do, there is an intersection point on the left and right subspan, and the intersections are calculated with the procedure described below. If there is equal depth-order, each subspan is tested for depth-overlap of the faces. If there is depth-overlap on a subspan, it is again subdivided, and the tests are repeated (see Figure 9). This process continues until either there is an intersection point in the subspan, or there is no depth-overlap, or the subspan becomes smaller than a pixel, in which case there might be two intersection points in one pixel, but these are discarded.

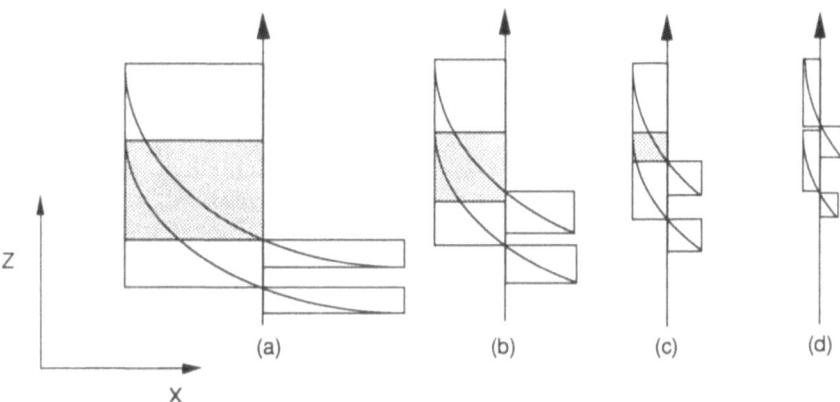

Figure 9.   *(a) , (b), (c) Depth-overlap only in left subspan, so subdivide*
subspan.
(d) No depth-overlap in subspans, so stop subdividing.

Intersection calculation

The intersection point of two faces with different depth-order on both sides of
the span is calculated as follows. First the smallest box in which the intersection
must lie is computed; actually this box is the intersection of the two bounding
boxes of the faces on the span. The central point of this box is the initial point for
a Newton-Raphson iteration of the system of the two quadratic equations
representing the intersecting faces (see Figure 10a). In most cases the iteration
will converge to the intersection point in the box within a few steps, but in some
cases it diverges or it converges to an intersection point outside the box. In that
case the box is subdivided, and the new intersection box and its central point are
computed for a repeated iteration (see Figure 10b). The process of subdividing
the box is repeated until convergence is achieved or the box's width becomes
smaller than a threshold value.

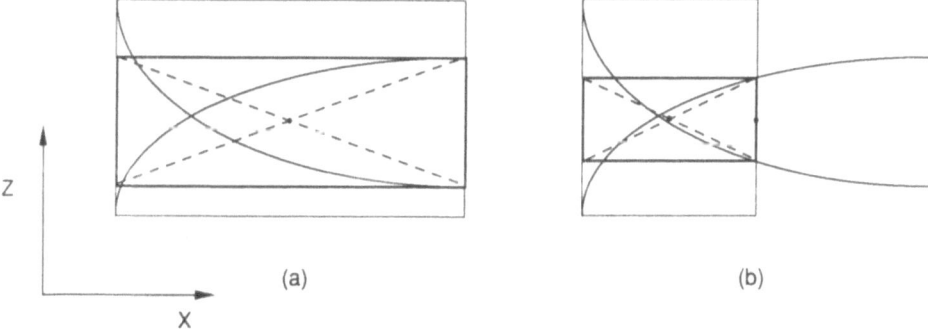

Figure 10.   *(a) Intersection box is the intersection of bounding boxes of*
faces.
(b) Intersection box after subdivision.

Span selection
The CSG scanline algorithm is an efficient display algorithm through its exploitation of several kinds of coherence (see Section 2). Displaying complex CSG models, i.e. models with 50 or more primitives, however may lead to a large number of very small spans, even when using exact representations. Exploiting span coherence in that case does not contribute much to the efficiency of the algorithm, since most spans are smaller than one pixel. In order to gain more from span coherence with complex models, an efficient procedure for selecting spans has been developed, which reduces the number of spans, and thereby increases their average length.

Left-edge selection
The left-edge selection procedure used here is based on the observation that when there is more than one span in the area of a pixel, only one span contributes to the colour of the pixel (see Figure 11).

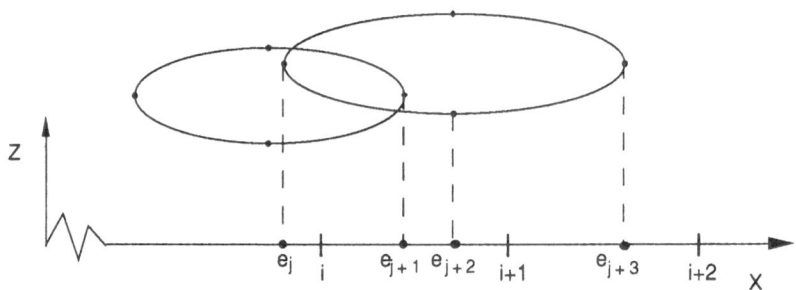

Figure 11. Smal spans .

Let $<e_j,e_{j+1}>$ be the last span processed by handlespan giving pixel i a colour. Now it is unnecessary to process span $<e_{j+1},e_{j+2}>$, because pixel i has its colour already; the next span to be processed is $<e_{j+2},e_{j+3}>$ for colouring pixel i+1. The left-edge selection procedure will skip the edge e_{j+1} and select e_{j+2} as the left boundary of the next span to be processed. Selecting left-edges this way gives a reduction in the number of spans up to 50% in very complex cases. Obviously the left-edge selection procedure cannot be used when doing anti-aliasing. Figure 12 gives a pseudo-code version of the left-edge selection procedure.

Right-edge selection
In order to exploit span coherence fully, spans should be as long as possible. When displaying complex models, there are often many spans smaller than possible, even when left-edge selection is used. This inefficiency is caused by the fact that the edge after the selected left edge in the AEL is regarded as the right span boundary, even if this edge does not result in another visible face (see Figure 13).

```
procedure select_left_edge ( leftedge );
{leftedge:        left span boundary to be selected     }
{nextedge:        next edge after leftedge in AEL        }
{spanbound:       boolean indicating whether leftedge is}
{                 span boundary                          }
begin
  leftedge := right edge of last processed span;
  spanbound := false;
  repeat
    if leftedge is last edge AEL then
      spanbound := true;
    else if X-value of nextedge - X-value of leftedge >= 1.0
    then
      spanbound := true;
    else
      leftedge := nextedge;
    update AFL;
  until spanbound;
end; {select_left_edge}
```

Figure 12. The pseudo code for left-edge selection.

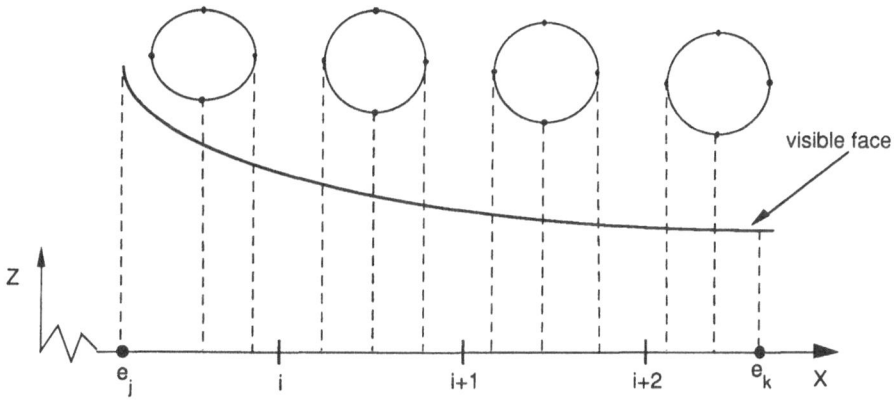

Figure 13. Edges without change of visible face.

Observing this fact, a technique was implemented to select an edge as the right boundary of a span only when this edge may change visibility. This is the case, if the edge satisfies one of the following conditions:

- the edge is in front of or on the visible face

- the edge belongs to a face that has overlap with the visible face, and so this face might intersect the visible face.

The right-edge selection procedure exploits invisibility coherence (Crocker 1984) on the span. Let edge e_j be selected as the left boundary of the span in Figure 13; the right-edge selection procedure will skip all the edges between e_j and e_k because these edges are behind the visible face. Figure 14 gives a pseudo-code version of the right-edge selection procedure.

Note that during selecting the right edge, the AFL is updated at every edge skipped; this complicates the handlespan procedure when intersection points are detected: the AFL may contain faces other then those active on the left subspan, so the AFL needs to be reset to its state at the intersection point.

```
procedure select_right_edge ( rightedge );
{rightedge:       right span boundary to be selected     }
{leftedge:        left span boundary already selected by}
{                 select_left_edge                        }
{xleft:           X-value of leftedge                     }
{spanbound:       boolean indicating whether rightedge   }
{                 is span boundary                        }
begin
  determine visible face at xleft;
  spanbound := false;
  rightedge := leftedge;
  repeat
    rightedge := next edge after rightedge from AEL;
    if rightedge is in front of or on visible face then
      spanbound := true;
    else if rightedge is not a left silhouette then
    begin
      {there is at least one face left of rightedge, so check}
      {this face for having overlap with the visible face   }
      if face overlaps with visible face then
        {there might be intersections}
        spanbound := true;
      if rightedge is a right silhouette then
      begin
        {there are two faces left of rightedge, so check }
        {other face the same way                          }
        if face overlaps with visible face then
          spanbound := true;
      end;
    end;
    if not spanbound  then
      update AFL;
  until spanbound or rightedge is last edge in AEL;
end; {select_right_edge}
```

Figure 14. Pseudo code for right-edge selection.

(a) A pipe with holes.

(b) A block with holes.

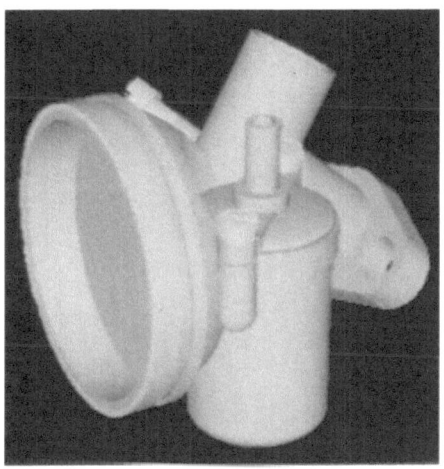

(c) A carburettor.

Figure 15. The test models

4. Results

The display algorithm is embedded in the CSG solid modelling system QUAMO (QUAdric MOdeller) developed at Delft University of Technology (van Kleij 1990). QUAMO is written in C and runs on an Apollo 4000 Domain under the BSD 4.2 UNIX operating system. For display, a graphics window of 512 x 512 pixels is used. In the algorithm the improvements mentioned by Bronsvoort (1986) were incorporated.

We give the results for the models of the three objects in Figure 15: a simple model with 4 primitives (see Figure 15a), an average complex model containing 28 primitives (see Figure 15b), and a complex model containing 60 primitives (see Figure 15c). The display times, ranging from 35 seconds for the simple model to 90 seconds for the complex model, are competitive with the display times of a polygon-based CSG modeler, and the shading is better.

The measurements were done with four versions of the algorithm: the 'naive' version without left- and right-edge selection, so every two successive edges in the AEL define a span, in the second version span selection is done only with the left-edge selection procedure, in the third version span selection is done only with right-edge selection, and in the fourth version span selection is a combination of left-edge selection and right-edge selection.

Chart 1 gives the number of processed spans in the different versions. Left-edge selection gives a reduction of the number of spans by up to 27%. Right-edge selection reduces the number of spans by up to 73%. Combining left-edge selection with right-edge selection gives only a few per cents more reduction: the right-edge selection procedure seems to skip many edges that are also skipped with left-edge selection.

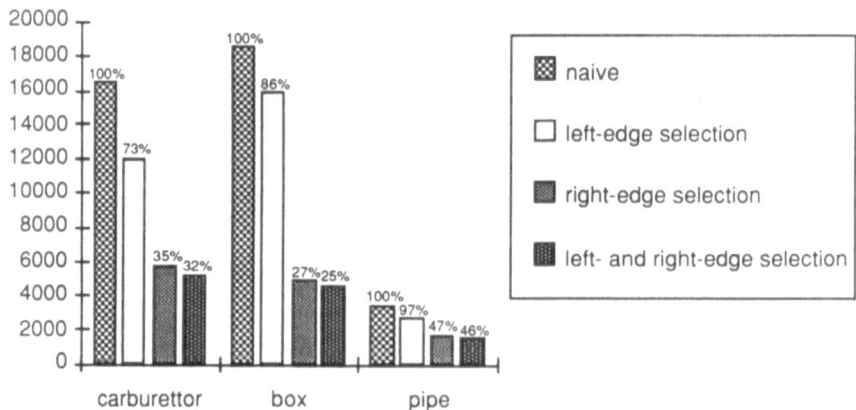

Chart 1. Number of spans processed by handlespan.

Chart 2 gives the execution times of the four versions of the algorithm in seconds. The right-edge selection procedure gives the best reduction in complex cases. The relative reduction in execution time is not equal to the relative reduction in number of spans. Left-edge selection seems to remove only spans on which the visible face is computed easily. In the right-edge selection procedure, more depth calculations than in the naive version are done, and there is some loss of coherence on the span, because the AFL may contain faces that are not in the right sorted order, in which case bubble sort is not efficient any more. Also with right-edge selection there is some overhead in updating the AFL in case of intersection points.

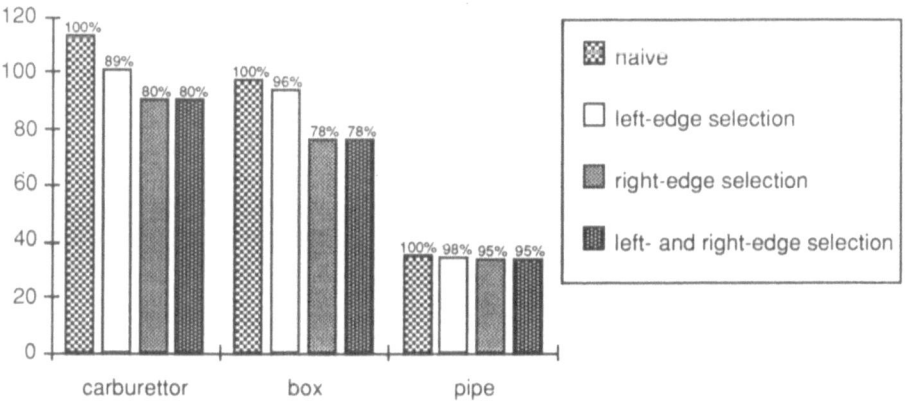

Chart 2. Display times in seconds.

5. Conclusions

We have presented a new and efficient algorithm for direct display of CSG models with quadric primitives that produces pictures of good quality in reasonable time. The use of monotonic scanplane sections requires the computation of the depths of the faces only at span boundaries. Only when there is depth overlap on a span, it is necessary to calculate a few more depths of the two overlapping faces to test for intersection points. Our algorithm differs from the algorithm of Pueyo and Mendoza (1987), in that we classify only the faces up to and including the visible surface of the composite object. It is also different from the algorithm of Chung (1984), in that we compute the depths of faces only at span boundaries, and we use intersection points to subdivide spans. A comparison between the algorithm of Chung, the algorithm of Pueyo and Mendoza, and our algorithm should be made to see which one is most efficient.

In our algorithm, the coherence between two successive scanlines is not fully exploited w.r.t. intersection points, which may be put into a hash-table, and the intersection points may be used as initial points for a Newton-Raphson iteration to compute the intersection points on the next scanline, as suggested by Mahl

(1972). The span selection procedures give reductions in execution times up to 22%, and may be combined with other techniques for reducing display times, such as invisibility coherence (Crocker 1984); they may also be incorporated in a CSG scanline algorithm for polyhedral objects to reduce execution times.

Further research will answer the question whether the use of exact representations for displaying CSG models with quadrics is more efficient than the use of polygon approximations. For exact representation, the number of geometric elements that must be transformed to and handled in image space, and the number of spans are much smaller than that for polygon representations. Also with parallel computing, the overhead in communication of the geometric data between processors is substantial when using polygons (Sato et al. 1985); using exact representations will reduce this overhead, and may lead to a reduction in the total display times.

Acknowledgements

We would like to thank Wim Bronsvoort and Erik Jansen for their valuable suggestions during the development of the algorithm, them and Denis McConalogue for clarifying the text, Xavier Pueyo for the discussions on the algorithm and the method for intersection calculation, Aadjan van de Helm and Peter Kailuhu for their technical support.

References

Atherton PR (1983) A scan-line hidden surface removal procedure for constructive solid geometry. *Computer Graphics* **17**(3): 73-82

Blinn JF (1984) The algebraic properties of homogeneous second order surfaces. Jet Propulsion Laboratory

Bronsvoort WF (1986) Techniques for reducing Boolean evaluation time in CSG scan-line algorithms. *Computer-Aided Design* **18**(10): 533-538

Bronsvoort WF (1988) Boundary evaluation and direct display of CSG models. *Computer-Aided Design* **20**(7): 416-419

Chung WL (1984) A new method of view synthesis for solid modelling. In: *Proceedings CAD '84*, Brighton, UK, pp 470-480

Crocker GA (1984) Invisibility coherence for faster scan-line hidden surface algorithms. Computer Graphics **18**(3): 95-102

Goldfeather J and Fuchs H (1986) Quadratic surface rendering on a logic-enhanced frame-buffer memory. *IEEE Computer Graphics & Applications* **6**(1): 48-59

Hakala DG, Hillyard RC, Nourse BE and Malraison PJ (1983) Natural quadrics in mechanical design. In: *Proceedings Autofact West*, pp 222 - 238

Mahl R (1972) Visible surface algorithms for quadric patches. *IEEE Transactions on Computers* **C-21**(1): 1-4

van Kleij R (1990) Implementation of a solid modelling system with quadratic surfaces. Report 90-41, Faculty of Technical Mathematics and Informatics, Delft University of Technology

Pueyo X and Mendoza JC (1987) A new scan line algorithm for the rendering of CSG trees. In: *Proceedings Eurographics '87*, G. Maréchal (ed), Elsevier Science Publishers, pp 347-361

Requicha AAG (1980) Representations of rigid solids: theory, methods and systems. *ACM Computing Surveys* **12**(4): 437-464

Roth SD (1982) Ray casting for modeling solids. *Computer Graphics and Image Processing* **18**(2): 109-144

Sato H, Ishii M, Sato K, Ikesaka M, Ishihata H, Kakimoto M, Hirota K and Inoue K (1985) Fast image generation of constructive solid geometry using a cellular array processor. *Computer Graphics* **19**(3): 95-102

Faculty of Technical Mathematics and Informatics, Delft University of Technology, 2628 Delft, The Netherlands

Determine Whether Two Line Segments Intersect

EMERY D. JOU

ABSTRACT

Determining whether two line segments intersect appears in various algorithms of geometric modeling and design. Given eight floating-point numbers, $x_1,y_1,x_2,y_2,x_3,y_3,x_4,y_4$, which define two line segments, $S_1=[(x_1,y_1),(x_2,y_2)]$ and $S_2=[(x_3,y_3),(x_4,y_4)]$. To determine the intersection of S_1 and S_2 requires to computing three expressions $(x_1-x_3)(y_3-y_4)-(y_1-y_3)(x_3-x_4)$, $(x_1-x_3)(y_1-y_2)-(y_1-y_3)(x_1-x_2)$, and $(x_1-x_2)(y_3-y_4)-(y_1-y_2)(x_3-x_4)$ without error. We use a two-stage process. First, we employ interval arithmetic. Only if interval arithmetic fails, we resort to multiple-precision arithmetic with a precision great enough to insure a correct result. This two-stage approach is necessary since the intersection can not be determined by floating-point arithmetic correctly, and worthwhile because most of the intersection can be decided with interval arithmetic.

Keywords: Line Intersection, Floating-point Number, Interval Arithmetic, Multiple-precision.

1. Introduction

A line in xy-plane which is not parallel to the y-axis can be specified by its slope a and its intercept b as $\{(x,y)|y=ax+b\}$. A more general specification of a line in xy-plane is as a triple (a,b,c), where the corresponding line is $\{(x,y)|ax+by+c=0\}$. Given two distinct points (x_1,y_1) and (x_2,y_2), a corresponding line triple (a,b,c) is $(y_1-y_2, x_2-x_1, x_1y_2-x_2y_1)$.

Given two lines $L_1 = (y_1-y_2, x_2-x_1, x_1y_2-y_1x_2)$ and $L_2 = (y_3-y_4, x_4-x_3, x_3y_4-y_3x_4)$. To determine whether L_1 and L_2 intersect, we compare the slope of L_1, $(y_1-y_2)/(x_1-x_2)$, with the slope of L_2, $(y_3-y_4)/(x_3-x_4)$. Due to floating-point rounding errors, two intersecting lines may appear to be parallel, i.e. the discriminator $D = (x_1-x_2)(y_3-y_4)-(y_1-y_2)(x_3-x_4)$ equals 0. We can not determine whether two line intersect correctly using only the floating-point arithmetic.

To avoid numerical errors in floating-point arithmetic, it requires using multiple-precision arithmetic to compute D such that the intersection can be determined without error [8, 9]. The product of two f-bit precision (mantissa) floating-point number is at most $2f$-bit. The difference of two f-bit floating-point numbers with the exponent in the range of 2^{-g} to 2^h requires up to $f+g+h$-bit precision. This is due to shifting the mantissa of the smaller floating-point number to the right by $g+h$-bit for raising its exponent to be equal to the exponent of the larger floating-point number. Thus, it requires $f+g+h$-bit precision to compute (x_1-x_2), (y_3-y_4), (y_1-y_2), and (x_3-x_4). The results of multiplying two such $f+g+h$-bit numbers, $(x_1-x_2)(y_3-y_4)$ and $(y_1-y_2)(x_3-x_4)$, are $2(f+g+h)$-bit numbers. Assume the products do not underflow or overflow, the final sum needs no more shifting, so D is a $2(f+g+h)$-bit number. Therefore, it requires $2(f+g+h)$-bit precision to compute D without error.

Another problem is to determine whether the x-coordinate of the intersection point of L_1 and L_2 lies between i and j. Let y_1^i and y_2^i be the y-coordinates of L_1 at i and L_2 at i respectively. Let y_1^j and y_2^j be the y-coordinates of L_1 at j and L_2 at j respectively. If $y_1^i>y_2^i$ and $y_2^j>y_1^j$, or $y_1^i<y_2^i$ and $y_2^j<y_1^j$, then L_1 and L_2 intersects between i and j. This involves computing expressions of the form $E = [y_1(i-x_2)+y_2(i-x_1)](x_3-x_4)$. Again, due to floating-point rounding errors, two lines may appear to intersect outside i and j, but actually they intersect inside. It requires more precision to compute exactly an expression like E than D.

There are many examples in [3] showing the geometric failures due to floating-point arithmetic, such as incidence asymmetry, incidence intransitivity, and topology violations. The line-intersection conditioning based on the condition number of a matrix indicates that for angles between two lines close to 0 or π, the intersection problem is ill conditioned and requires exact arithmetic to handle it accurately.

We assume exact input values and expect accurate results in determining whether two line segments intersect. It would be too costly to use the multiple-precision arithmetic which adds orders of magnitude to the computation than floating-point arithmetic. We find that interval arithmetic which is about twice more costly than floating-point arithmetic is appropriate for determining whether two line segments intersect exactly. The methodology of dealing with numerical problems by algorithms that work well in finite-precision arithmetic in [12] is what we follow.

The interval arithmetic is described in section 2. An implementation of multiple-precision arithmetic using integer arithmetic is presented in section 3. In section 4, a parametric line representation is used to derive the expressions required for determining whether two line segments intersect. A two-stage algorithm and testing results are shown in section 5. Section 6 contains the concluding remarks.

2. Interval Arithmetic

The operations, $\bullet \in \{+,-,*,/\}$, on a pair of closed intervals $A=[a,b]$ and $B=[c,d]$ are defined explicitly as [cf. 2, 6]

$$A+B=[a+_d c, b+_u d] \, ,$$

$$A-B=[a-_d d, b-_u c] \, ,$$

$A * B = [\min \{a *_d c, a *_d d, b *_d c, b *_d d\}, \max \{a *_u c, a *_u d, b *_u c, b *_u d\}]$,

$A / B = [a, b] * [1/d, 1/c]$, if B does not contain 0 ;

where $p \bullet_d q$ is the result of $p \bullet q$ rounded down (the floating-point neighbor to the left to the least significant bit) so that $p \bullet_d q \leq p \bullet q$, and $p \bullet_u q$ is the result of $p \bullet q$ rounded up (the floating-point neighbor to the right to the least significant bit) so that $p \bullet_u q \geq p \bullet q$.

The interval ratio, $C = A / B$, where $A = [a, b]$ and $B = [c, d]$, contains 0 when $a < 0$ and $b > 0$. If $A > 0$ and $B > 0$, C is strictly contained in the open interval $(0,1)$ when $b < c$; C is contained in $(1, \infty)$ when $a > d$; otherwise C contains 1. Similarly, if $A < 0$ and $B < 0$, C is strictly contained in the open interval $(0,1)$ when $a > d$; C is contained in $(1, \infty)$ when $b < c$; otherwise C contains 1. If $A > 0$ and $B < 0$ or $A < 0$ and $B > 0$, the interval ratio, $C = A / B$, is contained in $(-\infty, 0)$.

Here are the interval arithmetic routines and the two nearest neighbor routines.

DOWN(x):
> This machine dependent function calculates the nearest lower neighbor (round toward minus infinity) of a floating-point number x.

UP(x):
> This machine dependent function calculates the nearest upper neighbor (round toward plus infinity) of a floating-point number x.

addinterval(a, b, c, d, p, t):
> An output interval $[p, t]$ is calculated from the input intervals $[a, b]$ and $[c, d]$ so that $p = \text{DOWN}(a + c)$ and $q = \text{UP}(b + d)$.

subinterval(a, b, c, d, p, q):
> An output interval $[p, t]$ is calculated from the input intervals $[a, b]$ and $[c, d]$ so that $p = \text{DOWN}(a - d)$ and $q = \text{UP}(b - c)$.

multinterval(a, b, c, d, p, q):
> An output interval $[p, q]$ is calculated from the input intervals $[a, b]$ and $[c, d]$ so that $p = \text{DOWN}(\min(a*c, a*d, b*c, b*d))$ and $q = \text{UP}(\max(a*c, a*d, b*c, b*d))$.

divideinterval(a, b, c, d, p, t):
> An output interval $[p, q]$ is calculated from the input intervals $[a, b]$ and $[c, d]$ so that $[p, q] = [a, b] / [c, d] = [a, b] * [1/d, 1/c]$ if $[c, d]$ does not contain 0.

3. Multiple Precision Arithmetic

A multiple-precision number x, consisted of exponent and fraction like an floating-point number, is represented in a 32-bit integer array $a[0:n-1]$ as follows: The exponent of x is stored as a twos complement integer in $a[0]$. The fraction part of x is stored in twos complement form within $a[1:n-1]$. The leftmost bit (high bit) of $a[1]$ contains the sign bit. The high bits of $a[2:n-1]$ are set to 0 The low 31 bits in each successive 32-bit element of $a[2:n-1]$ contain the continuing digits of the fraction part of x. Thus, with n 32-bit integer, we have $31(n-1)$ bits of precision. We call such integer arrays representing multiple-precision numbers, *mp-arrays* (multiple-precision array) [cf. 10, 11].

The multiple-precision routines perform arithmetic on such mp-arrays using the integer operations. The multiple-precision arithmetic routines of interest are:

FTOMP(x,a):
> This machine-dependent procedure constructs the mp-array $a[0:n-1]$ which represents the double-precision (64-bit) floating-point number, x. $a[0]$ contains the exponent of x; $a[1]$ and $a[2]$ contain the fraction of x; and $a[3:n-1]$ contains 0.

addmp(a,b,c):
> This procedure adds the mp-array $a[0:n-1]$ to the mp array $b[0:n-1]$, placing the sum in the mp-array $c[0:n-1]$.

subtractmp(a,b,c):
> This procedure subtracts the mp-array $b[0:n-1]$ from the mp-array $a[0:n-1]$, placing the difference in the mp-array $c[0:n-1]$.

multiplymp(a,b,c):
> This procedure multiplies the mp-array $a[0:n-1]$ and the mp-array $b[0:n-1]$, placing the product in the mp-array $c[0:n-1]$.

dividemp(a,b,c):
> This procedure divides the mp-array $a[0:n-1]$ by the mp-array $b[0:n-1]$, placing the $31(n-1)$ bits of precision quotient into the mp-array $c[0:n-1]$. Newton's method is used to find the reciprocal of $1/b[0:n-1]$ which is then multiplied by $a[0:n-1]$ to get the quotient.

For a complete list of multiple-precision arithmetic package, we also include the ancillary routines.

EXTRACT(x,e,f)
> This machine-dependent procedure returns the exponent e and fraction f parts of the double-precision (64-bit) floating number x.

MPTOF(a,x)
> This machine-dependent routine constructs a double-precision (64-bit) floating-point number in x equivalent to the number represented in the integer array a.

normalize(a)
> This procedure normalizes the mp-array $a[0:n-1]$ so that the first bit to the right of the sign bit is 1 if the sign bit is 0 (positive), and 0 if the sign bit is 1 (negative).

shift(a,m)
> This procedure shifts $a[0:n-1]$ arithmetically $0 \leq m \leq 31(n-1)$ bits to the right.

negate(a,b)
> This procedure negates $a[0:n-1]$ by twos complementing and places the result in $b[0:n-1]$.

4. Line Intersection

A line containing the two points (x_1, y_1) and (x_2, y_2) can be specified parametrically as $\{(x, y) | (x, y) = (1-s)(x_1, y_1) + s(x_2, y_2), -\infty < s < \infty\}$. The position of a point on this line corresponds to a value of the parameter s. For $s < 0$, the point is before (x_1, y_1); for $s = 0$, the point is (x_1, y_1); for $0 < s < 1$, the point lies between (x_1, y_1) and (x_2, y_2); for $s = 1$, the point is (x_2, y_2); and for $s > 1$, the point is beyond (x_2, y_2). We denote this line as $((x_1, y_1), (x_2, y_2))$.

Given the following two lines $L_1 = \{(x, y) | (x, y) = (1-s)(x_1, y_1) + s(x_2, y_2), -\infty < s < \infty\}$ and $L_2 = \{(x, y) | (x, y) = (1-t)(x_3, y_3) + t(x_4, y_4), -\infty < t < \infty\}$. They intersect at the point where s and t satisfy the equations, $(1-s)x_1 + s x_2 = (1-t)x_3 + t x_4$ and $(1-s)y_1 + s y_2 = (1-t)y_3 + t y_4$, with the solution

$$s = \frac{(x_1-x_3)(y_3-y_4)-(y_1-y_3)(x_3-x_4)}{(x_1-x_2)(y_3-y_4)-(y_1-y_2)(x_3-x_4)} \quad \text{and} \quad t = \frac{(x_1-x_3)(y_1-y_2)-(y_1-y_3)(x_1-x_2)}{(x_1-x_2)(y_3-y_4)-(y_1-y_2)(x_3-x_4)}$$

Now, consider two line segments $S_1 = \{(x, y) | (x, y) = (1-s)(x_1, y_1) + s(x_2, y_2), 0 \le s \le 1\}$ and $S_2 = \{(x, y) | (x, y) = (1-t)(x_1, y_1) + t(x_2, y_2), 0 \le t \le 1\}$. To determine whether S_1 and S_2 intersect, we must decide if both $0 \le s \le 1$ and $0 \le t \le 1$ at the point of intersection. This involves computing three expressions $P = (x_1-x_3)(y_3-y_4)-(y_1-y_3)(x_3-x_4)$, $Q = (x_1-x_3)(y_1-y_2)-(y_1-y_3)(x_1-x_2)$, and $R = (x_1-x_2)(y_3-y_4)-(y_1-y_2)(x_3-x_4)$ without error. By using the multiple-precision routines of the last section with a suitable choice of n (size of mp-array), floating-point rounding errors can be avoided so that P, Q, and R can be computed correctly. The values of s and t can then be obtained by comparing P to R and Q to R respectively.

The results of using multiple-precision arithmetic for determining whether two line segments intersect are summarized below.

multiple	$t < 0$	$t = 0$	$0 < t < 1$	$t = 1$	$t > 1$
$s < 0$	no	no	no	no	no
$s = 0$	no	yes	yes	yes	no
$0 < s < 1$	no	yes	yes	yes	no
$s = 1$	no	yes	yes	yes	no
$s > 1$	no	no	no	no	no

How much does it cost to use multiple-precision arithmetic for computing P, Q, and R? Given eight floating-point numbers $x_1, y_1, x_2, y_2, x_3, y_3, x_4, y_4$ which have f-bit fraction with the exponent in the range of 2^{-g} to 2^h. It requires up to $2(f+g+h)$-bit precision to compute P, Q, and R without error. Note that there are $31(n-1)$ bits of precision in the mp-array. For VAX D-format floating-point numbers, f is 56 and the values of g and h are both 127, so for perfect VAX performance, $n = 21$ will suffice. For IEEE standard format on a SUN with an MC 68881 chip, f is 53, g is 1023, and h is 1022, so $n = 137$ for perfect performance. The multiple-precision arithmetic adds orders of magnitude to the computation than floating-point arithmetic.

Instead of multiple-precision arithmetic, we investigate using interval arithmetic to compute P, Q, and R for determining whether S_1 and S_2 intersect. In interval arithmetic, a floating-point number x is represented by $[x_d, x_u]$ where x_d is x's left neighbor and x_u is x's right neighbor. By using interval arithmetic, we obtain $P = [p_d, p_u]$, $Q = [q_d, q_u]$, and $R = [r_d, r_u]$. If both the interval ratios $s = P/R$ and $t = Q/R$ are strictly contained in the open interval $(0,1)$ (i.e., both $0 < s < 1$ and $0 < t < 1$), the line segments intersect, but not at an endpoint. If either s or t are contained in the open intervals $(-\infty, 0)$ or $(1, \infty)$ (i.e., $s < 0$, $s > 1$, $t < 0$, or $t > 1$), the line segments do not intersect (intersect outside at least one of the two line segments). If either s or t contain 0 or 1, we can not guarantee that $0 \leq s \leq 1$ and $0 \leq t \leq 1$. In this latter case, the intersection of the two segments S_1 and S_2 can not be determined with just this interval arithmetic method, we must resort to multiple-precision arithmetic.

The results of using interval arithmetic for determining whether two line segments intersect are summarized below. Note that the multiple-precision arithmetic is required at unspecified entries.

For $\alpha < 0 < \beta$, and $\mu < 1 < \nu$,

interval	$t \in (-\infty, 0)$	$t \in (\alpha, \beta)$	$t \in (0,1)$	$t \in (\mu, \nu)$	$t \in (1, +\infty)$
$s \in (-\infty, 0)$	out/out		out/in		out/out
$s \in (\alpha, \beta)$					
$s \in (0,1)$	in/out		yes		in/out
$s \in (\mu, \nu)$					
$s \in (1, +\infty)$	out/out		out/in		out/out

The interval arithmetic is about twice more costly than floating-point arithmetic. The testing results of 5,000 random pairs of line segments verify that most intersections are decided by interval arithmetic.

5. Algorithm and Results

Given eight floating-point numbers, $x_1, y_1, x_2, y_2, x_3, y_3, x_4, y_4$, determining the intersection of two line segments $S_1 = \{(x,y) | (x,y) = (1-s)(x_1,y_1) + s(x_2,y_2), 0 \leq s \leq 1\}$ and $S_2 = \{(x,y) | (x,y) = (1-t)(x_1,y_1) + t(x_2,y_2), 0 \leq t \leq 1\}$ is to decide if both $0 \leq s \leq 1$ and $0 \leq t \leq 1$ where

$$s = \frac{(x_1-x_3)(y_3-y_4)-(y_1-y_3)(x_3-x_4)}{(x_1-x_2)(y_3-y_4)-(y_1-y_2)(x_3-x_4)} \quad \text{and} \quad t = \frac{(x_1-x_3)(y_1-y_2)-(y_1-y_3)(x_1-x_2)}{(x_1-x_2)(y_3-y_4)-(y_1-y_2)(x_3-x_4)}.$$

For $s = 0$ or $s = 1$, and $t = 0$ or $t = 1$, S_1 and S_2 intersecting at the end-point of both line segments, (x_1, y_1) or (x_2, y_2), and (x_3, y_3) or (x_4, y_4), can be determined straightforwardly by comparison.

In general, we use a two-stage approach to determinting the intersection of S_1 and S_2.

First, $P = (x_1-x_3)(y_3-y_4)-(y_1-y_3)(x_3-x_4)$, $\quad Q = (x_1-x_3)(y_1-y_2)-(y_1-y_3)(x_1-x_2)$, $R = (x_1-x_2)(y_3-y_4)-(y_1-y_2)(x_3-x_4)$, s, and t are computed by interval arithmetic.

The routine *inform*(x1,y1,x2,y2,x3,y3,x4,y4,r1,r2) computes the interval [r1,r2] holding $(x_1-x_2)(y_3-y_4)-(y_1-y_2)(x_3-x_4)$ in interval arithmetic by the following steps:

subinterval(x1,x1,x2,x2,p1,p2), subinterval(y3,y3,y4,y4,q1,q2), multinterval(p1,p2,q1,q2,s1,s2),
subinterval(y1,y1,y2,y2,p1,p2), subinterval(x3,x3,x4,x4,q1,q2), multinterval(p1,p2,q1,q2,t1,t2),
subinterval(s1,s2,t1,t2,r1,r2).

Given two intervals $[a,b]$ and $[c,d]$, where $[c,d]$ does not contain 0, the routine *inratio*(a,b,c,d) is used to determine if the ratio of $[a,b]$ to $[c,d]$ is strictly contained in the interval (0,1), lies outside the interval (0,1), or contains either 0 or 1.

Only when interval arithmetic fails, s or t contain 0 or 1, we then resort to multiple-precision arithmetic to compute P, Q, R, s and t.

The machine-dependent routine *FTOMP* is used to convert the floating-point numbers x1, y1, x2, y2, x3, y3, x4, y4 into multiple-precision arrays fx1, fy1, fx2, fy2, fx3, fy3, fx4, fy4.

The routine *mpform*(fx1,fy1,fx2,fy2,fx3,fy3,fx4,fy4,frr) computes the multiple-precision array frr = (fx1-fx2)(fy3-fy4)-(fy1-fy2)(fx3-fx4) in multiple-precision arithmetic by the following steps:

subtract(fx1,fx2,fpp), subtract(fy3,fy4,fqq), multiply(fpp,fqq,fr1),
subtract(fy1,fy2,fpp), subtract(fx3,fx4,fqq), multiply(fpp,fqq,fr2),
subtract(fr1,fr2,frr).

Given two multi-precision arrays $a[0:n-1]$ and $b[0:n-1]$ with $b[0:n-1]$ does not equal 0, the routine *mpratio* (a,b) is used to determine if the ratio of $a[0:n-1]$ to $b[0:n-1]$ lies between 0 and 1.

A program to determine whether two line segments intersect is presented below.

/* The program INTERSECT has input of eight double-precision floating-point numbers, x1, y1, x2, y2, x3, y3, x4, y4, defining two line segments, $S_1=[(x1,y1),(x2,y2)]$ and $S_2=[(x3,y3),(x4,y4)]$. If S_1 and S_2 intersect, INTERSECT returns YES, otherwise INTERSECT returns NO. The program INTERSECT will never falsely claim or deny the intersection of S_1 and S_2. Note that n is a machine-dependent constant such as: $n=21$ (VAX) and n=137 (IEEE). */

```
#define YES 1
#define NO  0
```

```
#define and &&
#define or ||
#define ne !=
#define n    21 /* for VAX D-format floating-point number */

INTERSECT(x1,y1,x2,y2,x3,y3,x4,y4) double x1,y1,x2,y2,x3,y3,x4,y4;
{
    double p1,p2,q1,q2,r1,r2,s,t;
    int fx1[n], fy1[n], fx2[n], fy2[n], fx3[n], fy3[n], fx4[n], fy4[n], fpp[n], fqq[n], frr[n];
```

/* compute $(x_1-x_2)(y_3-y_4)-(y_1-y_2)(x_3-x_4)$ in interval arithmetic */
```
    inform(x1,y1,x2,y2,x3,y3,x4,y4,&r1,&r2);
    if (r1>0 or r2<0) { /* the interval [r1,r2] does not contain 0 */
```
/* compute $(x_1-x_3)(y_3-y_4)-(y_1-y_3)(x_3-x_4)$ in interval arithmetic */
```
        inform(x1,y1,x3,y3,x3,y3,x4,y4,&p1,&p2);
```
/* compute $(x_1-x_3)(y_1-y_2)-(y_1-y_3)(x_1-x_2)$ in interval arithmetic */
```
        inform(x1,y1,x3,y3,x1,y1,x4,y4,&q1,&q2);
        s = inratio(p1,p2,r1,r2);
        t = inratio(q1,q2,r1,r2);
        /* two line segments intersect */
        if ((s>0 and s<1) and (t>0 and t<1)) return(YES);
        /* intersect outside one or both segments */
        if ((s<0 or s>1) or (t<0 or t>1)) return(NO);
    }
    /* can't be decided by interval arithmetic; resort to multiple-precision arithmetic */
    /* convert double-precision floating-point numbers to multiple-precision arrays */
    FTOMP(x1,fx1); FTOMP(y1,fy1); FTOMP(x2,fx2); FTOMP(y2,fy2);
    FTOMP(x3,fx3); FTOMP(y3,fy3); FTOMP(x4,fx4); FTOMP(y4,fy4);
```

/* compute $(x_1-x_2)(y_3-y_4)-(y_1-y_2)(x_3-x_4)$ in multiple-precision arithmetic */
```
    mpform(fx1,fy1,fx2,fy2,fx3,fy3,fx4,fy4,frr);
    if (frr[1] ne 0) { /* the two line segments are not parallel */
```
/* compute $(x_1-x_3)(y_3-y_4)-(y_1-y_3)(x_3-x_4)$ in multiple-precision arithmetic */
```
        mpform(fx1,fy1,fx3,fy3,fx3,fy3,fx4,fy4,fpp);
```
/* compute $(x_1-x_3)(y_1-y_2)-(y_1-y_3)(x_1-x_2)$ in multiple-precision arithmetic */
```
        mpform(fx1,fy1,fx3,fy3,fx1,fy1,fx4,fy4,fqq);
        /* two line segments intersect (0<s<1 and 0<t<1) */
        if (mpratio(fpp,frr) and mpratio(fqq,frr)) return(YES);
        /* intersect outside one or both segments */
        else return(NO);
    }
    /* two parallel line segments */
    return(NO);
}
```

For 5,000 pairs of lines defined by distinguished line segments with randomly generated floating-point numbers as endpoint coordinates, we test our program on VAX 6220 (VAX D-format) and SUN 3/60 (IEEE format). We describe the testing results on

VAX 6220 in the following paragraphs with the testing results of SUN 3/60 enclosed in parenthesis. Note that the 5,000 pairs of lines used on VAX 6220 and SUN 3/60 are independently generated.

There are 4379 (4292) intersections, i.e. 87.6% (85.8%), which could be determined by interval arithmetic only where 747 (729) pairs intersect inside and 3632 (3663) pairs intersect outside; and 621 (708) intersections, i.e. 12.4% (14.2%) which have to be determined by multiple-precision arithmetic where 136 (154) pairs intersect inside and 485 (554) pairs intersect outside.

For the same input data, when the intersections are determined by floating-point arithmetic, there are 158 (179) errors, all of which happen in the cases where multiple-precision arithmetic should have been employed. It is obvious that no errors occur when the intersection could have been determined by interval arithmetic.

For the 158 (179) erroneous results, 149 (170) pairs of lines are claimed to intersect inside their distinguished segments, when in fact they intersect outside at least one segment; and 9 (9) pairs are claimed to intersect outside one or both distinguished segments, when in fact they intersect inside both segments.

The total error rate, 158 (179) errors in 5,000 pairs of lines, is 3.16% (3.58%) on VAX 6220 (SUN 3/60). If we consider errors within the class of the 621 (708) pairs which require multiple-precision arithmetic, the observed error rate is 25.4% (25.3%) on VAX 6220 (SUN 3/60).

6. Conclusion

We present a two-stage algorithm, using interval arithmetic as a sieve and following by multiple-precision arithmetic only in exigency, for determining whether two line segments intersect. Most cases of intersections can be determined by interval arithmetic. Only when interval arithmetic fails, one has to apply multiple-precision arithmetic.

A C language program which implements the two-stage algorithm to determining the intersection of two line segments is presented in [5]. The program will never falsely claim or deny the intersection (inside or outside) of two line segments. It takes into account all possible degenerate cases, such as one (or both) line segment is a point; one line segment is contained in another line segment; two line segments are overlapping; and two line segments are parallel. The intersection program is accompanied with a generic package of interval and multiple-precision arithmetic routines for VAX D-format, IEEE standard, and IBM 370 floating-point numbers. The interval and multiple-precision package has been used in computing union, intersection or difference of two polygons [7], 2D convex hull [4], and slope selection [1].

We are extending our two-stage algorithm on a parallel machine for determining the intersections of a set of line segments.

7. References

[1] Dillencourt, Michael B., Mount, David M. and Netanyahu, Nathan S., "A Randomized Algorithm for Slope Selection" Tech. Rep. No. CS-TR-2431, Dept. of Comput. Sci. Univ. of Maryland, March 1990.

[2] Good, D. I. and London, R. L., "Computer Interval Arithmetic: Definition and Proof of Correct Implementation", JACM, 17, 4, pp. 603-610, October 1970

[3] Hoffmann, Christoph M., "Geometric & Solid Modeling: An Introduction" Morgan Kaufmann Publishers, Inc., San Mateo, CA 94403, pp. 113-124, 1989.

[4] Kao, Thomas, C and Knott, Gary D., "An Efficient and Numberically Correct Algorithm for the 2D Convex Hull Problem" BIT 30, pp. 311-331, 1990.

[5] Knott, Gary D. and Jou, Emery D., "A Program to Determine Whether Two Line Segments Intersect" Tech. Rep. No. CS-TR-1884, Dept. of Comput. Sci. Univ. of Maryland, August 1987.

[6] Knuth, D. E., *The Art of Computer Programming: Seminumerical Algorithms*, 2nd Ed., Addison-Wesley, 1981

[7] Margalit, Avraham and Knott, Gary D., "An Algorithm for Computing the Union, Intersection or Difference of Two Polygons" Computers & Graphics, Vol. 13, No. 2, pp. 167-184, 1989.

[8] Plauger, P. J., "Programming on Purpose - you must be joking", Computer Language, pp. 15-19, April, 1987

[9] Scott, Norman R., *Computer Number Systems and Arithmetic*, Prentice Hall, 1985.

[10] Stallings, W., *Computer Organization and Architecture: Principles of Structure and Function*, Macmilliam, pp. 222-227, 1987

[11] Stroud, A. H. and Secrest, D. "A Multiple-Precision Floating-Point Interpretive Program for the Control Data 1604" Computer Journal, 6, pp. 62-66, 1963.

[12] Sugihara, Kokichi and Iri, Masao, "Construction of the Voronoi Diagram for One Million Generators in Single-Precision Arithmetic" the First Canadian Conference on Computational Geometry, August 21-25, 1989, Montreal, Canada.

Computer Science Center, University of Maryland, College Park, MD 20742, USA

Chapter 8

Visualization Models

Realistic Image Synthesis of Complex Objects Using a Simplified Model

KAZUFUMI KANEDA[1], HARUHIKO IRIYAMA[2], FUJIWA KATO[3], and EIHACHIRO NAKAMAE[1]

ABSTRACT

Even though rendering techniques in computer graphics have greatly progressed, it is still required that more realistic images with a short calculation time be generated. It is particularly desirable to put in objects without taking time and display these objects with a short calculation time. This paper proposes efficient techniques for rendering objects with rounded edges, complex objects composed of numerous simple elements such as transmission towers, and extremely thin objects such as transmission lines and curtains.

Key Words and Phrases: Realistic Image Synthesis, Rendering Model, Complex Objects, Thin Objects, Rounded Edges, Simplified Model, Pattern Mapping, Virtual Planes, Transmission Towers, Transmission Lines

1 INTRODUCTION

Most artificial objects such as frames of computers have rounded edges. These edges are often very attractive because of their highlights, even when the radius of the rounded edges is quite small. Therefore, the presence of rendering on rounded edges greatly influences the appearance of the object in computer graphics.

In many cases complex objects consist of relatively simple numerous elements, e.g., transmission towers and fences. If each element is put in as an object, it will take much time to model and render the complex objects. Although these objects can be simplified in their shapes, except when the objects are close-up, the accuracy in highlighting their surfaces, especially rounded edges, cannot be neglected.

Traditional techniques for rendering rounded edges can be classified into four types: A method based on set operations between primitives, a method of modeling rounded edges by using triangular patches and employing a smooth shading technique for rendering, a method of compositing a shaded image with a wire-frame image, and a method of emphasizing edges by making use of z-depth values. These techniques are outlined below.

Requicha et al. proposed a method of using set operations between primitives [Requicha '82]. In this method objects with rounded edges are constructed by using Boolean operation between primitives. In this method a couple of primitives are necessary for modeling each rounded edge. Furthermore, when the radius of the rounded edge is small, numerical calculation error may occur in the modeling step.

One of the authors et al. proposed a method for rendering rounded edges modeled by using curved surfaces [Okamura '83]. In their method, the rounded edges of objects are modeled by using Coons' patches. For rendering, these curved patches are divided into small triangular patches, and smooth shading is employed to display the rounded edges. If the radius of the rounded edge is small, this method is not efficient, because many small triangular patches are generated. This method also has the problem of numerical calculation error.

Saito et al. proposed the method for rendering rounded edges by using a wire-frame image [Saito '89a]. In this method, in order to generate images taking into account specular reflection on rounded edges, rounded edges are approximated to cylinders with small radii, and specular reflection of the cylinders is calculated. Then, the generated image is stored as a wire-frame image. Finally, the original image generated by taking no account of rounded edges and the wire-frame image are composited by taking into account depth from a viewpoint. However, this method has the possibility that the wire-frame image is hidden by the original image because of calculation error as the difference in depth between the wire-frame image and the original image is very small.

Saito et al. also proposed a method for emphasizing the edges of objects by employing depth values obtained in the process of generating images by using a z-buffer method [Saito '89b]. However, in this method generated images are insufficient from the view point of optical phenomena, because the main purpose is to put emphasis on the specular reflection of edges.

For displaying complex objects composed of numerous elements, texture mapping techniques [Blinn '76] have been used, and bump mapping techniques [Blinn '78] are able to render rough surfaces. In the case of rendering complex objects consisting of simple elements such as polygons and cylinders, texture mapping techniques are not available for rendering the shading effects of each element according to changes in the locations of light sources.

In order to render complex objects efficiently, hierarchical geometric models [Clark '76, Rubin '80] were proposed. In these methods the structure of object data are hierarchical, and the precision of object data used for rendering is varied according to the distance from the viewpoint. Thus, high quality rendering on reflection effects of distant objects cannot be expected.

This paper proposes an efficient method with two different models for displaying realistic images of polyhedrons with rounded edges and objects consisting of a number of relatively simple elements; i.e. a geometric model for perspective projection and hidden surface removal, and a rendering model for shading. That is, rounded edges are not taken into account in the input step of a geometric model, and only in the step of rendering are they taken into account. For complex objects composed of a lot of elements, the elements are modeled as patterns mapping onto virtual transparent planes in a geometric model, and in the shading process the objects are rendered by taking into account the real shapes of the patterns.

The simplified geometric modeling described above saves not only calculation time for perspective projection, hidden surface removal, and shadowing, but also generates realistic images including effects of specular reflection because of rendering by means of shading with real shapes of objects.

The proposed method has the following advantages.

For rendering rounded edges:

- No additional change of geometric models is required, when any rounded edges exist.
- Anti-aliased images are easily obtained, because the spans of rounded edges on a scanline can be calculated before shading.

For complex objects consisting of numerous elements:

- The complex objects can be easily modeled as patterns mapped onto virtual transparent planes.
- Each element modeled as a pattern can be rendered as if it is the real shape.

In the following sections, an efficient method for rendering rounded edges and realistic image synthesis of complex objects by using simple geometric models is described. Some examples of outdoor scenes, including transmission towers and transmission lines, and indoor scenes demonstrate the usefulness of the proposed method.

2   RENDERING OF ROUNDED EDGES

The proposed method for displaying rounded edges is based on rendering the rounded edges by taking into account the radius which has been set in the modeling step. Concerning rounded edges, the following conditions are assumed.

- Radii of rounded edges are relatively small.

- The viewpoint is not very close to the rounded edges.

In fact, the contour of an object with rounded edges is different from that without rounded edges. However, by introducing the conditions mentioned above, it can be assumed that the contour changes very little on a screen. Therefore, edges are rounded by the following steps.

1. In the first step, a traditional scanline method is employed; generating images without taking account of any rounded edges. In this step, the surface number intersecting with each scanline and depth values from the viewpoint are stored in a file.

2. Rounded edges and their radii are specified.

3. Rounded edges are rendered by using the data prepared in steps 1 and 2.

2.1   Classification of Rounded Edges

Rounded edges are classified into two cases:

- Only one surface between surfaces sharing a rounded edge is visible.

- Both surfaces sharing a rounded edge are visible.

In the following, how to render rounded edges in individual cases is discussed.

2.1.1   Rendering a Model for One Visible Surface

Let's assume that only one surface F_A between surfaces F_A and F_B whose common edge is rounded with radius r is visible as shown in Fig. 1. In this case, a rounding process is as follows (see Fig. 1).

1. The end point of the real rounded domain, P_A, is calculated.

2. Having defined that P_C is a point on the edge and P_v is a viewpoint, angle γ_A between $\overrightarrow{P_C P_A}$ and $\overrightarrow{P_C P_v}$ is obtained by the following inner product.

$$\gamma_A = \cos^{-1}\left\{ \frac{(\overrightarrow{P_C P_A} \cdot \overrightarrow{P_C P_v})}{|\overrightarrow{P_C P_A}| \, |\overrightarrow{P_C P_v}|} \right\}. \tag{1}$$

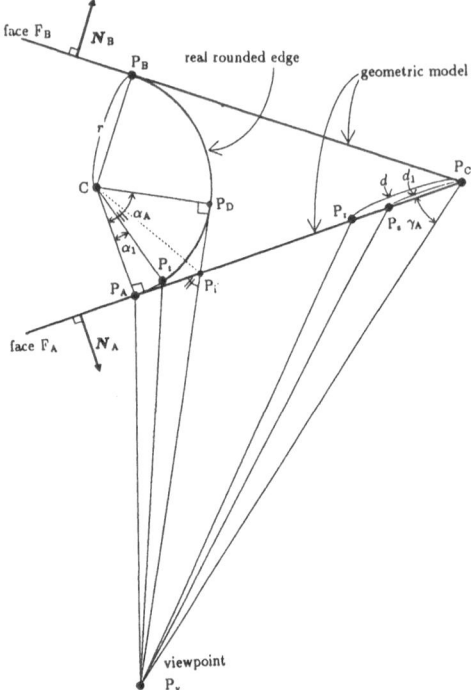

Figure 1: Rendering model for one visible surface.

Lines $\overline{P_C P_v}$ and $\overline{P_D P_v}$ can be assumed to be parallel because of the fact that the rounded area is fully distant from viewpoint, P_v, and then angle $\angle P_v P_i P_A$ can be set as to be γ_A, where P_i is the intersection point of $\overline{P_D P_v}$ and $\overline{P_A P_C}$. Therefore, angle α_A representing the visible part of the rounded edge is approximated by the following equation.

$$\alpha_A \simeq \gamma_A. \tag{2}$$

3. Distance d between the point P_c and P_r, where the latter is the beginning point of the rounded domain, is set to the length of $\overline{P_A P_i}$. That is, d is obtained by using the following equation.

$$d = r \tan \frac{\alpha_A}{2} = r \sqrt{\frac{1 - \cos \alpha_A}{1 + \cos \alpha_A}}. \tag{3}$$

4. For calculating the intensity at each point on surface F_A, normal vectors on the rounded edge are approximated as follows; the normal vector at point P_t on the real rounded edge is used for that of point P_s where the distance from point P_C is d_1 ($d_1 < d$). In order to determine point P_t, the angle between $\overrightarrow{CP_A}$ and $\overrightarrow{CP_t}$ (C is the center point of the real rounded edge) is approximated by using the following equation,

$$\alpha_1 = \frac{d - d_1}{d} \alpha_A. \tag{4}$$

In this way, normal vectors on the section, $P_r P_C$, are approximated to the real normal vectors on the rounded edge with radius r. Concerning the position of rounded edges, the larger the angle, $\angle P_A P_C P_B$, becomes, the smaller the error to the real rounded edge.

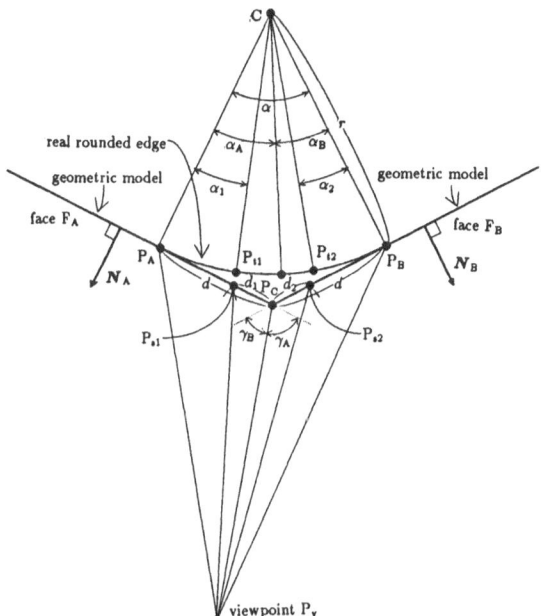

Figure 2: Rendering model for two visible surfaces.

2.1.2 Rendering a Model for Two Visible Surfaces

Let's assume that both surfaces F_A and F_B sharing a rounded edge are visible as shown in Fig. 2. In this case, the rounded domain to be rendered exists on both surfaces, F_A and F_B. The rounding process is as follows.

1. Both end points, P_A and P_B, of a rounded domain on F_A and F_B are calculated.

2. Having defined that P_C is a point on the edge and P_v is a viewpoint, the angle γ_A between $\overrightarrow{P_A P_C}$ and $\overrightarrow{P_C P_v}$ and the angle γ_B between $\overrightarrow{P_B P_C}$ and $\overrightarrow{P_C P_v}$ are obtained by the following inner products.

$$\gamma_A = \cos^{-1}\left\{ -\frac{(\overrightarrow{P_C P_A} \cdot \overrightarrow{P_C P_v})}{|\overrightarrow{P_C P_A}|\,|\,|\overrightarrow{P_C P_v}\,|} \right\}, \tag{5}$$

$$\gamma_B = \cos^{-1}\left\{ -\frac{(\overrightarrow{P_C P_B} \cdot \overrightarrow{P_C P_v})}{|\overrightarrow{P_C P_B}|\,|\,|\overrightarrow{P_C P_v}\,|} \right\}. \tag{6}$$

The ratio of rounded domain on the surfaces F_A and F_B is in proportion to these angles; angles α_A and α_B corresponding to the surfaces F_A and F_B, respectively, can be expressed by the following equation;

$$\alpha_A = \frac{\gamma_A}{\gamma_A + \gamma_B}\alpha, \tag{7}$$

$$\alpha_B = \frac{\gamma_B}{\gamma_B + \gamma_B}\alpha, \tag{8}$$

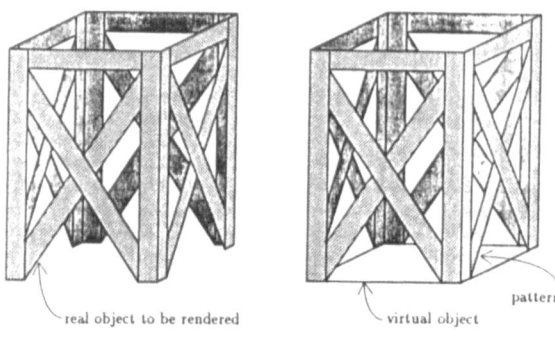

Figure 3: Concept of a virtual object.

where α is the angle of the real rounded domain.

3. Normal vectors for rendering rounded edges, $P_A P_C$ and $P_B P_C$, are calculated in the same manner of the steps 3 and 4 in the previous paragraph.

3   DISPLAYING COMPLEX OBJECTS USING A PATTERN MAPPING

Complex objects such as transmission towers and fences are composed of a number of relatively simple elements such as rectangles and cylinders. These elements are treated as opaque patterns mapped onto transparent planes, and shaded according to their real shapes.

3.1   Procedure of the Proposed Method

Procedure for rendering complex objects is as follows (see Fig. 3):

1. Modeling a few objects (called virtual objects) consisting of transparent planes (called virtual planes) based on the shapes of the original objects.

2. Mapping patterns corresponding to the elements of the objects onto the surfaces of the virtual objects.

3. Displaying only patterns by employing a scanline method; in the shading process each pattern is rendered according to the original shapes of the elements.

3.2   Geometric Model

The basic shapes of elements which can be rendered by the proposed method and how to define each element as a pattern are described.

Two types of patterns, convex polygons (called planar patterns) and cylinders (called cylindrical patterns), are prepared as the basic shape (see Fig. 4). From the view point of input, it is desired that these two patterns can be put in using almost the same format; the numerical data formats of both patterns are common, except only the giving of a flag to distinguish between a plane and a cylinder. By using this format, object data consisting of planar patterns, cylindrical patterns or even the patterns combining them can be easily put in.

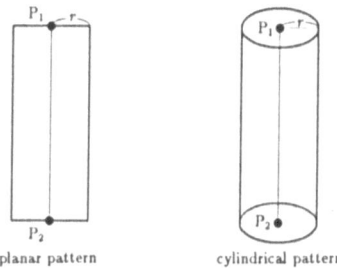

Figure 4: Two types of patterns.

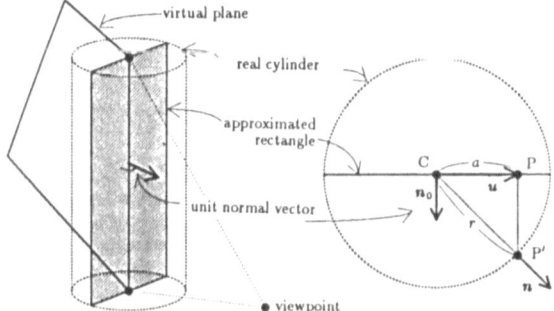

Figure 5: Calculation of the normal vector for a cylindrical pattern.

The shape of a cylindrical pattern can be approximated by the following rectangle except when the viewpoint is very close; the width is equal to the radius of the cylinder, and the normal of the rectangle always directs toward the viewpoint.

3.3 Rendering Model

planar patterns and cylindrical patterns mapped onto the virtual planes should be rendered faithfully with their real shapes. In the following, shading and shadowing are discussed.

3.3.1 Shading

Planar patterns are shaded by using the normal vectors of the virtual plane onto which the patterns are mapped.

In the case of cylindrical patterns, a normal vector at each point on an approximated rectangle is calculated taking into account the normal corresponding to the real cylinder; i.e., the normal vector at point P on the approximated rectangle is defined as that of point P' by mapping point P onto point P' on the surface of the cylinder (see Fig. 5). Finally, a unit normal vector at point P is obtained by using the following equation.

$$n = \frac{1}{r}(u + \sqrt{r^2 - a^2}\,n_0), \qquad (9)$$

where u is the vector $\overrightarrow{CP}$ (C is a point on the cylinder axis), r is the radius of the cylinder, a is the distance between P and C, and n_0 is the unit normal vector of the approximated rectangle.

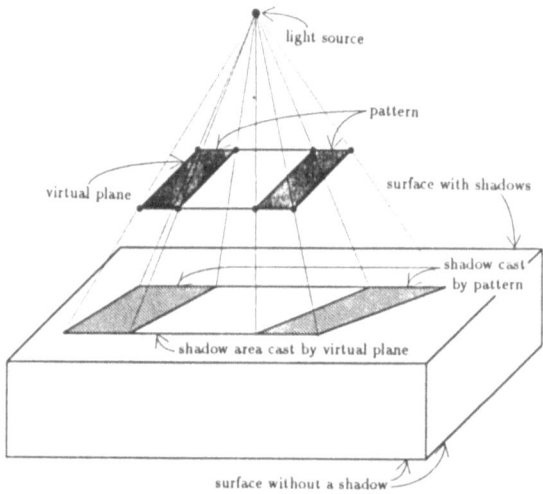

Figure 6: Efficient Shadowing.

3.3.2 Shadowing

The test of shadowing pattern by pattern takes an awful lot of calculation time, i.e., whether each pattern casts its shadow on which objects or not, because of a number of patterns. In order to address this problem, before the shadowing test on each pattern, whether a virtual plane where patterns are mapped casts its shadow on the objects or not, is tested (see Fig. 6). Only if the virtual plane casts a shadow, the shadowing of each pattern mapped onto the virtual plane is executed. By using this method, calculation time for shadowing can be greatly reduced.

3.4 Geometric Models of Various Objects

For modeling complex objects by using planar patterns and/or cylindrical patterns described before, the proposed modeling system has some primitive models for various objects, e.g., transmission towers, transmission lines, sets of insulators, fences, and curtains.

3.4.1 Modeling Transmission Towers

Transmission towers usually consists of planar elements and/or cylindrical elements. These elements are put in as planar patterns and/or cylindrical patterns mapped onto a virtual object composed of virtual planes; the external shape of a transmission tower is constructed as virtual objects, and then patterns corresponding to each element of the transmission tower are enrolled as a pattern on the surface of virtual objects. In order to set these patterns onto the virtual objects efficiently, the entry format is divided into three types; (1) planar patterns enrolled onto two virtual planes by a set of data, (2) planar patterns enrolled onto one virtual plane by a set of data, (3) cylindrical patterns on a virtual plane. Planar patterns are enrolled after clipping the edges flush with the virtual plane, while cylindrical patterns are enrolled as they are, even if they protrude from the plane (see Fig. 7).

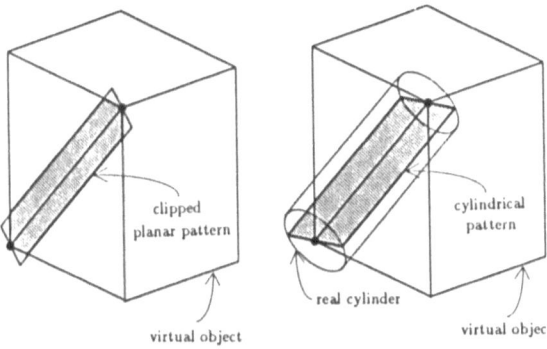

Figure 7: Modeling a transmission tower.

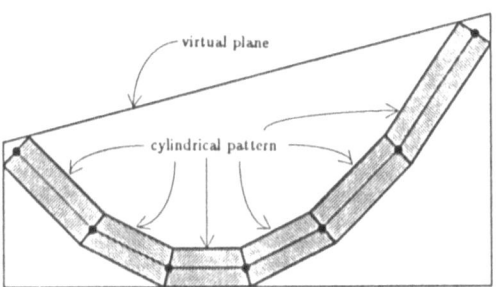

Figure 8: Modeling a wire of transmission lines.

3.4.2 Modeling Transmission Lines

A wire of transmission lines is represented as a set of cylindrical patterns mapped onto the virtual plane, which is set automatically (see Fig. 8).

The wires of a transmission line form catenary curves, but they are usually approximated as parabolic curves because of simple calculation [IEEJ '78]; parabolic curves are also employed for modeling transmission lines in this paper. It is well known that the parabolic curve representing a shape of a wire of transmission lines is expressed by the following equation.

$$y = c + \frac{x^2}{2c},\qquad(10)$$

where $c = T/W_c$, T is horizontal tension of the wire, W_c is weight of unit length of the wire. Using Eq. 10, the shape of the wire extended between the points (x_1, y_1) and (x_2, y_2) is expressed by the following equation.

$$y = \frac{(x - x_0)^2}{2c} + y_0,\qquad(11)$$

where

$$x_0 = \frac{1}{2}(x_1 + x_2) - c\frac{y_1 - y_2}{x_1 - x_2}$$

$$y_0 = \frac{1}{2}(y_1 + y_2) - \frac{1}{8c}(x_1 - x_2)^2 + \frac{c}{2}(\frac{y_1 - y_2}{x_1 - x_2})^2$$

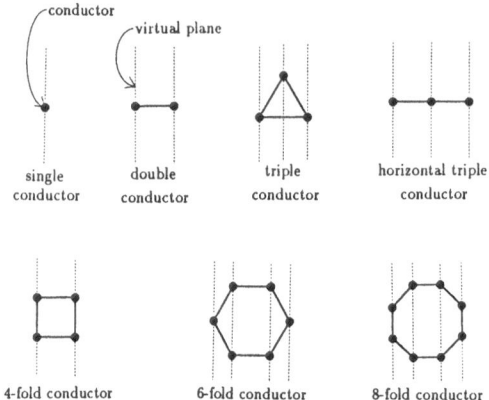

Figure 9: Setting virtual planes according to the transmission lines.

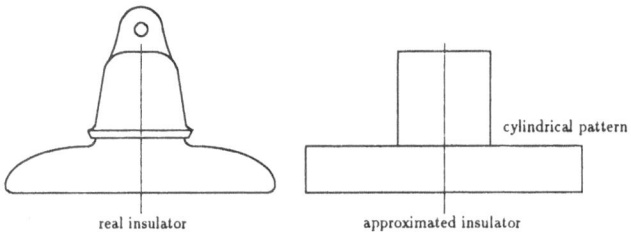

Figure 10: Modeling a insulator.

A wire is approximated as a set of line segments divided by n (n is the division number) along the x axis. There are two types of transmission lines: a single conductor type consisting of one conductor per one phase, and a bundle conductor type consisting of more than two conductors per one phase. The number of virtual planes necessary for mapping are set according to the type of the transmission lines as shown in Fig. 9 (the dotted lines are the locations of the virtual planes.)

3.4.3   Modeling Insulators

An insulator is modeled as a set of cylindrical patterns. For example, the proposed method can be employed to a suspension insulator shown in Fig. 10 (a) approximating it as two cylinders as shown in Fig. 10 (b); a virtual plane is enrolled for a set of insulators, and a set of two cylindrical patterns corresponding to one insulator is mapped onto the virtual plane.

3.4.4   Modeling Curtains

Let's consider curtains made of lace with gaps between very thin threads. In most cases, these threads are arranged in parallel and are periodic as shown in Fig. 11. Such a pattern can be defined by a radius of thread, gaps and colors of the threads. Then, in modeling the curtain, the external shape of a curtain is enrolled as some virtual objects, and then each periodical pattern corresponding to the threads is mapped onto them.

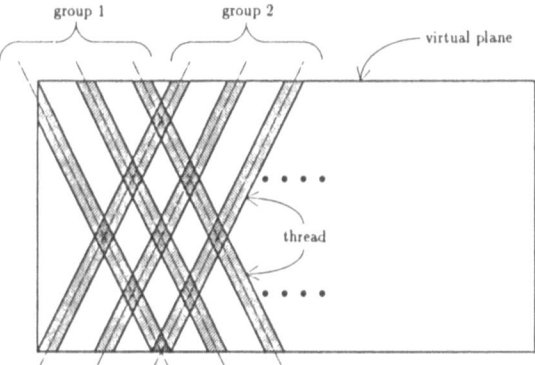

Figure 11: Modeling a curtain.

3.5 Anti-Aliasing of Extremely Thin Objects

For rendering extremely thin objects such as the electric wires of transmission lines and curtains made of lace it is very important to prevent the objects from disappearing and their intensity from changing erratically. For example, even when transmission lines are far from the viewpoint, both their wires' shapes and intensities should be minutely calculated, because their reflection effects cannot be ignored.

In the proposed method, a multi-scanning method [Nishita '84] is employed for anti-aliasing. This method introduces a virtual scanline (called sub-scanline) dividing a pixel equally, and removes aliasing by using a number of sub-scanlines. In order to render the reflection effects accurately, even if intersections between the cylindrical patterns and a scanline exist in the same pixel, intensities are calculated at several sampled points, whose number is specified beforehand.

For creating scenes with horizontal wires of transmission lines, the number of sub-scanlines in the area of the image with transmission lines must be considerably larger than that of the other area. Then, these images are generated by increasing the number of sub-scanlines, say fifteen lines per pixel; the range of increased sub-scanlines corresponds to the band of the virtual plane of the wires.

4 EXAMPLES

The proposed method is applied to rendering rounded edges; Fig. 12 (a) and (b) show the images of a cube without and with rounded edges, respectively. Every edge is 10 cm long and the radius of each rounded edge is 0.3 cm. In order to display highlights on the surfaces, Phong's model [Phong '75] is employed. In Fig. 12 (a), the boundary of the side surfaces is not recognized because of the equal brightness of both, while, in Fig. (b), edges are clearly observed although the radius of rounded edges is quite small.

Fig. 13 (a) and (b) show the images of a concave object. The length of long edges is 9 cm and the radius of the round one is 0.3 cm. Fig. 13 (b) demonstrates that the proposed method can deal with a fillet.

In the following, some examples of complex and/or thin objects are displayed. Fig. 14 (a) and (b) show the close-up scenes of transmission towers consisting of planar patterns and of cylindrical patterns, respectively.

Table 1: Comparison of the CPU time.

	number of object	number of pattern	CPU time [sec.]
proposed method	9	128	61.9
ordinary method	158	0	102.1

(computer: SiliconGraphics IRIS-4D/120GTX)

Tab. 1 shows the comparison of the CPU time to render Fig. 14 (a) between the proposed method and an ordinary method in which the transmission tower are modeled by using objects. In the proposed method, the transmission tower consists of 9 virtual objects and 128 planar patterns. The CPU time of the proposed method is about 40 percents shorter than the ordinary method. In regards to the comparison of the rendering time of Fig. 14 (b), we could not get the CPU time of the ordinary method, because it is quite difficult to model the transmission tower by using cylinders under the condition of no interference of objects. This means that the more complex the objects are, the more valuable the proposed method is.

Fig. 15 shows the scenes including transmission lines. Fig. (a), (b), and (c) demonstrate single conductor transmission lines, four-fold conductor transmission lines, and eight-fold conductor transmission lines, respectively. A multi-scanning method with 20 sub-scanlines is employed on the vertical planes for anti-aliasing; the transmission towers consist of cylindrical patterns, and the background image is generated by mapping aerial photographs onto a terrain model constructed by using contour data from a map [Kaneda '89]. The reflection effects of the transmission lines appear, although each wire of the transmission lines occupies less than a pixel on a screen. Depicting such reflection effects is quite difficult should line drawings be used.

Fig. 15 (d) demonstrates transmission towers with sets of suspension insulators. In the case of a close-up view of the insulators, such as those set on the closest transmission tower, their shapes look somewhat awkward, while for a distant view, their shapes look natural.

Fig. 16 shows a interior scene with a curtain. The curtain is modeled by using 18066 cylindrical patterns set onto 144 virtual planes. A multi-scanning method with 20 sub-scanlines is also employed. These cylindrical patterns are arranged by using two patterns of vertical and horizontal threads. The vase is also modeled by using cylindrical patterns, and edges of both the desk and the vase rest are rounded.

5 CONCLUSIONS

Generating realistic images with rounded edges and complex and/or very thin objects has been realized by using a simplified model, and has demonstrated the usefulness of the proposed method.

The proposed method has the following advantages:

- Rounded edges can be efficiently rendered because the proposed method is not based on smooth shading of triangular patches but on mapping normal vectors.

- Relatively distant complex and/or thin objects whose reflection effects cannot be ignored for realistic images can be easily modeled and efficiently rendered by using patterns set onto virtual planes.

The following points remain as further studies. For rendering rounded edges, the proposed method should be improved to deal with variable radius. For modeling and rendering complex objects, a pattern expressing the frustum of a cone should be prepared. By improving these points, more realistic images can be expected.

289

(a) without a rounded edge (b) with rounded edges

Figure 12: Effects of rounded edges.

(a) without a fillet (b) with a fillet

Figure 13: Effects of a fillet.

(a) Planar patterns (b) Cylindrical patterns

Figure 14: Close-up scenes of a transmission tower.

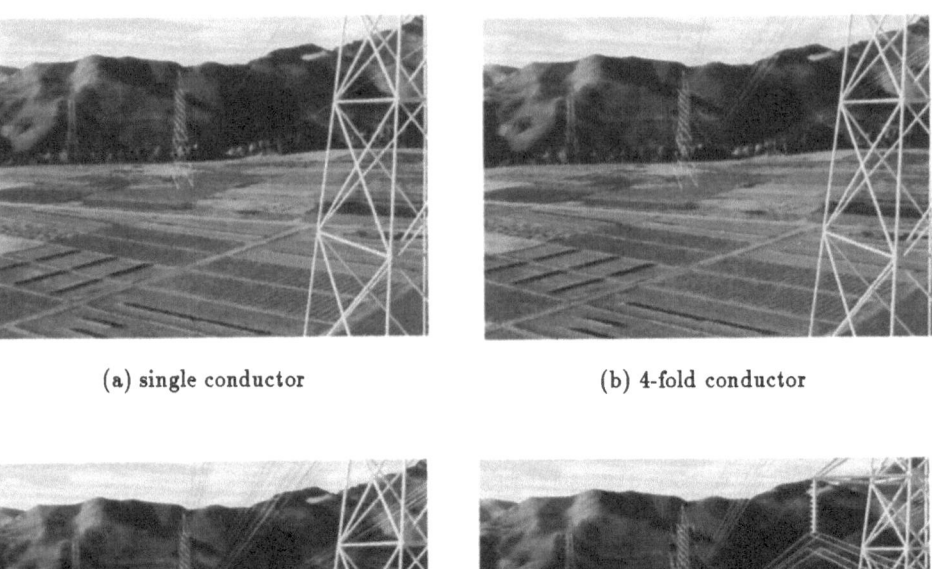

(a) single conductor   (b) 4-fold conductor

(c) 8-fold conductor   (d) sets of suspension insulators

Figure 15: Transmission lines.

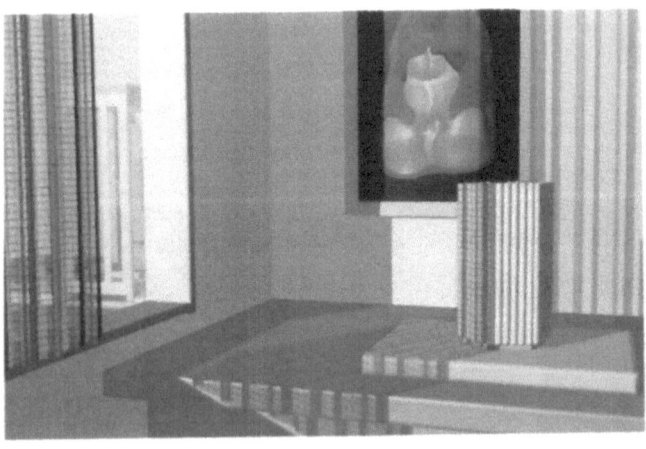

Figure 16: A interior scene with a curtain.

REFERENCES

[Blinn '76]   Blinn, J. F. and Newell, M. E. (1976), Texture and Reflection in Computer Generated Images, Comm. ACM 19(10), 542-547.

[Blinn '78]   Blinn, J. F. (1978), Simulation of Wrinkled Surfaces, Computer Graphics 12(3).

[Clark '76]   Clark, J. H. (1976), Hierarchical Geometric Models for Visible Surface Algorithms, Comm. ACM 19(10), 547-554.

[IEEJ '78]   IEE of Japan, ed. (1978), Electric Engineering Handbook, IEE of Japan, Tokyo.

[Kaneda '89]   Kaneda, K., Kato, F., Nakamae, E., Nishita, T., Tanaka, H., and Noguchi, T. (1989), Three Dimensional Terrain Modeling and Display for Environmental Assessment, Computer Graphics 23(3), 207-214.

[Nishita '84] Nishita, T. and Nakamae, E. (1984), Half-Tone Representation of 3-D Objects with Smooth Edges by Using a Multi-Scanning Method, Trans. IPS Japan 25(5), 703-711.

[Okamura '83] Okamura, T., Harada, K., Nakamae, E., and Nishita, T. (1983), A Half-Tone Representation of Curved Surfaces by Using Triangular Approximation, IECE Technical Report, IE82-92, 19-24.

[Phong '75]   Phong, B. T. (1975), Illumination for Computer-Generated Pictures, Comm. ACM 18(6), 311-317.

[Requicha '82] Requicha, A. A. G. and Voelcker, H. G. (1982), Solid Modeling, A Historical Summary and Contemporary Assessment, IEEE Computer Graphics & Applications 2(3), 9-24.

[Rubin '80]   Rubin, S. M. and Whitted, T. (1980), A 3-Dimensional Representation for Fast Rendering of Complex Scenes, Computer Graphics 14(3), 110-116.

[Saito '89a]   Saito, T., Shinya, M., and Takahashi, T. (1989), Highlighting Rounded Edges, New Advances in computer Graphics (Proc. CG International '89), Springer-Verlag Tokyo, 613-629

[Saito '89b]   Saito, T. and Takahashi, T. (1989), Edge Enhancement in Computer Generated Images, Proc. 39th Annual Convention IPS Japan, 913-914.

[1]Faculty of Engineering, Hiroshima University, Hiroshima, 724 Japan
[2]ASCII Corporation, Minato-ku, Tokyo, 107 Japan
[3]Tokyo Electric Power Co. Ltd., Chiyoda-ku, Tokyo, 100 Japan

Graphics Modeling As a Basic Tool for Scientific Visualization

J.L. Encarnação, P. Astheimer, W. Felger, M. Frühauf, M. Göbel, and K. Karlsson

keywords: scientific visualization, graphics modeling, visualization toolkit, volume visualization, visual analysis, visual comparison of data, 4D modeling

1 Introduction

The task of systems for the visualization of scientific data is to compute images representing the contents of a given data set. This data set, of course, cannot be altered in order to compute better images. Therefore, modeling is not used to create data sets describing objects, as e.g. in CAD systems. Modeling in scientific visualization means to find the method and the way to compute an image from a given data set, which presents certain features in that data set in the best possible manner to the user.

This paper describes modeling tasks in scientifc visualization and the concepts and the architecture of visualization systems. Moreover, it presents examples of modeling in scientific visualization from already implemented systems at FhG-AGD.

The main tasks of modeling in the process of scientific visualization are introduced in chapter 2. Modeling in traditional computer graphics is compared with modeling in scientific visualization. This demands a brief overview of main tasks in scientific visualization and the architecture of visualization systems as given in chapter 3.

One task of modeling in scientific visualization is the process of mapping data to graphical primitives and corresponding attributes. As an example of this modeling task, the interactive specification of parameters and attributes for the rendering of regular volume data sets is described in chapter 4.

Chapter 5 emphasizes mainly on the mapping of data obtained from Finite Element simulations in mechanical engineering to graphical primitives, e.g. lines, surfaces or voxels. The interactive modeling of the graphical representation of the data as handled in ISVAS is described. ISVAS is a system for the analysis of the results of finite element simulations in fracture mechanics developed at FhG-AGD. It covers modeling in scientific visualization from data preprocessing to the calculation of the final image.

The comparison of real world observations and simulation results aids to improve and refine simulation techniques and helps to understand ongoing events. Chapter 6 presents some reflections on that topic.

Time is an important clue which affects many features of todays visualization systems. The impact and realization of time on various aspects in visualization is explored in chapter 7.

2 Modeling in Scientific Visualization

In traditional Computer Graphics, modeling is understood as the process for mapping application data onto geometrical or graphical objects and onto corresponding object attributes. Modeling also is seen as the technique of combining separately defined geometrical objects in space with the intention to define complex scenes using these predefined objects.

Standard graphics systems like PHIGS support the second aspect in modeling by providing corresponding transformations and attribute inheritance functions. The first aspect in modeling, the decision which graphical primitive or geometrical object is used for representing an application data set, is left to the application programmer. Of course, the programmer's design decision is heavily influenced by common sense, i.e. traditional modeling methods which provide a widely accepted technique for representing the specific data set in a visual manner.

In Scientific Visualization, modeling processes for application data are conceptual similar to modeling in Computer Graphics although modeling is more complex due to the great amount of data and the unconfirmed correlations between data. A programmer in Computer Graphics has a concrete idea about the visual presentation of the data, whereas a scientist in scientific computing uses well-known visualization techniques without knowing which type of presentation offers the most insight into the data. There is no guarantee that a scientist will see what is hidden in billions of numbers.

This is indeed one main difference between modeling in Computer Graphics and modeling in Scientific Visualization: in the first field, data may be manipulated until the visual representation fits; in visualization, the visual representation of data - not the data to be visualized - may be manipulated until new coherence in the data is discovered. In both areas modeling describes rather interactive processes than static and non flexible rules.

The great challenge in modeling as a basic tool in Scientific Visualization is to find appropriate data processors and visualizers for a particular data set [McDF-87]. Modeling therefore takes place at different layers in the overall visualization process, e.g. at the application layer in defining simulation parameters, at the visualization layer in selecting one or more visualization techniques, at the rendering layer in choosing a specific rendering quality, etc. In visualization the scientist needs to have access to various alternative data mapping modules to control the visual presentation of the data at each level in the visualization pipeline. This pipeline stands for the overall process of data modeling form raw application data to displayable images.

Orthogonal to data modeling in the visualization pipeline there is a demand to combine data from various sources, e.g. satellite data, terrain data and simulation data, within one visualization object. The aim is to generate one image out of these very complex visualization objects which contains both variant and non variant data. Modelers allow to combine scientific data in not only in space and but also in time. At each level in a visualization system, modeling tools are established which allow to puzzle together data with corresponding semantics.

Besides mapping of data onto images and combining data for images, modeling in visualization includes the modeling of application data by interacting with images and subsequent image regeneration triggered by interactive control of the visualization process.

3   A model for visualization systems

The system model in Scientific Visualization can be represented as a bipartit graph [FFGG-90], encompassing data and processes (see figure 1). Data is handled by a particular process as soon as it is accessible for the process. Each process converts input data to output data under parameter control. This view is data flow oriented, whereby the data flow through the entire system describes the modeling cascade in Scientific Visualization.

Data is produced by data sources (i.e. numerical processes, monitoring systems, etc.) and consumed by data absorbers (in general graphical devices). Each process is associated to a specific layer within the system. All processes of a certain layer accept data of the same semantical level. Processes of a layer i can make use of the processes within the same layer and the layer i-1. Each layer comprises a data storage to retain objects for fast image regeneration which has to be performed any time the user interferes interactively in the visualization process. In particular, retained objects are of great importance for interactive visualization systems. A specific path of one application data set through the network of processes is called visualization pipeline, i.e. an interactively defined sequence of processes to model data.

The visualization system model consists of six layers: the data source layer, the filtering layer, the mapping layer, the rendering layer, the imaging layer and the display layer.

1.   The data source layer contains data sources, like sensors or numerical simulations which deliver a huge amount of experimental data or simulation data (e.g. satellite images, medical images, computations in finite element methods, fluid dynamics or physics). The data is pre-processed (e.g. elimination of transmission errors) in order to provide the basic application data to be transferred to the underlying processes.

2.   In the data filter layer are such processes located, which reduce the basic application data to the data records of the user's interest. New data is derived from the basic data, e.g. gradients, and if necessary, a conversion to a standard data format is undertaken. Examples for filter processes are interpolation, segmentation and other data enhancement techniques.

296

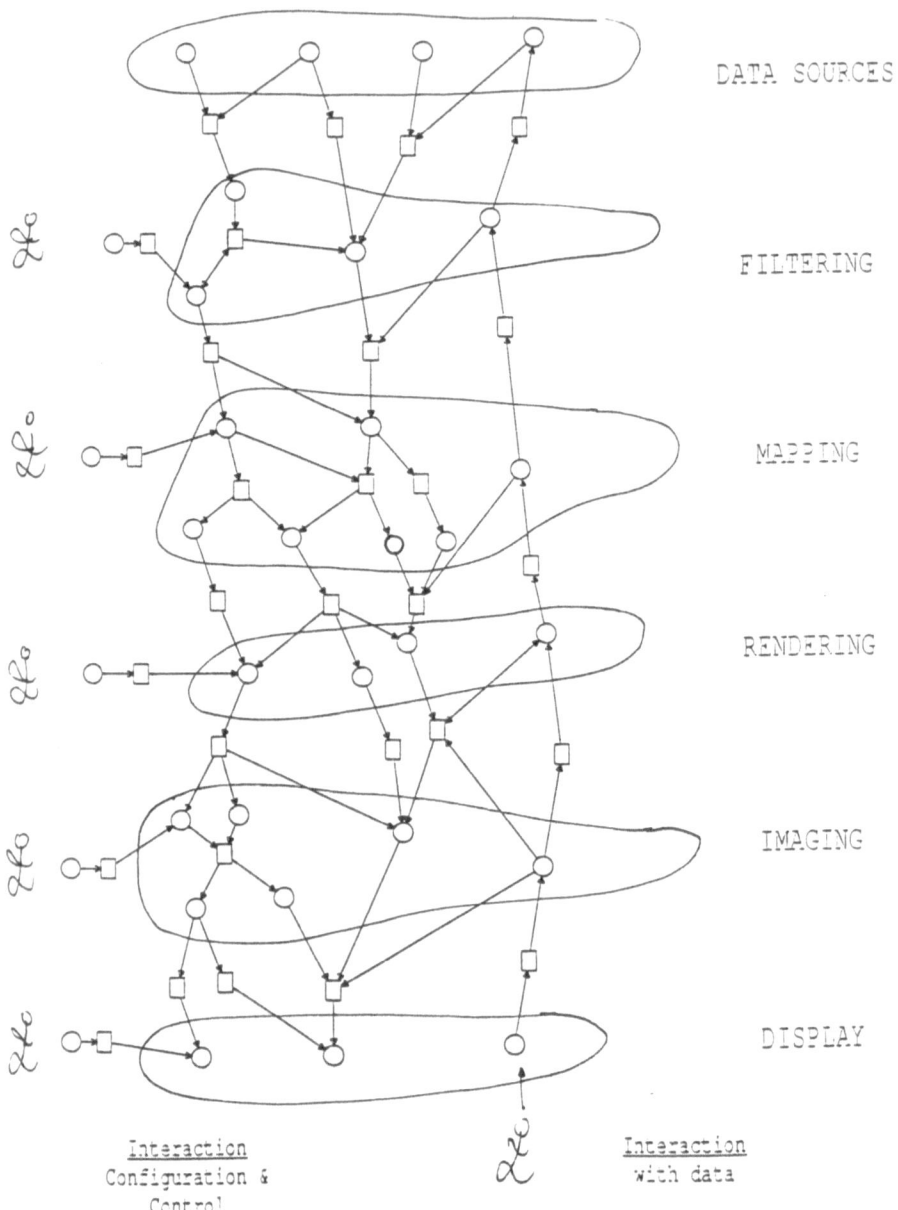

Figure 1: Network of Processes in Scientific Visualization

3. The mapping layer provides processes which map data onto visualization techniques, such as colour-coded contour lines, trajectories, hedgehogs, vectors etc. In a multimedia context these techniques are not restricted to address only the visual perception of information, but also for instance the acustic or tactile perception. Visualization objects represent combined application data which is to be display as a whole choosing one out of alternative visualization techniques. Visualization techniques are realized by rendering objects, i.e. the retained data structure of the next layer.

4. The processes within the rendering layer generate virtual images (pixmaps) in a standard format from rendering objects (e.g. lines, surfaces, volumes, etc.). Rendering objects are derived from visualization objects after selecting a specific visualization technique. Integrated rendering of geometric data, volumetric data and analytical functions is provided by the visualization system.

5. The imaging layer contains processes which perform image-to-image transformations. These are in general: linear projections (translate, scale, etc.), image presentation and image enhancement, binary operators as well as image format conversion and interpolation in image space.

6. The display layer is realized by window management systems. This layer is responsible for displaying virtual images, for specifying the display space and for handling user interaction on basis of windows (local scaling, image refresh, etc).

3.1 Interaction model in visualization systems

Interactivity is essential for stimulating scientists to evaluate unknown combinations of data [EnSc-88]. Interaction must be controlled by an extremely comfortable and easy-to-use user interface that supports the scientist to experiment with data, trying different visual presentations or identifying data by visual means.

Interactivity is classified into two aspects: one to configure and control the visualization system and a second to perform interaction with application data.

1. Control and configuration of the visualization process is allowed at each layer i. Each module has parameters, which can be modified by the user in interactive mode and which will normally cause a new data flow through the output pipeline to update the displayed image. In time invariant data visualization this update will cause an (immediate) image regeneration; in time dependent data visualization, the modification of parameters will be applied to subsequent images.

2. A comfortable but also very difficult feature is to relate image data (pixel) to data emerged earlier in the visualization pipeline. Interaction with application data is generated from basic graphical input like pointing and positioning in images. Reverse processes in each layer allow to regenerate semantics of the specific layer, e.g. picking one pixel of the virtual image allows to compute a position in 3D when knowing about the 3D object space and the corresponding transformations. Applying this technique subsequently, a pick input may identify an application data set, provided that the reverse processes exist and that data is retained at each layer or that information of the data modeling processes is held with each particular pixel.

Generating semantical input needs a sophisticated echo handling. Echo techniques for supporting both types of interaction are either provided by an user interface managment system or generated by specific echo processes within the visualization process network.

3.2 The VIS-A-VIS system

FhG-AGD is currently developing a visualization toolkit for scientific applications. The aim of the VIS-A-VIS project is the development of a toolkit for high quality, interactive visualization in scientific computing on parallel system architectures. The basic idea is to develop a hardware-independent, network-transparent tool set for experimental interactive inspection of complex data. The tool set will be be configurable to the need of each particular application and allows to integrate application models (numerical simulations). The toolkit provides an open system which may be extended with additional modules if required by specific applications. The anticipated user interface is based on OSF/Motif. The envisaged hardware platforms for the VIS-A-VIS toolkit are LAN-based distributed systems, parallel machines and massive parallel machines.

The VIS-A-VIS system consists of three basic layers.:

- the application layer,
- the visualization toolkit,
- the integrated rendering system.

The rendering system provides the interface to the graphics facilities of workstations at the lower level. A number of interfaces will be available, including the Image Interchange Format (IIF) of the coming Imaging Standard [ISO-90], virtual pixmaps, X11 compatible images and higher level maschine dependent interfaces. The renderer provides an integrated solution for geometric data [HaMa-90], for volumetric data [EFFK-90] and for the rendering of analytic functions [AsFe-90].

The visualization toolkit uses the rendering interface for image generation and for object (data) identification input. The toolkit consists of modules which provide visualization techniques, such as vector fields, iso surfaces, contour lines etc. Visualization objects are data structures which may be combined with other visualization objects in space and time, e.g. combine terrain data with a satellite image and with measured data from environmental sensors. Each visualization object can be set into a visual presentation by choosing one (out of alternative) visualization technique.

The application layer of VIS-A-VIS mostly is covererd by application projects (see Chapter 5). Application specific data filters and numerical models will be integrated into the VIS-A-VIS framework, so that the control of application models by a user will be available using the same interaction and echo techniques within the Motif environment as at the visualization level.

3.3 The visualization toolkit

The overall concept of the toolkit focus on the modularity and interactivity of the complete system. The modular design supports the mapping of application visualization goals to a simple visualization pipeline or even to a more complex visualization network, which consists of toolkit modules. So, the toolkit is a framework for a variety of modules including different tools to edit application and graphic data and the data flow between modules in a visualization environment.

Similiar approaches are realized in [Dyer-90, Upso-89]. In both systems the graphical output plays the dominant role and user input can only modify module parameters. A real user interaction with the application data is not possible. This drawback will be overcome with the VIS-A-VIS toolkit.

In VIS-A-VIS, each module transforms input data to output data under parameter control. A module obeys to a set of interface description rules, so that additional modules can be developed and tested stand-alone and then be integrated in the framework. They are invoked by a supervisor process if their action is necessary. There are several module classes, e.g. mapper (from application data to geometry) and renderer (from geometry to pixel). VIS-A-VIS destinguishes between different module classes, such as:

application:	NULL	-->	data
data filter:	data	-->	data
mapper:	data	-->	geometry
map&renderer:	data	-->	image
geo filter:	geometry	-->	geometry
renderer:	geometry	-->	image
image filter:	image	-->	image
display:	image	-->	display space.

Additionally to those classes, VIS-A-VIS allows to integrate tools of the following classes:

geo_modeler:	NULL	-->	geometry
scanner:	NULL	-->	image.

Each module within one class may be represented by one process. This allows a well-tailored distribution of the system over an available computational network. Moreover the power of parallel computers can be exploited. According to the data flow model in VIS-A-VIS, communication between the modules is based on standard communication mechanisms, like message passing or pipes. This is one advantage in supporting massive parallel computers with distributed memory. All modules are data-driven, i.e. they execute on new or changing data or parameter. There are a bunch of standard data types, like geometry, scene description, pixel and application data.

The display of images is only one aspect of output. Application data can also be modeled by sound (or smell) to be perceptible by humans. For an ergonomic interaction there are advanced input devices necessary. Available today are besides mouse et. al. spaceball, data glove, etc. Time is an important factor for both display and control. Application data will be transformed according its time requirements, control will be possible with time or event specification.

4   Interactive specification of parameters and attributes for volume visualization

One task of modeling in scientific visualization is the process of mapping data to graphical primitives and corresponding attributes. As an example of this modeling task, the interactive specification of parameters and attributes for the rendering of regular volume data sets is described in this chapter. Data sets that depend on three spatial dimensions are called volume data. The dependent variables of the data can be scalar, vector or tensor fields.

The methods for calculating shaded 3D presentations of scalar volume data in scientific visualization can be divided in two different categories. The first category are surface-oriented representations. Surfaces representing certain features of the data are explicitly calculated from the volume data set in hand. These surfaces are then rendered with "conventional" methods. Here, the calculation of the surface representation is computing-intensive or can be realized only with the support of the user, whereas the shaded representation of the surfaces can be produced relatively fast. Moreover, surface rendering is supported by the hardware of the graphics workstations for polygon shading.

In the second category there are volume-oriented representations. Volume rendering procedures compute shaded 3D representations directly from the volume data set in hand (figure 2). Here, the complete volume data set is always the basis for the calculation of the representation. Only a few preparing, simple data convertions have to be made prior to rendering. The representation method and quality as well as the emphasis of single features of the data set in hand are determined by choosing the representation parameters. Since the whole data set is always in hand, this kind of 3D representation of volume data in scientific visualization is very computing-intensive and therefore very time-costly. High-quality representations cannot be calculated on graphics workstations in spaces of time which allow for an interactive analysis of the data sets.

The interactive analysis of complex volume data sets and the interactive finding of the best possible representation for the required features is a precondition for achieving scientific insights. Modeling of the best graphical representation of a scientific volume data set is heavily influenced by the specification of the visualization parameters.

Therefore methods have to be developed and implemented, with which the parameters for controlling volume-oriented representation procedures can be chosen. These methods have to be appropriate to judge the effects on the final representation, after having chosen the parameters. The user has to be able to create the echo of the choice of the parameters in short time, in order to support interactive work for the data analysis. The choice of the parameters should largely be realized in an interactive way and not by a command language. We have implemented a graphical interactive user interface for the specification of parameters and attributes for volume visualization using X and OSF/Motif. The functionality and the concept of that user interface is described in the following paragraphs.

The most challenging part of the user interface is the real-time interactive definition of viewing parameters for volume rendering. Viewing parameters in this case are the viewpoint and cut planes through the volume data set. We use an approach for the fast rendering of volume data which is based on a scanline-based texture mapping on a cube's surface. The user interface solves the problem of realtime rotation and slicing of huge data sets on graphics workstations. It follows the natural understanding of rotation and is operated by using the workstation's mouse. Furthermore we have developed tools for interactive colour assignment, lighting, segmentation and contour extraction which are included in the user interface.

4.1 Attributes and parameters

The volume visualization procedure we are using for volume rendering [Früh-90], applies the following parameters to specify the representation to be created:
- Scalar volume data set
- Viewpoint or rotation angle
- Cut planes through the volume
- Visibility
- Rendering method
- Method for the calculation of normals
- Shading method
- Method for the calculation of samples
- Light source position
- Reflection parameters
- Colour
- Transparency
- Resolution of final image

Visibility, colour and transparency are individually defined for each volume element (voxel). They are defined by means of functions depending on the scalar value of the voxel. Such functions can be piecewise linear or piecewise constant. For these functions threshold values are then interactively specified. For the transparency and colour assignment to the voxels, as well as for the setting of the visibility attribute, the following chapter presents suitable echo types.

One of the most difficult tasks in volume data visualization is to develop a tool, with which even large data sets (e. g., 256^3) on graphics workstations can be rotated and cut in realtime. The following paragraph also presents a method for that task (see also [FrKa-90]).

The choice of the most appropriate methods for the actual procedure of volume visualization can understandably not be simulated by other methods. Here the user depends on his experience with the single methods. In order to accelerate the generation of the representation, pictures with lower resolution can be calculated. In general, however, these will only provide a rough impression of the representation quality to be expected. Methods, therefore are chosen from menues.

4.2   Echoes

Colour and transparency assignment

Colour and transparency assignments on voxels are realized, in the simplest case, by means of threshold values in the range of values of the data. The definition of the threshold values is effected after the analysis of selected data set layers. The result of the assignment is exemplarily checked on these or other layers. Transparency values are mapped onto grey values. The interactive specification of the threshold values is supported by two devices: first, by inquiring about the value of single, mouse-identified data points, and second, by displaying a chosen threshold value in context with the histogram of a scanline in one data set layer . All these operations can be carried through in realtime on one data set layer each. Precondition for the implementation of these tools is, however, that one single pixel can be identified with the workstation's mouse (figure 3).

Viewpoint and Cut Planes

Volume data is often arranged in a regular grid. Thus, a data cube is obtained from a stack of images. This simplifies the algorithm for the interactive specification of the viewpoint immensly. The user recognizes the cube's position from the position of the edges and vertices of the cube. Top and bottom, left and right, front and back are recognized on the basis of the inner structure of the cube's surfaces. Therefore we project 2D pixmaps from the volume data set onto the six surfaces of the cube (figure 4). In the simplest case, the outermost layers of the data set are used for that purpose. If these layers, however, do not contain sufficient information, the volume data is orthogonally projected onto the cube's surfaces, above a threshold value having been defined by the user. This technique is especially appropriate for data sets which are not present in cube form. The calculation of these six pixmaps is effected during the preprocessing. They are kept in the main memory of the workstation while using the tool.

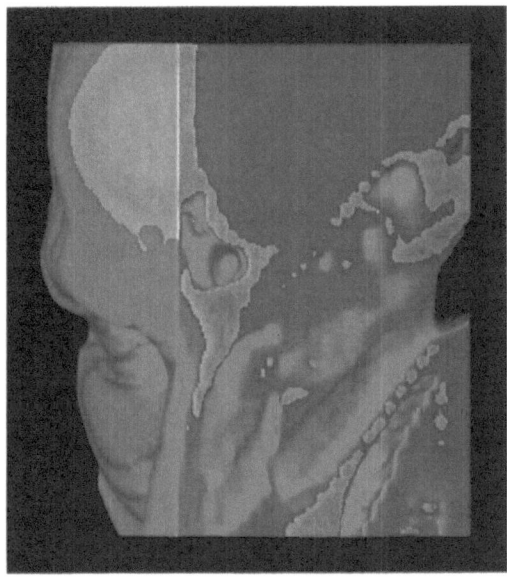

Figure 2: Volume Rendering of a Computer-Tomogram (CT) data set of the human nose

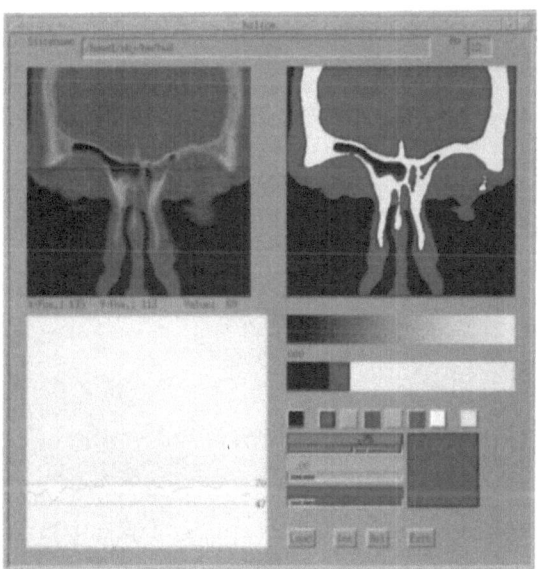

Figure 3: Interactive colour assignment to a slice of the CT data set

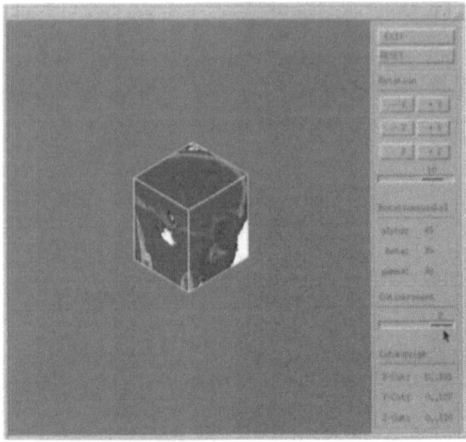

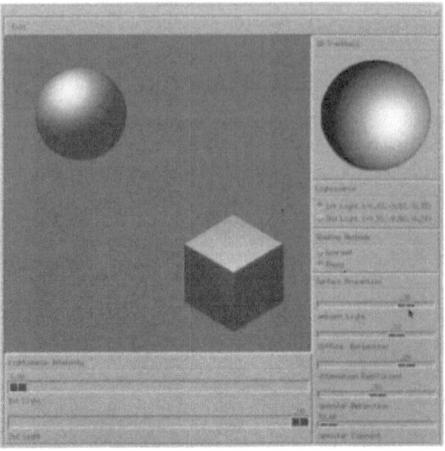

Figure 4: Interactive rotation and cutting of   Figure 5: Interactive specification of lighting
the CT data set   parameters for volume rendering

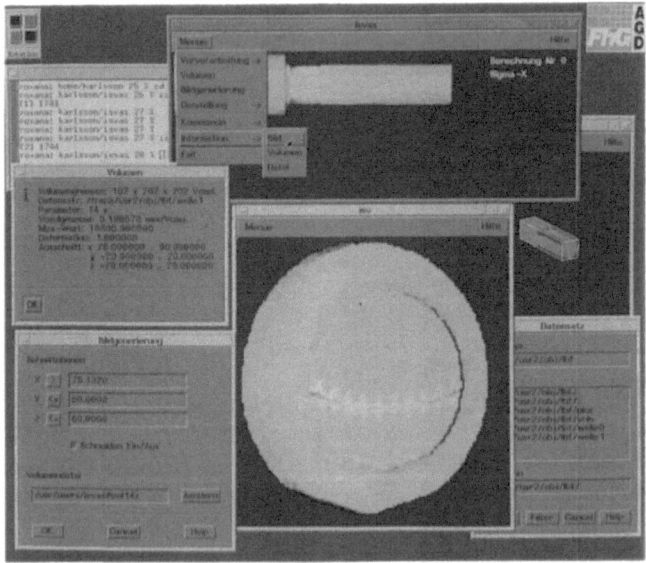

Figure 6: Analysis of finite element data with ISVAS

During the rotation of the data cube, only the eight verticess of the cube are transformed. At any time, at most three faces of the cube are visible. The visible faces are identified by the aid of the normal vector. The orthogonal projection of the cube's faces onto the image plane is effected by simply eliminating the z-coordinate. The corresponding pixmaps are mapped onto the thus developing parallelograms by scaling and shearing. For that a scanline-based fill algorithm is used [Hofm-89].

Cuts through the volume are specified by successively removing visible surfaces of the cube. In this case only one of the six pixmaps has to be recalculated. The quick recalculation of one pixmap is here supported by information from its z-buffer. In case of removing one layer, the neighbouring faces are only reduced by one pixel.

For the recalculation of the visible layers it is important, that the complete data set is present in the main memory during transit time. Our experience shows that the benefit of the tool is not restricted, when large data sets are reduced by the factor two for this purpose.

Light source and reflection parameters

The user interface has to explain the effects of specifying the light sources and reflection parameters to users, who are not familiar with the principles of the 3D representation in computer graphics (lighting and shading). Since shading with regard to complex scenes cannot be effected in realtime, the echo generation to the lighting parameters is realized by means of a simple scene from geometric solids. Here especially one scene offers itself, consisting of a sphere and a cube (figure 5). For such a simple scene, the shading can be calculated very quickly on a workstation.

5 Interactive visual analysis of volume data

ISVAS (Interactive Software for the Visual AnalysiS of fracture mechanics) is a visualization system for the analysis of the results of finite element simulations in fracture mechanics. The finite element method is used to simulate tests, in which specimens are subjected to stresses under fluctuating loads. The simulations produce very large amounts of data, where stress - a second-order tensor field, containing bending and shear stress - and displacement are calculated for each node in the finite element mesh. Although ISVAS is being developed for fracture mechanics, the general conception makes it possible to visualize any kind of volume data, e. g. from medicine, fluid dynamics etc.

ISVAS allows an interactive modeling of the data and the graphical representation of the data throughout the visualization process, from the preprocessing until the final image (see figure 6).

At the preprocessing of the data functions are available, that enable the creation of new aspects of the data, like interpolation between data sets, combination of stress components and calculation of derived variables, e. g. the von Mises stress. It is also possible to make some changes in the data, e. g. to scale the displacements in order to detect and analyze small deformations and cracks in the material.

In the mapping process there are many ways to represent the finite element data graphically using different graphics primitives and attributes. The methods used in ISVAS will be briefly described here.

The simplest graphics primitive to display the data is the point. The finite element nodes are mapped to points, where the point size, type and colour represent the stress value at the node.

The geometry of the object under study can also be mapped to curve primitives, displaying the finite element mesh as a wire-frame model. The stress field is mapped onto colour or onto other primitives added to the wire-frame display. Such primitives can be symbols, icons or three-dimensional arrows, where the length, direction and colour of the arrow present information about the stress. As the finite element mesh normally is much denser in the regions with high gradient it is often a reasonable to distribute the arrows on a regular grid instead of placing them on the nodes.

More realistic images can be achieved with surface primitives. Polygons or spline surfaces can be used to represent the surface of the object. The stress field is in this case represented by textures and colours. To give a better three-dimensional impression of the image shading may be applied. However, the variation in intensity due to shading often disturbs the presentation of the stress field in colours. The mapping of the field values onto colour and the grade of shading must be modifiable, in order to obtain an optimal image.

Another type of surface oriented mapping are iso-surfaces [GaNa-89]. This is an interesting case, where field values are mapped onto geometry. Nested iso-surfaces could be displayed transparently or another field component could be mapped onto colour, showing two dimensions in the same image to analyze their correlation.

Points, curves and surfaces can be rendered fast enough to allow interactions like rotation, scaling etc. in real-time on a graphics workstation. However, the three-dimensional volume information has been reduced to a point, a curve or a two-dimensional surface. The information about the entire complexity and inhomogenity of the volume is lost. When analyzing the inner parts of the objects by cutting away parts of the volume, the finite elements must be cut and the surface must be reconstructed from the original data. If non-convex finite elements are used, the elements may be cut up into several smaller elements by each cut surface.

Therefore ISVAS is using a three-dimensional volume primitive. The volume is built up of voxels, each voxel containing a scalar value. The irregular finite element mesh is transformed into the regular voxel model by scan-conversion of the finite elements [Kauf-87a, Kauf-87b], representing the geometry of the object, and trilinear interpolation of the stress field. The stress value domain is segmented into intervals and a colour is assigned to each interval. By using few intervals - e. g. 16 - iso-lines will be visible on the surface of the object, which by many users is considered an advantage over a continuous colour scale.

The volume is in ISVAS rendered with Back-to-front projection [FrGR-85] and Z-buffer gradient shading [GoRe-85].

During volume rendering parts of the volume are cut away to make inner information visible. The parts to cut are specified by planar and cylindrical cut surfaces and also combinations of surfaces. The rendering parameters, like view point, scaling, cutting etc., are specified by the user with the aid of special tools, which allow the interactive real-time rotation of the object [ChMS-88], positioning of the cut surfaces, light sources etc. Special rendering techniques, producing low-quality, sketchy but fast images, are used as echoes in these tools, as the normal volume rendering methods are too slow for interactive work [FrKa-90]. (See chapter 4.)

In the final image the presentation of the data can be modeled by changing the colour table. The mapping of stress value intervals onto colour as well as the grade of shading can be adjusted to obtain the optimal presentation of the data in each individual case.

6   Interactive and visual comparison of application data

In order to provide the scientist with insight views on his application data, a sophisticated method to present and investigate visualization results must be achieved. One drawback of current visualization systems besides realtime viewing and interaction to investigate the data, is the lack of support for comparing numerical data. Experiments and simulations produce a huge amount of data (e.g. in Computational Fluid Dynamics). And for dynamic proceedings data is delivered at different timesteps. When the graphical data interpretation produce a sequence of images, it is difficult to compare the frames in mind. But such a comparison is of great importance for the data analyst, in order to find out data correlations, especially in non-consecutive data records.

It should be possible to compare arbitrary data records of one or more simulation runs or experiments. So, it is essential to present two or more data records (represented by static images) in a comparable manner. A comparison can operate on complete data records as well as on selected subareas. In general we distinguish comparison techniques, which (a) operate on the original application data or (b) perform a filtering and merging of the original data and operate on this results. In case (a) the observer rely for the comparison only on his visual perception and in case (b) he is supported by the system.

There are several techniques to model, present and merge data records in a static or dynamic way:

1.   Visualization of two data records in two neighbourhood screen areas and simultaneous presentation.

2.   Visualization of two data records in one screen area and alternating presentation.

3.   In the case of symmetrical data records, merge two data records along their symmetry axis and visualize the result.

4.   Visualization of two data records in one screen area in the way that one image is put on top of the other image by utilizing a transparency technique.

5.   Animation of data records (e.g. to interpolate smoothly between two data records to be compared).

6.   Merge two data records and visualize the result. Merging can be done for instance by subtraction or integrated display of e.g. arrows in different colours.

7.   Give history information about user selected data points.

(Note, technique 1 to 3 base only on the comparison ability of the human visual system.)

The selection of data records to be compared can be achieved in several ways. The simplest method is to determine the approbriate numbers of data records. In a time-oriented selection the user choose the time and the system generates the corresponding data records. Another technique uses the application data value of one data record at an identified location and offers data records with the same data value at this location for comparison.

Graphic images for example with colour coding technique give a fairly good overview of the numerical data material. For the detailed analysis of the data often graphical representations like colours are too unprecise; an identification of image areas should return the exact values of related data by computing reverse functions.

With reference to the system model described in chapter 2 the interactive visual data comparison is involved in the following modeling aspects:

-   interaction with application data (data probe)

-   time modeling (e.g. generation of animation sequences and history plots)

-   data modeling within the filtering and imaging layer (e.g. data merging)

7   4D Modeling

4D modeling in the context of scientific visualization is the incorporation of time in the visualization process. The term 4D - which is geometrically interpreted not representable in our world - initially characterized the handling of a scene composed of 3D objects plus an additional parameter - namely time. But there are more aspects to be considered in respect of time: the integration of time parameters in application and graphic data structures, the efficient evaluation of time in an animated image sequence, direct manipulative input and echo techniques and a lot more related topics.

The realization of time through the generation of several image frames per second (e.g. in a flight simulator) and by sophisticated interaction techniques (e.g. 3D Cursor) had been a problem mainly due to lack of computing power. To produce an animation sequence the common procedure is to compute every single frame seperately (takes some minutes or even up to several hours) and copy it consecutively on a video tape. With the new generation of parallel Graphics Workstations [EnSc-89] and their coming still improved successors some realtime features will be possible which were accomplished in the past only by specialized hard- and software. This chapter will concentrate on aspects concerning the integration and realization of time in the visualization process; an example will illustrate the realization of time aspects.

7.1 Applications

Time as applied to an animated image sequence is an important clue which contributes significantly to the comprehension of application phenomena. There are many application areas which benefit from animation like computational fluid dynamics, medicine, astro physics or structural mechanics.

7.2 Modeling Techniques

There are two principal techniques how to apply the time parameter.

The first application is the handling of time like any other independant variable. With this approach all standard static visualization techniques are available. Time is usually mapped to one spatial dimension, e.g. 2D plot diagrams with one coordinate axis as the value (e.g. temperature) and the other time. Furthermore there are techniques which try to preserve the time parameter in static representations. Examples are the simultaneous display of images side by side or one on top of the others on the screen.

The other, more challenging application, is the evaluation of the time parameter in an animated sequence.

7.3 Realtime

When time is evaluated in the visualization process it is not only important that there is an animation sequence running but that it proceeds at a speed analogous to the simulation it is driven from. Realtime, strictly applied, is the in-time visualization of phenomena. There are many proceedings which are too slow or fast to monitor in reality (e.g. plant growth, nuclear disintegration). Visualization now offers tools to slow down or accelerate reality and display graphical representations at a sensible speed. In either case realtime visualization of simulation or sensor data should be a well defined (linear or perhaps sometimes logarithmic) mapping from world time to system time to support cognitive processes.

Realtime visualization can be achieved by two approaches. One method is to precompute the necessary image frames off-line and record them on video tape for replay (suitable for longer sequences / high resolution images) or record them on disk for display (suitable for shorter sequences / low resolution images). This procedure is common for most animation and visualization applications and due to time consuming large-scale simulation and graphic algorithms and lack of sufficient computation power.

The other method demands for a higher system performance to realize the on-line generation of image frames. Here every module in the image generation pipeline - simulation or retrieval of data, data filter, data-to-geometry mapper, renderer and display system - has to be quite efficient. Usually a trade-off between simulation and image quality and generation speed has to be made.

Regardless the difficulty to predict module runtimes the question whether a system performance is high enough for on-line generation of image frames does not only depend on the machine's capabilities to generate at least 25 frames per second of random complexity but on constraints put up by human viewers. There is a limit of human perception and comprehension of anminated sequences. It depends on

- how much space of the display is involved in the animation,

- how many centers of interest there are,

- how quick objects change attribute values (position, shape, look).

These "viewing constraints" put a natural limit to the technical possible. Although complex simulations and elaborated rendering techniques will ever succeed to exhaust machine power there is a fair chance to realize on-line visualization applications.

The consecutive display of image frames requires special system features to control the sequence. In todays UNIX-environments the display of image frames can be appropriately controlled with alarm clock signals.

7.4 Data Structures

In a visualization pipeline there are many different data types (figure 7). Time is a parameter which affects the data structures on all system levels and modules. A data structure is a net consisting of objects and relations between objects. An object is an instantiation of a class and is characterized by an identifier plus an additional set of attributes which can be inherited. Main categories are the application data, the graphic data (scene description, geometric primitives, 2 and 3D raster primitives) and pixel data. A geometric primitive for instance has geometric and material attributes, illumination model and existance attribute.

These data can either be retained data (information is kept during the whole session) or non-retained data (temporary structures are created when modules become active). Retained data has the great advantage, that when some parameter of a module is changed and the image must be updated, only the data downstream the visualization pipeline has to be recomputed. For a new camera position it is only necessary to rerender the scene and not to initiate a new simulation run. Non-retained data imply a complete refresh cycle with recomputation of all previous data structures when parameters of any module changes. Some retained data is always necessary, minimal initial data to start the simulation. Here a trade-off between speed and storage has to be made. For visualization speed and as basis for realtime applications retained data is very important.

Now time can be integrated in each object's attribute list. An attribute is either static or dynamic and depends on time or other object attribute values. The evaluation of dynamic attributes is based on an attached function. An object looks like:

object:

    ...

    attribute$_i$: if <condition> then <action>

    ...

The condition is a boolean function with time and other attribute values as input parameters. The action function affects other objects and attributes. For instance an object "ghost" can have an attached procedure for its attribute "existance" returning true for time period 0^{00}h - 1^{00}h, else false. This concept is similar to the frame data structure in artificial intelligence. A control logic decides when to evaluate the attached functions.

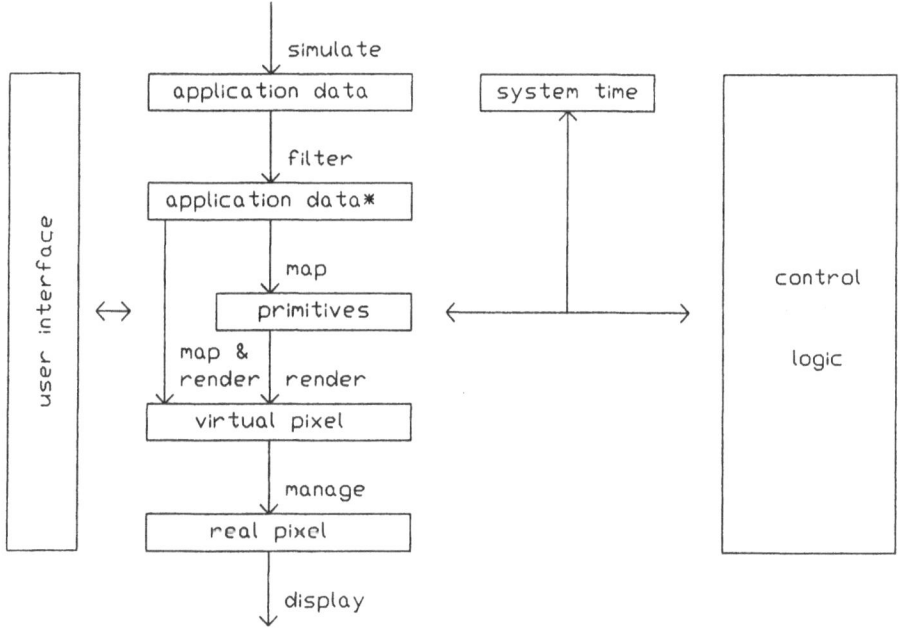

Figure 7: Time in visualization data structures

An example is the visualization task of tracking a satellite's path through our solar system. The application delivers the initial data of our solar system (position and radii of planets with gravitational potential) and the mass and the initial velocity vector of the satellite. Visualization objects map to the overall potential field (can be converted to a pixel representation by a volume renderer) and the satellite, which is first converted to a geometrical description, rendered and combined with the representation of the potential. A simulation computes a series of locations according to the satellite's path through space. These locations cause frames to be updated. In a realization with non-retained data the simulation on top has to provide new locations which initiate reprocessing the whole output pipeline. With retained data in the display layer and appropriate attached functions it is possible to update the pixel representation of the satellite.

7.5 Visualization Control

As the example shows, visualization speed can be significantly improved with retained data and carefully chosen rendering techniques. A control logic supervises the execution of to the object attributes attached functions. This approach contributes a great deal to reduce computation overhead. With attached functions it is possible to download application methods near the end of the pipeline and just start the system time clock. The control logic has to check for each time step which altered conditions match and execute the following action list. The matching procedure is either done by searching methods or by using precomputed information structures.

7.6 Input

For sophisticated interactive man machine dialogues special echo techniques have to be provided. These echo techniques support the method of direct manipulation, i.e. a user sees an immediate response to his physical input. In three dimensional environments fast and efficient computation of echoes is a basis for direct manipulation. In this context realtime is not a well defined mapping of different time clocks but means "as fast as possible" as there is no temporal relation between input and echo.

7.7 Example

An example for the application of 4D modeling aspects is the visualization of the interaction between a probe and a target under the influence of their potential fields. In this case study various aspects of 4D modeling are realized.

Probe and target are located in a world cube which extends in three dimensions. Both objects are mapped to constant density spheres, the potential around the target is mapped to a 3D gaslike cloud. To support three dimensional impression the world cube is visualized as a cage (open to the viewer) and shadows of the probe on left, down and far side are generated during the simulation run (figure 8).

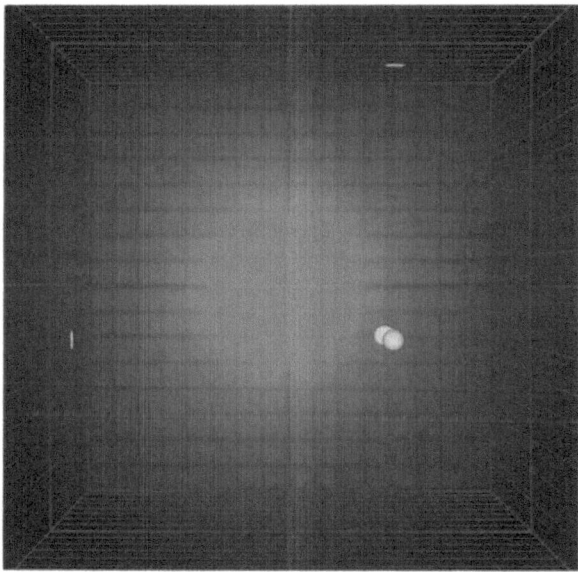

Figure 8: Probe in potential field

The simulation evaluates for each time step a new location of the probe according to the surrounding potential field. The simulation stops when the probe leaves the world cube or hits the target.

This visualization application is generated on-line in realtime. Alarm clock signals initiate the display of image frames. Constraints worry about the animation of the probe. Constraints limit either probe movement (controls time steps) or time increment. Visualization speed is at least 5 frames per second on a Iris 4D/25 with a resolution of 1024^2 in full colour.

The objects have to be generated very fast to get a reasonable image frequence. The potential of the target is inherently an algebraic function which can be rendered directly to a pixel representation [AsFe-90]. This is accomplished by a novel type of volume renderer which evaluates algebraic functions which describe volume densities like a potential field. The intensity i.e. accumulated density values can be evaluated by a curve integral. The rendering of algebraic functions e.g. a potential as a 3D gaslike cloud is reduced to the evaluation of an intensity function. The main advantages of this approach are the linear computation times in respect to screen resolution and no storage overhead of any auxiliary or intermediate values as in traditional volume renderers. The computation expense per pixel is the evaluation of an intensity function.

A user interface permits to set and modify the initial conditions for the simulation run. Parameters are the initial location and velocity vector of the probe. Handling of parameters is accomplished via direct manipulation of location, length and orientation of an arrow representation.

9 Conclusion

The aim of this paper was to introduce to various aspects of modeling in the area of Scientific Visualization. The three most important aspects are:

- modeling of visualization techniques in the visualization pipeline,

- modeling of data by combining different data sources and

- the modeling of application data by interaction with images.

These aspects have been prototyped in current projects at FhG-AGD. The examples in the previous chapters focus on modeling with respect to volume visualization, structural analysis and comparative data studies.

4D modeling is evidently needed in Scientific Visualization. Concepts as presented in this paper will be realized in the very near future. One precondition for demonstrating 4D modeling is the availibility of high performance workstations. The generation of available multiprocessor graphics workstations will now allow to perform 4D modeling in realtime.

10 Acknowledgements

The work reported in this paper was granted by the German Ministry of Research and Technology under grant ITR 9001/1 (VIS-A-VIS) and by the Fraunhofer Society (ISVAS).

11 References

[AsFe-90] Astheimer,P., Felger,W.: Direct Visualization of Algebraically Defined Volume Densities, FhG-AGD, Bericht FAGD-90i026

[BeGr-89] Bergeron,R.D., Grinstein,G.G.: A Reference Model for the Visualization of Multi-dimensional Data, Eurographics 1989, Hamburg

[ChMS-88] Chen, M.; Mountford, S. J.; Sellen, A.: A Study in Interactive 3-D Rotation Using 2-D Control Devices, Computer Graphics, Vol. 22, No. 4 (1988)

[Dyer-90] Dyer, D. Scott: A Dataflow Toolkit for Visualization, IEEE CG&A, July 1990, pp. 60-69

[EFGK-90] Encarnacao, J.L., Frühauf, M., Göbel, M., Karlsson K.: Advanced Computer Graphics Techniques for Volume Visualization, HP Workshop, Mai 1990, Böblingen

[EnSc-88] Encarnacao, J. L.; Schönhut, J.: High Performance, Visualisation and Integration - The Computer Graphics Headlines for the 90's, in: Proc. IFIP TC 5 Conference on CAD/CAM Technology Transfer, Mexico City; North-Holland, Amsterdam (1988)

[FFGG-90] Felger, W., Frühauf, M., Göbel, M., Gnatz, R., Hofmann, G.R.: Towards a Reference Model for Scientific Visualization Systems, erscheint in: Grave, M. (ed.): Eurographics Workshop on Visualization in Scientific Computing, Spinger Verlag, Berlin, Heidelberg, New York

[FrGR-85]   Frieder, F.; Gordon, D.; Reynolds, R. A.: Back-to-front display of voxel-based objects, in: IEEE Computer Graphics and Applications, Vol. 5, No. 1 (1985)

[FrKa-90]   Frühauf, M.; Karlsson, K.: The Rotating Cube: Interactive Specification of Viewing for Volume Visualization, Eurographics Workshop on Visualization in Scientific Computing, Clamart, France (1990)

[Früh90]   Frühauf, M.: Volume visualization on workstations: image quality and efficiency of different techniques, Computers & Graphics, Vol 14 No 4 (1990)

[GoRe-85]   Gordon, D.; Reynolds, R. A.: Image space shading of 3-dimensional objects, in: Computer Vision, Graphics and Image Processing, Vol. 29, pp. 361-376 (1985)

[GaNa-89]   Gallagher, R. S.; Nagtegaal, J. C.: An Efficient 3-D Visualization Technique for Finite Element Models and Other Coarse Volumes, Computer Graphics, Vol. 23, No. 3 (1989)

[HaMa-90]   Haas.S., de Martino,J.M: DESIRe Distributed Environment System for Integrated Rendering, to be presented at IEEE EPUSP Workshop, Sao Paulo, December 1990

[Hofm89]   Hofmann, G. R.: Non-planar polygons and photographic components for naturalism in computer graphics. In: Eurographics '89 / Hansmann, W.; Hopgood, F. R. A.; Strasser, W. (Eds.). North-Holland, 1989.

[Kauf-87a] Kaufman, A.: An Algorithm for 3D Scan-Conversion of Polygons, in: Proc. Eurographics '87, Elsevier Science Publishers B. V. (1987)

[Kauf-87b] Kaufman, A: Efficient Algorithms for 3D Scan-Conversion of Parametric Curves, Surfaces and Volumes, Computer Graphics, Vol. 21, No. 4 (1987)

[McDF-87]   McCormick, B. H.; DeFanti, T. A.; Brown, M.: Visualisation in Scientific Computing, Computer Graphics, Vol.21, No.6 (1987)

[Upso-89]   Upson, C. et al.: The Application Visualization System: A Computational Environment for Scientific Visualization, IEEE Comp Graph App, July 1989, pp. 30-41 (1989)

Fraunhofer-Arbeitsgruppe für Graphische Datenverarbeitung, 6100 Darmstadt, Germany

PART 3

Applications of Modeling

Chapter 9

Modeling of Art Painting

Drawing Chinese Traditional Painting by Computer

Pang Yun-Jie and Zhong Hui-Xiang

ABSTRACT

The paper presented here introduces a computer painting system which draws Chinese traditional painting by controlling real brush pens on "Xuan" paper, a kind of paper specially used for drawing Chinese painting. An additive device is fixed on a plotter for holding the brush pen to draw strokes. Basic strokes are generated to compose complex pictures. And realizing skills of Chinese painting by a computer is discussed. Some paintings drawn by the system are shown here.

KEY WORDS

Chinese painting, plotting, brush pen, stroke.

INTRODUCTION

Chinese traditional painting is a kind of old and profound art. Using computer to draw Chinese painting is a new subject. To imitate various skills of drawing Chinese painting by controlling a real brush pen with a computer is the aim of the subject.

Some works for simulating brush paintings have been presented (Richard 1985, Steve 1986, Pang et al 1987,1988). These works are not working on controlling a real brush pen to draw strokes. We should mention the work (Shi et al 1986) that is a calligraphic brush writing system. The system was used to write perfectly calligraphic character by controlling a real brush pen.

We began to work on the system from the early days of 1985 and displayed at the exhibition of China national science and technology in May 1986. In the five years the system has been much improved. All works for developing the system are in our own ways separately and independently. The works to be different from the previous works are briefly stated as follows:
1. Made an additive device for getting a brush pen up and down slowly. The device can be fixed on the carriage of a plotter, so it must be light and steady.

2. Made brush pens. Each brush pen has a tube filled with ink.   The
ink must steady leak from the tube to the brush, and must not leak   out
of the brush when the pen is off the plotting plane, or when the pen is
setting in liesure time. Brush pens can be set on holders of the
plotter, and the computer can choose a brush pen as normal plotting
pens. Leakages of ink in brush pens are different. So that we can   get
various densities of ink.
3. Made ways with which the desirable stroke can be generated.

We will introduce the main ideas of drawing Chinese paintings with the
system.

BASIC IDEA

The system consists of a microcomputer (IBM/PC), a   tablet,   a plotter
(a six-pen plotter SEKONIC SPL-400) and an additive device with
special brush pens.

The additive device mounted on the plotter has a board for   pressing   a
brush pen up or down (see Fig.1)

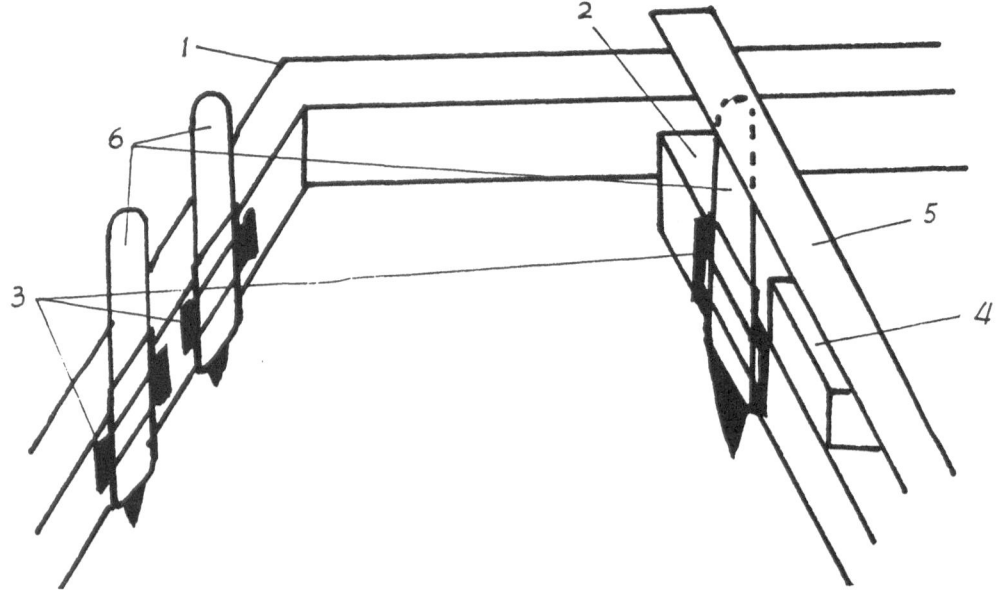

Fig.1 the plotter with an additive device
1. plotter   2. carriage   3. pen holder   4. additive device
5. board   6. brush pen

Brush pens are set on holders of normal plotting pens.   A brush pen
consists of three parts, a brush (i.e, a Chinese hair pencil), a tube
filled with ink, a spring for forcing the brush off the plotting plane
(see fig.2).

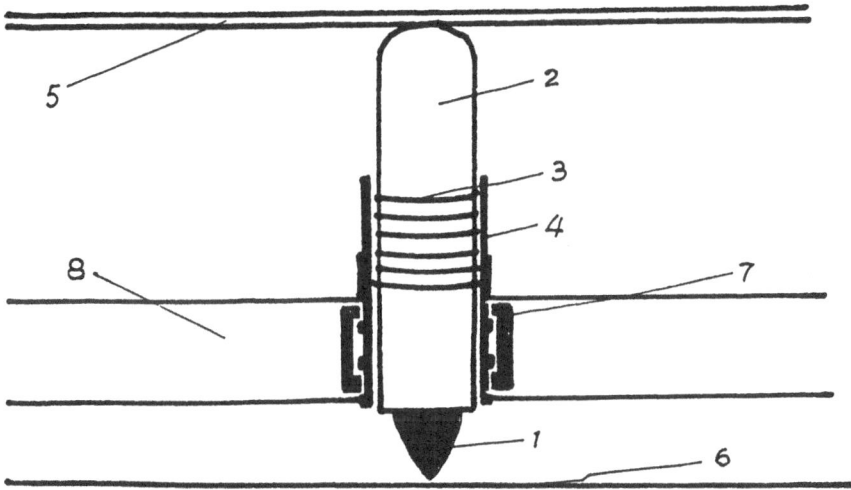

Fig.2 a section drawing of the brush pen
1. brush   2. tube   3. spring   4. pen shell tube   5. board
6. plotting plane   7. pen holder 8. pen carriage

The computer instruction for getting a pen down has become a signal for
starting a micromotor in the additive device. The micromotor can tow
the board down slowly, and the board can press the pen down slowly too.
The computer instruction for getting a plotting pen up can make the
motor run reversely. Then the motor can tow the board up slowly. The
spring in the brush pen forces the brush up. It takes an invariant
time from the tip of the brush touching the plotting plane (it is to
say, that the pen is at a high position) till the pen getting down the
lowest vertical position (that the pen is at a low position) (see
Fig.3).

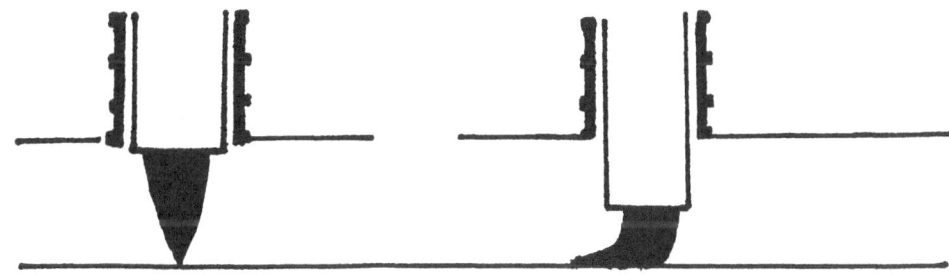

The high position   The low position
Fig.3 pen positions

Otherwise, it also takes an invariant time interval when the brush from
the low position getting up to the high position. The control of a
stroke's width can be taken in processes of the brush being down or up.

At a medial time when the pen being down, giving the instruction of
raising pen can make the stroke begin to become thin. Whereas, when
the pen being up, giving the instruction of pressing pen, we can make
next". At P7, we end the stroke, giving a mark for terminating a
sequence.

Fig.4   a seven points stroke   Fig.5   a nine points stroke

At P4, the most thick of the stroke was taken. That means, when the
brush from high position going down to low position, the pen can move
from P1 through P2,P3 to P4. If we insert P1' between P1 and P2, P2'
between P2 and P3, F1' and F2' are simply "moving to the next", then
the stroke may become as shown on Fig.5. The stroke became the most
thick from P2' to P4.

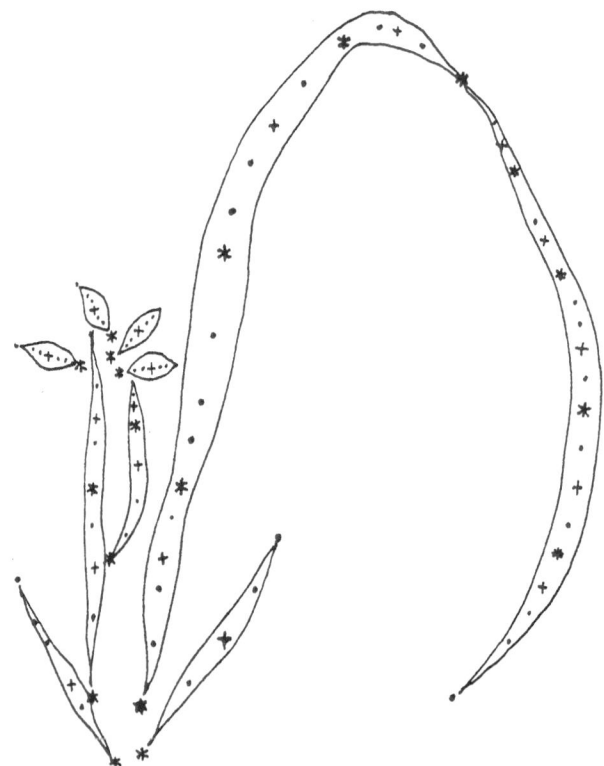

Fig.6   the sample points of picture 1
* indicates "pressing pen down" at the point
+ indicates "raising pen up" at the point
∘ indicates "moving to the next" at the point

the stroke begin to become thick. Also, the spans of the pen moving can be used to control the shape of a stroke. For drawing a desirable stroke, giving a proper sequence of points, and at each point, giving one of the instruction of making the brush down, up or ahead to the next point fitly. Let the pen be controled by the sequence of points, then we can obtain the desirable stroke, so the problem of making various strokes became that of making corresponding sequences of points.

A Chinese painting can be considered as a collection of strokes. We focus on the generating strokes in this paper, and leave others in future.

MAKE STROKES

Let (Xi,Yi) be the coordinate of a point in the device coordinate system, Fi be one of the instructions of raising pen, pressing pen or moving pen to the next point at (Xi,Yi), Pi be $(Xi,Yi,Fi),i=1,2,\ldots,n$. Then
$$A=(P1,P2,P3,\ldots\ldots,Pn)$$
represents a stroke, A picture can be represented by a sequence of strokes:
$$Picture=(A1,A2,\ldots\ldots,Am)$$

There are two opposite problems:
1. For a certain stroke, how to make the corresponding sequence of points;
2. For a certain sequence of points, what shape of stroke would be.

In practice, the former is solved from the latter. While we have more strokes and their corresponding sequences of points, we do have more experiences of making sequences of points fitting certain stroke. The simple way to solve the latter problem is drawing a stroke following by the sequence. To solve the former, we take some sample points of the stroke, then draw a stroke followed by the sample points by the system. If the drawn stroke is not suitable, revise the sequence of points.

The revision of a sequence of points can be done with
1. adding points inserted in sample points;
2. deleting some points from the sequence;
3. altering some points in the sequence;
4. using interpolation to the points;
5. using B-spline to the points.

What are the rules for revision? We would like to illustrate the rules diagrammatically.

Figure 4 shows a seven points stroke. At point P1, the brush was at the high position, and the width of the stroke is thinnest. The F1 was "pressing pen down". At P2,P3, the F2,F3 were "moving to the next". At P4, the F4 was "raising pen". At P5,P6, the F5,F6 were "moving to the

Picture 1

Picture 2 (a)   Picture 2 (b)

Picture 3

Picture 4

Taking the idea shown on Fig.4 and Fig.5, we can make more complex revisions. In practice, revisions are made by using a tablet to input sample points, and looking the central line of the stroke displayed on screen, and drawing the stroke on paper, interactively and refinedly.

Standard strokes can be made for general use or as references of generating strokes. Geometric transformations can be used to the points to reconstruct strokes.

Figure 6 shows the sample points of picture 1 displayed after the text.

DISCUSSION

The aim of developing the system is to draw painting by computer. But the system will not be limited in drawing Chinese painting. In computer aided animations, the system may be used to draw inbetweens or scenery. In office work the system may also be used to draw diagram. More skills of Chinese traditional painting need to be realized. Fully utilizing the computer's features to form a kind of painting art with a unique artistic style is of great significance.

Some results displayed here show some effects of computer drawing.
Picture 1 shows the picture with the sample points shown on figure 6.
Picture 2, a bamboo, (a) and (b) show the degree of reproducebility.
Picture 3, an orchid, shows the variety of strokes.
Picture 4, a Chinese calligraphy, shows the capability of the system for writing Chinese calligraphy.

REFERENCES

Richard Greene (1985) The Drawing Prism: A Versatile Graphic Input Device. Computer Graphics, 1 (3):103-117.
Steve Strassmann (1986) Hairy Brushes. Computer Graphics 20 (4): 225-232.
Pang Yun-Jie, Yang Shu-Xun, Chi Yu (1987) Combining cmputer graphics with Chinese traditional painting. Compt & Graphics 11 (1): 63-68.
Pang Yun-Jie Wang Zheng-Xuan (1988) Using parameterized strokes to compose images, automatika 1-2: 25-30.
C.Shi, Y.Aoki, K.Onda (1986) A calligraphic Character Generation and Brush Writing System. Trans. IECE Japan (section E), 69 (9): 1030-1040.

Department of Computer Science, Jilin University, Changchun, 130023 China

Modeling the Diffuse Paintings of 'Sumie'

QINGLIAN GUO and TOSIYASU L. KUNII

ABSTRACT

Diffuse painting, or 'Nijimi', which is the most remarkable feature of black ink painting (called 'Sumie' in Japanese), is produced by letting the ink diffuse into the absorbent paper. The diffusion of the ink usually results in a delicate blurred image. A model for simulating the nijimi effect with computers has been developed. It is based on the physical analysis of the construction of the paper, the characteristics of liquid flow and particle adsorption, and the interaction between the liquid and the paper. The images generated by this model are proved to fit well with the observed patterns.

KEYWORDS

Nijimi, Colloidal liquid, Capillary phenomenon, Disordered system, Physical simulation

1. INTRODUCTION

In this paper, an integrated graphical model for simulating the 'Nijimi' phenomenon is presented. Nijimi is one of the remarkable techniques of black ink painting, which is the art produced with ink and brushes, and is called 'Sumie' in Japanese. The nijimi image is created by letting ink spread beyond the original border of a stroke. As the ink seeps into the special painting paper with high absorbency, a feathery, blurred edge as illustrated in Fig. 1 is obtained. During the course of our research, it is realized that nijimi is a complex and interesting physical phenomenon, which cannot be completely simulated by the conventional graphical techniques such as texture mapping or the creation of degradation functions. On the other hand, the definition of the research is also not limited to black ink painting. As the ink is a kind of colloidal liquid, the nijimi phenomenon can be considered as a typical instance of the diffusion of a colloidal liquid in an absorbent solid. By simulating the nijimi phenomenon with computers, it is possible to bridge the gap between experimental facts and physical principles on the surface phenomena.

The nijimi phenomenon is a new topic that has not been studied by computer graphics researchers. Although some previous work has been done for modeling painting strokes (Lewis 1984; Greene 1985; Strassmann 1986) or liquid flow (Fournier 1986; Peachey 1986), the nijimi effect has not been discussed. Traditional descriptions of diffusion phenomena concern the transportation of particles from higher to lower concentration caused by the chaotic Brownian motion of the particles. In the case of nijimi, the diffusion of the ink is caused by the hydrodynamic forces and the surface tension of the fibers of the absorbent paper. The interaction between the liquid and the fibers determine the motion, the transportation, and the spatial distribution of the colloidal particles in the mesh. The traditional diffusion functions are not enough to describe all these complex factors and thus cannot be used for simulating nijimi.

For developing an appropriate model to simulate the nijimi phenomenon, it is necessary to be aware of its physical mechanism. An experiment, called capillary phenomenon, has to be reviewed first. If a thin tube is placed upright in water, the liquid will rise inside the tube. The final liquid surface inside the tube is higher than that of the outside (Fig. 2). The capillary phenomenon can also be observed in the nijimi phenomenon. Looking through a microscope, we can see that the paper is a mesh of fibers as shown in Fig. 3. The small holes or spaces between the fibers act as thin tubes to carry liquid away from the initial area, and create diffusion.

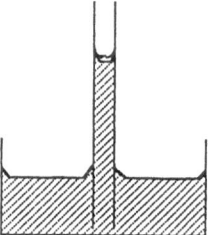

Fig. 2 The capillary phenomenon

From the above explanation, it follows that the simulation of nijimi can be carried out by modeling the following basic factors: (*i*) The construction of the fiber mesh. The mesh is made from numerous fibers. Randomness appears as a local feature of the distribution of the fibers, while regulation or uniformity appears as a global feature. Both these two properties should be considered; (*ii*) The change of ink density during the diffusion procedure. This change is caused by the interaction between the mesh and the liquid; (*iii*) The delicate variation of image intensity. It results from the dynamic variation of the state of liquid flow and particle adsorption according to the local structure of the mesh. Based on the modeling of these factors, the nijimi images can be created with the variation in time. Some information obtained from experiments and physical analysis on the phenomenon, and some mathematical techniques are used for formulating and modeling these factors.

The discussion in this paper is organized as follows: in the next section, the model to construct the mesh is presented. Section 3 discusses the interaction of the mesh with liquid density and section 4 models the local image intensity variation. The diffusion image generation procedure is summarized in section 5, together with the discussion and evaluation on the change in image with time. Section 6 shows an application of our method to ink painting strokes. Section 7 concludes this paper.

2. CONSTRUCTION OF THE MESH

For constructing the mesh, it is indispensable to decide an appropriate data format to represent the mesh structure. Traditionally, network format is used, but in our case the complexity and randomness of the fiber distribution will make the data be too enormous to manage. Instead, we used a two dimensional array with entries denoting the distribution density of the fibers to represent the structure of the mesh. For each pixel on a mesh, the distribution density is defined as the number of fibers passing through it. The construction of a mesh is determined by the density value of the pixel itself and those of the surrounding pixels.

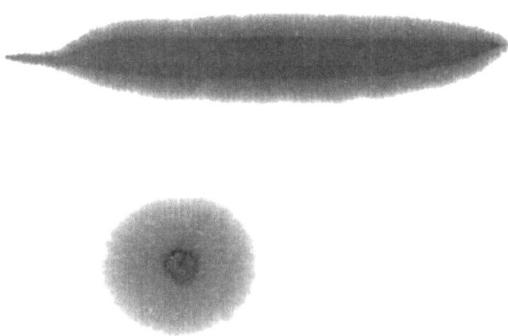

Fig. 1 An example of 'Nijimi'

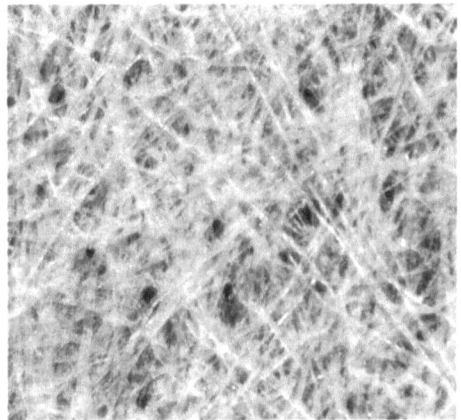

Fig. 3 The detail of fiber structure I (The picture is taken through a microscope with the magnification of 500.)

Fig. 4 The detail of fiber structure II (The picture is taken through a microscope with the magnification of 60.)

To model the construction of the mesh, the properties of fiber distribution need to be considered. Figure 3 and 4, taken through microscope with different magnifications, show a piece of paper in detail. The local property of fiber distribution is illustrated in Fig. 3, where the position and orientation of the fibers vary randomly. In contrast, the global property of fiber distribution appears uniform as in Fig. 4. For constructing the mesh with these properties, the principles of disordered systems (Ziman 1979) are used. The basic idea of the disordered systems is that: the physical situation at some point r is exactly or approximately reproduced at every other point which are regularly positioned like lattices. It can be mathematically represented as

$$F(r + R) \sim F(r).$$

The situation function F and the range R are related to the properties of the systems. Hence, a mesh is created by dividing a field into several regions and distributing the fibers according to the rule that for each region, the average fiber distribution is the same, but within each region, the fiber distribution varies randomly.

There is also a need to enable the user to control the structure of the mesh. Some parameters related to the characteristics of the mesh, such as the average length of the fibers, the quantity of the fibers, and the size of the mesh are used for this purpose. By changing the values for these parameters, various kinds of interesting meshes can be constructed.

Suppose a mesh consisted of n_0 fibers and has the area of $X \times Y$. Each fiber is represented by a curved line, and the longest fiber has a length of l. The mesh is constructed using the following procedure:

- Divide the entire field of the mesh by vertical and horizontal parallel lines into $\lceil X/R \rceil \lceil Y/R \rceil$ regions. R is user-specified to indicate the width of each region. The number of fibers in each region n is given by

$$n = \lceil \frac{n_0}{\lceil X/R \rceil \lceil Y/R \rceil} \rceil. \tag{1}$$

- For each region, perform the following steps by n times.

  - Randomly select a start position p_0 within the region.
  - Randomly select a direction θ.
  - Draw a curved line from p_0 in the direction of θ with length l.
  - For each pixel through which the curved line passes, increment the value of the variable denoting the number of fibers.

In Fig. 5, two meshes created with different fiber quantities are shown.

3. CHANGE OF INK DENSITY

During the formation of nijimi, the change in liquid density occurs because of interaction with the mesh. Colloidal liquid is made by mixing particles of solid with water. For instance, ink is made by mixing powdered carbon and glue with water. The density of a colloidal liquid is decided by the average size of the particles in it (van de Ven 1989). When the liquid begins to diffuse into the mesh, an observable change of liquid density will occur at the start points. This is because only those particles that are smaller than the space between fibers can seep into the mesh along with water. It is as if a filter is embedded in the mesh. The influence of the filter effect results in a change in liquid density, as well as in a global change in image intensity.

To model the filter effect, it is important to consider the relationship between the liquid density and the size distribution of the particles. Suppose the biggest particles are of the size S, the probable distribution $p(s)$ should satisfy the normal density function (Montroll 1979) as shown in Fig. 6. Then, liquid density U_0 can be described as

$$U_0 \approx \int_0^S p(s)sds/V, \tag{2}$$

where, V represents the quantity of the liquid.

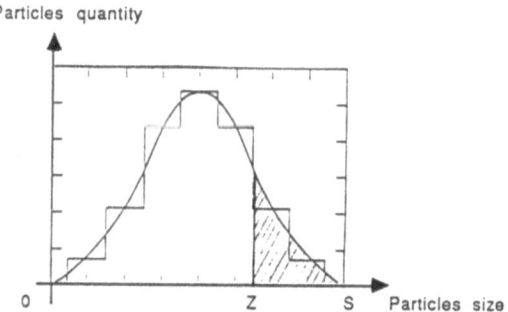

Fig. 6 The distribution of the particles of a colloidal liquid

To evaluate the filter effect, a passing function is defined according to the principle that only the particles which are smaller than the size of the space between fibers can diffuse into the mesh. Assume that Z represents the average size of the space between the fibers, which is decided by the average density of the mesh. The passing function $f(s)$ is

$$f(s) = \begin{cases} 1 & \text{for } s < Z \\ 0 & \text{for } s >= Z. \end{cases} \tag{3}$$

If the initial density is U_0, the change in density Δ_U due to the filter effect can be decided as

$$\Delta_U \approx U_0 - \int_0^Z p(s)sds/V. \tag{4}$$

The change in liquid density can be observed until the size of the particles get to be sufficiently small. From the time a drop of liquid ink falls on the paper, until the diffusion process is completed, three areas of different in liquid density are formed as shown in Fig. 7.

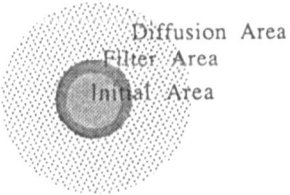

Fig. 7 The three areas of a nijimi image

First is the initial area where ink is applied. Then there is the filter area through which the ink seeps into the paper. The range of the filter area is decided by the initial ink density and ink quantity. The change of ink density during this area is determined by equation (4), and can be represented by a linear decreasing function. The third is the diffusion area where only the particles smaller than the average size of the spaces between fibers exist. For this area, adsorption of the ink particles on the fibers is the main reason to cause the change in liquid density. The change is much like that in heat transfer and it can be represented by a decreasing function of the distance from the initial area.

4. THE LOCAL VARIATION OF IMAGE INTENSITY

The intensities of the pixels in the diffusion area are decided not only by the density of the liquid but by the characteristics of liquid flow and particle adsorption in the mesh. It is observed that liquid will first flow through the fibers, and then fill the empty spaces between the fibers. The liquid flows to the empty spaces only after it has passed through the surrounding fibers. This characteristic causes some points of the empty spaces to be untouched by the ink when a limited liquid remains. Along with the liquid flow, another process takes place. It is the adsorption of the particles of the colloidal liquid on the fibers of the mesh. According to the physical principle of adsorption the quantity of adsorbed particles is in proportion to the surface area of the solid. It is easy to understand that there will be more particles adsorbed at the points through which fibers pass than that at the points with no fibers passing through. In other words, the state of particle adsorption varies with the structure of the mesh. Due to the characteristics of liquid flow and uneven particle adsorption in the mesh, the delicate local variation of intensity (the blur) is produced in the diffusion images.

For modeling the image intensity variation, we applied statistical analysis on the construction of meshes, and classified the states of the fiber structure at each point into a number of individually distinct cases. For each case, the state of liquid flow and particle adsorption is decided dynamically, and then the intensity is calculated to generate the image.

According to these cases, the pixels of the meshes are classified into four types as in Fig. 8. To determine the type of a pixel, not only the number of fibers at the pixel but also that at the surrounding pixels are used as reference.

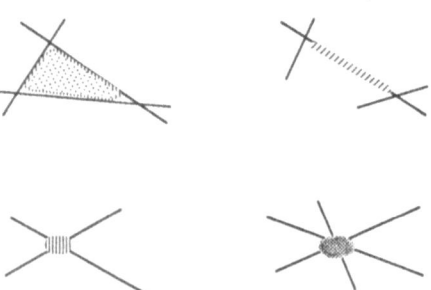

Fig. 8 The classification of the pixels in the meshes

- Type 1: a pixel through which no fiber passes. Not only the pixel itself but more than half of its surrounding pixels have no fiber passing through them.

- Type 2: a pixel through which only one fiber passes.

- Type 3: a pixel through which two fibers pass.

- Type 4: either a pixel where more than two fibers pass or a pixel which is surrounded by pixels not being type 1.

Suppose the liquid density is U_0, the parameters are defined as $\mu > 0$, $\beta > 0$ and $\beta > \mu$. The adsorption density for these four kinds of pixels need to be adjusted according to equation (5). The image intensity of these pixels can be determined from the adsorption densities.

$$\dot{U} = \begin{cases} U_0 - \mu & \text{for pixel of type 1} \\ U_0 & \text{for pixel of type 2} \\ U_0 + \mu & \text{for pixel of type 3} \\ U_0 + \beta & \text{for pixel of type 4.} \end{cases} \tag{5}$$

A part of the type 1 pixels may not be reached by the ink, and this tends to increase along with the decrease in ink quantity. An additional procedure is applied on the type 1 pixels by randomly selecting some of the pixels and changing their intensity to 1.0 (white). The proportion of the white pixels among the type 1 pixels increases with the distance from the initial area.

5. IMAGE GENERATION PROCEDURE

For generating the delicate images of nijimi, it is required to illustrate the details which go beyond the resolution of the screen. Our simulation schema, as illustrated in Fig. 9 , is therefore designed to complete an image in two steps. The first is to generate a fine and detailed image on the microscopic domain based on the modeling introduced in previous sections. The second step is to transform the detailed image to the true nijimi image on the resolution domain of the screen. The transformation can be completed simply by averaging the intensities of neighboring pixels from the final image.

It is important to simulate nijimi images with change in time. The image variation with time can be viewed as the extension of the range of the diffusion area. Experimental data shows that the rate of the extension approximately satisfies the relation

$$v(t) = e^{-kt}. \tag{6}$$

The parameter k is determined by the initial quantity of the liquid, the clarity of the liquid and the average density of the paper. Further observation makes it clear that the liquid transport in a mesh is completed in steps. The length of a step is decided by the density of the mesh. In each step, the dynamics of liquid transport appears to be that the liquid flows through the fibers first, and then fills the empty spaces between the fibers.

For giving the animation of nijimi image realistically, the idea of multi-level motion control is applied (Bruderlin 1989; Thalmann 1989). The low level control decides the extension of the diffusion distance in each time interval. The high level control simulates the dynamics of liquid flow in the mesh. For each time interval, the extension of the distance is further divided into steps. The pixels within a completed step, will all be rendered, but for an incomplete step, only the pixels through which fibers pass are rendered. The empty pixels will not be rendered until the step is completed.

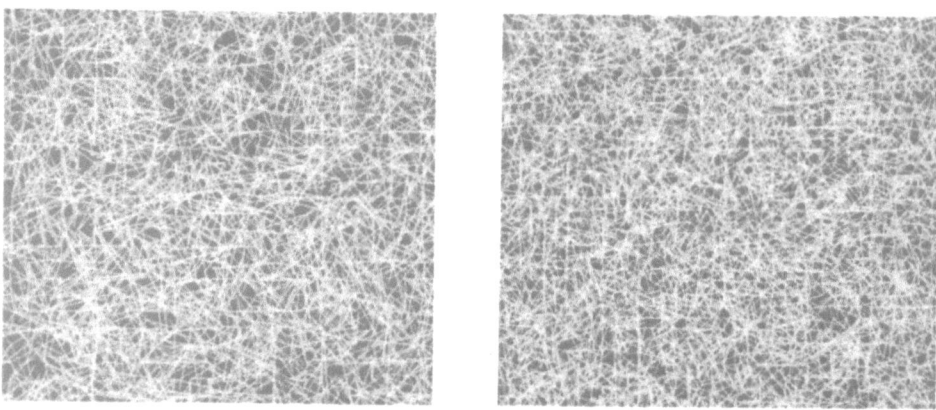

Fig. 5   The meshes generated by a computer

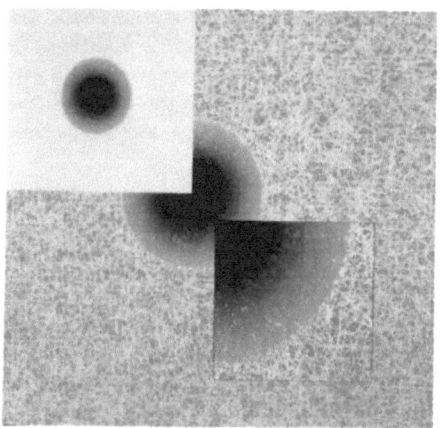

Fig. 9   Generation of the nijimi image

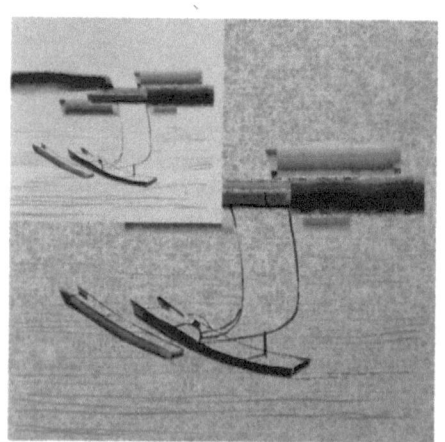

Fig. 11   A computer-generated sumie with nijimi on some of the strokes

Suppose the length of a step is specified as L, the nijimi image generating procedure can be unified as follows:

- Generate a mesh with the model presented in section 2.

- Decide the extension distance of nijimi image D_i in ith time interval by

$$D_i = v(i)\Delta_t. \tag{7}$$

- Determine the number of the completed steps N_i and the length of the incomplete step l_i in this time interval by

$$N_i = (D_i + l_{i-1}) \bmod L, \tag{8}$$

and

$$l_i = (D_i + l_{i-1}) - LN_i. \tag{9}$$

- Render the pixels in the N_i completed steps and the pixels through which fiber passes in the incomplete step according to the principles expressed in section 3 and section 4.

- While $v(i) \neq 0$, return to the second process and repeat for the next time interval.

6. APPLICATION

We have used our this model to generate nijimi on painting strokes. In Strassmann's method, a stroke is approximated by a list of successive polygons along the path the brush has moved through. Users define the format of a stroke by specifying a list of position and width samples. Both position and width are interpolated using the piecewise parametric spline (Plass 1983). In our approach, the polygons of the original stroke are extended in the direction of the width as in Fig. 10. The original stroke corresponds to the initial area, while the extended parts denote the filter and diffusion areas. Figure 11 shows an example of black ink painting generated by computer. In the upper part of the painting, there are some strokes, which describe the fog over the lake. These blurred strokes are created with the effect of nijimi.

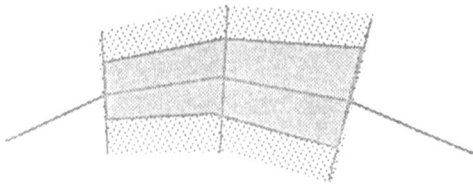

Fig.10 Generate nijimi on a stroke

7. CONCLUSIONS

A model for simulating the nijimi phenomenon has been introduced. The model was developed by splitting up the phenomenon into some parts and then analyzing their characteristics and relationships. The absorbent painting paper, which is the key point in our simulation, is modeled using the concepts of disorder systems. The change in liquid density resulting in the interaction between the ink and the mesh is discussed and evaluated. For modeling the local variation of image intensity, the characteristics of liquid flow and particle adsorption are considered. With our model, realistic images with natural variation in time can be generated effectively.

An implementation has been carried out on the Asahi Stellar work-station. All code has been written in C language. As an application of our model, black ink painting strokes with the nijimi effect have been generated.

The current version of the model is limited to the two dimensional simulation. It is possible for it to be extended to higher dimensional cases. Extensions to other areas of application are also possible.

REFERENCES

Bruderlin A, Calvert TW (1989) Goal-Directed, Dynamic Animation of Human Walking. Computer Graphics 23(3):233-242

Fournier A (1986) A Simple Model of Ocean Waves. Computer Graphics 20(4):75-84

Greene R (1985) The Drawing Prism: A Versatile Graphic Input Device. Computer Graphics 19(3):103-117

Lewis JP (1984) Texture Synthesis for Digital Painting. Computer Graphics 18(3):245-252

Montroll EW, Lebowitz JL (1979) Studies in Statistical Mechanics-VII. North-Holland Publishing Company

Peachey DR (1986) Modeling Waves and Surf. Computer Graphics 20(4):65-74

Plass M, Stone M (1983) Curve-Fitting with Piecewise Parametric Cubics. Computer Graphics 17(3):229-238

Strassmann S (1986) Hairy Brushes. Computer Graphics 20(4):225-232

Thalmann D (1989) Motion Control: From Key-frame to Task-Level Animation. Proceedings of Computer Animation '89, State-of-the-art in Computer Animation 1-17

van de Ven TGM (1989) Colloidal Hydrodynamics. Academic Press

Ziman JM (1979) Models of Disorder - The theoretical physics of homogeneously disordered systems. Cambridge University Press

Department of Information Science, Faculty of Science, The University of Tokyo, Bunkyo-ku, Tokyo, 113 Japan

Chapter 10

Modeling of Computer-Aided Design

Interactive Data Input System
for Tetrahedral Element Generation

H. YAMASHITA, Y. TANIZUME, and E. NAKAMAE

Abstract

The 3-D finite element method is a powerful numerical analysis tool, however one of its disadvantages is the trouble in constructing tetrahedral elements. Even though the automatic element generation methods which have already developed can be used for dividing an analysis field into tetrahedra, analysts have still to feed in data such as shapes, dimensions, and positions of objects. As this data is 3-D data, feeding it is troublesome for the analysts, and such operations easily cause data errors. Then, constructing a superior man-machine interface system on data input is required: An interactive data input system implemented into a graphics work station, which puts in 3-D data types without any difficulty or error is proposed.

Keywords: F.E.M., CAD, Pre-processor, Automatic element generation, Interactive data input system.

1. INTRODUCTION

The 3-D finite element method has become more popular as a powerful numerical analysis method in various fields. In order to execute the 3-D finite element analysis, it is necessary to divide the analysis field into finite elements, usually formed by tetrahedra. Yamashita (1980) pointed out this process is very complex compared with 2-D field problems and it is regarded as one of major drawbacks in putting the 3-D finite element analysis to practical use. Several authors(Phai 1982; Cavendish 1985; Miyamoto 1989) have developed some automatic tetrahedral element generation methods. Even though these automatic element generation methods can be used for dividing an analysis field into tetrahedra, analysts have still to feed in data such as shapes, dimensions, and positions of objects. As this data is 3-D data, drawing up and feeding it are troublesome for the analysts, and such operations easily cause data errors. Constructing a superior man-machine interface system on data input is required because in traditional automatic element generation methods the following problems exist:

In Reference of Phai(1982), every coordinate of all points consisting of tetrahedra has to be fed by using digitizers; to set all these points suitably by hand is quite difficult and complicated work.

In Reference of Cavendish(1985), in the first step, an analysis field is divided into coarse tetrahedral elements, which are then subdivided into more dense elements by using the Delaunay algorithm; for making the coarse subdivision map, a user slices objects with several parallel planes. And then the user has to feed in the coordinates of every point on each plane, where the points include not only those defining the objects but also those inserted by taking into account the suitable density of the element distribution.

In Reference of Miyamoto(1989), the analysis field is manually divided into small regions consisting of several convex polygonal poles, then the tetrahedral elements are automatically generated by subdividing by suitable numbers given in advance. The amount of input data in this method is small compared with that of Phi(1982) and Cavendish(1985); one of disadvantages is that the user has to prepare the 3-D data defining small regions in numerical form by hand. The recent works on the mesh generation, for example the references of Schroeder(1988) and Baker(1989), make users to feed the geometric information of the materials and mesh control information, even though they gave no information about how to feed.

As mentioned above, in previous tetrahedral element generation methods users have to put in the 3-D input data in numerical form by hand; that work is tedious and easily causes data errors. In order to easily put in 3-D data and prevent errors, it is much better if that data is put in interactively and is visualized as a figure.

The authors have already proposed an automatic tetrahedral element generation method(Yamashita 1991) mapping a topological cubic lattice frame, a 3-D grid, onto objects. The method has the following properties:

(1) Mesh density control is easy, (2) the shapes of generated elements are closer to those of a regular tetrahedron, and (3) the processing time for generating elements is short. The input data consist of 3-D coordinates expressing the shapes, the dimensions, and the positions of objects in the field, and the subdivision numbers of the objects and 3-D grids; therefore the amount of data is relatively small. This data is classified into two types, real and integer numbers, geometric coordinates expressing dimensions and topological coordinates expressing subdivision numbers, respectively.

In this paper, we describe an interactive data input system implemented into a graphics work station, which puts in those two 3-D data types without any difficulty or error. The system has the two kinds of coordinate systems mentioned above, and can confirm input data in visual.

The proposed system has the following advantages:

(1) Data is put in non-numerical form by using a mouse as much as possible, and lattice scales are available for three orthographs; plane, front, and side views.

(2) Two kinds of coordinate systems, with real and integer types, facilitate the input of data concerning the size, location, and subdivision numbers of the objects in a 3-D analysis field.

(3) The three orthographs mentioned above and an isometric view make it easy to confirm input data in visual and to avoid incorrect input.

In the following, the definition of technical terms, the overviews of the tetrahedral element generation method(Yamashita 1991), and its input data are described. Then the components and functions of the proposed interactive data input system are presented, and finally the usefulness of the system is demonstrated through an example.

2. DEFINITION AND CHARACTERISTICS

Let's discuss a 3-D analysis field in the XYZ-rectangular coordinate system, and define some technical terms.

Region R_i and the R_i-coordinate system

An analysis field is divided into n_r pieces of rectangular shaped regions for the purpose of mesh density control. The i-th region is called "region R_i". Region R_i can include other smaller regions, but two regions which do not include each other are not permitted contact. Fig. 1(a) shows an example in which an analysis field is divided into four regions, where the outermost region R_4 includes three smaller regions R_1, R_2, and R_3. Fig. 1(b) shows the i-th region; the original point O_i is the cardinal point of R_i expressing a rectangular coordinate system called the "R_i-coordinate system": By using this coordinate system, real number expressing the data concerning dimensions of 3-D objects and locations of subdividing regions can be easily treated.

3-D grid G_i and the G_i-coordinate system

In order to divide region R_i into tetrahedral elements with a simple algorithm in a short time, a cubic lattice frame as shown in Fig. 2 is

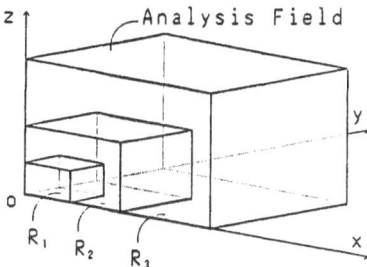

(a) Analysis Field and Regions

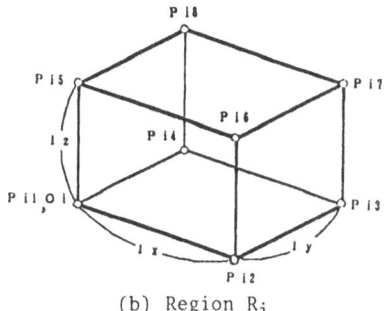

(b) Region R_i

Fig. 1 Region

used. The frame is called "3-D grid G_i" or simply " G_i "; G_i is assigned to region R_i. The 3-D grid has a discrete coordinate system with a topological 3-D grid; the coordinates in the 3-D grid are expressed by the numbers of three directions assigned to each intersection of the frame. This coordinate system is called the "G_i-coordinate system". The subdivision numbers of a 3-D grid are given by the three components (b_x, b_y, b_z) which express the subdivision numbers for the three directions respectively, as shown in Fig. 2. The subdivision numbers are given by integer numbers; G_i-coordinate system is used to feed these integer numbers. As region R_i can include other smaller regions or be included in larger ones, 3-D grid G_i also has the same relationship as that of R_i.

Lattice node

Each intersection of the 3-D grid's frame is called a "lattice node". Eight lattice nodes corresponding to the eight vertices of the 3-D grid G_i($N_{11}, \cdots, N_{18}$ shown in Fig. 2) are mapped onto the eight respective vertices($P_{11}, \cdots, P_{18}$) of region R_i, as shown in Fig.1(b). The other lattice nodes on the contour surfaces are also mapped onto the corresponding surfaces of region R_i. In case there are some objects in region R_i, some assigned lattice nodes on the surfaces of the objects are mapped, and the geometric coordinates of the other lattice nodes are moved just like an elastic cord. All these lattice nodes consist of the nodes of tetrahedral elements.

Primitives

To facilitate the data input of objects, the following primitives are defined:(1) a rectangular prism, (2) a triangular pole, (3) a

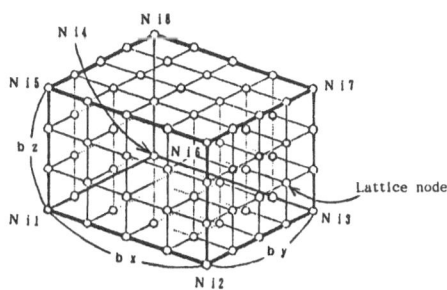

Fig.2 3-D grid G_i

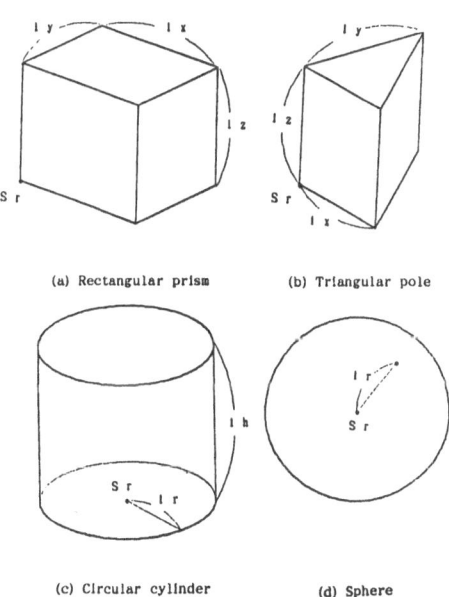

(a) Rectangular prism

(b) Triangular pole

(c) Circular cylinder

(d) Sphere

Fig.3 Primitives(R_i-coordinate system)

344

circular cylinder approximated by a polygon, and (4) a sphere approximated by a polyhedron.
Figs. 3 and 4 show primitives expressed by the R_i and G_i-coordinate systems respectively.

3. INPUT DATA AND OVERVIEW OF TETRAHEDRAL ELEMENT GENERATION METHOD

Before input of data for tetrahedral element generation by using the proposed data input system explained later, the only requirement for the user is to prepare the data concerning size and locations of objects existing in his analysis fields. The user may interactively input the following data in order by looking on a screen and manipulating a mouse:
(1) Rectangular shaped regions $R_i (i=1, \cdots, n_r)$; region R_i is usually fed in order from the inmost region to the outmost region, and the size of R_i is decided on trial by estimating the size of tetrahedral elements generated in R_i, (2) primitives; in the case that some objects such as cores or coils exist in region R_i, each object is composed of some primitives, and (3) the 3-D grid $G_i (i=1,2, \cdots, n_r)$; after adequacy of the size of $R_i (i=1,2, \cdots, n_r)$ and primitives on the screen are confirmed visually by the user, the subdivision numbers of $G_i (i=1,2, \cdots, n_r)$ are finally decided. If modification of size of $R_i (i=1,2, \cdots, n_r)$ is necessary, the process should be returned to (1).
After feeding these data, tetrahedral elements are automatically generated by using the following algorithm.

The algorithm for the i-th region is described; the process to divide regions into tetrahedral elements is done in order from the inmost region to the outmost region.
Step 1: Generate the 3-D grid G_i in region R_i. In this step, the intervals of the lattice nodes are even in the R_i-coordinate system.
Step 2: When some primitives exist in region R_i, map the lattice nodes of G_i onto the corresponding vertices and surfaces of the primitives and set the geometric positions of the other lattice nodes by moving the frames just like an elastic cord(Fig. 5 shows an example in 2-D case.).
Step 3: If a region R_k is included in region R_i, delete the lattice nodes of G_i existing in region R_k(see Fig. 6).
Step 4: Generate

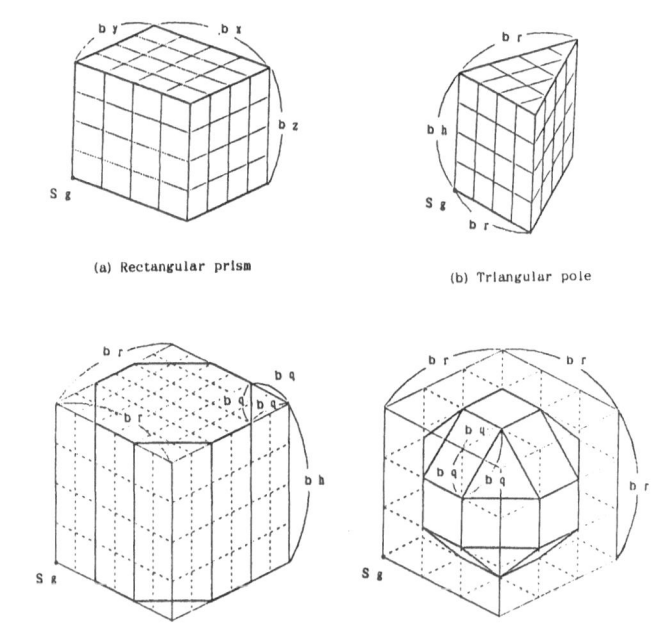

(a) Rectangular prism
(b) Triangular pole
(c) Circular cylinder approximated by a polygon (d) Sphere approximated by a polyhedron

Fig. 4. Primitives(G_i coordinate system)

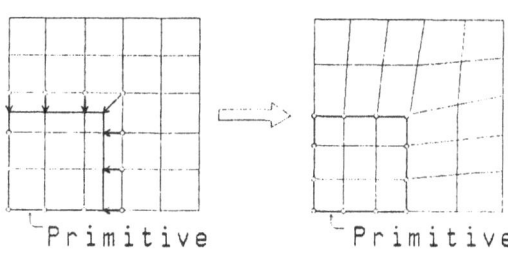

Fig. 5. Mapping of lattice nodes

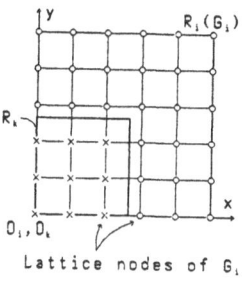

Lattice nodes of G_i

x:deleted nodes

Fig. 6. Delete of lattice nodes

hexahedra from the cubic lattice frames of the 3-D grid G_i.
Step 5: Divide the hexahedra into tetrahedra by taking account of the conformity with the surfaces of objects and tetrahedra which already have been generated in R_k.
Step 6: Repeat from Step 1 to Step 5 for all 3-D grids.

Input data required in the tetrahedral element generation method mentioned above is as follows:

(1) Input data of R_i and G_i
(i) In case R_i is included in R_j, the R_j-coordinates of cardinal point O_i(see Fig.1(a)) of region R_i and G_j-coordinates of cardinal point N_{i1}(see Fig.2) of G_i.
In case R_i is not included in any region, the XYZ-rectangular coordinates of cardinal point O_i.
(ii) Dimensions of R_i(l_x, l_y, and l_z)(see Fig.1(b)).
(iii) Subdivision numbers of G_i(b_x, b_y, and b_z)(see Fig.2).
(iv) The number of 3-D grid G_k included into G_i.

(2) Input data of primitives included in region R_i(see Figs. 3 and 4)
(i) For the cardinal points, S_r(see Fig. 3) and S_g(see Fig. 4), of each primitive, the R_i and G_i-coordinates, respectively.
(ii) For each primitive the number expressing material.
(iii) For each primitive:
  (a) Rectangular prism: Dimensions(l_x, l_y, and l_z) and subdivision numbers(b_x, b_y, and b_z).
  (b) Triangular pole: Dimensions(l_x, l_y, and, l_z) and subdivision numbers(b_h and b_r).
  (c) Circular cylinder: Radius(l_r), the height of cylinder(l_h), and subdivision numbers(b_h, b_r, and b_g).
  (d) Sphere: Radius(l_r), and subdivision numbers(b_r and b_q).

As mentioned above the types of input data are classified into the following:
(i) 3-D data(real numbers) expressing the dimensions and the positions of region R_i(i=1,$\cdots$,n_r) and primitives.
(ii) 3-D data(integer numbers) expressing the subdivision numbers and the locations of 3-D grid G_i and primitives.
(iii) The grid number expressing the relationships of inclusion in each other.
Data of (i) is expressed by a real number and data of (ii) and (iii) by an integer number. To facilitate the 3-D data input of (i) and (ii), the proposed data input system connects two types of coordinate systems as will be mentioned later.

4.INTERACTIVE DATA INPUT SYSTEM

First, the basic idea of the unified treatment of input data mentioned in the previous section and two coordinate systems are explained, and then the compo- nents and the functions of the proposed interactive data input system are described.

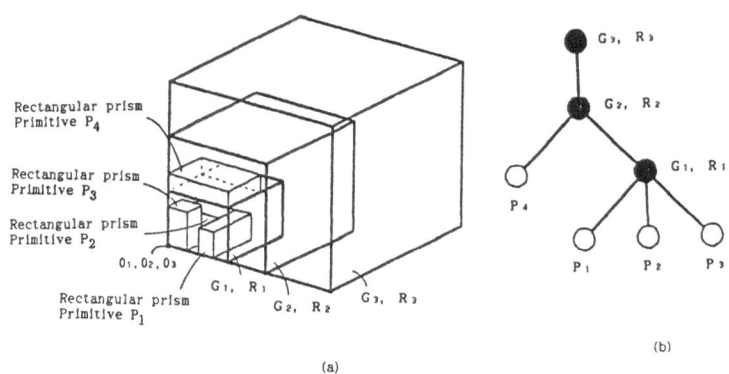

Rectangular prism Primitive P_4

Rectangular prism Primitive P_3

Rectangular prism Primitive P_2

O_1, O_2, O_3

G_1, R_1

Rectangular prism Primitive P_1

G_2, R_2 G_3, R_3

(a)

G_3, R_3

G_2, R_2

G_1, R_1

P_4

P_1 P_2 P_3

(b)

Fig. 7. Relationship of input objects' inclusion

In the following, all n_r rectangular regions, the n_r 3-D grids, and primitives are called generically an "input object".

4.1 Data with a tree structure and the two coordinate systems

Let's explain the relationships between the two coordinate systems, and the data of input objects by using a simple example shown in Fig. 7, where a coil(Primitives P_1 and P_2), a core(Primitive P_3), and an aluminum plate(Primitive P_4) are displayed in a one-eighth quadrant. The relationships concerning inclusion in regions R_1, R_2, R_3, and primi- tives in R_1 and R_2 shown in Fig. 7(a) can be expressed by the tree structure shown in Fig. 7(b). In this manner, input data of a 3-D grid (parents node) and its child nodes(some input objects) can be generally treated as a one unit group. For example, the input objects correspond- ing to the child node of G_2 are G_1 and P_4, then G_2, G_1, and P_4 are treated as one group. That is, the input data concerning one node in a tree structure graph is treated in the coordinate system of it's parents node. By using this method, the treatment of input data can be unified. The proposed data input system is based on the idea mentioned above. Further, in order to realize feeding data by using a mouse and lattice scales of the coordinate system instead of keyboard, the two coordinate systems, R_1 and G_1-coordinate systems, are installed in the proposed system for two types of data, real and integer types, respectively, as mentioned in the next section.

4.2 The interactive data input system and its functions

In order to feed and edit data, two kinds of windows, an "input window" and an "editing window", are prepared. The former is for the input and change of dimensions and/or subdivision numbers of an input object, while the latter is for the movements and copies of input objects and for the selection of a 3-D grid and/or a primitive as an object for editing(see Fig. 8). A 3-D grid indicated for editing is called a "current grid", and an input object among child nodes of the current grid can be chosen as the object for editing; it is called a "current object".

To feed in the data without any difficulty or error, a data input system should have the following functions:

(i) Input of coordinates data by using a lattice scale and a mouse, and

(ii) Visual confirmation of input data

In order to realize functions (i) and (ii), three orthographs(plane, front, and side views) and one isometric view are introduced to both the input window and the editing window(see Fig.9). Each view has two scales for R_i and G_1-coordinate systems, of which either can be chosen as occasion calls, and these are displayed with input objects. By indicating with a mouse a near point of an intersection of the scale, the coordinates at the inter-section are automatically obtained. This function is available for both scales, real and inte-

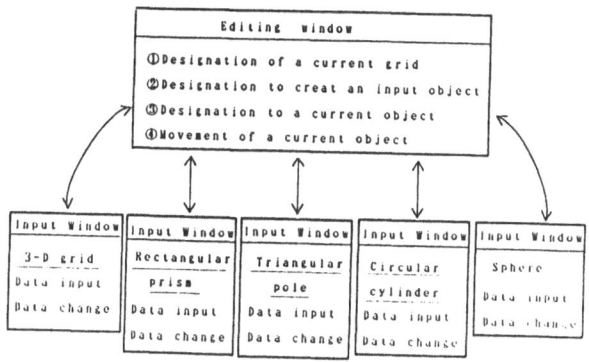

Fig. 8. Function of editing and input windows, and their mutual relationship

ger types, but in the former, if it is somewhat difficult to express by using the scale, input from a keyboard is available. The input data of an object is simultaneously displayed in all four views, thus making visual confir-mation quite easy and accurate. In addition to the four views, both windows have a menu area in which functions facilitate data feeding without error(see Fig.9).

The functions of both windows are explained in the following.

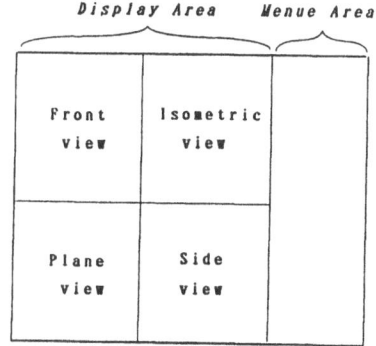

Fig. 9. Screen structure of editing and input windows

(1) Functions of the editing window
i) Designation of a current grid
One 3-D grid is designated as a cur-rent grid from the 3-D grids which already have been fed in; this is done by indicating a grid's number in the menu area. By this operation the current grid and the input objects corresponding to its child nodes are displayed in every view; the current grid is displayed in red and input objects in black for easy recognition.
ii) Designation to create an input object
In "CREATE menu" at the menu area, there are designated buttons for each input object, for example, GRD for a 3-D grid and HEX for rectangular prism, and so on. By indicating one of these buttons, the window changes to the input window and then an input object with default values of subdivision numbers and dimensions appears in the input window. After that, the input object is created by resetting those values as mentioned later.
iii) Designation of a current object
One of input objects corresponding to the child nodes of the current grid is designated as a current object; this operation is easily done by indicating the input object displayed in any one of the four views; the current object is displayed in green in order to distinguish it from the others.
iv) Movement of a current object
Any current object can be moved to the desired position in the current grid by using a mouse; the movement is available in both the R_i and G_i-coordinate systems.
v) Designation of relationships of inclusion among 3-D grids
In case a current grid includes 3-D grid G_k, by indicating the number k in the menu area, G_k is included with in the current grid. For example, assuming that (G_1, P_1, P_2, P_3), (G_2, P_4), and (G_3) in Fig. 7 already have been fed in as three groups, in order to make up a tree structure

as shown in Fig. 7(b), G_3 is designated as a current grid, and then the number 2 is indicated. A similar operation is also required for G_2.

(2) Functions of the input window
An input window is opened for feeding in every input object, and subdivision numbers and dimensions of each input object are fed in by using three orthographs in the G_1 and R_1-coordinate systems respectively. The material of every primitive is designated by indicating one of material numbers prepared in the menu area. For example, input of a rectangular prism is done by the following processes:
Indicating "HEX" in the CREATE menu in the editing window, the window automatically changes to the input window, and a rectangular prism with default values of subdivision numbers and dimensions appears. Then the user can reset the subdivision numbers and dimensions by indicating a location on any of three views or by feeding from a keyboard.

4.3 Other functions

In the proposed system, the following functions are also developed for better operations.
* Size of the lattice scale
In order to enable the treatment of various sizes of objects, the intervals on the lattice scale can be changed from 0.01 to 100 every ten times.
* Magnification of display
Magnifying power for display of three orthographs and isometric view can be changed from 0.01 to 100 times roughly every double value.
* Movement of display view
Indicating a point in any three orthographs in the editing window by mouse, all three orthographs and the isometric view are scrolled as the point is set at the center in each view.
* Modification of input data
For modifying the data of input objects which have already been fed in, designation of any desired input object as a current object is available.

5.APPLICATION

The proposed method is applied to the model shown in Fig. 10(a), which consists of one core, one coil, and two aluminum plates with a hole at the center of the plate. The analysis field is one eighth of the field because of the symmetry of this model. The number of 3-D grids fed in is seven; they are numbered from 1 in due order from the innermost 3-D grid to the outermost(see Fig. 10(b)).
The innermost 3-D grid, G_1, includes ten primitives which comprise a core, a coil, and an aluminum plate. Fig. 11 shows the editing window, where G_1 is chosen as a current grid and a rectangular prism of the core is chosen as the current object. Fig. 11(a) shows the editing window for the R_1-coordinate system: By designating each input object existing inside G_1 as a current object, its dimensions, positions, and the mutual relationships between input objects can be confirmed in visual. On the other side, Fig. 11(b) is displayed by the G_1-coordinate system; the subdivision numbers of each object are also confirmed visually, but the relative dimensions of objects are different from the real ones.
Next, let's show the procedure of input of region R_2. First, designate "GRD" button of "CREATE menu" in the editing window, then the window changes into the input window as shown in either Fig. 12(a) which is used for input of the dimensions of R_2 or Fig. 12(b) which is used for input of the subdivision numbers of G_2. The interchange from the input window (Fig.(a)) to the other (Fig.(b)) or from Fig.(b) to Fig.(a), is done by choosing the buttons of "subdivision" or "size" in the menu area, respectively. The data of the dimensions of R_2(the subdivision

numbers of G_2) are fed interactively by using the three orthographs in $R_2(G_2)$ coordinate system; the user may input one data point by indicating and clicking the location on two of the three orthographs, the coordinates of the nearest intersection of lattice scale to that location are fed. In case that the coordinates of the input data are not equal to that of the intersection of the lattice scale in R_2-coordinate system, the user can input the correct data from a keyboard. By pushing another mouse button, the window changes back to the editing window. Then, by indicating in order "R_1", "inclusion", and "R_2" in the menu, R_1 is included in R_2; Fig. 13(a) and (b) show the relationships of R_2 and R_1, and G_2 and G_1, respectively.

Fig. 14 shows the subdivision maps of the model shown in Fig. 10, the elements near the central region in the analysis field are divided into dense tetrahedral elements and the further from the central region the coarser of the elements; the distribution seems adequate. Table 1 shows input and output data, and CPU time for processing: The input data is very little, and the processing time is also extremely short.

Table 1 Input and Output, and CPU time

INPUT	No. of regions	7
	No. of primitives	10
OUTPUT	No. of tetrahedra	2922
	No. of nodes	642
	CPU time [sec.]	13.2

Computer : SiliconGraphics IRIS-4D/20C

By using the proposed data input system, the burden of work for feeding data and confirming the adequacy of the data is greatly lightened as operation of the data input becomes quite easy.

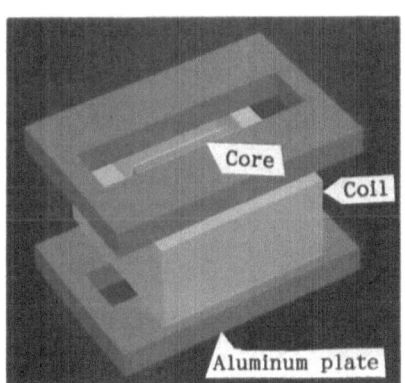

(a) Model

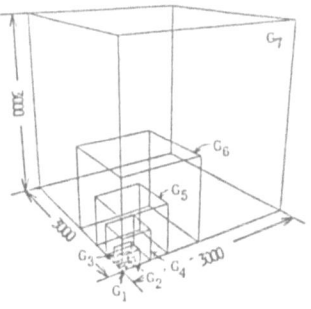

(b) Relationship of 3-D grids' inclusion

Fig. 10. Model and 3-D grids

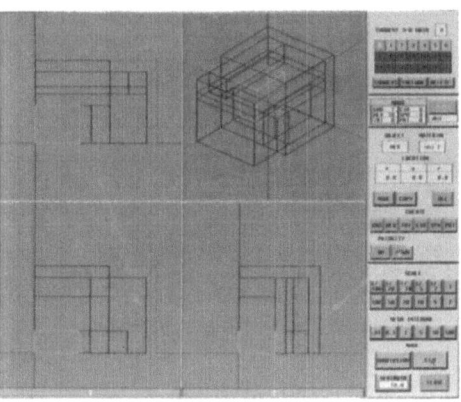

(a) R_i coordinate system

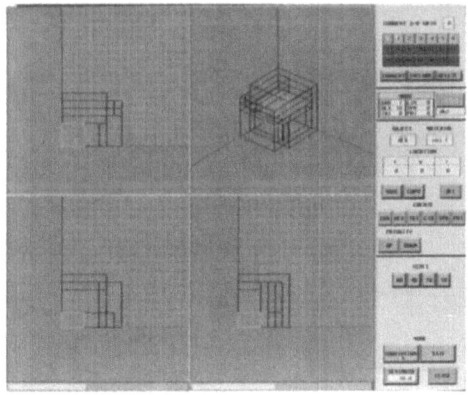

(b) G_i coordinate system

Fig. 11. Editing window

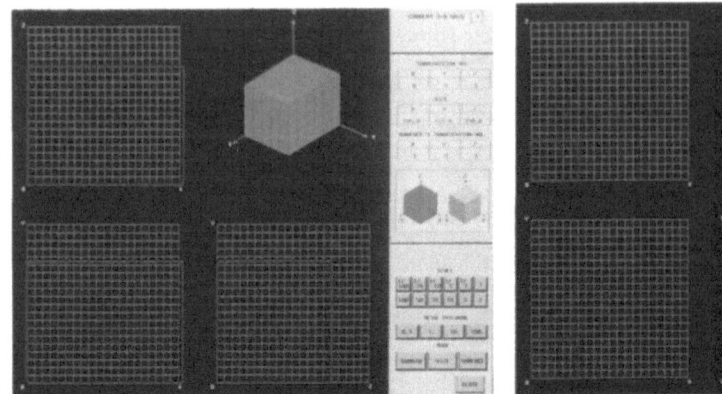

(a) Input of dimension of R_2 (b) Input of subdivision numbers of G_2

Fig. 12   Input window

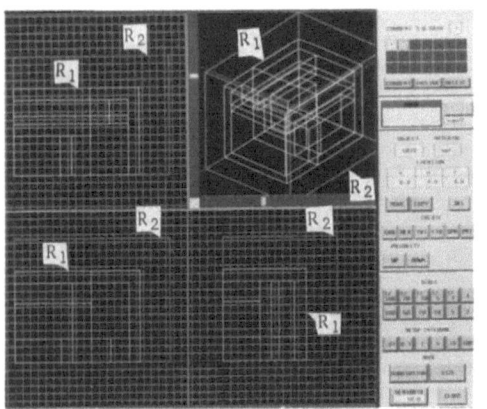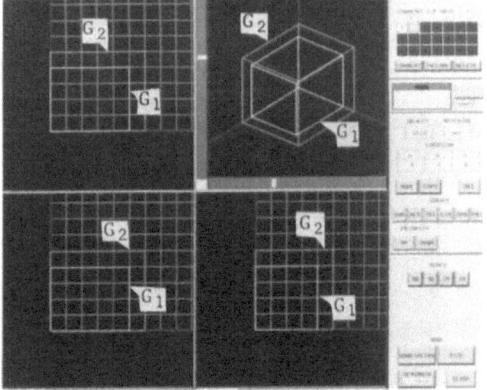

(a) R_2 coordinate system   (b) G_2 coordinate system

Fig. 13   Editing window

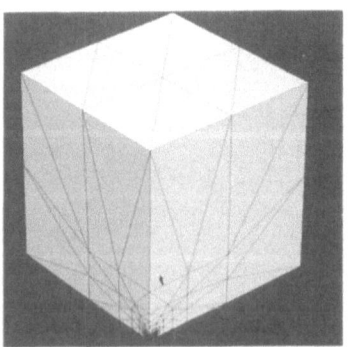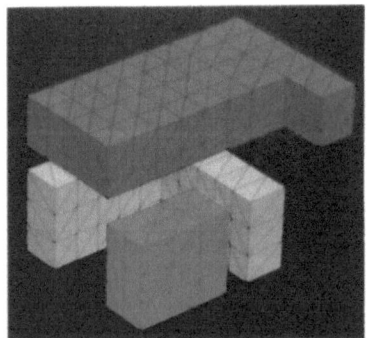

(a) All analysis region   (b) Coil, core, and aluminum plate

Fig. 14. Subdivision maps

6.CONCLUSION

An interactive data input system for the tetrahedral element generation system (Yamashita 1991) was discussed; all data is interactively fed in by using three orthographs, an isometric view, and some menus mainly with a mouse. The data input operation is quite simple, and avoidance of errors can be expected. The availability of this system has been demonstrated by using examples.

As a pre-processor for finite element analyses, the proposed data input system which has achieved labor saving for the input of data should be unified by the following two systems:
(1) The automatic tetrahedral element generation system (Yamashita 1991); the processing time is short, the control of mesh density is easy, and the shape of generated elements is closer to that of regular tetrahedra.
(2) A display system of subdivision maps; the confirmation of whether the subdivision maps are suitable or not is easy.
At present, this unified system is under development.

REFERENCES

Baker TJ(1989) Automatic Mesh Generation for Complex Three-Dimensional Regions Using a Constrained Delaunay Triangulation. Engineering with Computers 5:161-175
Cavindish JC, Filed DA, Frey WH(1985) An Approach to Automatic Three Dimensional Finite Element Mesh Generation. Int. J. Numer. Meth. Eng. 21:329-347
Miyamoto K, Yamashita H, Nakamae E(1989) An Automatic Finite Element Generation Method for Three Dimensional Magnetic and Electric Field Analysis. Trans. IEE of Japan 109-D(6):431-438
Phai NV(1982) Automatic Mesh Generation with Tetrahedron Elements. Int. J. Numer. Meth. Eng. 18(3):273-289
Schroeder WJ, Shephard MS(1988) Geometry-based Fully Automatic Mesh Generation and The Delaunay Triangulation. Int. J. Numer. Meth. Eng. 26:2503-2515
Yamashita H, Nakamae E(1980) An Automatic Triangular Mesh Generation for Finite Element Analysis. Information Proceeding in Japan 21(3):183-190
Yamashita H, Tanizume Y, Nakamae E(1991) Faster Automatic Tetrahedral Elements Generation using Topological Mapping. to be appeared on Trans. IEE of Japan 111(3)

Faculty of Engineering, Hiroshima University, Hiroshima, 724 Japan

CAD System for Steel Frame Structures as Packing Cage (Design Expert System and Graphic Support)

Yukio Tada[1], Ryuichi Matsumoto[2], Masashi Yano[3], and Nobuaki Miwa[4]

ABSTRACT

Because in general, the data which are treated in the expert system are technical and not well known by the user of the system, it is necessary for the expert system to have a good user interface in its input and output parts so that the system may be easy to deal with. This study aims to prepare a user interface for the CAD system with function as expert system which is being developed to support the design works of steel frame structures as packing cage. The system is designed so that receiving the order for packing, which is composed of the weight of the cargo and outer sizes of the frame, it might give the style of the frame structure or allocation of steel members, the selection of member types or shapes of steel and the sizing of members according to the experience and standard. For the satisfaction of the strength and economic requirement, the frame design includes the structural analysis and optimization. The proposed system is mainly supported by graphics. First, except for two items from the packing order, the data are inputted, if necessary, by a selective method. That is, the user chooses data among recommended ones accompanied with appropriate figures. Second, the results of design are outputted by several methods depending on the data types. Moreover, the use of multiple windows yields good convenience.

KEY WORDS

Design Engineering, CAD, Expert System, User Interface, Graphic Support, Steel Packing Frame

1. INTRODUCTION

The expert system has the possibility to be introduced in several stages of the production process (Roth et al. 1983; Nilsson 1980). In the design stage also, the expert system has been developed because design works need a lot of technical knowledges (Akagi & Fujita 1990). One of problems in the use of the expert system is that the data which are treated in the expert system are technical and, in many cases, not well known by the user of the system. As the countermeasures, it is

necessary to use such an expression of data in the input and output
parts that could be understood easily by the users. For the purpose,
the expert system must have a better user interface. The authors have
been developing a design expert system which supports the design works
for packing frames that are used in the shipping transportation (Tada
et al. 1990). The system creates automatically the overall configurations of the frame structure and the boundary conditions for the
analysis such as the loading and supporting ones by using the technique of knowledge information processing, which were dependent on the
experienced ability of the experts. Furthermore, in order to minimize
the total weight of the frame materials the system optimizes the
cross-sectional areas of the frame members considering the strength
constraints (Tada et al. 1988). The data treated in this system
involve technical ones such as principal directions of the cross
sections and stresses, and it is hard to understand the three-dimensional configuration of the frame and positions of the loading points
only by numeric data. Therefore, in its input and output parts, it is
necessary to use intelligible expressions by appending examples and
figures. This study aims to develop a user interface for the input
and output parts of the CAD system mainly by the use of graphics.

2. SYSTEM CONFIGURATION

The outward form of the frame structure which is used for packing is a
rectangular parallelepiped as shown in Fig.1, and on its six faces
which are called frontal, side, top and bottom faces, steel members of
the frame are allocated in various manners such as vertically, horizontally and diagonally, which are called patterns of the faces in
this paper. Which pattern is used for each face, the adoption of
cross-sectional shape for each member and decision of boundary conditions for structural analysis are dependent on the packing order such
as the sizes and weight of the cargo and how to transport it. The
size of the frame is 10m in length in the largest case, and the cargo
with weight of at most several tons is packed. The works of stevedoring are classified into resting (singly and piling up) and the loading
and unloading by a crane and a forklift, and the ways of transporta-

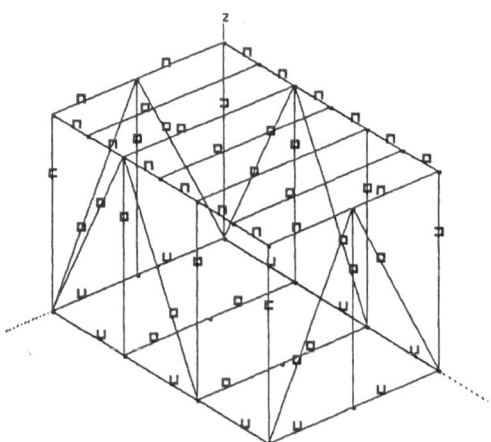

Fig.1   Frame configuration and cross-sectional shapes of members

tion are by a truck, railroad, shipping and so on. These differences in form of works and transportation cause different loads to the frame and for this reason the designer must determine appropriate boundary conditions for the structural analysis in his design work.

The present system is composed of the following four parts.
(1) The inputting part of order informations for packing: From the order for packing, order informations such as the outward sizes of the frame and the weight of the cargo are inputted.
(2) The part of creating data for the structural analysis: From the order informations, the structural shape of the frame and the data necessary for the structural analysis and optimization are created automatically by applying knowledge data base, and these data are outputted being transformed into the format for the analysis program (Tada et al. 1990). First, for the creation of structural shape, the pattern of each face is determined according to the order informations and considering the manufacturing process of frame itself, and nodal numbers, nodal coordinates and member numbers are created. Besides, the nodal numbers of end points in every members are extracted. Next, the fixed points and their constrained degrees of freedom are set depending on the way of the stevedoring, and the loading points and values of loads in each directions are determined depending on the way of stevedoring, the weight of the cargo, the area of the top face, and the dynamic loading factors which have been estimated from the way of stevedoring and the way and paths of transportation. The settlement of these boundary conditions, that is, what and where outer loads are acting and where and how the structure is supported, is difficult in practice and most important as in the case of making models of finite element analysis (Seguchi et al. 1985). Finally, the cross-sectional shape of each member is selected and the local coordinate system is set corresponding to each shape. The steels which are used for the steel frame are C-, I-, H- and L-shape ones and square pipes and so on, and the shapes adopted are limited to some types for their allo-cated positions from experiences, similarly to the case in selecting patterns for each face. The local coordinate of each member is de-rived from the principal axes of its cross-sectional shape and the position of the face on which it is mounted. This part is main one of the present expert system. In the system, the data are stored in the form of linear lists for the free addition of new elements such as nodes and finite elements in the process of automatic data generation.
(3) The part of structural analysis and optimization: For the struc-ture and under the boundary conditions both created in the second part, structural and stress analyses and optimization of member sizes are carried out (Tada et al. 1988). The frame as packing cage has a three-dimensional Rahmen structure and is analyzed by the finite element method. In the stress analysis, in order to consider combined loadings, this system adopts the shear strain energy theory and uses the equivalent stresses as the criterion of strength, which are de-rived from nodal forces obtained in the structural analysis. Moreo-ver, the buckling stress is also taken into consideration in compres-sed members. Comparing these stresses with the reference stress, the cross-sectional area of each member is renewed by the use of a simple algorithm;

$$A^* = A(S_e/S_a)^m ,$$

where A and A^* are cross-sectional areas before and after the reforma-tion, S_e and S_a are generated stress and the reference stress, respec-tively, and m is a positive constant. This alogorithm is efficient in the viewpoint of computational time (Gallagher 1973). By repeating these analysis and renewal of member sizes, the frame structure is optimized so as to have an approximately minimum weight. In this

Table 1   Data to be inputted

Outer sizes	Frontal and side lengths and height of frame
Weight	Weight of cargo
Stevedoring	Resting (singly or piling up in double), Crane, Forklift
Pattern of face	Pattern 1 (combination of N type and no-diagonal type), Pattern 2 (K type), Pattern 3 (combination of H type and HK type)
Cross-sectional shape of member	C-shape, I-shape, H-shape (3 types), L-shape (2 types), square pipe (2 types)

optimization process,   as the sizes of the steel which can be   adopted are   provided   by the industrial standard,   those which   have   minimum cross-sectional   areas   within the feasible domain are selected   among standardized articles.
(4)   The output part of design and analysis results: The   structural shape   of   the   frame,   optimum sizes of members and related   data   are outputted.

The   part of analysis and optimization is developed on IBM 6100 or IBM 3083, and other parts are implemented on MACINTOSH II of APPLE.   MACIN TOSH   II has abundant user-friendly functions such as   color   graphics and multi-window,   but it is not suited for numerical computation of a large   scale.   Then,   this system allots given several works to their respective suitable machines, and the data are transmitted between two computers through floppy discs.

3. PART FOR INPUTTING DATA

3.1 Data to be Inputted

As   mentioned before,   the outer sizes of frame and the weight of   the cargo   and   ways   of stevedoring are inputted as   order   informations. Besides these items,   in case of manual input,   patterns of faces   and types   of   steel for members must be inputted.   Except for the   frame sizes and cargo weight, all data are inputted by the selective method. The works of data input are done dialogically in the form of   replying to the request from the system.   By using this style of input,   users can   carry   out   the design work without a manual for the use   of   the design system. Table 1 shows the data to be inputted.

3.2 Input of Numerical Value

In the input of the frame sizes and cargo weight, a dialogue box which shows   the items to be inputted appears on the display.   By   clicking the   mouse at the item which is to be inputted and typing the   numeric value with the keyboard, the value is written in the corresponding box as shown in Fig.2.   When all data have been inputted,   "OK" button is clicked   to   tell the system the completion of   input.   Untill   this clicking, the correction of the data is possible.

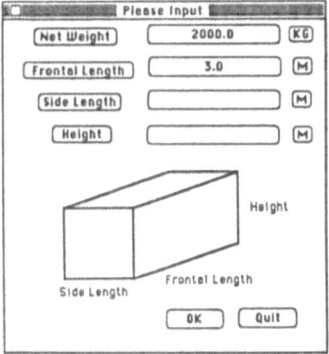

Fig.2 Dialogue box

3.3 Input by Selective Method

All other data are inputted by selective method. With the process of
the design, the lists of candidates to be selected are displayed with
appropriate figures as shown in Figs.3 and 4. These candidates are
those to which possible designs were narrowed down to some degree
according to the experience and standard of packing companies.   Following instructions from the system, the user takes his pick by clicking the mouse, and clicking the "OK" button subsequently feeds the
selected data to the system.   Or, the data are inputted directly by
double-clicking, that is, clicking the mouse twice in quick succession
at the candidate which the user wants to choose.

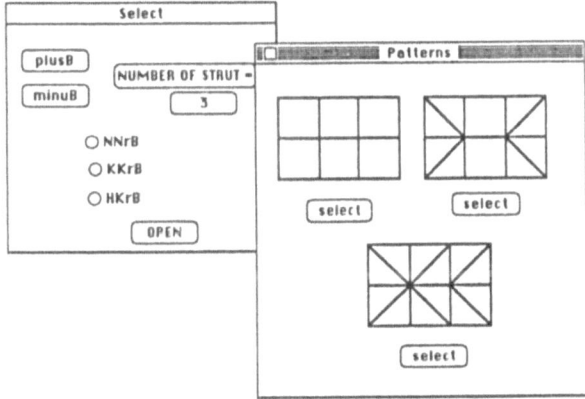

Fig.3 List of candidates for frontal face and their figures

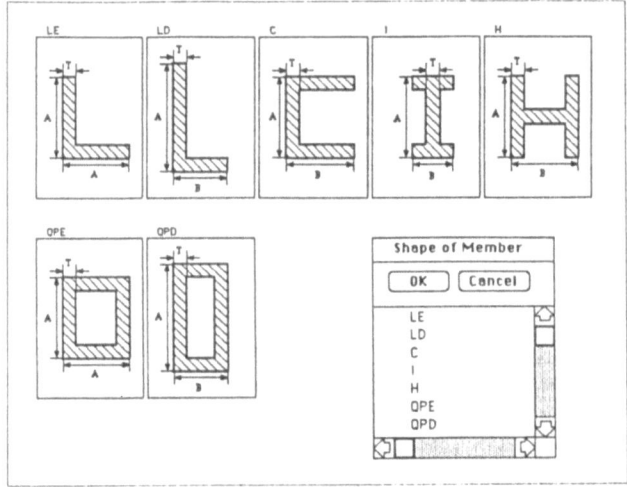

Fig.4 List of candidates for shape of member

4. PART FOR OUTPUTTING DATA

4.1 Construction of Output Part

The data which are outputted from the present system are the configuration of the frame created in Part (2) and the optimum sizes of
members and results of structural analysis obtained in Part (3) as
shown in Table 2.

On the monitor, three types of windows are used for data output; a
main window which shows the data by figures, several chart windows
which show the numeric results, and subwindows which assist the chart
windows by illustrations. These windows can be translated and changed
in size with the mouse.

Table 2   Outputted data

Frame configuration	Nodal number and coordinates, Member number, Cross-sectional shape and its principal direction
Boundary conditions	Fixed point and constrained degrees of freedom, Loading point and direction, Value of load
Result of structural analysis	Nodal forces and moments at two end-points of member, Nodal displacements and rotational angles at two end-points of member, Nodal displacements and rotational angles in global structure
Result of stress analysis	All stress components, compressive stress and critical buckling stress of member
Result of optimization	Judgment on structural safety (OK or NO), Sizes of cross-section, length and weight of member, Total weight of frame structure

Table 3 Menu of output part

Main window	Nodal numbers, Member numbers, Fixed points, Loading points, Cross-sectional shapes of members, Deformed state
Scale	Frame --- (x0.5, x1.0, x1.5, x2.0) Deformation --- (x1, x5, x10, x50, x100)
Rotation	Horizontal Direction (-180, ···, -30, 0, 30, ···, 180) Vertical Direction (-90, ···, -30, 0, 30, ···, 90)
Chart window	Frame configuration, Nodal forces and displacements, Nodal moments and rotational angles, Result of stress analysis, Result of optimization
Print	Print out of data

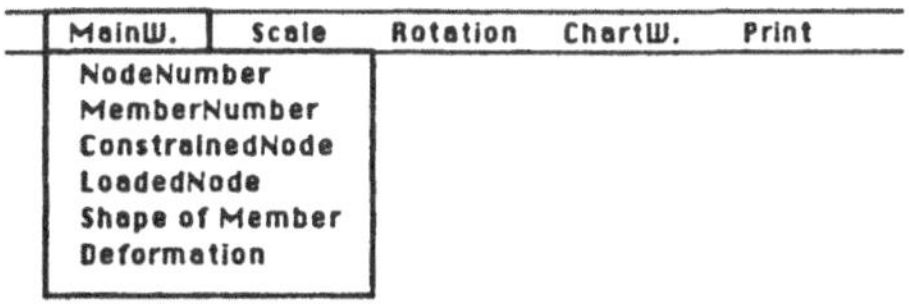

MainW.	Scale	Rotation	ChartW.	Print
NodeNumber MemberNumber ConstrainedNode LoadedNode Shape of Member Deformation				

Fig.5 Menu bar

Outputting can be performed almost only by selecting required data from a menu and list with the mouse. The prepared menu in the present system is shown in Table 3. A menu bar is set on the top line of the monitor, and by clicking the mouse at the desired item its contents are displayed. Fig.5 shows the state where the main window is open.

4.2 Main Window

In the main window, the configuration of the obtained frame, created boundary conditions for the analysis, the deformation of the frame, and the judgment on the structural safety are shown with figures.

At first, only the frame is displayed. Each member of the frame is drawn in black if it satisfies the stress and buckling constraints, and otherwise, drawn by red. If a desired item is selected from the menu, its data are superimposed on the original figure. By typing the space key, the scene of the monitor returns to the original figure where only the frame is displayed. The figures shown in the window can be changed in their scales and be rotated. Similarly, on the figure of deformation, the displacement of nodal points are magnified and added to the coordinates of the corresponding nodes so as to show the deformed state legibly.

Symbols which express the cross-sectional shapes and directions of members, the fixed points and degrees of freedom, and the loading points and directions are stored as figures in the memory. When they are requested to be shown, they are called out from the memory. Other figures such as that of the frame are drawn every time when requested.

4.3 Chart Window and Subwindow

There are six types in chart window; two for the result of structural (deformation) analysis, and four for the frame construction, the boundary conditions, the result of stress analysis and the result of optimization, respectively. They appear on the display by being selected from the menu in the main window. In the cases of selecting results of structural and stress analyses, the list of member numbers are displayed, and then by choosing a desired member number, the informations about the member are manifested with figure in a subwindow. By typing the space key, the chart window appears again.

There are three types in subwindow; that is, for the nodal forces and displacements, nodal moments and rotational angles, and stress. The data shown in the subwindow of stress are the compressive stress and the critical buckling stress of the member chosen. If the compressive stress is less than the buckling stress, the member is safe in regard to buckling. In the subwindows of nodal forces and displacements, the axes of the local coordinate system are drawn with the illustration of the member, and the nodal forces and displacements at two end points of the member are superimposed with their nodal numbers. In the right of the member figure, the figure of the whole frame is drawn in a reduced scale so as to show the position of the object member in the whole structure. In the subwindow of nodal moments and rotational angles, the manifestation is done similarly.

The figures drawn in the subwindows are outputted as resources by being called through a program. That is, in this treatment, the whole figure is treated as the set of codes in unit of bit.

4.3 Print Out of Data

The data in a subwindow can be printed out by choosing the "print" command if the subwindow is in active state. The main window can be printed out singly or with subwindow superimposed. The system also can print out all final data in a lump.

5. EXAMPLE OF DESIGN

This chapter shows an example of designing a steel frame structure with this system. The weight of the object cargo is 2000.0±kg], the outward sizes of the frame are 3.0x2.0x2.0±m], and the structural analysis at the state being rested singly is used for judgment of the safety.

5.1 Input of the Packing Order

In the followings, the scene in the case of a manual input is shown.

(1) The outer sizes of the frame and the weight of the cargo:
Fig. 2 shows the dialogue box in inputting.

(2) The ways of stevedoring:
From the list shown in Fig.6, "Placed(Single)" is selected.

(3) Pattern for each face:
For four types of faces (front, side, top and bottom ones), patterns are selected from the lists of their respective recommended ones as shown in Fig.3, and the frame shown in Fig.7 is created.

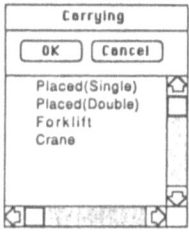

Fig.6 List for stevedoring

(4) Cross-sectional shape of member:
Referring to a list and figures of cross-sectional shape as shown in Fig.4, which is recommended depending on the positions for the member to be allocated, the cross-sectional shape for each member is determined. The chosen shapes are also shown in Fig.1.

5.2 Output of Results of Design and Analysis

(1) Main Window:
The first scene of the main window is the obtained frame configuration as shown in Fig.7. Every members are drawn by black, which shows that they all satisfy the stress constraint. Superimposition of the symbols of the loading and fixed points and the deformation to this figure yields Fig.8, and we can know the deformed state well. Returning to the original figure and calling the member numbers, Fig.9 is displayed.

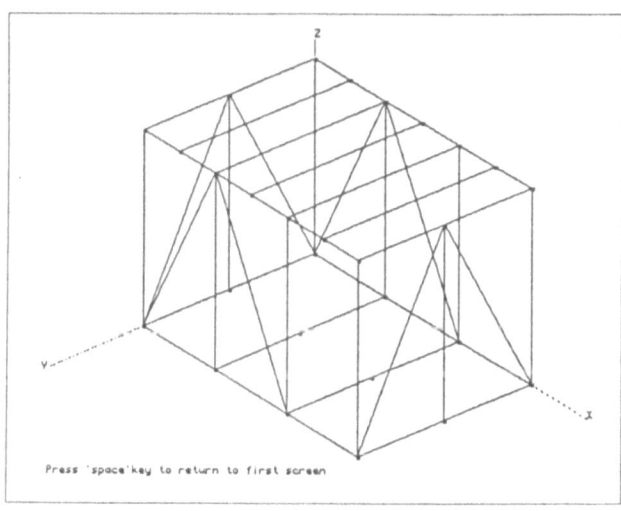

Fig.7 Created frame structure

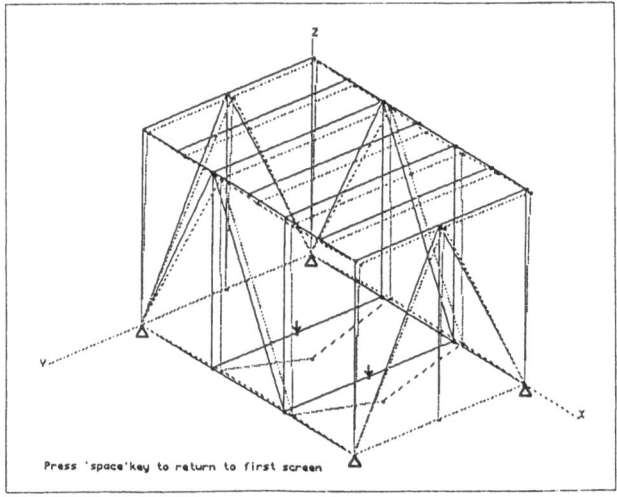

Fig.8   Loading and fixed points, and deformation of frame

(2) Subwindow:
Figs.8 and 9 show that the members FG310, FG311, FG320 and FG321 have
large deformations.   By subwindows such as Figs. 10 to 12, detailed
data for members are manifested. For the member FG310, it is observed
from Fig.10 that the displacement in the z direction at node 9 is
large, from Fig.11 that the moment about y axis at node 9 is large,
and from Figs.10 and 12 that this member is in compressive state but
there is no danger of buckling.

(3) Chart Window:
In Fig.13, the chart window of the stress analysis shows the allowable
stresses (written as "PERMISSIVE"), the equivalent stresses (written
as "STRESS"), the critical buckling stresses (written as "BUCKLING
LIMIT") and the compressive stresses for individual members.   For
members in tension state, "0.0000e00000" is written as the compressive
and critical buckling stresses.   It is found that the equivalent
stress of the member FG310 is maximum, and its value is close to the
allowable stress due to the optimization of sizing in member cross-
sections. The reason why the equivalent stresses for many members are
cosiderably less than the allowable stress and have too much margin is
that according to the industrial standard, there are no steels which
have smaller cross-sectional areas.

6. CONCLUSIONS

This study developed the input and output parts of the CAD system for
frame structures as packing cage. The input by the selective method,
variable output ways depending on the data types, and the use of
window functions such as the translation and alteration in scales
improved the user interface of the system.   The approaches taken in
the present system have some common points which are useful and effective in other systems.

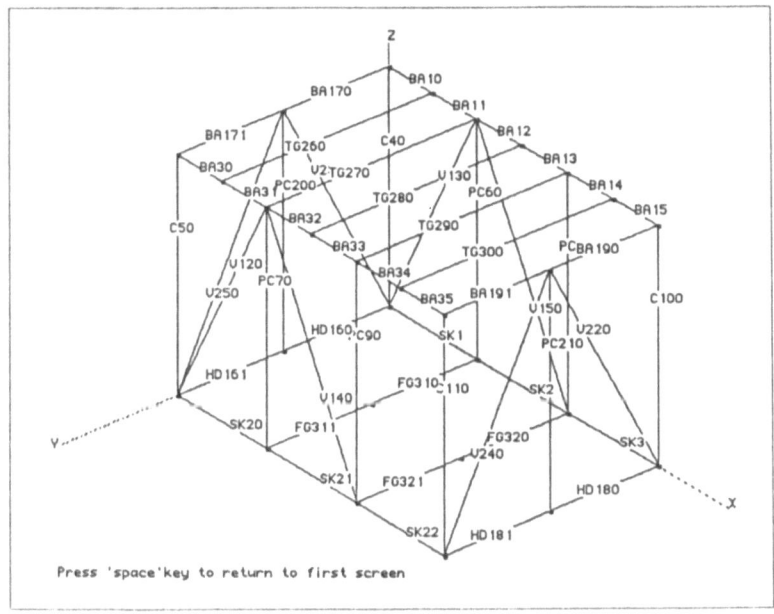

Fig.9   Member numbers

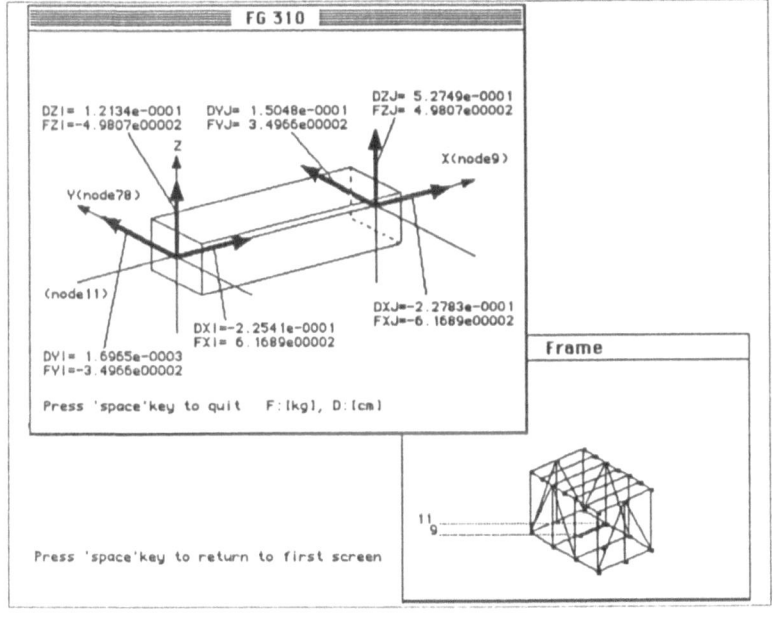

Fig.10   Nodal displacements and nodal forces in member FG310

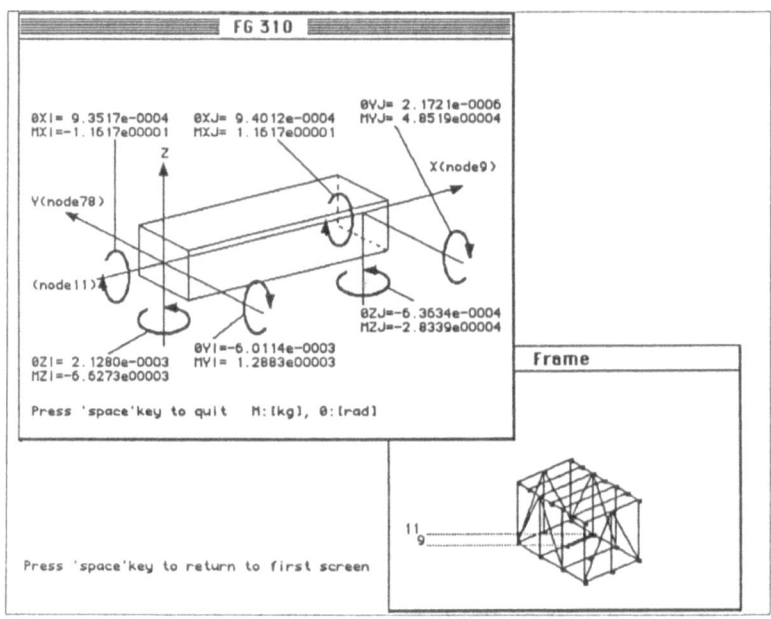

Fig. 11   Nodal rotational angles and nodal moments in member FG310

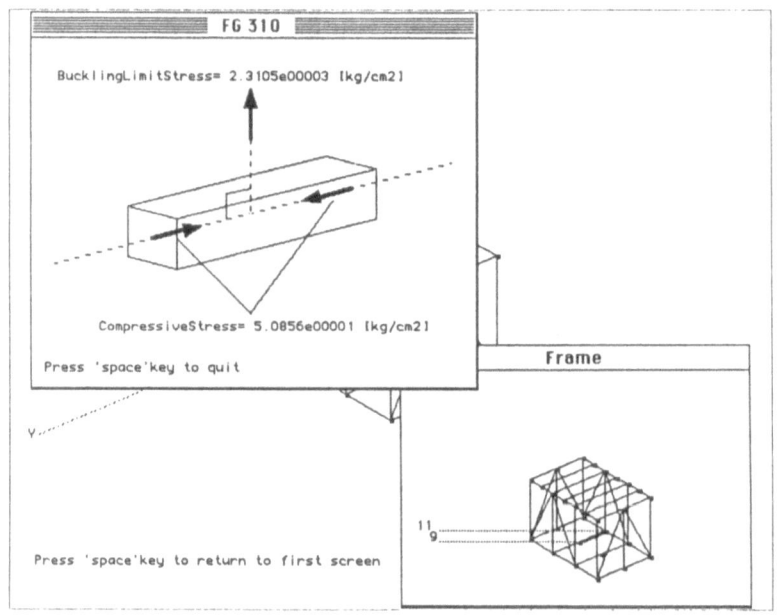

Fig.12   Compressive stress in member FG310

MEMBER	PERMISSIVE	STRESS	BUCKLING LIMIT	COMPRESSIVE --[KG/CM^2]
SK 1	2.4000e00003	9.8316e00002	0.0000e00000	0.0000e00000
SK 2	2.4000e00003	9.6972e00002	0.0000e00000	0.0000e00000
SK 3	2.4000e00003	1.6263e00003	2.2436e00003	4.6397e00001
BA 10	2.4000e00003	7.7173e00001	2.1147e00003	9.9629e-0001
BA 11	2.4000e00003	8.6002e00001	2.1147e00003	9.4048e-0001
BA 12	2.4000e00003	1.5965e00002	2.1147e00003	8.4862e00000
BA 13	2.4000e00003	2.3731e00002	2.1147e00003	8.4794e00000
BA 14	2.4000e00003	3.3739e00002	2.1147e00003	6.7822e00000
BA 15	2.4000e00003	3.3264e00002	2.1147e00003	6.7985e00000
SK 20	2.4000e00003	1.4372e00003	0.0000e00000	0.0000e00000
SK 21	2.4000e00003	1.2037e00003	2.2436e00003	3.4605e00000
SK 22	2.4000e00003	9.9828e00002	2.2436e00003	3.9365e00001
BA 30	2.4000e00003	9.5810e00001	2.1147e00003	1.5516e00000
BA 31	2.4000e00003	4.7664e00001	2.1147e00003	1.5679e00000
BA 32	2.4000e00003	1.4201e00002	2.1147e00003	9.3313e00000
BA 33	2.4000e00003	2.7781e00002	2.1147e00003	9.3151e00000
BA 34	2.4000e00003	3.4417e00002	2.1147e00003	7.4858e00000
BA 35	2.4000e00003	4.0012e00002	2.1147e00003	7.4368e00000
C 40	2.4000e00003	1.0063e00002	4.1508e00002	1.1589e00000
C 50	2.4000e00003	1.1245e00002	4.1508e00002	1.2181e00000
PC 60	2.4000e00003	6.3384e00002	0.0000e00000	0.0000e00000
PC 70	2.4000e00003	7.7253e00002	0.0000e00000	0.0000e00000
PC 80	2.4000e00003	5.0825e00002	0.0000e00000	0.0000e00000
PC 90	2.4000e00003	6.2197e00002	0.0000e00000	0.0000e00000
C 100	2.4000e00003	4.3146e00002	4.1508e00002	1.1538e00001
C 110	2.4000e00003	4.3506e00002	4.1508e00002	1.1656e00001
BA 170	2.4000e00003	3.4245e00001	0.0000e00000	0.0000e00000
BA 171	2.4000e00003	5.5828e00001	1.4392e00003	8.0091e-0001
HD 180	2.4000e00003	6.6531e00001	1.4889e00003	1.1229e-0003
HD 181	2.4000e00003	6.4493e00001	0.0000e00000	0.0000e00000
BA 190	2.4000e00003	4.6588e00001	1.4392e00003	2.0990e-0001
BA 191	2.4000e00003	8.4462e00001	1.4392e00003	1.0882e00000
PC 200	2.4000e00003	1.5036e00001	0.0000e00000	0.0000e00000
PC 210	2.4000e00003	4.3275e00001	0.0000e00000	0.0000e00000
V 220	2.4000e00003	1.5909e00002	7.1058e00002	3.4313e00000
V 230	2.4000e00003	5.3108e00001	7.1058e00002	3.9420e00000
V 240	2.4000e00003	1.6243e00002	7.1058e00002	3.6555e-0001
V 250	2.4000e00003	6.4995e00001	7.1058e00002	8.8075e-0001
TG 260	2.4000e00003	3.8365e00001	0.0000e00000	0.0000e00000
TG 270	2.4000e00003	1.2176e00002	1.2359e00002	9.8352e00000
TG 280	2.4000e00003	1.8965e00001	1.2359e00002	3.9760e00000
TG 290	2.4000e00003	1.3800e00002	1.2359e00002	5.5428e00000
TG 300	2.4000e00003	4.0689e00001	0.0000e00000	0.0000e00000
FG 310	2.4000e00003	2.1059e00003	2.3105e00003	5.0856e00001
FG 311	2.4000e00003	2.0866e00003	0.0000e00000	0.0000e00000
FG 320	2.4000e00003	2.0677e00003	2.3105e00003	3.0038e00001
FG 321	2.4000e00003	2.0900e00003	0.0000e00000	0.0000e00000

Fig.13 Chart window showing stress states

RERERENCES

Akagi S., Fujita K. (1990) Principles and Applications of Expert Systems for Engineering Design, Corona Publishing, (in Japanese), Tokyo.
Gallagher R.H. (1973) Fully Stressed Design. In: Gallagher R.H., Zienkiewicz, O.C. (ed) Optimum Structural Design (Theory and Applications). John Wiley & Sons, London New York Sydney Toronto, pp 19-32.
Nilsson N.J. (1980) Principles of Artificial Intelligence, Tioga Publishing Co.
Roth F.H., Waterman D.A., Lenat D.B. (1983) Building Expert Systems, Addison-Wesley.
Seguchi Y. et al. (1985) An Approach to Construction of Expert System for Modeling by Finite Element Method. In: Proceedings of the 31th Annual Convention IPS Japan, pp 925-926, (in Japanese).
Tada Y, Matsumoto R., Yamamoto K. (1988) Development of CAD System for Frame Structure as Packing Cage (1st Report: Stress Analysis and Optimum Design of Frame Structure). Trans. of JSME, Vol.54, No.507, A :2069-2073, (in Japanese).
Tada Y., Matsumoto R., Yano M. (1990) CAD System for Steel Frame Structure as Packing Cage. In: Proceedings of 1990 Japan-USA Symposium on Flexible Automation -A Pacific Rim Conference-, Volume III, ISCIE, Kyoto, Japan, pp 1249-1252.

[1]Department of Systems Engineering, Faculty of Engineering, Kobe University, Kobe, 657 Japan
[2]Faculty of Econoinformatics, Himeji Dokkyo University, Himeji, 670 Japan
[3]Systems Development Laboratory, Hitachi Ltd., Kawasaki, 215 Japan
[4]Division of Quality Control, Atsugi Works, Sony Corporation, Atsugi, 243 Japan

A Connectionist Approach to Geometrical Constraint-Solving

Nami Kin[1], Yoshiaki Takai[2], and Tosiyasu L. Kunii[1]

ABSTRACT

This paper proposes a new way to solve geometrical constraints by using the extended Boltzmann machine which is a kind of an artificial neural network. An energy function associated with the network is defined to include terms of higher-order than quadratic ones with respect to the binary states of units building up the network. The extended Boltzmann machine works as a minimizing machine for the polynomial energy function. We show that this machine is a good solver of nonlinear geometrical constraints, and suitable for drawing pictures such as graphs, trees, and flowcharts which represent the relationships among discrete objects.

Keywords: Boltzmann machines, connectionism, geometrical constraint, neurographics, nonlinear optimization problem, picture description

1 INTRODUCTION

Geometrical constraints are a very powerful technique used to describe pictures in an intuitive and declarative way (Sutherland 1963; Nelson 1985; Leler 1988; Kin et al. 1989). Satisfying geometrical constraints, however, is a difficult problem in most cases. This is because a number of constraints are described in the form of nonlinear equations; constraints on the length of line segments in Euclidean space are represented as simultaneous quadratic equations. Therefore, to simplify the problem, most constraint-based systems resort to numerical methods, and are restricted to only linear constraints (Wyk 1982; Kamada 1989). A quick and stable method of solving nonlinear constraints is desired to support intuitive picture drawing systems.

On the other hand, connectionist models have been applied to rapidly solve some combinatorial optimization problems (Hopfield 1982). Connectionist models stand for artificial neural networks based explicitly on an abstraction of our current understanding of the information processing properties of biological neurons (Feldman and Ballard 1982; Pfeifer et al. 1989). Hopfield demonstrated that mutually connected artificial neural networks can be programmed to find near-optimal solutions of NP-complete problems in polynomial time. Such a network reaches an optimal solution by searching for a minimum of the energy function which is defined as a quadratic form with respect to the states of units building up the network. Thus, the class of simultaneous equations that are converted to minimization problems which can be directly mapped to the networks, are restricted to linear (Takeda and Goodman 1986; Tank and Hopfield 1986).

In drawing a geometrical picture, a human being can easily and quickly call up its image and manipulate it. In this cognitive process, he/she unconsciously solves some nonlinear geometrical constraints in the brain. If this conjecture is true, then neural computation is expected to provide an effective method of geometrical constraint-solving in declarative and intuitive picture drawing.

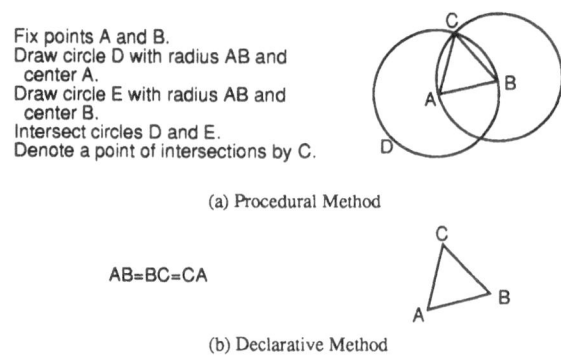

(a) Procedural Method

AB=BC=CA

(b) Declarative Method

Fig.1 Two Methods of Drawing an Equilateral Triangle ABC

This paper describes an initial attempt to integrate constraint-based picture drawing and neural computation. We first review geometrical constraints and classify them by their order. Then, we extend the energy function associated with neural networks. We focus specifically on a Boltzmann machine which is a kind of mutually interconnected neural network, and try to solve nonlinear optimization problems using this machine. Lastly, we show how we can apply the extended Boltzmann machine to nonlinear geometrical constraint-solving, and evaluate our method through some experimental results on a prototype system that has been developed.

2 GEOMETRICAL CONSTRAINTS

There are two methods of picture description: procedural and declarative. Figure 1 illustrates these two methods to describe an equilateral triangle ABC (Fuller and Prusinkiewicz 1988; White 1988). The procedural method gives an algorithm to construct a picture in a stepwise fashion. On the contrary, the declarative method gives only the conditions a picture must satisfy. A set of these conditions is referred to as *geometrical constraints*. The users of constraint-based picture drawing systems need not convert their constraints to the corresponding sequence of procedural imperatives. This is done automatically by the system. In general, when users draw a picture, they first think in terms of not the construction process but the desired *features* of a picture. Therefore, from a viewpoint of the user interface, the declarative method using geometrical constraints is a better form which minimizes the semantic gap between users and the system.

The geometrical constraints given by a user, however, may not always be sufficient to construct pictures (exactly-determined). They might be incomplete (under-determined) or redundant (over-determined) (Kin et al. 1989). If the constraints are under-determined, there are infinitely many solutions, and if over-determined, a consistent solution might not exist. In addition, exactly-determined constraints might merely guarantee that the number of the solutions is finite. In the case where a constraint has more than one solution, on what criterion does the system choose a solution? We have classified pictures into two types according to their primary concerns (Noma et al. 1989):

Table 1 The Order of Some Geometrical Constraints

Order	Constraint	
1	horizontality	$y_1 - y_2 = 0$
	verticality	$x_1 - x_2 = 0$
	fixation	$x - a = 0, \quad y - b = 0$
2	parallel	$(x_1 - x_2)(y_3 - y_4) - (x_3 - x_4)(y_1 - y_2) = 0$
	orthogonality	$(x_1 - x_2)(x_3 - x_4) + (y_1 - y_2)(y_3 - y_4) = 0$
	equidistance	$(x_1 - x_2)^2 + (y_1 - y_2)^2 - k^2 = 0$
		$(x_1 - x_2)^2 + (y_1 - y_2)^2 - (x_3 - x_4)^2 - (y_3 - y_4)^2 = 0$

1. the pictures where the abstract relationship among objects represented by a set of discrete geometrical entities is of importance;

2. the pictures where the geometrical information of each constituent entity is of importance.

Pictures of the first type come out in the fields of data visualization and the layout problem of graphs, and have some degrees of freedom in geometry. In other words, any picture is *legal* if it satisfies some geometrical constraints. On the other hand, the pictures of the second type such as mechanical drawings, are desired to be *unique* and *unambiguous*. Therefore, in the first case the picture drawing system can choose any solution, but in the second case it must choose only the exact one. In this paper, we focus our attention on pictures of the first type.

To treat pictures with geometrical ambiguity, drawing systems are desired to solve inconsistent constraints in some degree (White 1988; Kamada 1989). The usual methods of solving inconsistent constraints are the least square method for linear constraints, and the Newton-Raphson method for nonlinear ones (Kamada 1989). The least square method can solve over-constrained linear constraints uniquely. But in the case of nonlinear constraints, large computation time is required and only a locally minimal solution can be obtained. That is why nonlinear constraint-solving is a difficult problem in general. However, nonlinearity plays an important role in geometrical constraints. Table 1 shows the order of some geometrical constraints. For example, an equidistance constraint $AB = CD$ in Euclidean geometry is represented as a quadratic equation:

$$(x_A - x_B)^2 + (y_A - y_B)^2 = (x_C - x_D)^2 + (y_C - y_D)^2$$

$$A : (x_A, y_A), \ B : (x_B, y_B), \ C : (x_C, y_C), \ D : (x_D, y_D)$$

Nonlinearity is hard to solve but inevitably essential in the field of geometrical constraint-solving. That is, a good constraint solver for drawing pictures with some geometrical ambiguity has to deal with (1) incomplete constraints, (2) inconsistent constraints, and (3) nonlinear constraints.

Compared with usual numerical methods, the connectionist approach described here has three main potential advantages:

1. It can reach a global minimum with the probability of one.

2. It requires only iteration of very simple threshold operations.

3. It can resort to massively parallel processing more easily.

Especially, if a suitable and sufficient hardware system for the parallel computation could be provided, it might make full use of its its real ability.

3 AN EXTENDED BOLTZMANN MACHINE

In this section, we describe a connectionist model to meet the requirements of the geometrical constraint solver. This model is based on a Boltzmann machine which works to minimize the energy function associated with the network. Firstly, we review the Boltzmann machine, the energy function of which is extended to deal with nonlinear constraints directly.

3.1 Boltzmann Machines

A Boltzmann Machine can be viewed as a network consisting of a number of two-state units which are mutually connected (Ackley et al. 1985; Aarts and Korst 1989). The network is represented by a pseudograph $B = (U, C)$, where U denotes a finite set of units and C is a finite set of unordered pairs of elements of U denoting the connections between the units. A *unit* u is either "1" or "0". A *connection* $\{u, v\}$ joins the units u and v. Usually, a connection $\{u, u\}$ is called a *loop* or a *bias connection*. With a connection $\{u, v\}$, a *connection strength* $w_{\{u,v\}} \in R$ is associated. A *configuration* k of a Boltzmann machine is given by a global state of the Boltzmann machine and is uniquely defined by a sequence of length $|U|$, whose u_{th} component $k(u) \in \{0, 1\}$ denotes the *state* of unit u in configuration k.

An energy function $E(k)$ assigns to each configuration k a real number defined by

$$E(k) = - \sum_{\{u,v\} \in C} w_{\{u,v\}} k(u) k(v)$$

The objective of a Boltzmann machine is to reach a configuration with minimal energy. To reach the minimal configuration, a state transition mechanism is introduced. This mechanism allows the units to adjust their states by a stochastic function of states of the neighbors and the corresponding connection strengths. This means that a state transition increasing the energy is also allowed with some probability. Hence, a Boltzmann machine can escape from local minimal configurations in the same manner as a *simulated annealing algorithm*, which is a stochastic computational technique derived from statistical mechanics for finding near globally-optimal solutions to large combinatorial optimization problems. Basically, each state transition of a unit is composed of three steps denoted as follows:

Step 1: Select one unit u at random.

Step 2: Calculate the sum of input to the unit u, $g(u)$.

$$g(u) = \sum_{\{u,v\} \in C} w_{\{u,v\}} k(v) + w_{\{u,u\}}$$

Step 3: Set the state of u at "1" with probability P denoted by

$$P = \frac{1}{1 + exp(\frac{-g(u)}{T})}, \qquad T: temperature \text{ of the network}$$

Since units evaluate their state transitions locally, Boltzmann machines facilitate the use of parallelism. Therefore, we may have many different approaches that can be pursued to realize parallel state transitions in a Boltzmann machine.

After a sufficiently large number of iterations of the state transitions at a fixed value T, a Boltzmann machine can reach an equilibrium state, which is corresponding to the *Boltzmann distribution* at the temperature T. Therefore, by gradually decreasing the temperature associated with the network, the probability to reach a configuration with globally minimal energy converges asymptotically to one. A manner of decreasing temperature, which is so-called a *cooling schedule*, plays a definitive role to ensure the quick convergence to sub-optimal solutions. The discussion on the detailed cooling schedule, however, is beyond the scope of this paper.

Note that the energy function associated with a configuration of a Boltzmann machine has a quadratic form with respect to the unit states. Thus, a Boltzmann machine can solve only linear simultaneous equations, which means the minimization of the quadratic objective function as follows:

$$E = \sum_j \lambda_j |\sum_i a_{ij} x_i - b_j|^2, \qquad x_i \in \{0,1\}, \qquad a_{ij}, b_j, \lambda_j : \text{constant}$$

In other words, a conventional Boltzmann machine searches a least square solution of the linear simultaneous equation. Of course, by using a learning mechanism, it is not impossible to treat higher-order constraints (Hinton et al. 1984). The learning algorithm of the Boltzmann machine, however, is too slow to apply to the geometrical constraint solver. Therefore, to quickly solve nonlinear optimization problems in a more straightforward manner, the energy function must be extended to include terms of higher-order than quadratic ones with respect to the unit stats. We then introduce the extended energy function which includes terms of higher-order.

3.2 Extension of the Energy Function

3.2.1 Definitions
Given a finite set of *free units*

$$U = \{u_1, u_2, \ldots, u_n\}, \qquad n \geq 1,$$

a set of *logical connections* L is defined as

$$L = 2^U - \emptyset$$

where 2^U means a power set of U.
Then, we introduce a *connection strength function* $W : L \to \mathbf{R}$, and define an extended energy function $E(k)$ as follows:

$$E(k) = -\sum_{c \in L} W_c \cdot S_c, \qquad S_c = \prod_{u \in c} k(u)$$

Apparently, this multilinear function is a natural extension of the conventional energy function described in the former Section since the energy function defined above includes quadratic terms with respect to the unit states.

Now, we define the *quasi-unit* $\bar{u}_c$ for each free unit u included in a logical connection c. The state of a quasi-unit is determined by other free units belonging to c:

$$k(\bar{u}_c) = S_{c-\{u\}} = \prod_{v \in c-\{u\}} k(v)$$

Here, we call $\{u, \bar{u}_c\}$ a *physical connection* of the free unit u on the logical connection c. In the case of $c = \{u\}$, $k(\bar{u}_c)$ is defined as follows:

$$k(\bar{u}_c) = S_{c-\{u\}} = S_{\{\}} = 1$$

This means that the quasi-unit $\bar{u}_c$ in the above case is a *tautologous unit* whose state is clamped to always "1". A connection between a free unit and a tautologous unit corresponds to a bias connection. When $|c - \{u\}| = m$, $\bar{u}_c$ is called a m_{th}-*order* quasi-unit. Clearly, a free unit is also a first-order quasi-unit. In addition, all physical connections on c are equally associated with the connection strength w_c.

Higher-order extension of Boltzmann machines is not limited to the way described here. Similar approaches are found in (Maxwell et al. 1986; Sejnowski 1986).

3.2.2 Ljapunov Stability

In this subsection, we show the Ljapunov stability of the extended energy function. Ljapunov stability, in this paper, means that the energy function associated with a Boltzmann machine is decreased by a single state transition of a free unit.

Let a network be in a configuration k, then a *neighboring configuration* k_u is defined as the configuration which is obtained from k by changing the state of the free unit u. We derive Ljapunov stability by showing that the difference of the energy functions denoted by

$$\triangle E_k(u) = E(k_u) - E(k)$$

is always nonpositive. In the energy function, $W_c \cdot S_c(u \notin c)$, which does not include u in the logical connection, has no contribution to the energy difference $\triangle E_k(u)$. Thus, we consider only the logical connections including u. Neighboring configurations can be represented as follows:

$$k_u(v) = \begin{cases} k(v) & \text{if } u \neq v \\ 1 - k(v) & \text{if } u = v \end{cases}$$

Then, the energy function of k_u is denoted by

$$E(k_u) = - \sum_{c \in L, c \ni u} W_c \cdot (1 - k(u)) \cdot S_{c-\{u\}}$$

Hence, using the relation $S_{c-\{u\}} = k(\bar{u}_c)$, we obtain

$$\triangle E_k(u) = (2k(u) - 1) \sum_{c \in L, c \ni u} W_c \cdot k(\bar{u}_c)$$

The above formula means that if the input to the free unit u, which is determined by the states of the all quasi-units of u and the corresponding connection strengths, is nonnegative, by setting the state of u at 1, and if the input is negative, by setting the state at 0, the energy of the entire network can always be decreased (or unchanged).

In searching a globally minimal configuration, local minima are easily avoided by the stochastic relaxation technique, which is the same method as the conventional Boltzmann machine. Thus, except for the parts corresponding to a cooling schedule, the fundamental algorithm of minimizing the extended energy function is described as follows:

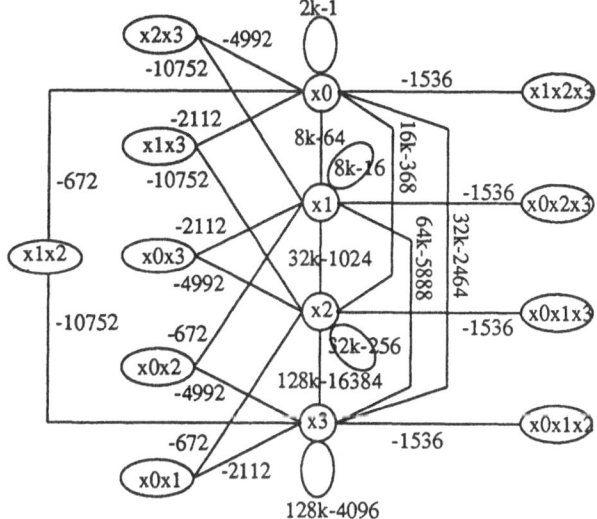

Fig. 2 An Extended Boltzmann Machine Calculating the 4-bit Square Root of k

Step 1: Select a free unit u at random.

Step 2: Calculate the sum of input to u, $g(u)$.

$$g(u) = \sum_{c \in L, c \ni u} W_c \cdot k(\overline{u}_c)$$

Step 3: Set the state of u at 1 with probability P denoted by

$$P = \frac{1}{1 + exp(\frac{-g(u)}{T})}, \qquad \text{T: temperature of the network}$$

Step 4: Reset the all quasi-units associated with u.

Compare the above algorithm with one shown in Section 3.1. Except for the last step, the both algorithms have almost the same sequence.

3.2.3 An Example

As a simple example, we try to solve a quadratic equation $x^2 = k$ ($k > 0$). This problem can be regarded as the minimization problem of the objective function $f = |x^2 - k|^2$. Therefore, if x is represented as a n-bit binary number, the extended Boltzmann machine consisting n free units asymptotically converges to a solution $x = \sqrt{k}$ from any initial values of x.

In the case of $n = 4$, the objective function f has a forth-order form as follows:

$$f = |(x_0 + 2x_1 + 4x_2 + 8x_3)^2 - k|^2$$

If we expand the above formula paying attention to $x_j^n = x_j$ ($n \geq 2$) and compare the coefficients with the extended energy function, the connection strength of each physical connection can be determined easily. Figure 2 shows the extended Boltzmann machine which calculates the square root. In this figure, free units also function as first-order quasi-units.

4 CONNECTIONIST CONSTRAINT-SOLVING

This section describes how we can apply the connectionist model defined to the geometrical constraint-solving through some examples. Moreover, we discuss some problems remained to solve in future.

4.1 Linear Constraints

Linear constraints, such as horizontality of a line through two points, can be represented in the form of an inner product of two vectors as follows:

$$a_1 x_1 + a_2 x_2 + \cdots + a_m x_m = b, \quad a_i, b: \text{constants}, \quad x_i: \text{coordinate value}$$

If we represent coordinate values with n-bit binary numbers, the above constraint can be easily solved by a Boltzmann machine which minimizes the energy function below:

$$E = |\sum_{i=0}^{m-1} a_i (\sum_{j=0}^{n-1} 2^j u_{ij}) - b|^2$$

$$u_{ij} \in \{0,1\}: \text{the state of the unit}, \quad x_i = \sum_{j=0}^{n-1} 2^j u_{ij}$$

Apparently, above formula has a quadratic form with respect to u_{ij}.

When we treat several constraints simultaneously, the linear combination of all the energy functions corresponding to the constraints is considered:

$$E = \lambda_1 E_1 + \lambda_2 E_2 + \cdots + \lambda_r E_r$$

Here, λ_i is an empirical constant which denotes the strength of each constraint. In other words, λ means the relative desirability to hold the corresponding constraints. Therefore, we can easily deal with inconsistent constraints as well as consistent ones in a framework of the constraint hierarchy.

In the case of linear constraints, if the number of coordinate values is m and each coordinate value can be represented by a n-bit binary number, a Boltzmann machine consisting of mn units can solve these constraints. Figure 3 shows the Boltzmann machine in the case of $m = 2$ and $n = 3$.

4.2 Nonlinear Constraints

Nonlinear constraints are treated by the extended Boltzmann machine described in Section 3.2. For example, think of solving a geometrical constraint $AB = d$, which means that the length of the line segment AB is d. Note that this geometrical constraint is incomplete to define a picture since no constraints related to the position of the line segment are given. We first represent x and y coordinates of points A and B with binary digits, then make a network which minimizes the extended energy function as follows:

$$E = |(\sum_j 2^j (u_{0j} - u_{2j}))^2 + (\sum_j 2^j (u_{1j} - u_{3j}))^2 - d^2|^2$$

$$A : (x_A, y_A), \quad x_A = \sum_j 2^j u_{0j}, \quad y_A = \sum_j 2^j u_{1j}$$

$$B : (x_B, y_B), \quad x_B = \sum_j 2^j u_{2j}, \quad y_B = \sum_j 2^j u_{3j}$$

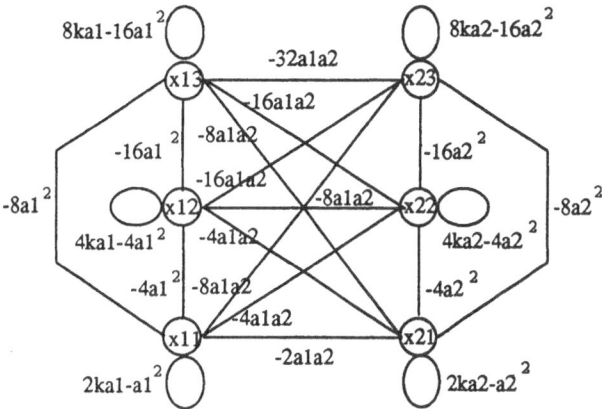

Fig. 3 A Boltzmann Machine Solving a Linear Constraint

Each connection strength is:

$$
\begin{aligned}
W_{\{u_{ij}\}} &= 2^{2j+1}d - 2^{4j} \\
W_{\{u_{ij},u_{kl}\}} &= sign(i,k)2^{j+l+2}d - 2^{2j+2l+1} - sign(i,k,i,k)2^{2j+2l+2} \\
&\quad -sign(i,i,i,k)2^{3j+l+2} - sign(i,k,k,k)2^{j+3l+2} \\
W_{\{u_{ij},u_{kl},u_{mn}\}} &= -sign(i,i,k,m)2^{2j+l+n+2} - sign(i,k,i,m)2^{2j+l+n+3} \\
&\quad -sign(i,m,k,k)2^{j+2l+n+2} - sign(i,k,k,m)2^{j+2l+n+3} \\
&\quad -sign(i,k,m,m)2^{j+l+2n+2} - sign(i,m,k,m)2^{j+l+2n+3} \\
W_{\{u_{ij},u_{kl},u_{mn},u_{pq}\}} &= -(sign(i,k,m,p) + sign(i,m,k,p) \\
&\quad +sign(i,p,k,m))2^{j+l+n+q+3}
\end{aligned}
$$

where

$$
sign(i,k,m,p) = sign(i,k) \cdot sign(m,p)
$$

$$
sign(i,k) = \begin{cases} 1 & \text{if } i = k \\ -1 & \text{if } i = k \pm 2 \\ 0 & \text{otherwise} \end{cases}
$$

Given an arbitrary line segment AB as an initial configuration of the network, by iterating state transitions, the extended Boltzmann machine converges to a line segment the length of which is d. In this case, the position of the segment is determined only in a probabilistic way because no stationary constraints are given. Therefore, using this method, it is possible to solve the incomplete geometrical constraints shown in Figure 1(b). That is, we can transform any triangle to an equilateral triangle. Of course, it is also easy to join other consistent and/or inconsistent constraints together in a way shown in Section 4.1.

Figure 4 shows some results of the equilateral triangle constraint obtained by the prototype constraint solver which realizes a sequential algorithm of the extended Boltzmann machine. The prototype solver was implemented on Sun-4 SPARCstation 330 which is a well-known 32-bit Unix

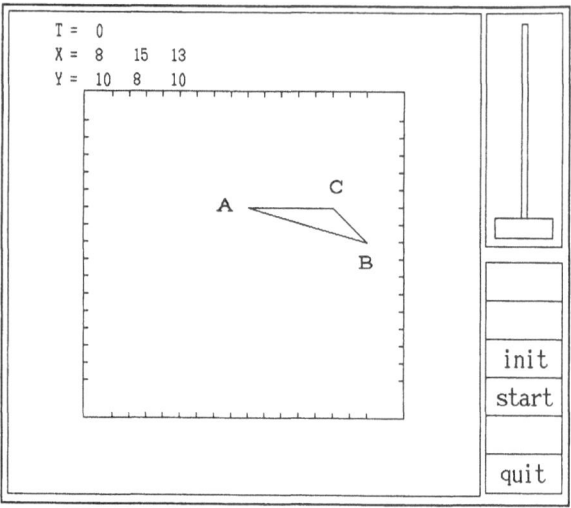

(a) The Initial State

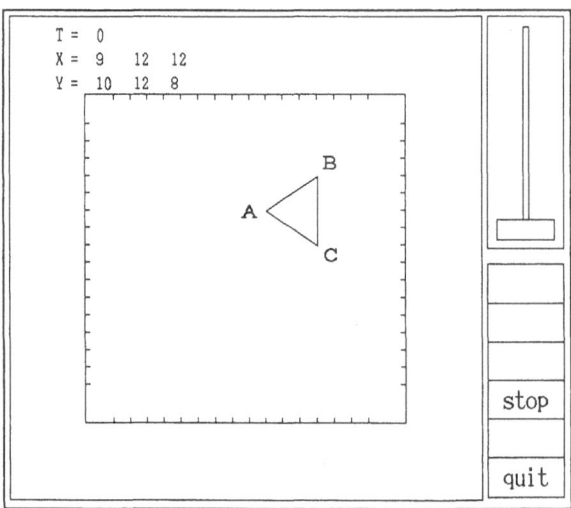

(b) The Converged Equilateral Triangle with Edge Length 4

Constraint: $AB = BC = CA = 4$

Fig. 4 The Examples of the Prototype System Screen

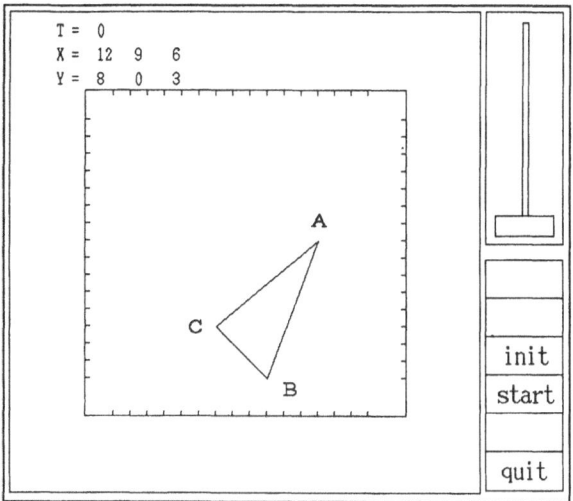

(c) The Initial State

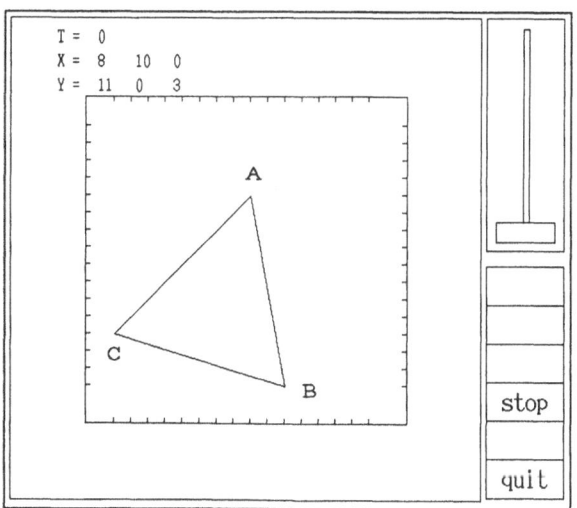

(d) The Converged Equilateral Triangle with Edge Length 10

Constraint: $AB = BC = CA = 10$

workstation equipped with the X-window system. In these figures, each coordinate value is represented by a 4-bit binary number, and initial conditions are given arbitrarily by a user in an interactive manner. The network temperature is set at any time by moving a slider lever on the window, and annealing is automatically performed according to the cooling schedule programmed in advance. The experiments by the prototype system show that the convergence to a near-optimal solution is remarkably quick. In the case of the above example, we can obtain a solution in a few seconds. Moreover, we need no sophisticated cooling schedule to escape from local minima; the network temperature is set to nearly zero from the beginning. To solve more complicated constraints including many free points, however, we might have to consider an elaborate cooling schedule.

4.3 Discussion

To deal with constraints associated with the line length, as the energy function E has a 4th-order form of u_{ij}, second- and third-order quasi-units are required to construct an extended Boltzmann machine. Therefore, if the coordinate values are represented by 8-bit binary numbers, the number of free units required is only 32. The number of second-order quasi-units, however, is $_{32}C_2 = 496$, and that of third-order quasi-units is $_{32}C_3 = 4960$. Explosive increase of the number of quasi-units is a practical problem which should be overcome. When an extended Boltzmann machine is simulated using a sequential computer, however, quasi-units are not necessary. Logical AND operations of binary states of the free units can play a role of them.

Another problem remained lies in the summation of the connection strengths. In the above example, the number of free units is $4n$, where n is the number of bits. Then, the number of the connections is:

$$\text{the number of the connections per unit}$$

$$4n \left(\underbrace{1}_{1st} + \underbrace{_{4n-1}C_1}_{2nd} + \underbrace{_{4n-1}C_2}_{3rd} + \underbrace{_{2n-1}C_3 +_{2n-1} C_1 \times_{2n} C_2}_{4th} \right) = 4n \left(\frac{16}{3}n^3 + \frac{8}{3}n \right)$$

$$= \frac{32}{3}n^2(2n^2 + 1)$$

Fortunately, it is unusual in most geometrical constraints that the coefficients of constraints have different values. This fact results in a desirable feature that the variety of the values of the connection strengths is considerably limited. Therefore, we can represent the weights of connections in a rather simple and regular form as shown in section 4.2. Thus, by using such regularity in the connection strength summation, the reduction of calculation complexity and/or memory space could be available.

5 CONCLUSION

In this paper, we proposed a brand-new connectionist approach to solve geometrical constraints based on the extended Boltzmann machine. This machine can be used to solve nonlinear geometrical constraints, and is particularly good at drawing pictures such as undirected graphs, trees, and flowcharts which represent the relationships among discrete objects with some geometrical ambiguity. The advantage of using the connectionist model lies in that it can solve inconsistent, incomplete, and nonlinear geometrical constraints, and generate the most adequate picture in a very short time. We conclude that our brand-new approach developed, say *neurographics*, which is an integration of the artificial neural networks and computer graphics, provides a breakthrough in the constraint-based picture drawing.

We considered geometrical constraints from the viewpoint of an orthogonal coordinate system, which is suitable for the conventional numerical computation. This might not be a good way to fully utilize the advantages of the connectionist models however. It is one of the future problems to evaluate another geometrical index system for the connectionism.

ACKNOWLEDGEMENTS

We are grateful to Ms. Deepa Krishnan for her thoughtful comments.

REFERENCES

Aarts E and Korst J (1989) *Simulated Annealing and Boltzmann Machines.* John Wiley & Sons

Ackley DH, Hinton GE, and Sejnowski TJ (1985) A learning algorithm for Boltzmann machines. *Cognitive Sciences* 9:147–169

Feldman JA and Ballard DH (1982) Connectionist models and their properties. *Cognitive Science* 6:205–254

Fuller N and Prusinkiewicz P (1988) Geometric modeling with Euclidean constructions. In: Magnenat-Thalmann N and Thalmann D (eds) *New Trends in Computer Graphics*, Proc. CG International '88. Springer-Verlag, pp 379–391

Hinton GE, Sejnowski TJ, and Ackley DH (1984) Boltzmann machines: constraint satisfaction networks that learn. Carnegie-Mellon University, *Technical Report CMU-CS-84-119*

Hopfield JJ (1982) Neural networks and physical systems with emergent collective computational abilities. *Proc. National Academy of Sciences.* 79:2554–2558

Kamada T (1989) *On Visualization of Abstract Objects and Relations.* PhD thesis, Dept. of Information Science, Faculty of Science, The University of Tokyo

Kin N, Noma T, and Kunii TL (1989) PictureEditor: a 2D picture editing system based on geometric constructions and constraints. In: Earnshaw RA and Wyvill B (eds) *New Advances in Computer Graphics*, Proc. CG International '89. Springer-Verlag, pp 193–207

Leler W (1988) *Constraint Programming Languages: Their Specification and Generation.* Addison-Wesley

Maxwell T, Giles CL, Lee YC, and Chen HH (1986) Nonlinear dynamics of artificial neural systems. In: Denker JS (ed) *Neural Networks for Computing*, AIP Conf. Proc. 151. Snowbird(UT), pp 299-304

Nelson G (1985) Juno, a constraint-based graphics system. *ACM SIGGRAPH Comput. Graph.* 19(3):235–243

Noma T, Kunii TL, Kin N, Enomoto H, Aso E, and Yamamoto T (1989) Constructive picture description with Euclidean geometry. *The Visual Computer* 5(1/2):40–52

Pfeifer R, Schreter Z, Fogelman-Soulie F, and Steels L (1989) Putting connetionism in perspective. In: *Connectionism in Perspective*. North-Holland, pp xi–xxi

Sejnowski TJ (1986) Higher order Boltzmann machines. In: Denker JS (ed) *Neural Networks for Computing*, AIP Conf. Proc. 151. Snowbird(UT), pp 398-403

Sutherland IE (1963) Sketchpad: a man-machine graphical communication system. In: *Proc. Spring Joint Computer Conf.* pp 329–346

Takeda M and Goodman JW (1986) Neural networks for computation: Number representations and programming complexity. *Applied Optics* 25(18):3033–3046

Tank DW and Hopfield JJ (1986) Simple neural optimization network: an A/D converter, signal decision circuit, and a linear programming circuit. *IEEE Trans. on Circuits and Systems* 33(5):533–541

White RM (1988) Applying direct manipulation to geometric construction systems. In: Magnenat-Thalmann N and Thalmann D (eds) *New Trends in Computer Graphics*, Proc. CG International '88. Springer-Verlag, pp 446–455

Wyk CJ Van (1982) A high-level language for specifying pictures. *ACM Trans. on Graphics* 1(2):163–182

[1] Department of Information Science, Faculty of Science, The University of Tokyo, Bunkyo-ku, Tokyo, 113 Japan

[2] Division of Information Science, Faculty of Engineering, Hokkaido University, Sapporo, 060 Japan

List of Contributors

Citation Index

Keyword Index